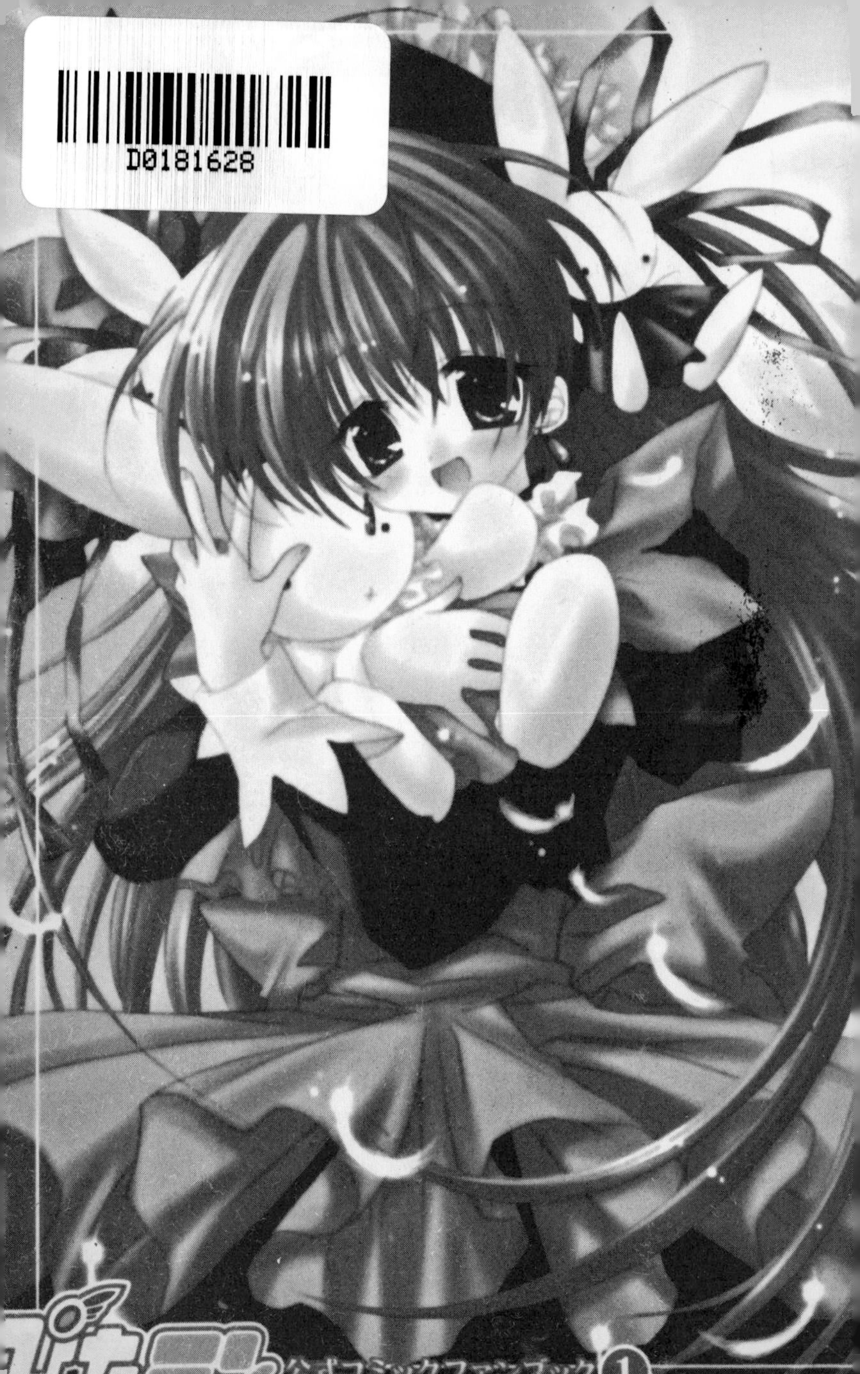

公式コミックファンブック ①

PITA-TEN
Official Fan Book

Volume 1
by
Koge-Donbo

TOKYOPOP®

HAMBURG // LONDON // LOS ANGELES // TOKYO

Pita Ten Official Fan Book Vol.1
Created by Koge-Donbo

Translation - Nan Rymer
English Adaptation - Adam Arnold
Copy Editors - Eric Althoff and Hope Donovan
Retouch and Lettering - Irene Woori Choi
Production Artist - Gloria Wu
Cover Design - Al-Insan Lashley

Editor - Paul Morrissey
Digital Imaging Manager - Chris Buford
Production Managers - Jennifer Miller and Mutsumi Miyazaki
Managing Editor - Lindsey Johnston
VP of Production - Ron Klamert
Publisher and E.I.C. - Mike Kiley
President and C.O.O. - John Parker
C.E.O. - Stuart Levy

A  Manga

TOKYOPOP Inc.
5900 Wilshire Blvd. Suite 2000
Los Angeles, CA 90036

E-mail: info@TOKYOPOP.com
Come visit us online at www.TOKYOPOP.com

ISBN: 1-59816-106-7

First TOKYOPOP printing: November 2005
10 9 8 7 6 5 4 3 2 1
Printed in Canada

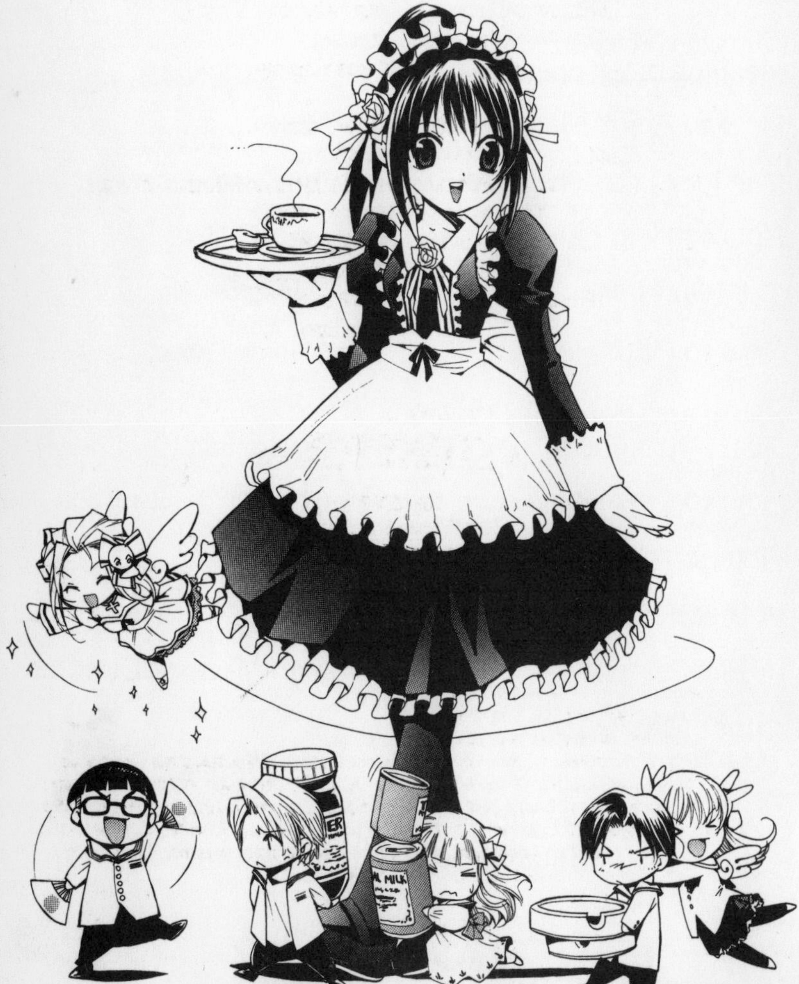

Table of Contents

Cover Illustration: Koge-Donbo
Inside Illustration: Izumi Sakurazawa

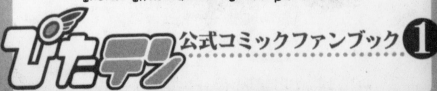

公式コミックファンブック ①

PITA-TEN
Official Fan Book
1

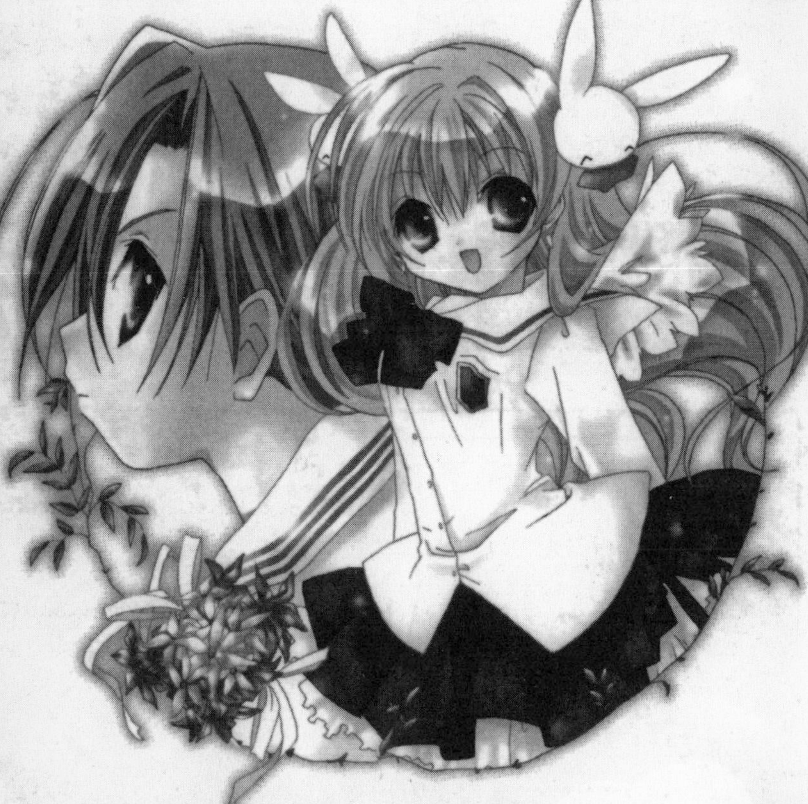

PITA-TEN OFFICIAL FAN BOOK 1

Pita-Ten's Cast of Characters

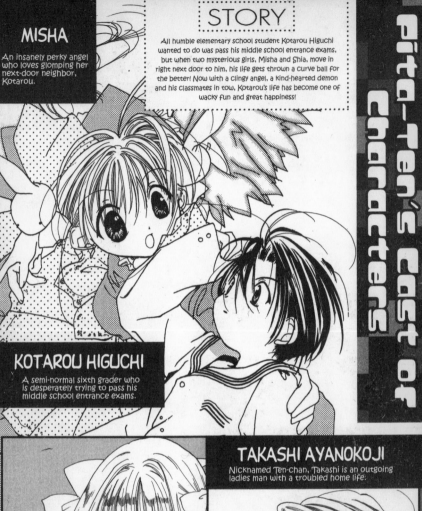

STORY

All humble elementary school student Kotarou Higuchi wanted to do was pass his middle school entrance exams, but when two mysterious girls, Misha and Shia, move in right next door to him, his life gets thrown a curve ball for the better! Now with a clingy angel, a kind-hearted demon and his classmates in tow, Kotarou's life has become one of wacky fun and great happiness!

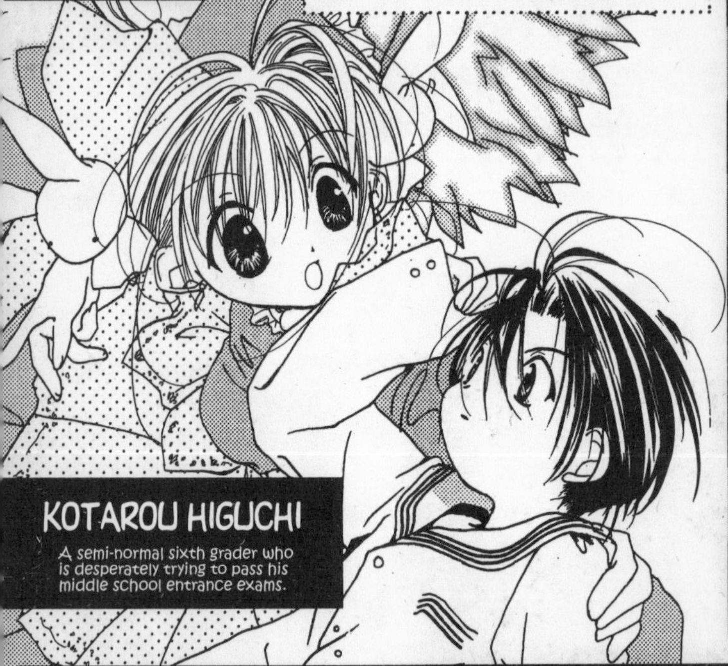

MISHA

An insanely perky angel who loves glomping her next-door neighbor, Kotarou.

KOTAROU HIGUCHI

A semi-normal sixth grader who is desperately trying to pass his middle school entrance exams.

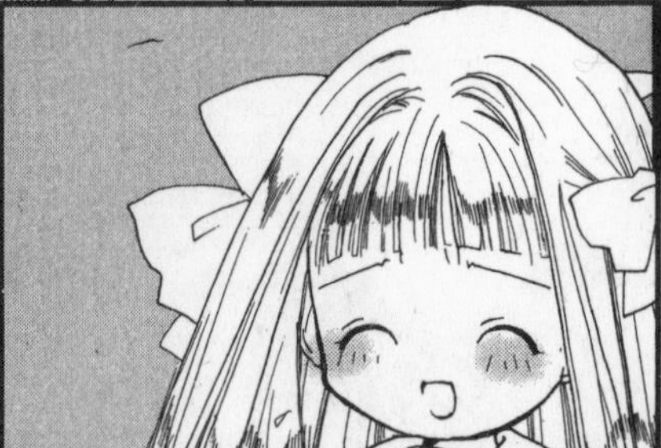

TAKASHI AYANOKOJI

Nicknamed Ten-chan, Takashi is an outgoing ladies man with a troubled home life.

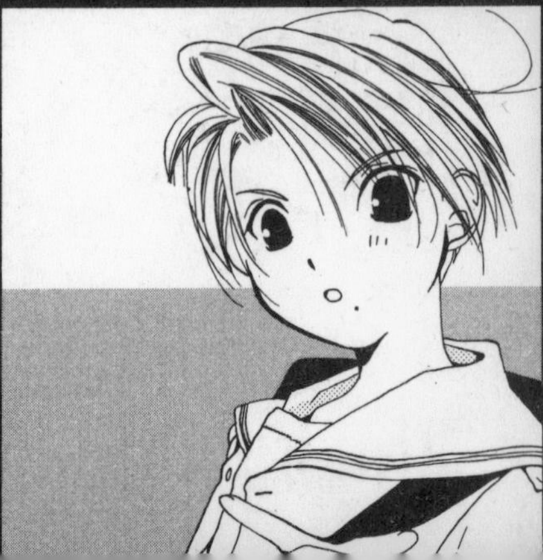

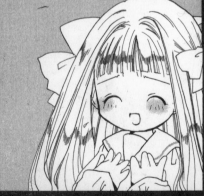

KOBOSHI UEMATSU

This semi-sweet loudmouth and advice-giver has the hots for Kotarou.

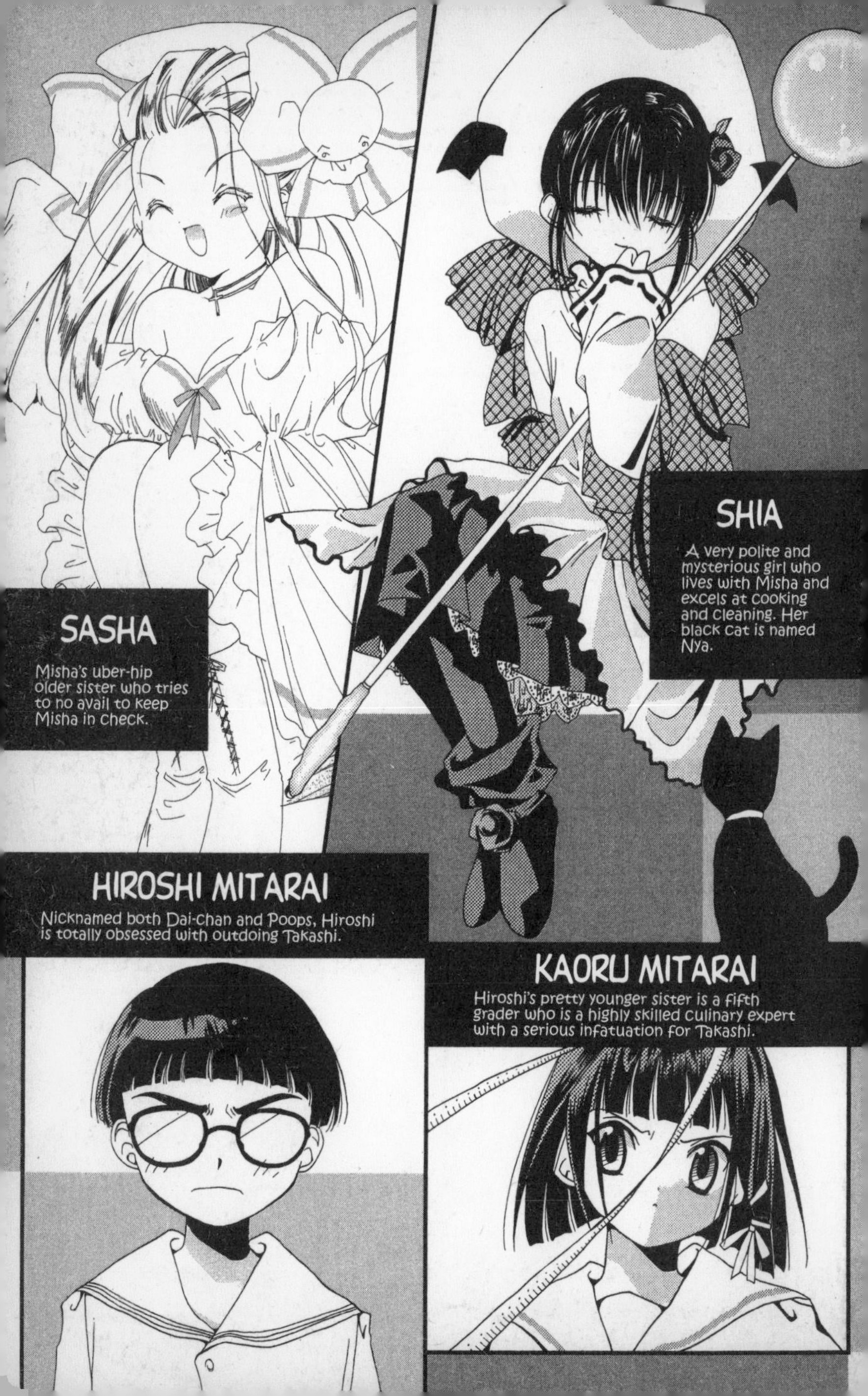
SHIA
A very polite and mysterious girl who lives with Misha and excels at cooking and cleaning. Her black cat is named Nya.
SASHA
Misha's uber-hip older sister who tries to no avail to keep Misha in check.
HIROSHI MITARAI
Nicknamed both Dai-chan and Poops, Hiroshi is totally obsessed with outdoing Takashi.
KAORU MITARAI
Hiroshi's pretty younger sister is a fifth grader who is a highly skilled culinary expert with a serious infatuation for Takashi.

♪ La la laaa ♪

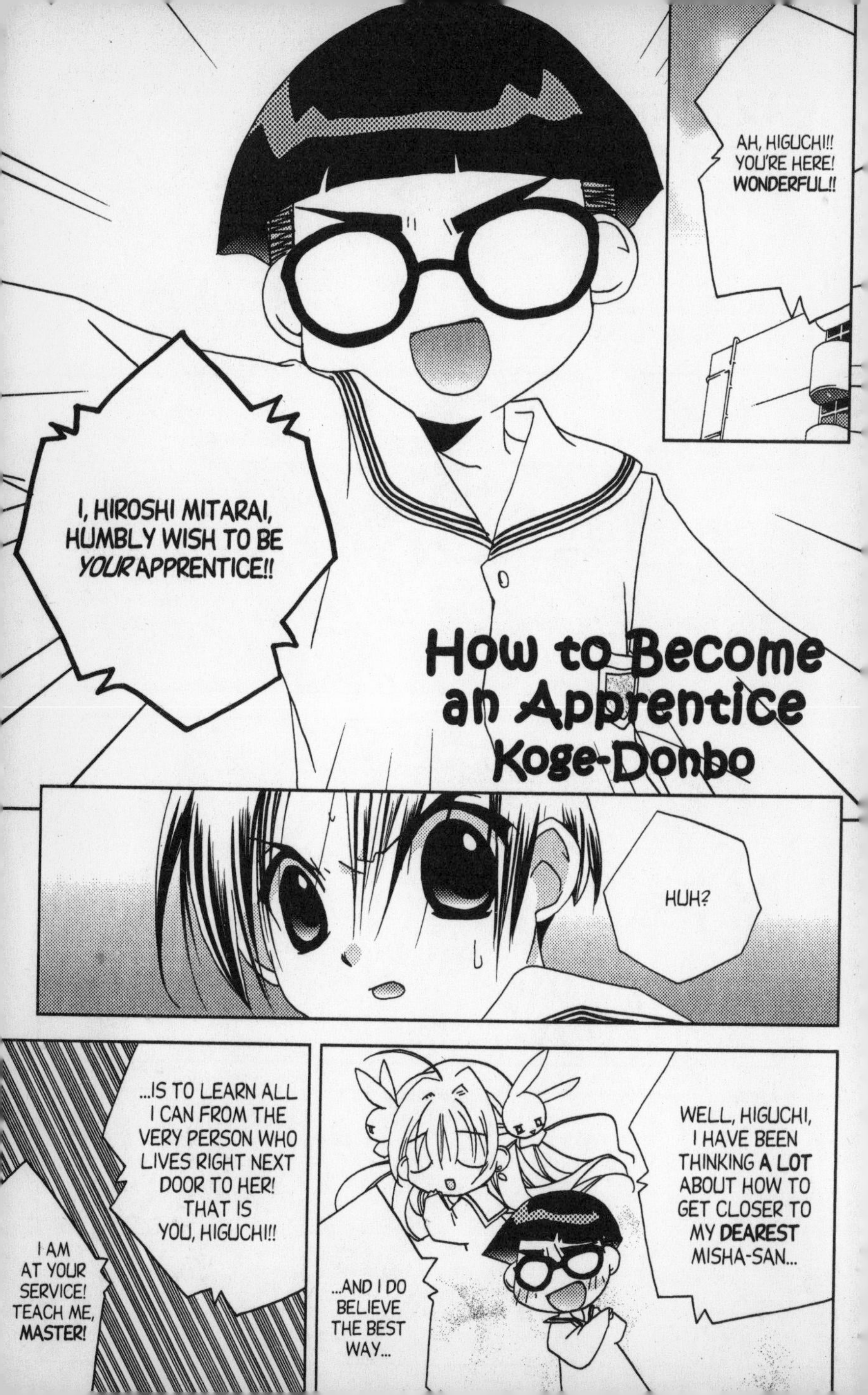

AH, HIGUCHI!! YOU'RE HERE! WONDERFUL!!
I, HIROSHI MITARAI, HUMBLY WISH TO BE YOUR APPRENTICE!!
How to Become an Apprentice
Koge-Donbo
HUH?
WELL, HIGUCHI, I HAVE BEEN THINKING A LOT ABOUT HOW TO GET CLOSER TO MY DEAREST MISHA-SAN...
...AND I DO BELIEVE THE BEST WAY...
...IS TO LEARN ALL I CAN FROM THE VERY PERSON WHO LIVES RIGHT NEXT DOOR TO HER! THAT IS YOU, HIGUCHI!!
I AM AT YOUR SERVICE! TEACH ME, MASTER!

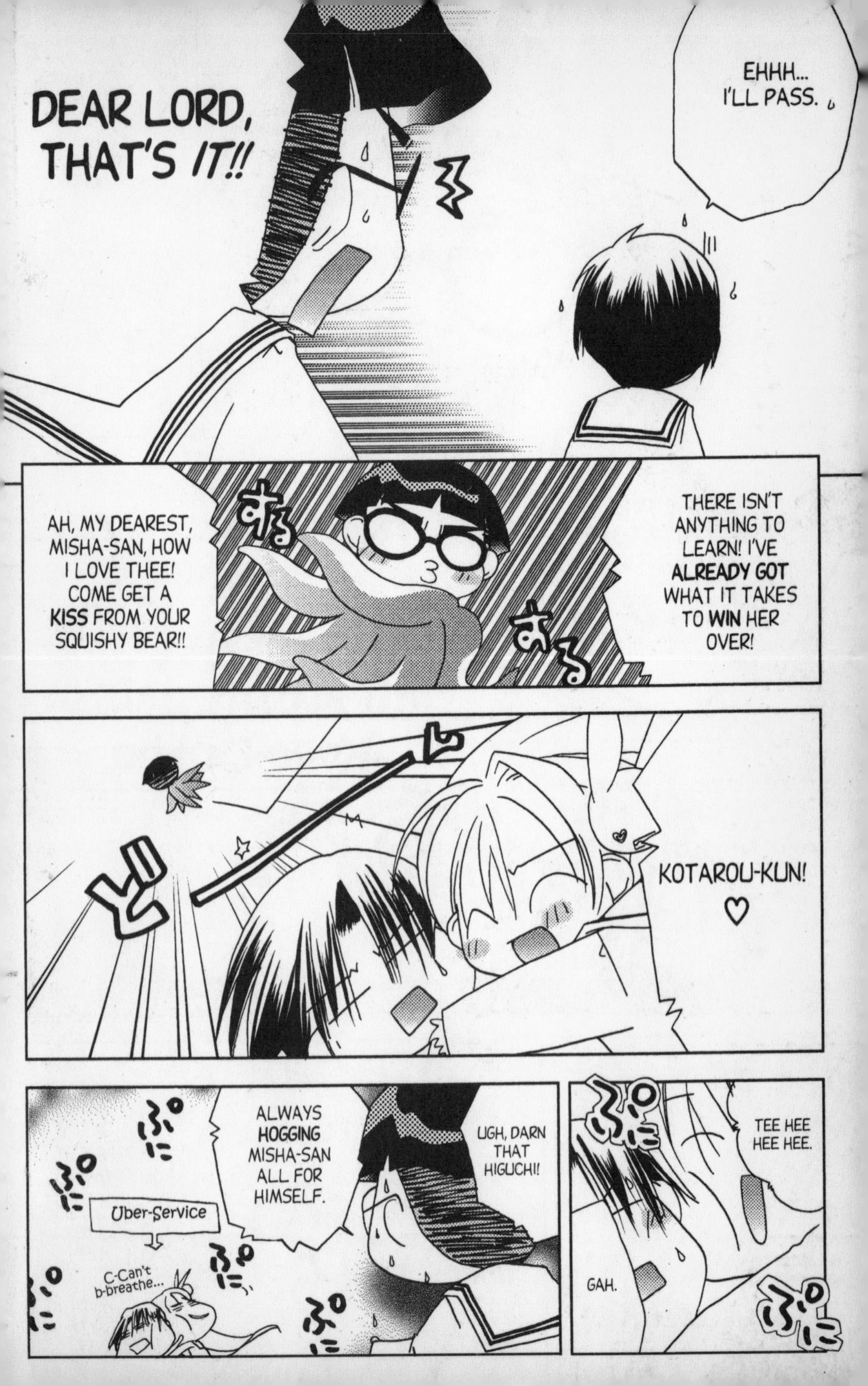
EHHH... I'LL PASS.
DEAR LORD, THAT'S IT!!
THERE ISN'T ANYTHING TO LEARN! I'VE ALREADY GOT WHAT IT TAKES TO WIN HER OVER!
AH, MY DEAREST, MISHA-SAN, HOW I LOVE THEE! COME GET A KISS FROM YOUR SQUISHY BEAR!!
KOTAROU-KUN! ♡
TEE HEE HEE HEE.
GAH.
ぷに
UGH, DARN THAT HIGUCHI!
ALWAYS HOGGING MISHA-SAN ALL FOR HIMSELF.
ぷに
Uber-Service
C-Can't b-breathe...

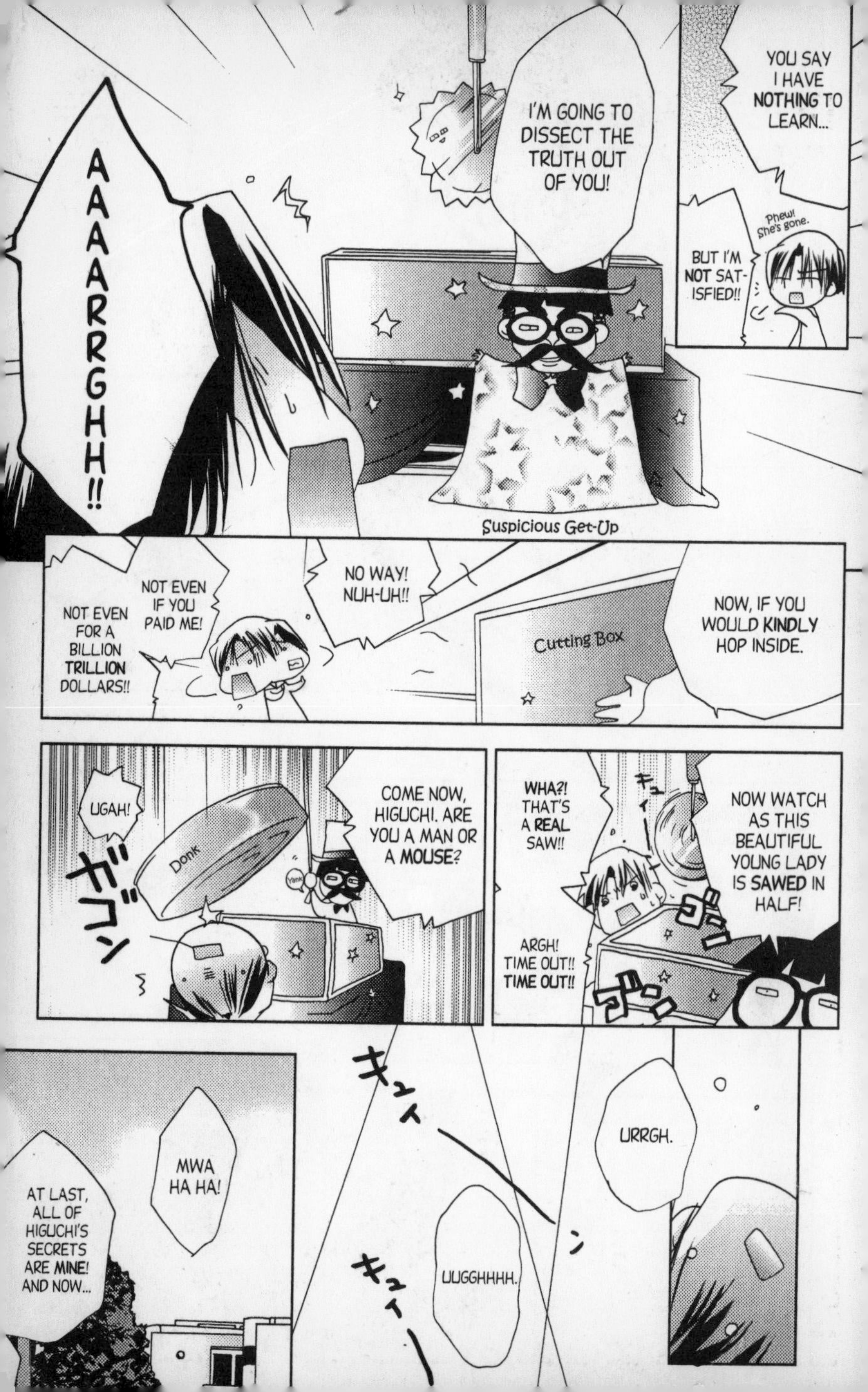
YOU SAY I HAVE NOTHING TO LEARN...
Phew! She's gone.
BUT I'M NOT SATISFIED!!
I'M GOING TO DISSECT THE TRUTH OUT OF YOU!
AAAARRGHH!!
Suspicious Get-Up
NOW, IF YOU WOULD KINDLY HOP INSIDE.
Cutting Box
NO WAY! NUH-UH!!
NOT EVEN IF YOU PAID ME!
NOT EVEN FOR A BILLION TRILLION DOLLARS!!
NOW WATCH AS THIS BEAUTIFUL YOUNG LADY IS SAWED IN HALF!
WHA?! THAT'S A REAL SAW!!
ARGH! TIME OUT!! TIME OUT!!
COME NOW, HIGUCHI. ARE YOU A MAN OR A MOUSE?
Yank
UGAH!
Donk
ガゴン
URRGH.
キュイーン
UUGGHHHH.
キュイー
MWA HA HA!
AT LAST, ALL OF HIGUCHI'S SECRETS ARE MINE! AND NOW...

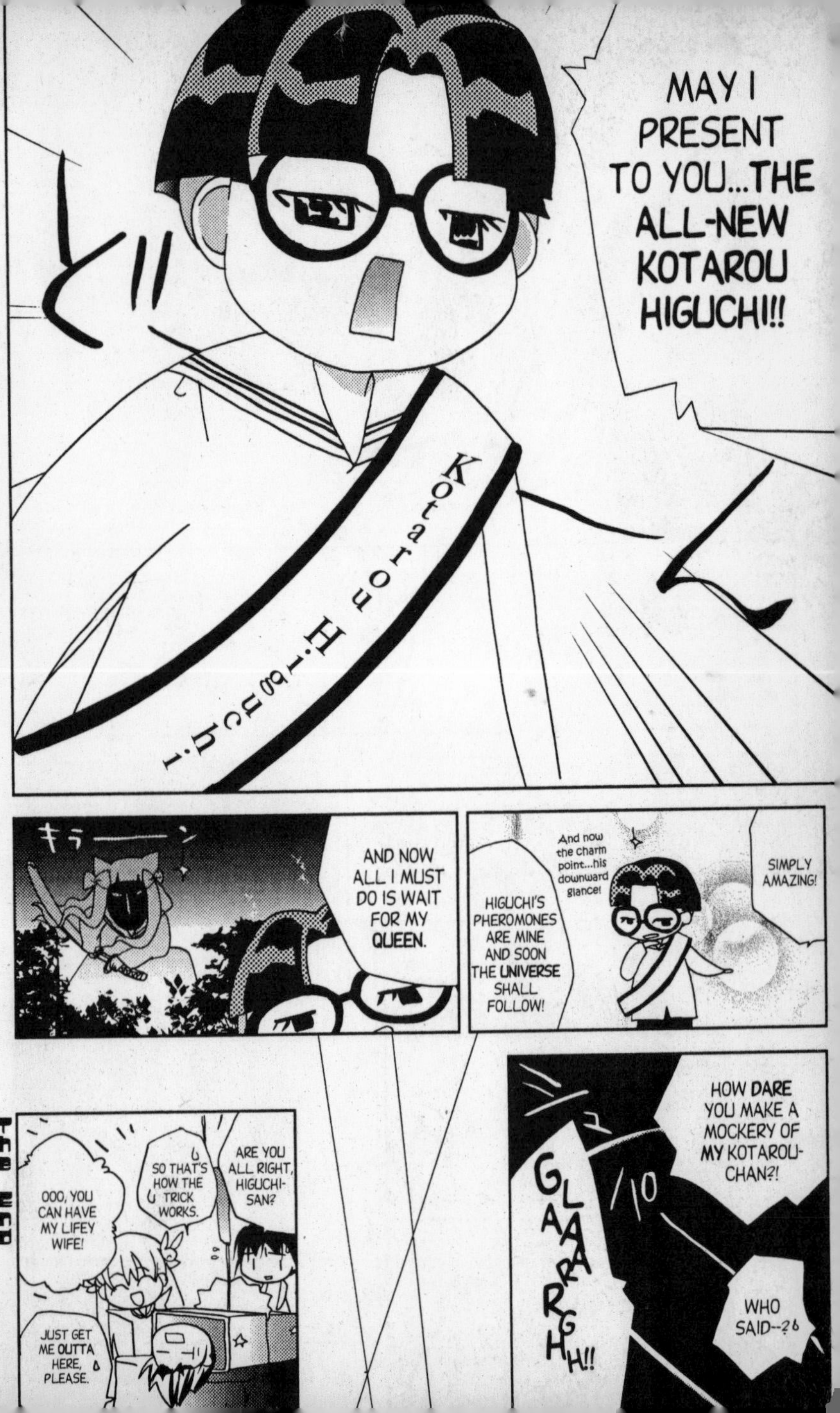
MAY I PRESENT TO YOU...THE ALL-NEW KOTAROU HIGUCHI!!
Kotarou Higuchi
SIMPLY AMAZING!
And now the charm point...his downward glance!
HIGUCHI'S PHEROMONES ARE MINE AND SOON THE UNIVERSE SHALL FOLLOW!
キラーーーン
AND NOW ALL I MUST DO IS WAIT FOR MY QUEEN.
HOW DARE YOU MAKE A MOCKERY OF MY KOTAROU-CHAN?!
GLAAARRGHH!!
WHO SAID--?!
ARE YOU ALL RIGHT, HIGUCHI-SAN?
SO THAT'S HOW THE TRICK WORKS.
OOO, YOU CAN HAVE MY LIFEY WIFE!
JUST GET ME OUTTA HERE, PLEASE.
The End

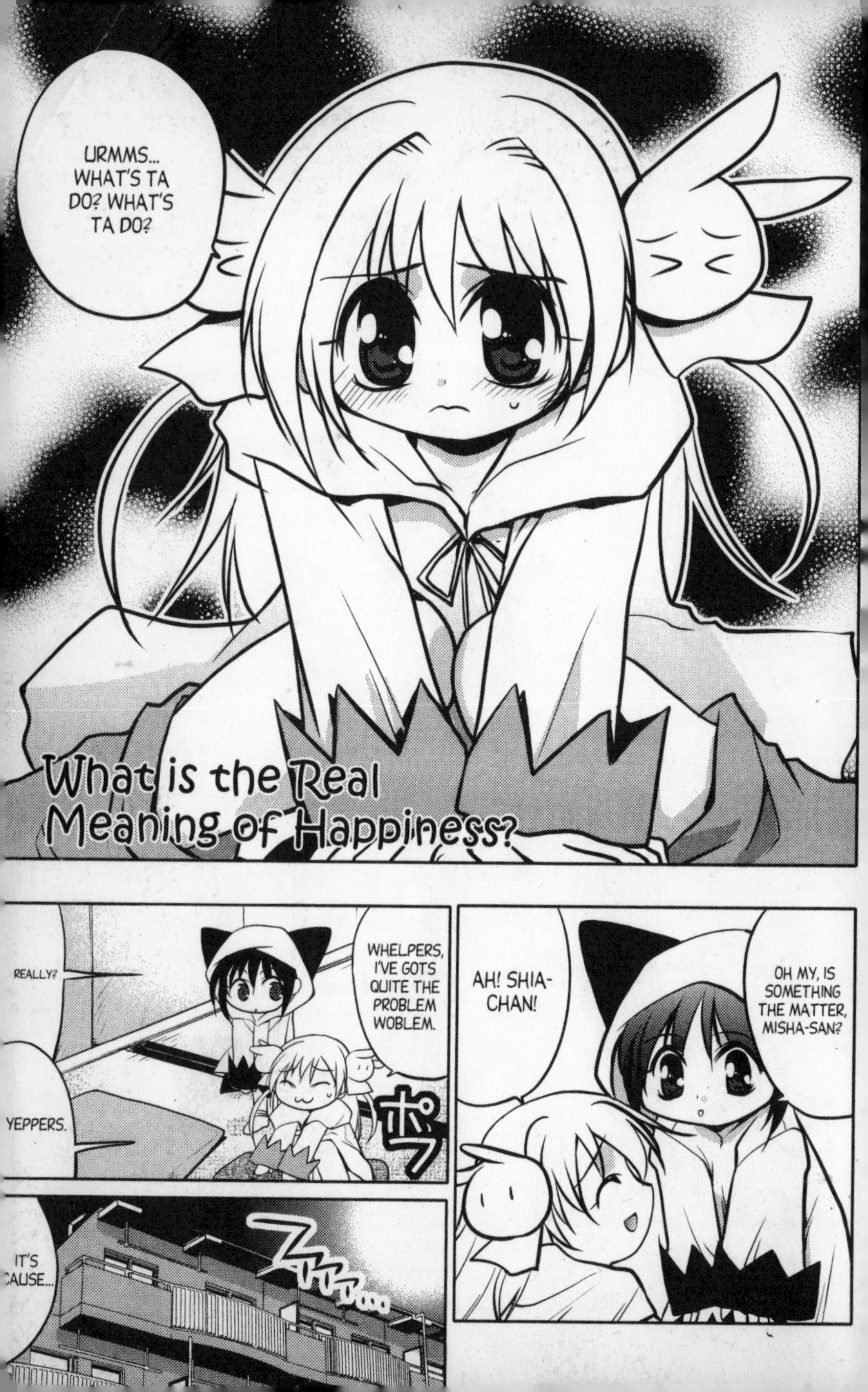
URMMS... WHAT'S TA DO? WHAT'S TA DO?
What is the Real Meaning of Happiness?
OH MY, IS SOMETHING THE MATTER, MISHA-SAN?
AH! SHIA-CHAN!
WHELPERS, I'VE GOTS QUITE THE PROBLEM WOBLEM.
ポフ
REALLY?
YEPPERS.
IT'S CAUSE...

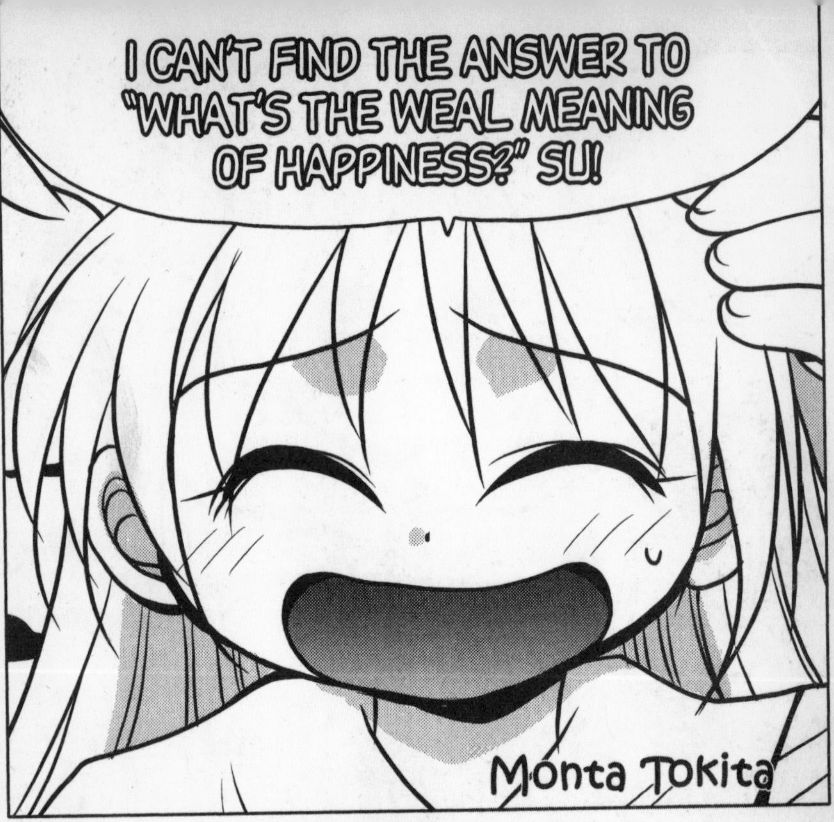

I CAN'T FIND THE ANSWER TO "WHAT'S THE WEAL MEANING OF HAPPINESS?" SU!
Monta Tokita

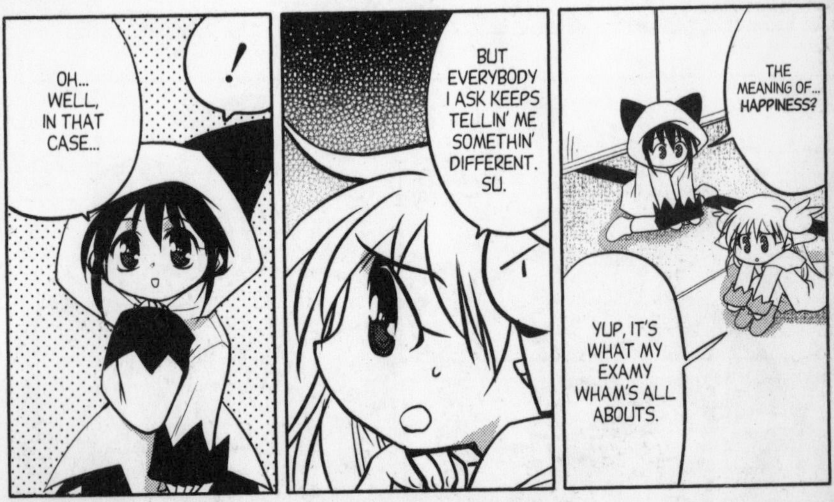

THE MEANING OF... HAPPINESS?
YUP, IT'S WHAT MY EXAMY WHAM'S ALL ABOUTS.
BUT EVERYBODY I ASK KEEPS TELLIN' ME SOMETHIN' DIFFERENT. SU.
!
OH... WELL, IN THAT CASE...

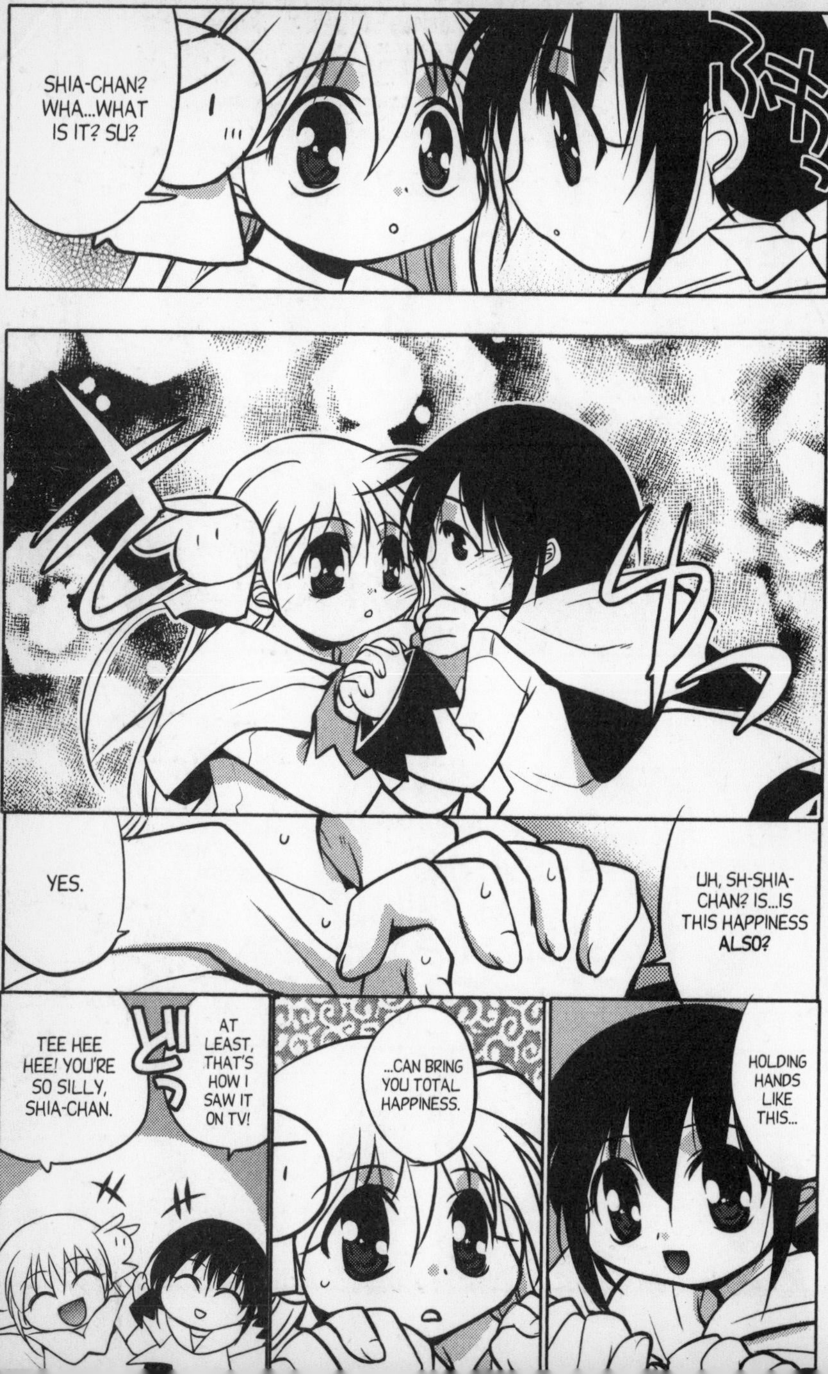
SHIA-CHAN? WHA...WHAT IS IT? SU?
UH, SH-SHIA-CHAN? IS...IS THIS HAPPINESS ALSO?
YES.
HOLDING HANDS LIKE THIS...
...CAN BRING YOU TOTAL HAPPINESS.
AT LEAST, THAT'S HOW I SAW IT ON TV!
TEE HEE HEE! YOU'RE SO SILLY, SHIA-CHAN.

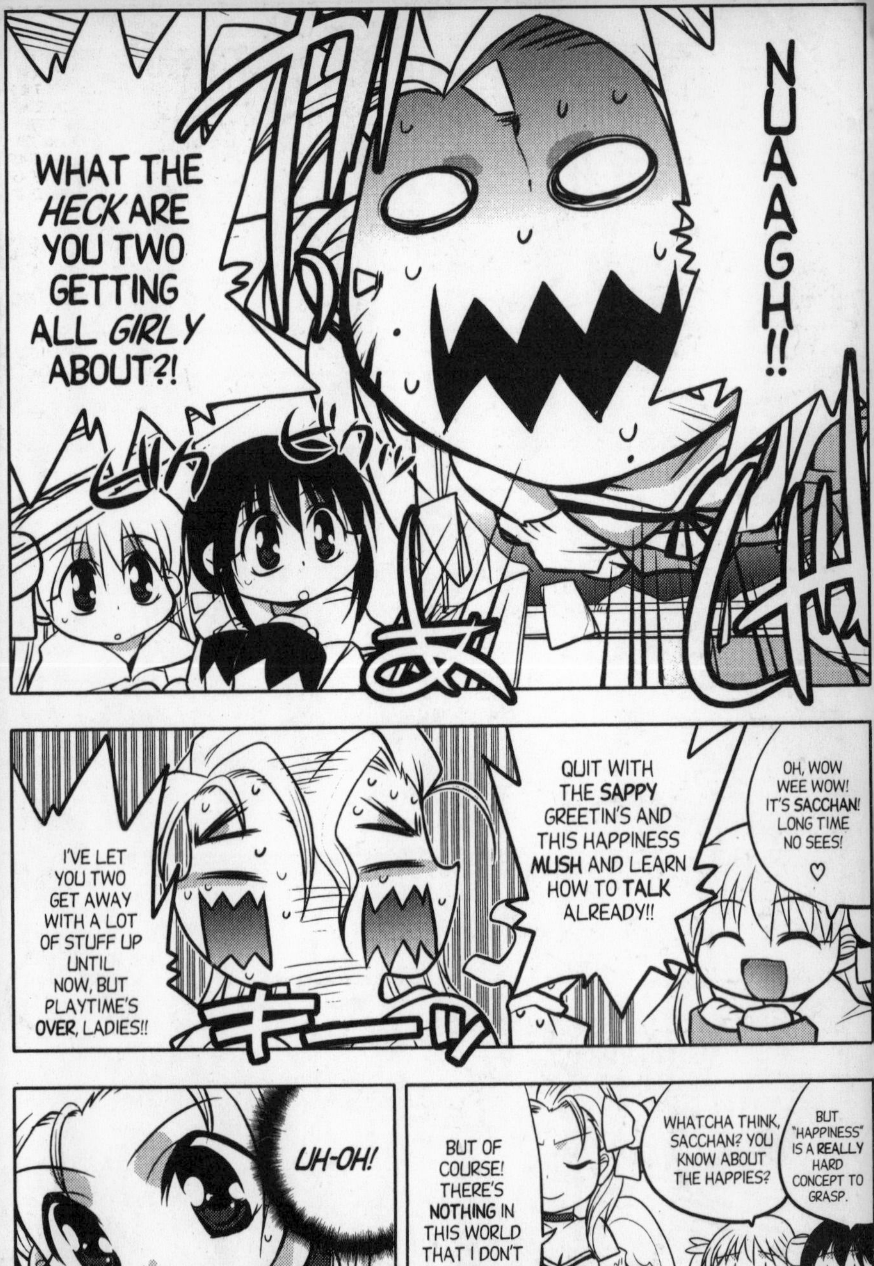
NUAAGH!!
WHAT THE HECK ARE YOU TWO GETTING ALL GIRLY ABOUT?!
OH, WOW WEE WOW! IT'S SACCHAN! LONG TIME NO SEES! ♡
QUIT WITH THE SAPPY GREETIN'S AND THIS HAPPINESS MUSH AND LEARN HOW TO TALK ALREADY!!
I'VE LET YOU TWO GET AWAY WITH A LOT OF STUFF UP UNTIL NOW, BUT PLAYTIME'S OVER, LADIES!!
BUT "HAPPINESS" IS A REALLY HARD CONCEPT TO GRASP.
WHATCHA THINK, SACCHAN? YOU KNOW ABOUT THE HAPPIES?
BUT OF COURSE! THERE'S NOTHING IN THIS WORLD THAT I DON'T KNOW!
UH-OH!

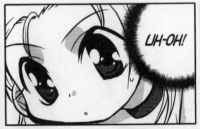

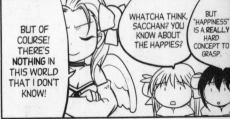

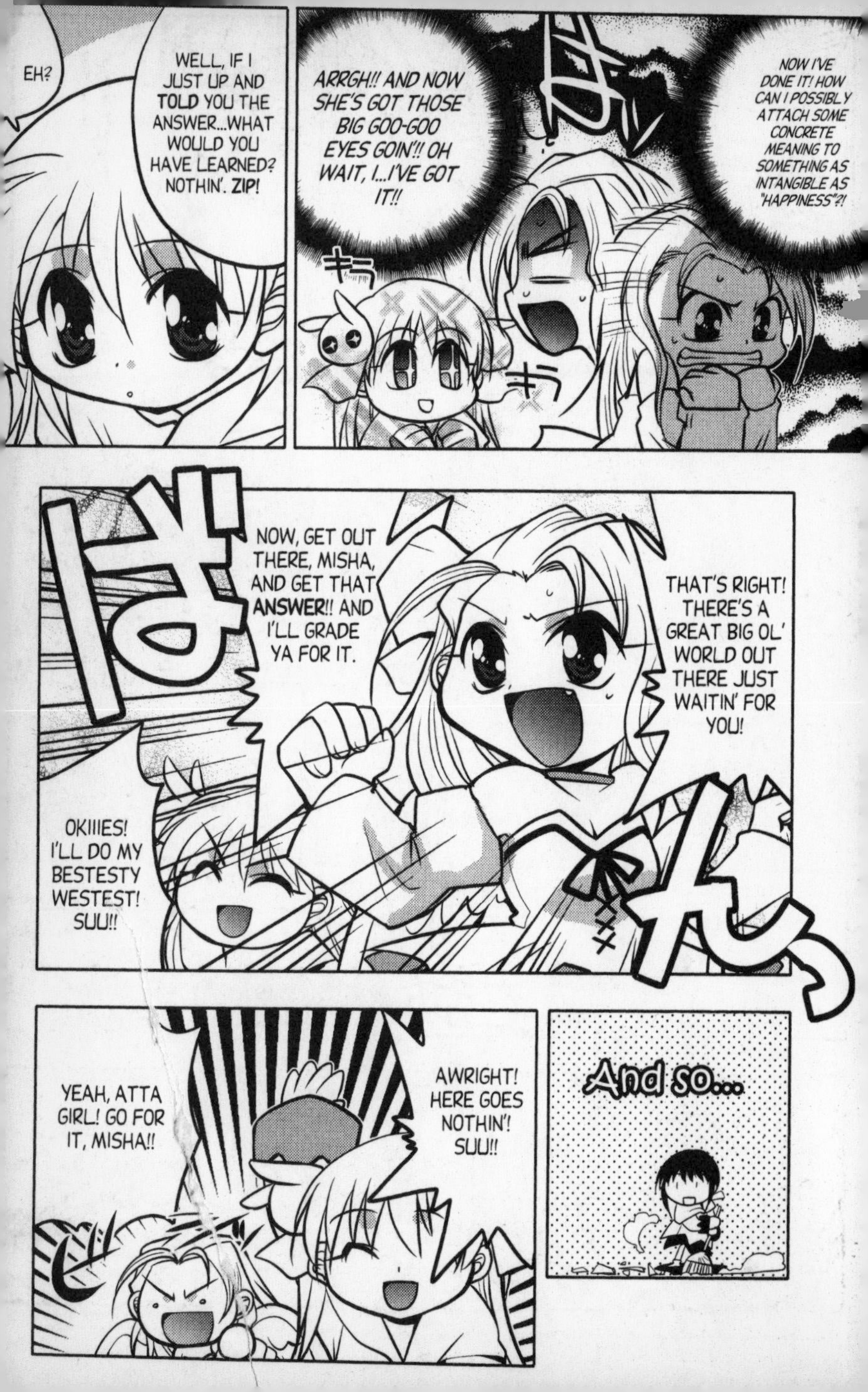
NOW I'VE DONE IT! HOW CAN I POSSIBLY ATTACH SOME CONCRETE MEANING TO SOMETHING AS INTANGIBLE AS "HAPPINESS"?!
ARRGH!! AND NOW SHE'S GOT THOSE BIG GOO-GOO EYES GOIN'!! OH WAIT, I...I'VE GOT IT!!
WELL, IF I JUST UP AND TOLD YOU THE ANSWER...WHAT WOULD YOU HAVE LEARNED? NOTHIN'. ZIP!
EH?
NOW, GET OUT THERE, MISHA, AND GET THAT ANSWER!! AND I'LL GRADE YA FOR IT.
THAT'S RIGHT! THERE'S A GREAT BIG OL' WORLD OUT THERE JUST WAITIN' FOR YOU!
OKIIIES! I'LL DO MY BESTESTY WESTEST! SUU!!
And so...
AWRIGHT! HERE GOES NOTHIN'! SUU!!
YEAH, ATTA GIRL! GO FOR IT, MISHA!!

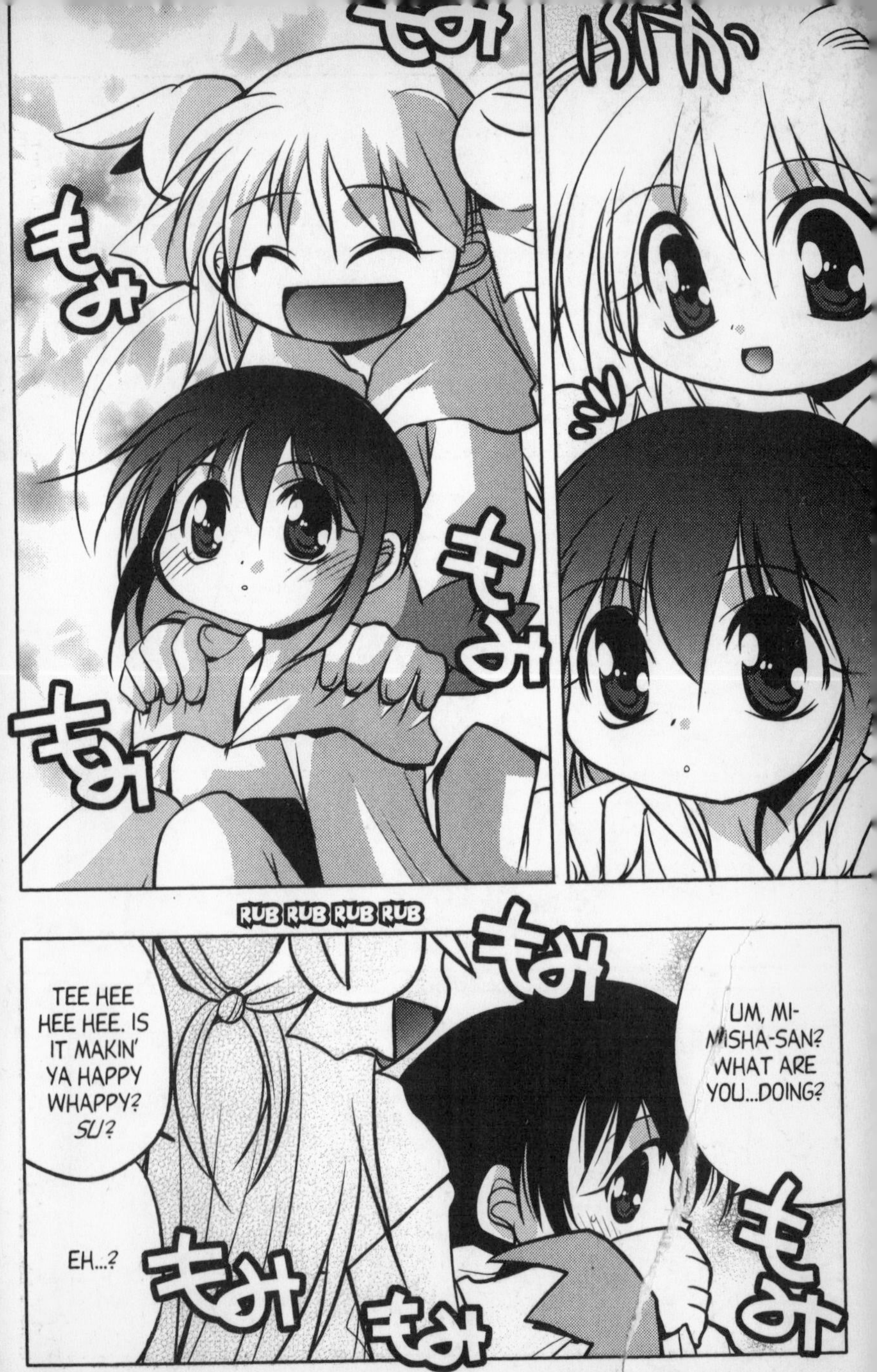
ふわ、
もみ
もみ
もみ
もみ
RUB RUB RUB RUB
もみ
UM, MI-MISHA-SAN? WHAT ARE YOU...DOING?
TEE HEE HEE HEE. IS IT MAKIN' YA HAPPY WHAPPY? *SU*?
もみ
もみ
EH...?
もみ

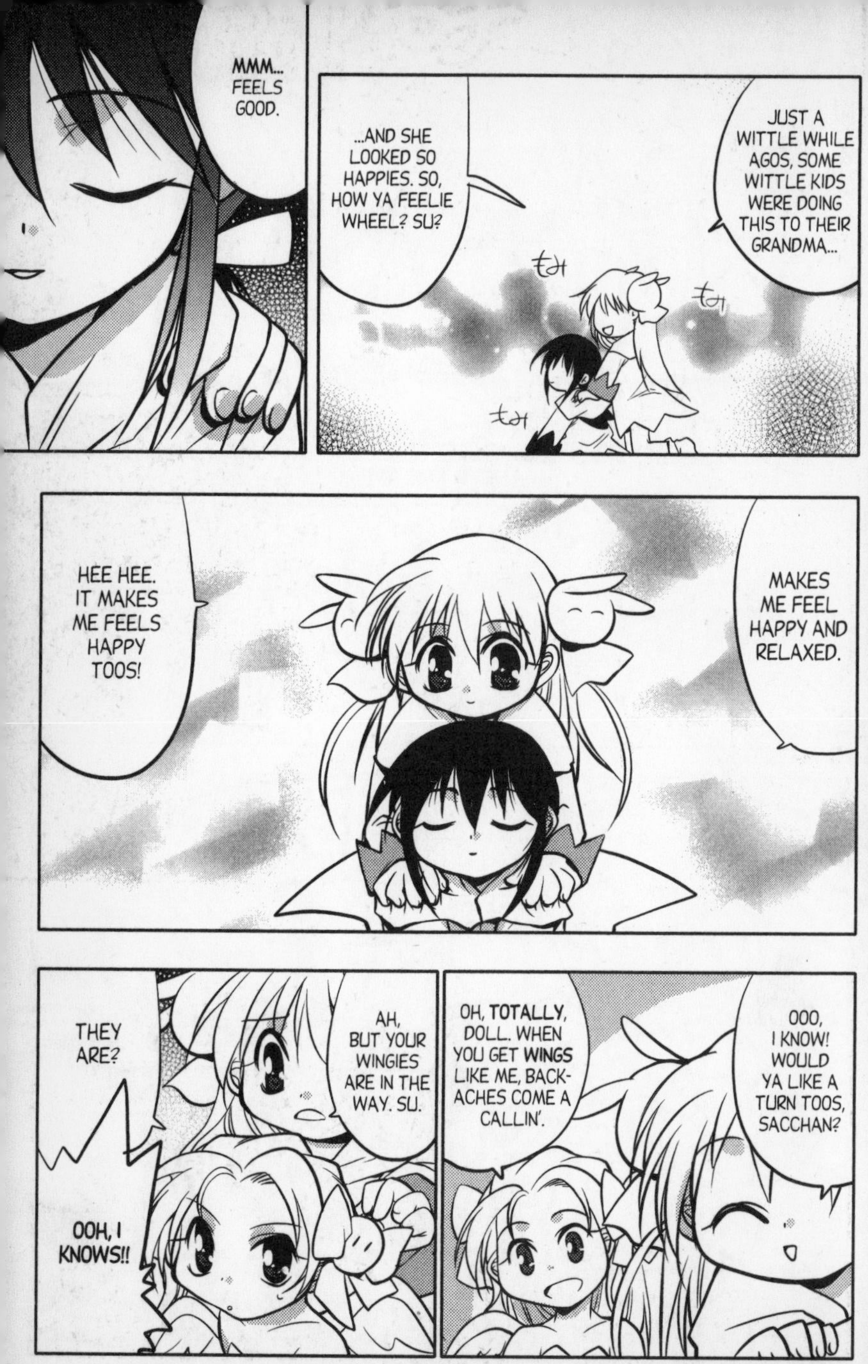
JUST A WITTLE WHILE AGOS, SOME WITTLE KIDS WERE DOING THIS TO THEIR GRANDMA...
...AND SHE LOOKED SO HAPPIES. SO, HOW YA FEELIE WHEEL? SU?
もみ
もみ
もみ
MMM... FEELS GOOD.
MAKES ME FEEL HAPPY AND RELAXED.
HEE HEE. IT MAKES ME FEELS HAPPY TOOS!
OOO, I KNOW! WOULD YA LIKE A TURN TOOS, SACCHAN?
OH, **TOTALLY**, DOLL. WHEN YOU GET **WINGS** LIKE ME, BACK-ACHES COME A CALLIN'.
AH, BUT YOUR WINGIES ARE IN THE WAY. SU.
THEY ARE?
OOH, I KNOWS!!

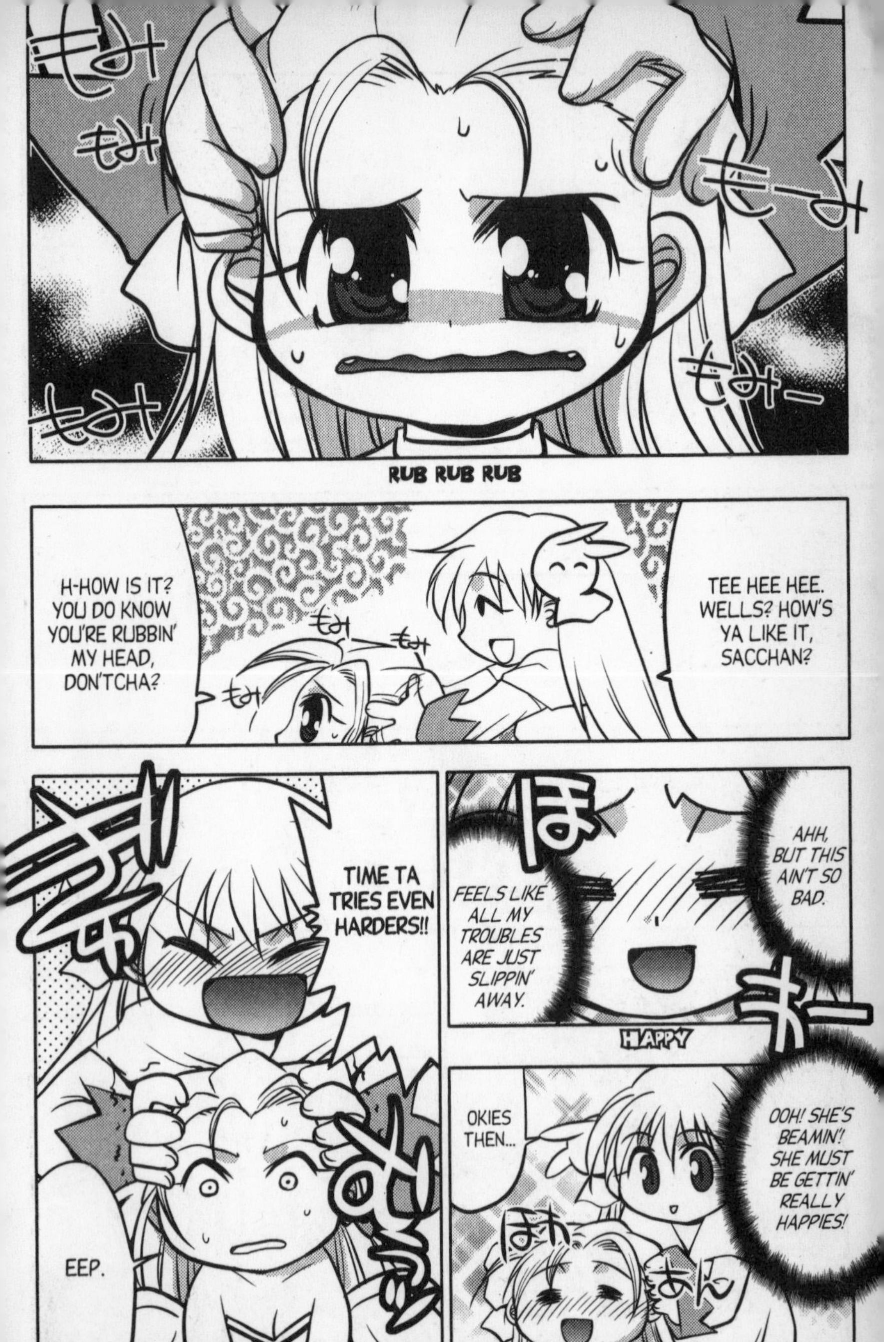
RUB RUB RUB
TEE HEE HEE. WELLS? HOW'S YA LIKE IT, SACCHAN?
H-HOW IS IT? YOU DO KNOW YOU'RE RUBBIN' MY HEAD, DON'TCHA?
AHH, BUT THIS AIN'T SO BAD.
FEELS LIKE ALL MY TROUBLES ARE JUST SLIPPIN' AWAY.
HAPPY
OOH! SHE'S BEAMIN'! SHE MUST BE GETTIN' REALLY HAPPIES!
OKIES THEN...
TIME TA TRIES EVEN HARDERS!!
EEP.
CRUNCH

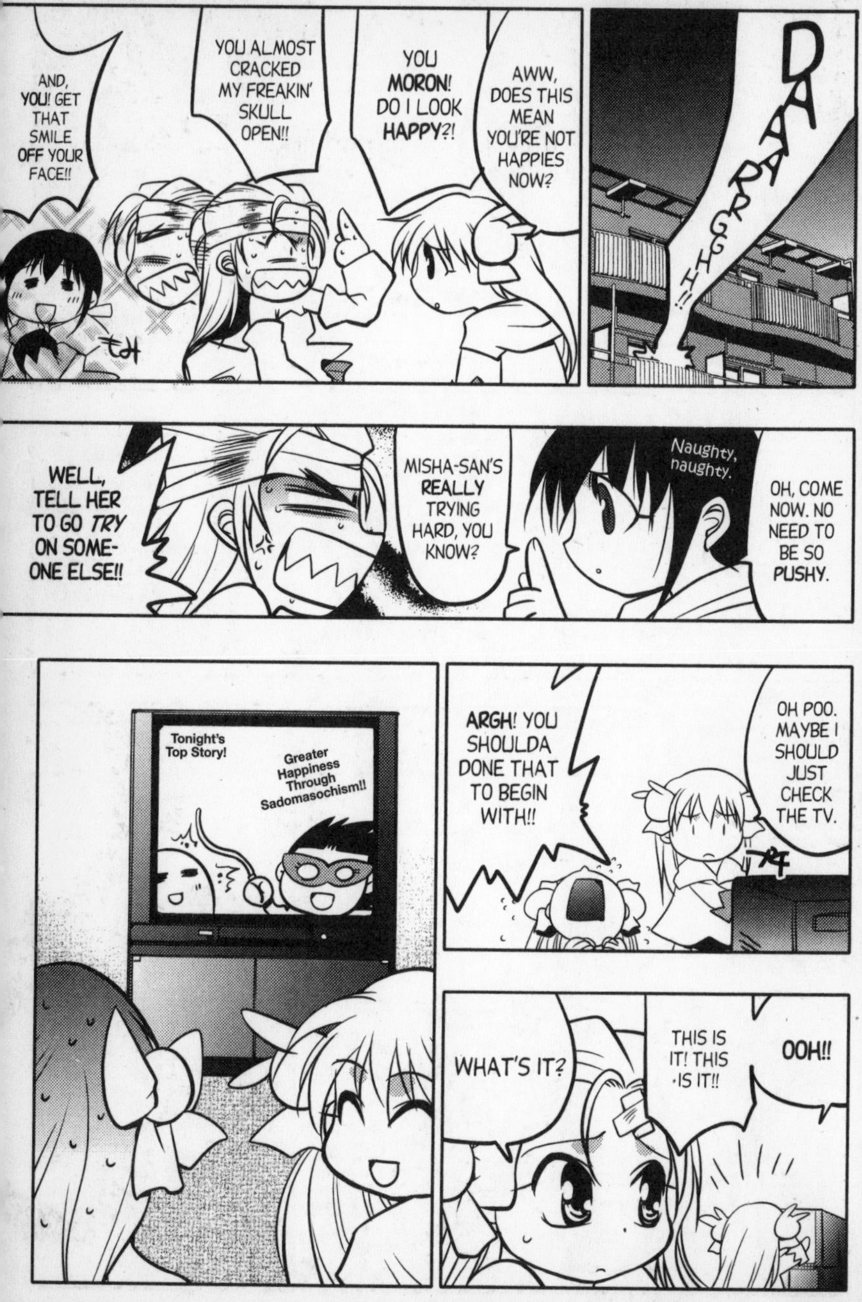

DAAARRGHH!!
AWW, DOES THIS MEAN YOU'RE NOT HAPPIES NOW?
YOU MORON! DO I LOOK HAPPY?!
YOU ALMOST CRACKED MY FREAKIN' SKULL OPEN!!
AND, YOU! GET THAT SMILE OFF YOUR FACE!!
OH, COME NOW. NO NEED TO BE SO PUSHY.
Naughty, naughty.
MISHA-SAN'S REALLY TRYING HARD, YOU KNOW?
WELL, TELL HER TO GO TRY ON SOME-ONE ELSE!!
OH POO. MAYBE I SHOULD JUST CHECK THE TV.
ARGH! YOU SHOULDA DONE THAT TO BEGIN WITH!!
OOH!!
THIS IS IT! THIS IS IT!!
WHAT'S IT?
Tonight's Top Story!
Greater Happiness Through Sadomasochism!!

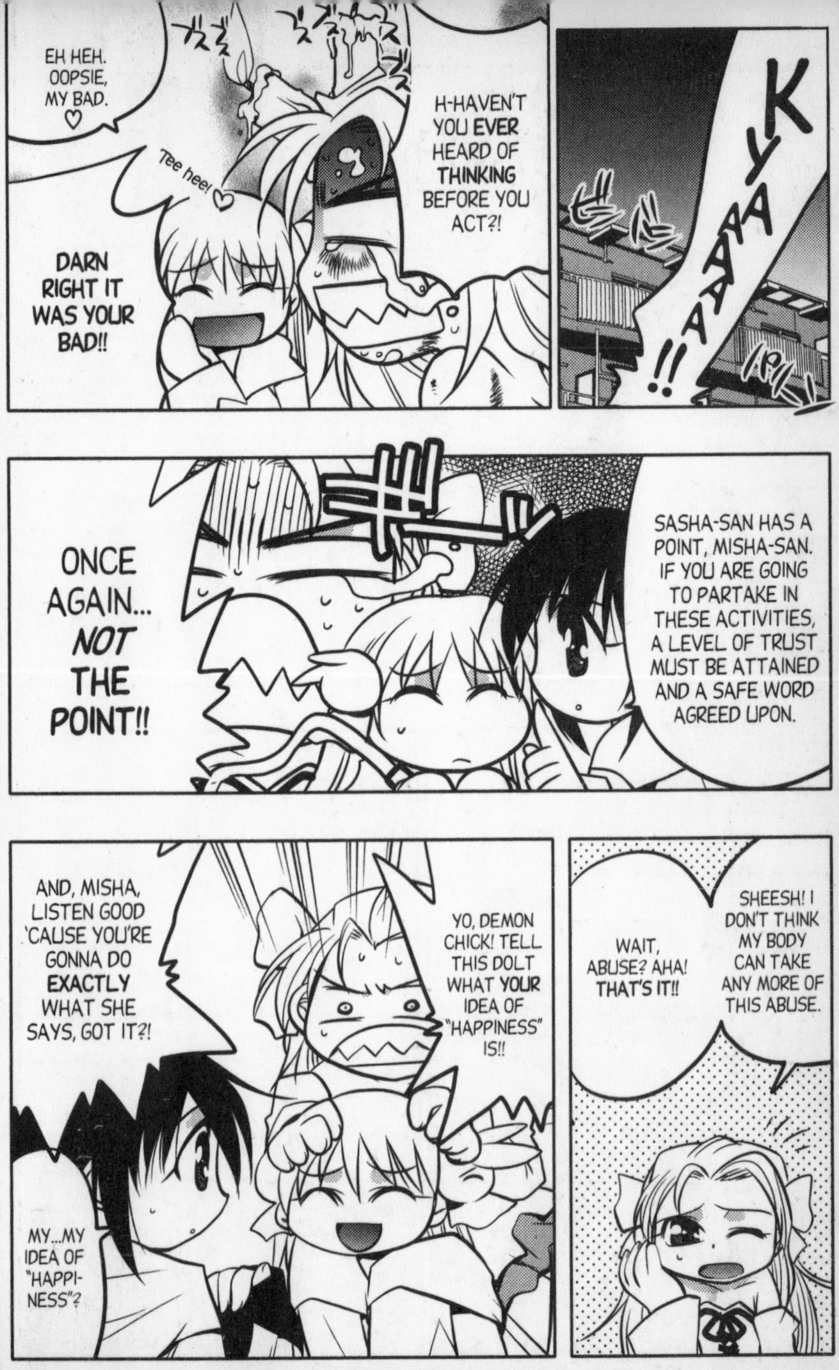
KYAAAAAA!!
EH HEH. OOPSIE, MY BAD. ♡
H-HAVEN'T YOU EVER HEARD OF THINKING BEFORE YOU ACT?!
Tee hee! ♡
DARN RIGHT IT WAS YOUR BAD!!
SASHA-SAN HAS A POINT, MISHA-SAN. IF YOU ARE GOING TO PARTAKE IN THESE ACTIVITIES, A LEVEL OF TRUST MUST BE ATTAINED AND A SAFE WORD AGREED UPON.
ONCE AGAIN... NOT THE POINT!!
SHEESH! I DON'T THINK MY BODY CAN TAKE ANY MORE OF THIS ABUSE.
WAIT, ABUSE? AHA! THAT'S IT!!
YO, DEMON CHICK! TELL THIS DOLT WHAT YOUR IDEA OF "HAPPINESS" IS!!
AND, MISHA, LISTEN GOOD 'CAUSE YOU'RE GONNA DO EXACTLY WHAT SHE SAYS, GOT IT?!
MY...MY IDEA OF "HAPPI-NESS"?

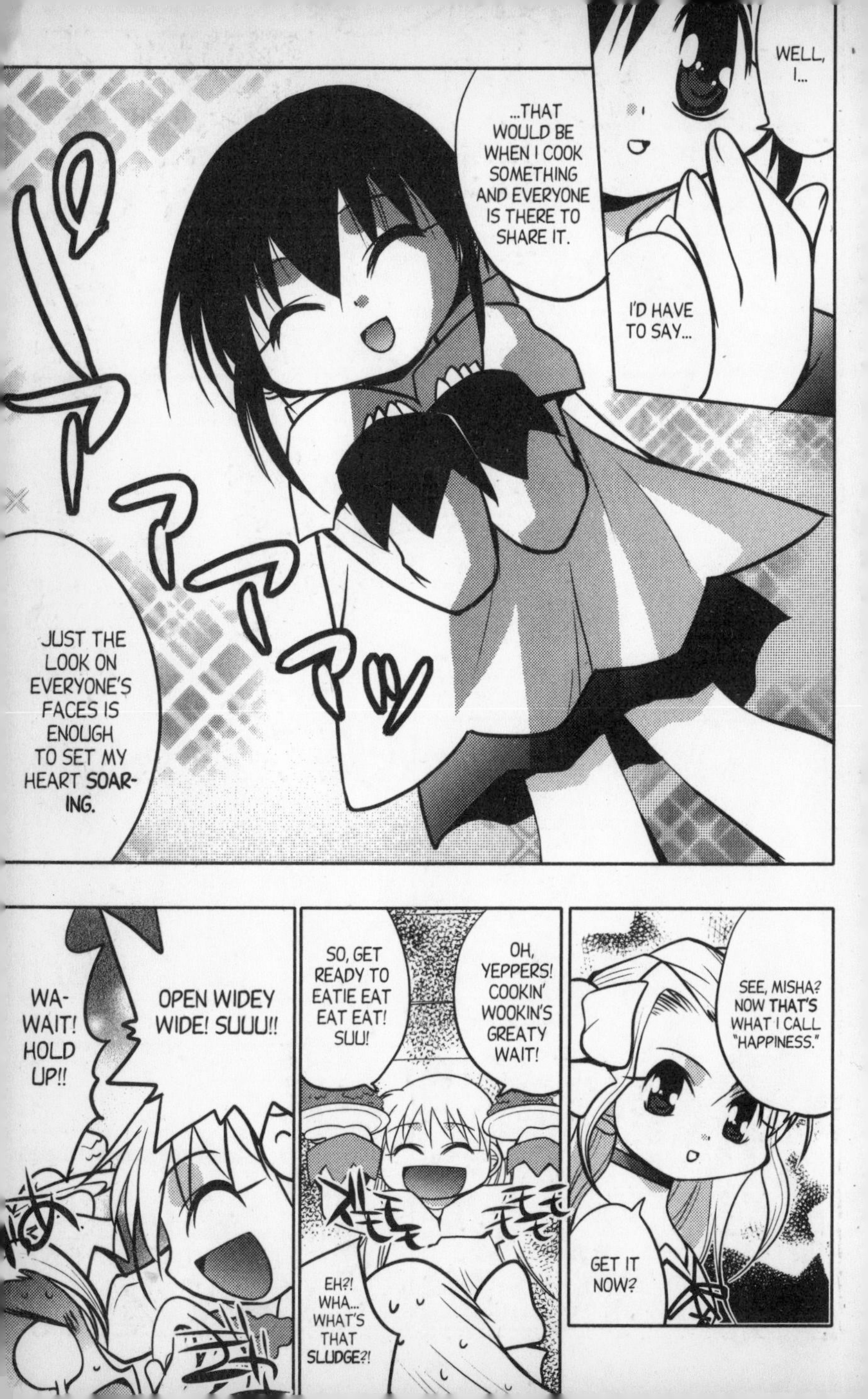

WELL, I...
I'D HAVE TO SAY...
...THAT WOULD BE WHEN I COOK SOMETHING AND EVERYONE IS THERE TO SHARE IT.
JUST THE LOOK ON EVERYONE'S FACES IS ENOUGH TO SET MY HEART SOAR-ING.
SEE, MISHA? NOW THAT'S WHAT I CALL "HAPPINESS."
GET IT NOW?
OH, YEPPERS! COOKIN' WOOKIN'S GREATY WAIT!
SO, GET READY TO EATIE EAT EAT EAT! SUU!
EH?! WHA... WHAT'S THAT SLUDGE?!
OPEN WIDEY WIDE! SUUU!!
WA-WAIT! HOLD UP!!

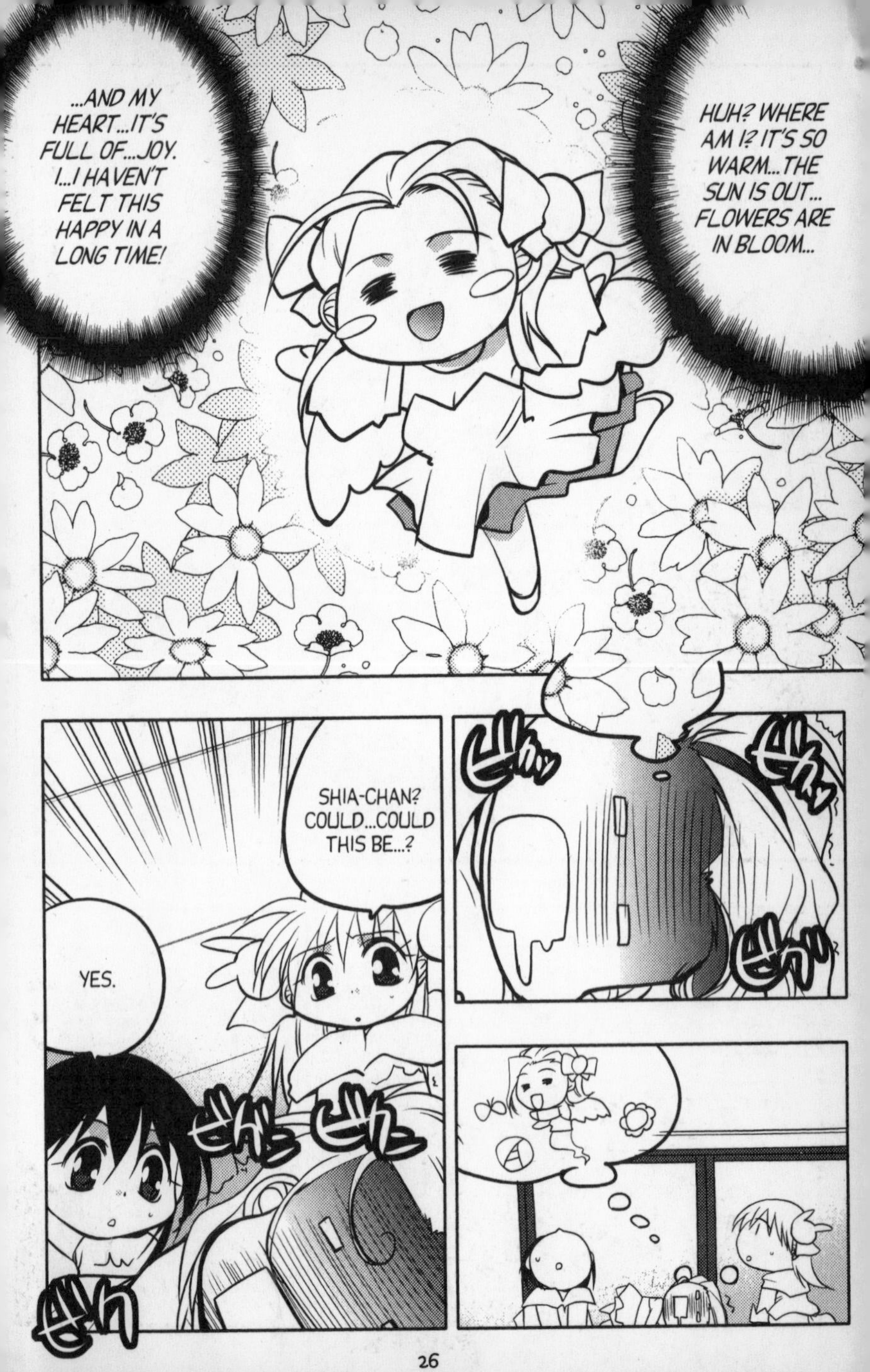
HUH? WHERE AM I? IT'S SO WARM...THE SUN IS OUT... FLOWERS ARE IN BLOOM...
...AND MY HEART...IT'S FULL OF...JOY. I...I HAVEN'T FELT THIS HAPPY IN A LONG TIME!
SHIA-CHAN? COULD...COULD THIS BE...?
YES.

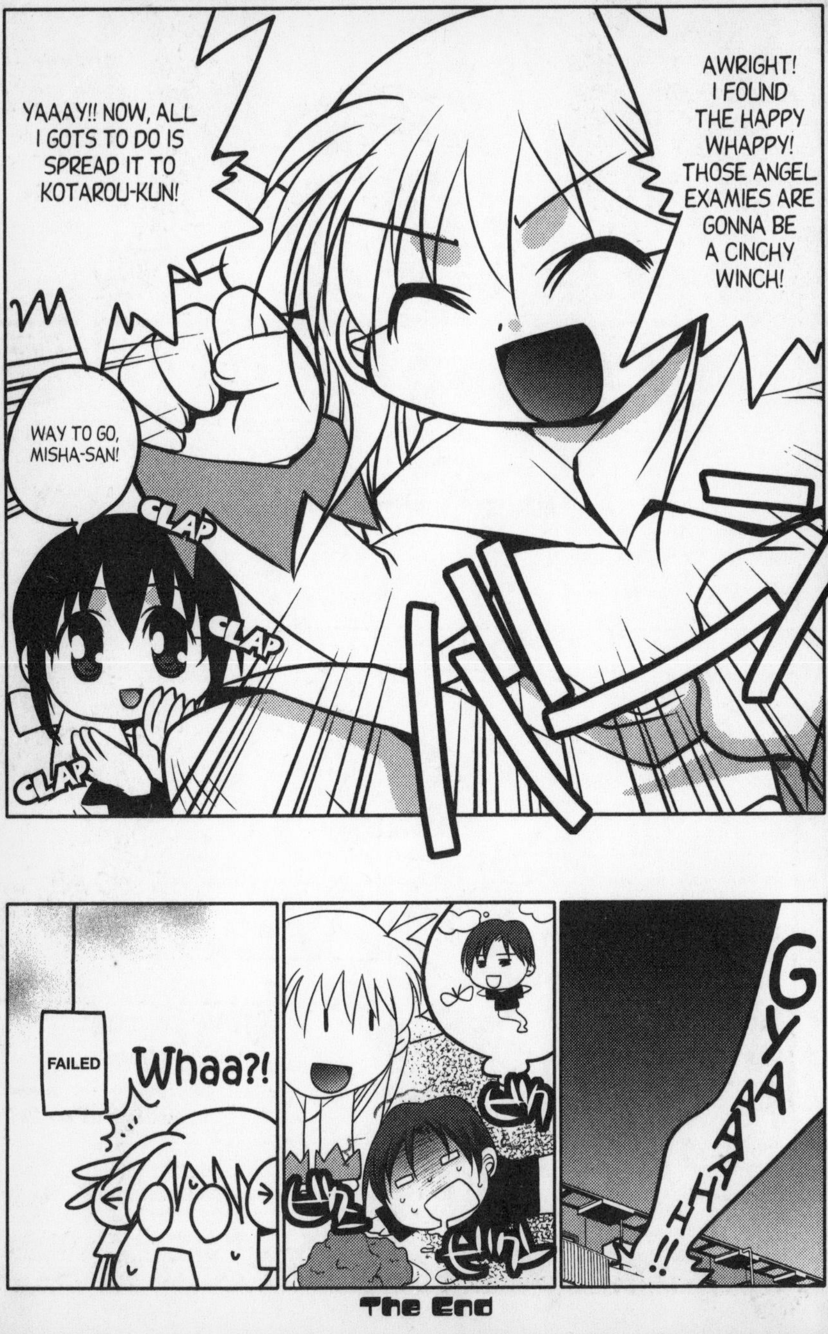
AWRIGHT! I FOUND THE HAPPY WHAPPY! THOSE ANGEL EXAMIES ARE GONNA BE A CINCHY WINCH!
YAAAY!! NOW, ALL I GOTS TO DO IS SPREAD IT TO KOTAROU-KUN!
WAY TO GO, MISHA-SAN!
CLAP
CLAP
CLAP
GYAAAAAHHH!!
FAILED
Whaa?!

The End

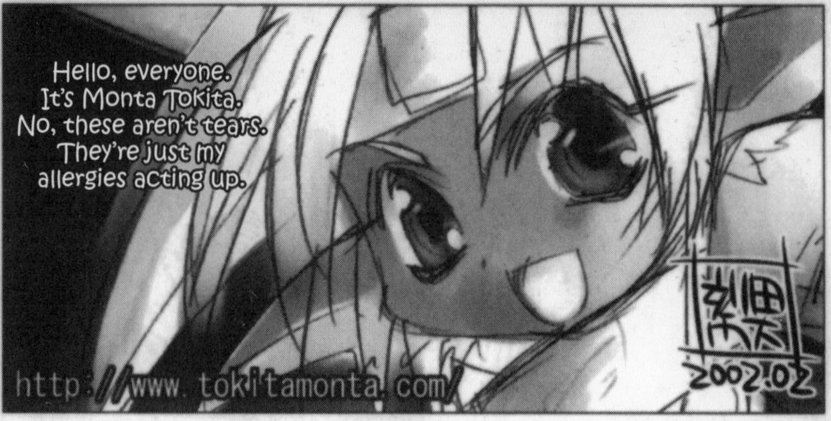
Hello, everyone.
It's Monta Tokita.
No, these aren't tears.
They're just my
allergies acting up.
http://www.tokitamonta.com/
2002.02

P.15
Monta Tokita

Writer's Talk

P.29
Mukku

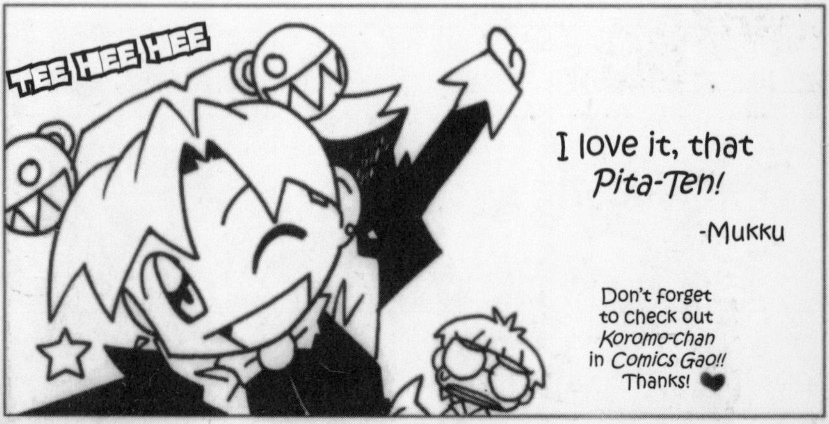
TEE HEE HEE
I love it, that
Pita-Ten!
-Mukku
Don't forget
to check out
Koromo-chan
in *Comics Gao!!*
Thanks!

Lesson X

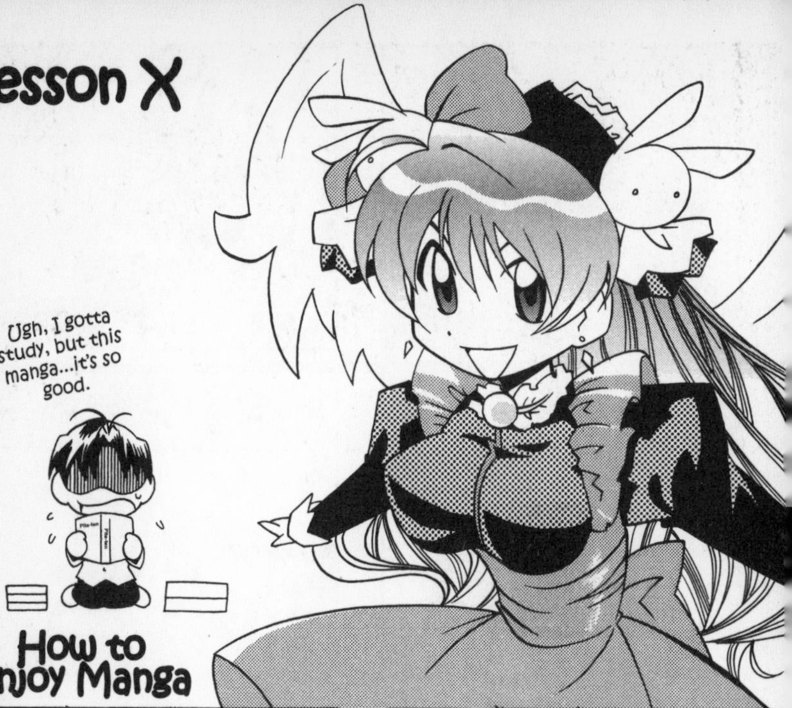

Ugh, I gotta study, but this manga...it's so good.
Pita-ten

How to Enjoy Manga

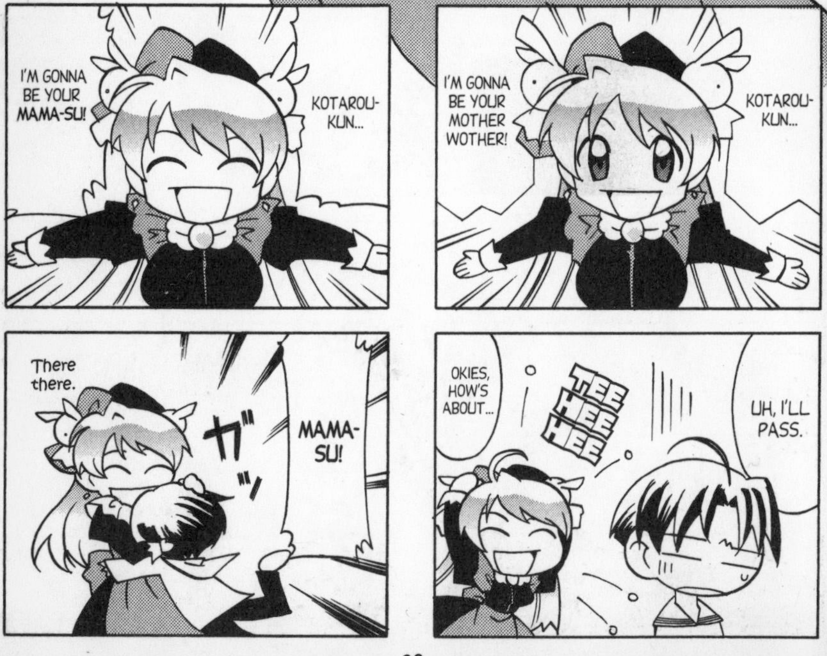

KOTAROU-KUN...
I'M GONNA BE YOUR MOTHER WOTHER!
KOTAROU-KUN...
I'M GONNA BE YOUR MAMA-SU!
UH, I'LL PASS.
TEE HEE HEE
OKIES, HOW'S ABOUT...
MAMA-SU!
ガ
There there.

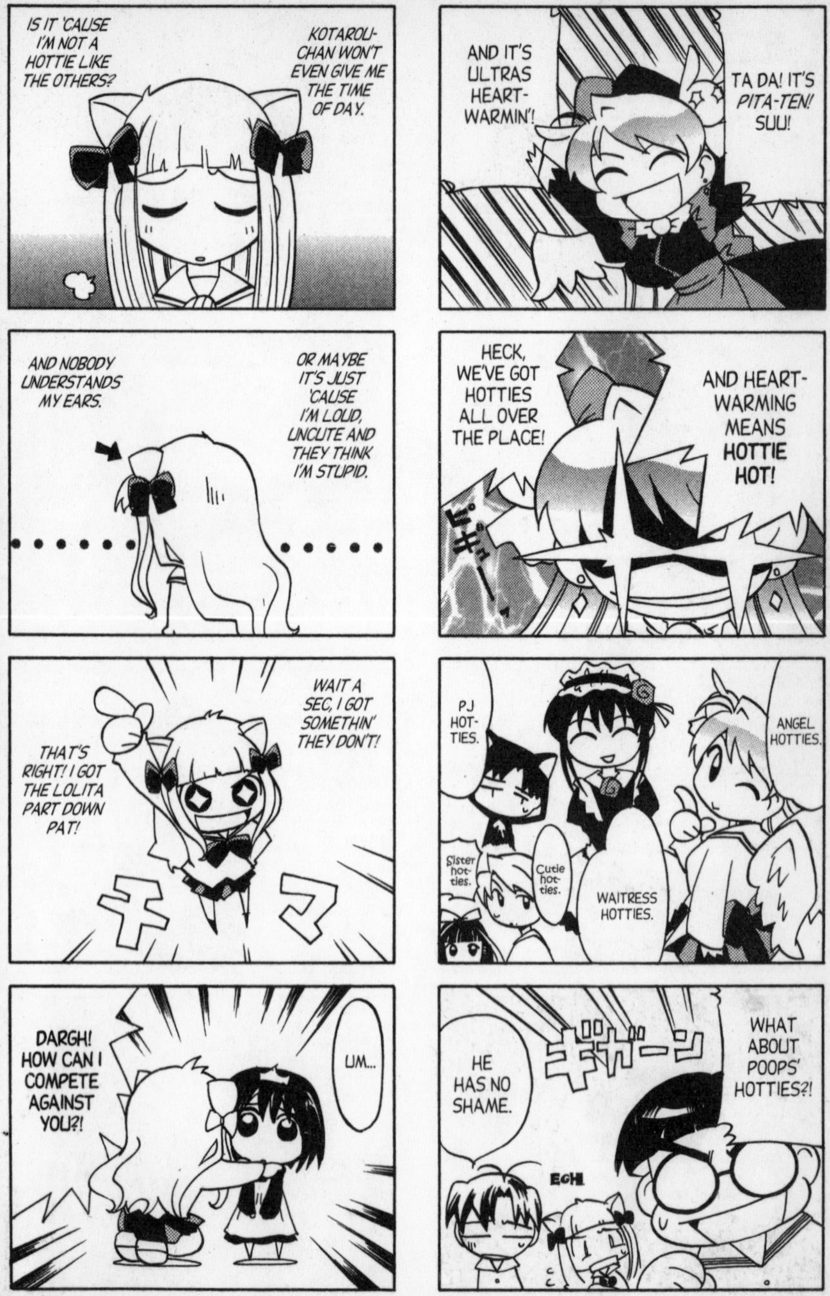
TA DA! IT'S PITA-TEN! SUU!
AND IT'S ULTRAS HEART-WARMIN'!
AND HEART-WARMING MEANS HOTTIE HOT!
HECK, WE'VE GOT HOTTIES ALL OVER THE PLACE!
ANGEL HOTTIES.
PJ HOTTIES.
WAITRESS HOTTIES.
Cutie hotties.
Sister hotties.
WHAT ABOUT POOPS' HOTTIES?!
ギガーン
HE HAS NO SHAME.
EGH
KOTAROU-CHAN WON'T EVEN GIVE ME THE TIME OF DAY.
IS IT 'CAUSE I'M NOT A HOTTIE LIKE THE OTHERS?
OR MAYBE IT'S JUST 'CAUSE I'M LOUD, UNCUTE AND THEY THINK I'M STUPID.
AND NOBODY UNDERSTANDS MY EARS.
WAIT A SEC, I GOT SOMETHIN' THEY DON'T!
THAT'S RIGHT! I GOT THE LOLITA PART DOWN PAT!
UM...
DARGH! HOW CAN I COMPETE AGAINST YOU?!

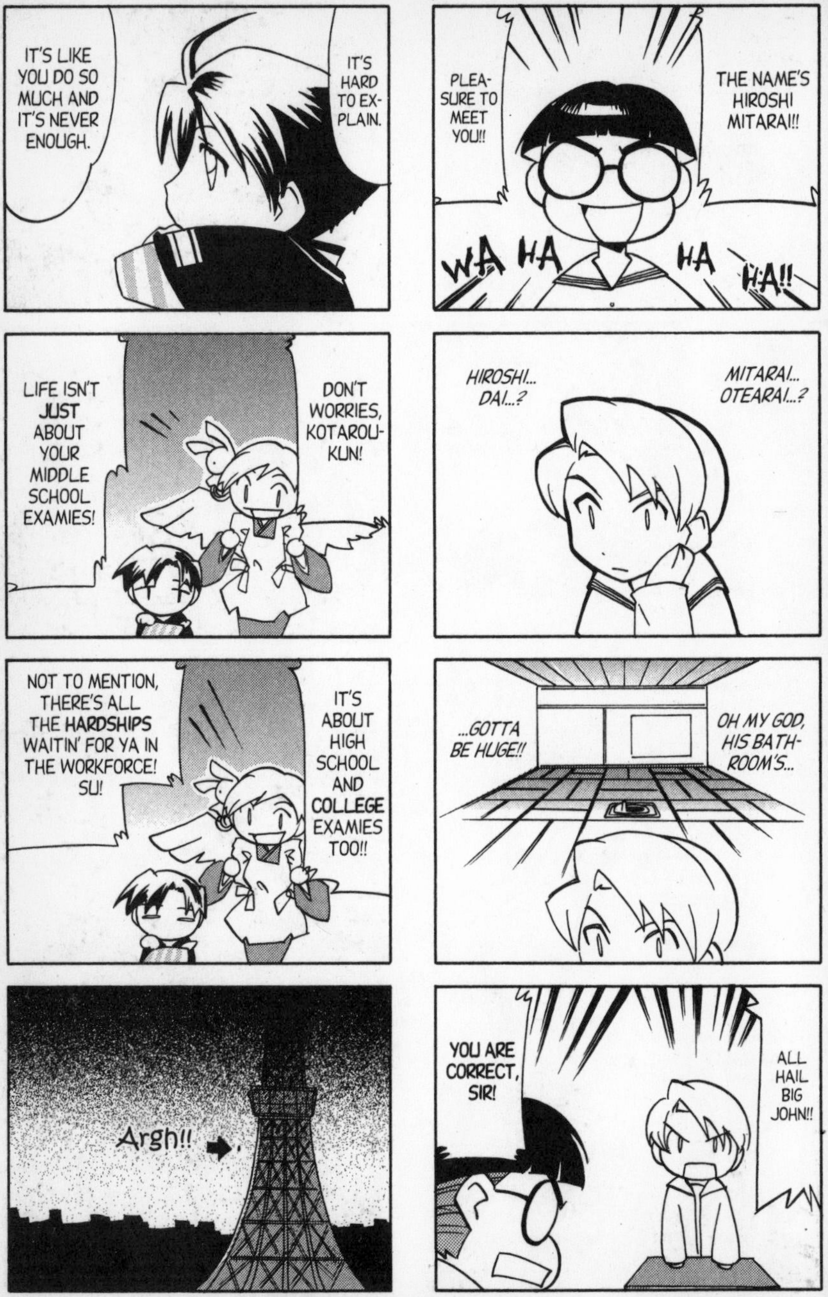
THE NAME'S HIROSHI MITARAI!!
PLEASURE TO MEET YOU!!
WA HA HA HA!!
MITARAI... OTEARAI...?
HIROSHI... DAI...?
OH MY GOD, HIS BATHROOM'S...
...GOTTA BE HUGE!!
ALL HAIL BIG JOHN!!
YOU ARE CORRECT, SIR!
IT'S HARD TO EXPLAIN.
IT'S LIKE YOU DO SO MUCH AND IT'S NEVER ENOUGH.
DON'T WORRIES, KOTAROU-KUN!
LIFE ISN'T JUST ABOUT YOUR MIDDLE SCHOOL EXAMIES!
IT'S ABOUT HIGH SCHOOL AND COLLEGE EXAMIES TOO!!
NOT TO MENTION, THERE'S ALL THE HARDSHIPS WAITIN' FOR YA IN THE WORKFORCE! SU!
Argh!!

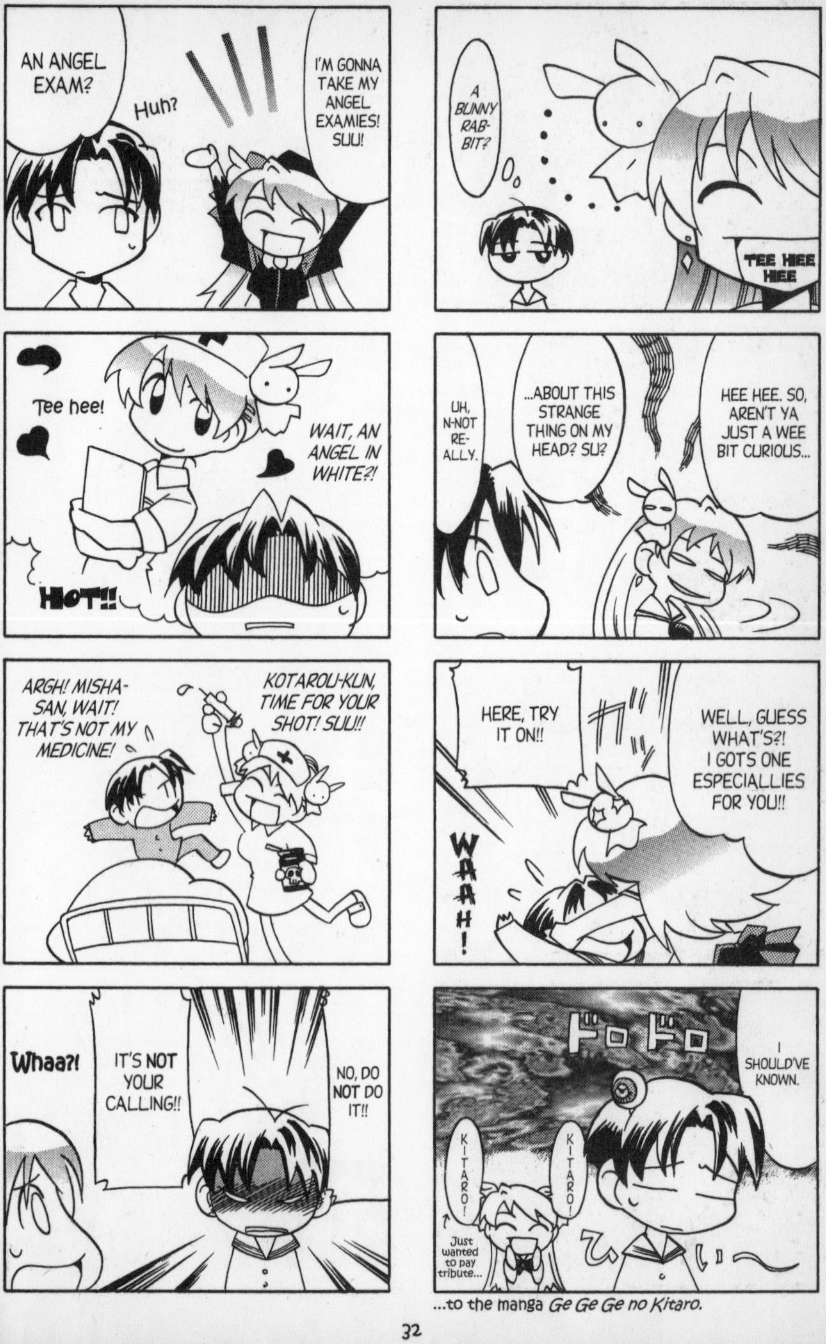
A BUNNY RAB-BIT?
TEE HEE HEE
HEE HEE. SO, AREN'T YA JUST A WEE BIT CURIOUS...
...ABOUT THIS STRANGE THING ON MY HEAD? SU?
UH, N-NOT RE-ALLY.
WELL, GUESS WHAT'S?! I GOTS ONE ESPECIALLIES FOR YOU!!
HERE, TRY IT ON!!
WAAAH!
ドロドロ
I SHOULD'VE KNOWN.
KITARO!
KITARO!
Just wanted to pay tribute...
I'M GONNA TAKE MY ANGEL EXAMIES! SUU!
Huh?
AN ANGEL EXAM?
WAIT, AN ANGEL IN WHITE?!
Tee hee!
HOT!!
KOTAROU-KUN, TIME FOR YOUR SHOT! SUU!!
ARGH! MISHA-SAN, WAIT! THAT'S NOT MY MEDICINE!
NO, DO NOT DO IT!!
IT'S NOT YOUR CALLING!!
Whaa?!

...to the manga *Ge Ge Ge no Kitaro.*

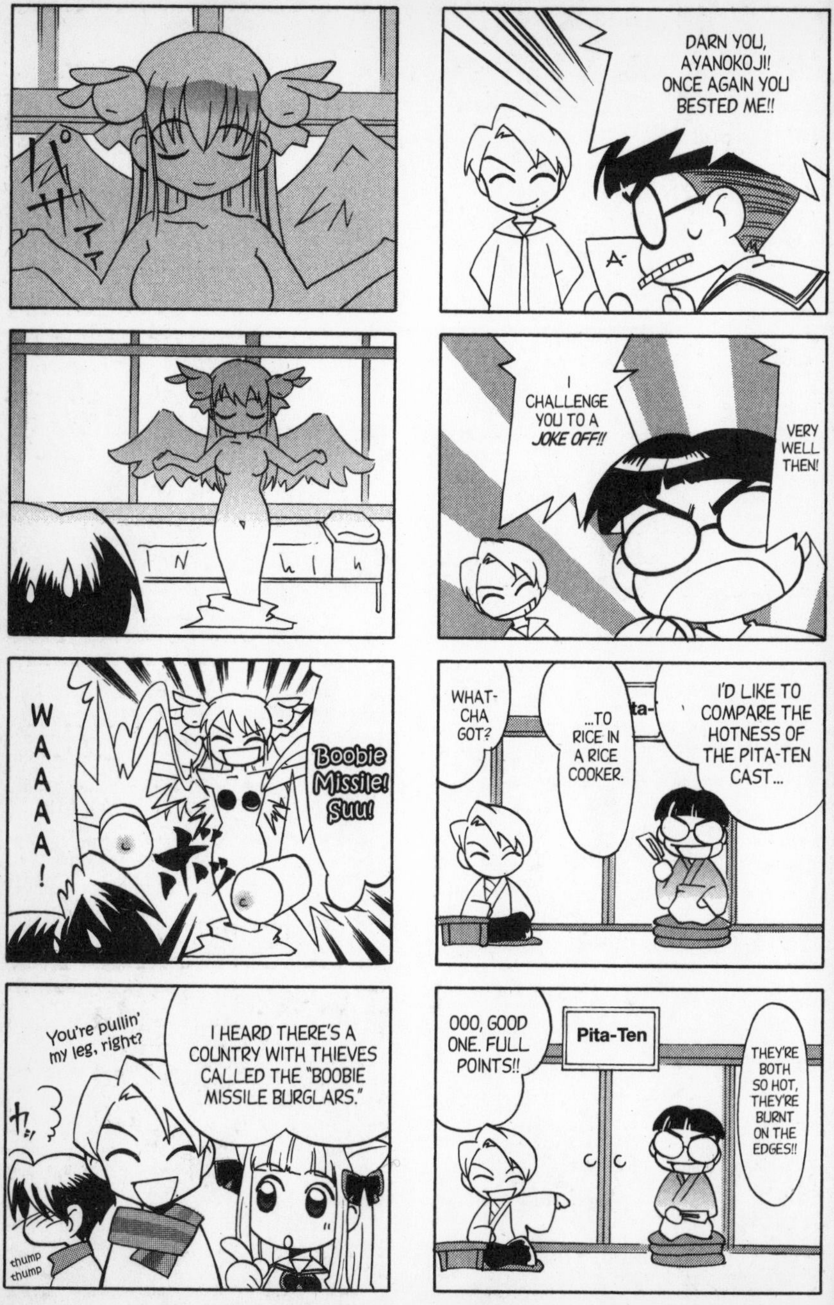
DARN YOU, AYANOKOJI! ONCE AGAIN YOU BESTED ME!!
A-
I CHALLENGE YOU TO A JOKE OFF!!
VERY WELL THEN!
I'D LIKE TO COMPARE THE HOTNESS OF THE PITA-TEN CAST...
...TO RICE IN A RICE COOKER.
WHAT-CHA GOT?
THEY'RE BOTH SO HOT, THEY'RE BURNT ON THE EDGES!!
Pita-Ten
OOO, GOOD ONE. FULL POINTS!!
Boobie Missile! Suu!
WAAAAA!
I HEARD THERE'S A COUNTRY WITH THIEVES CALLED THE "BOOBIE MISSILE BURGLARS."
You're pullin' my leg, right?
thump thump

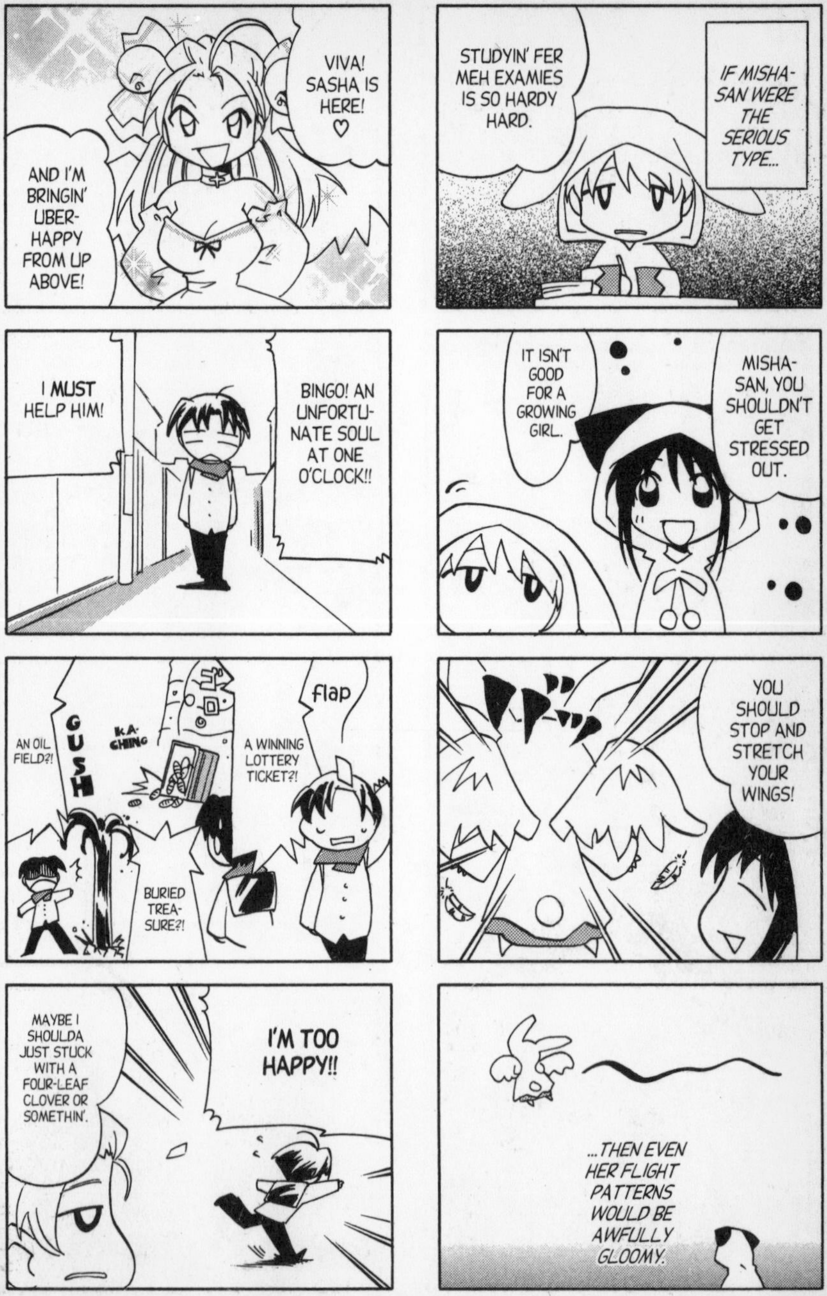
IF MISHA-SAN WERE THE SERIOUS TYPE...
STUDYIN' FER MEH EXAMIES IS SO HARDY HARD.
MISHA-SAN, YOU SHOULDN'T GET STRESSED OUT.
IT ISN'T GOOD FOR A GROWING GIRL.
YOU SHOULD STOP AND STRETCH YOUR WINGS!
...THEN EVEN HER FLIGHT PATTERNS WOULD BE AWFULLY GLOOMY.
VIVA! SASHA IS HERE! ♡
AND I'M BRINGIN' UBER-HAPPY FROM UP ABOVE!
BINGO! AN UNFORTUNATE SOUL AT ONE O'CLOCK!!
I MUST HELP HIM!
flap
A WINNING LOTTERY TICKET?!
KA-CHING
BURIED TREASURE?!
GUSH
AN OIL FIELD?!
I'M TOO HAPPY!!
MAYBE I SHOULDA JUST STUCK WITH A FOUR-LEAF CLOVER OR SOMETHIN'.

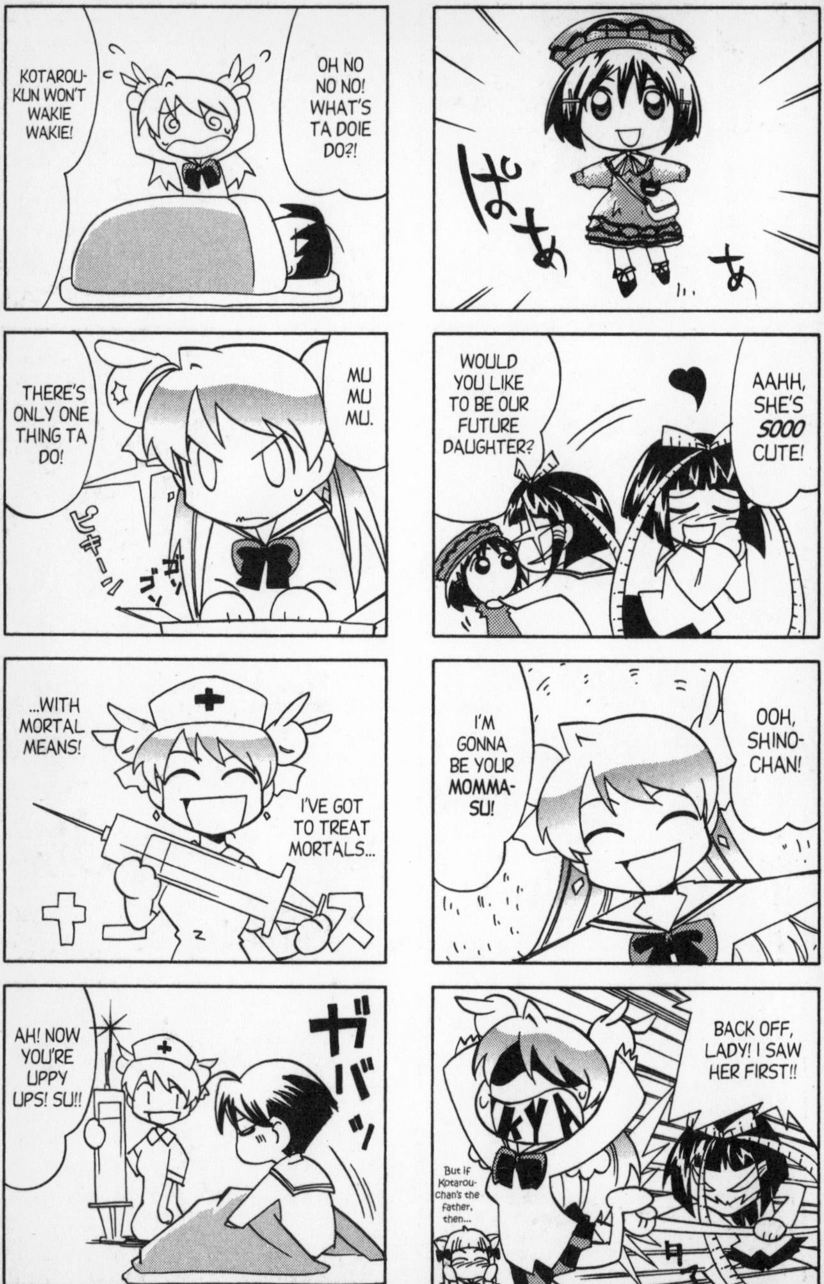
ぱあ
あ
AAHH, SHE'S SOOO CUTE!
WOULD YOU LIKE TO BE OUR FUTURE DAUGHTER?
OOH, SHINO-CHAN!
I'M GONNA BE YOUR MOMMA-SU!
BACK OFF, LADY! I SAW HER FIRST!!
KYA
But if Kotarou-Chan's the father, then...
OH NO NO NO! WHAT'S TA DOIE DO?!
KOTAROU-KUN WON'T WAKIE WAKIE!
MU MU MU.
THERE'S ONLY ONE THING TA DO!
ピキーン
I'VE GOT TO TREAT MORTALS...
...WITH MORTAL MEANS!
ナース
ガバッ
AH! NOW YOU'RE UPPY UPS! SU!!

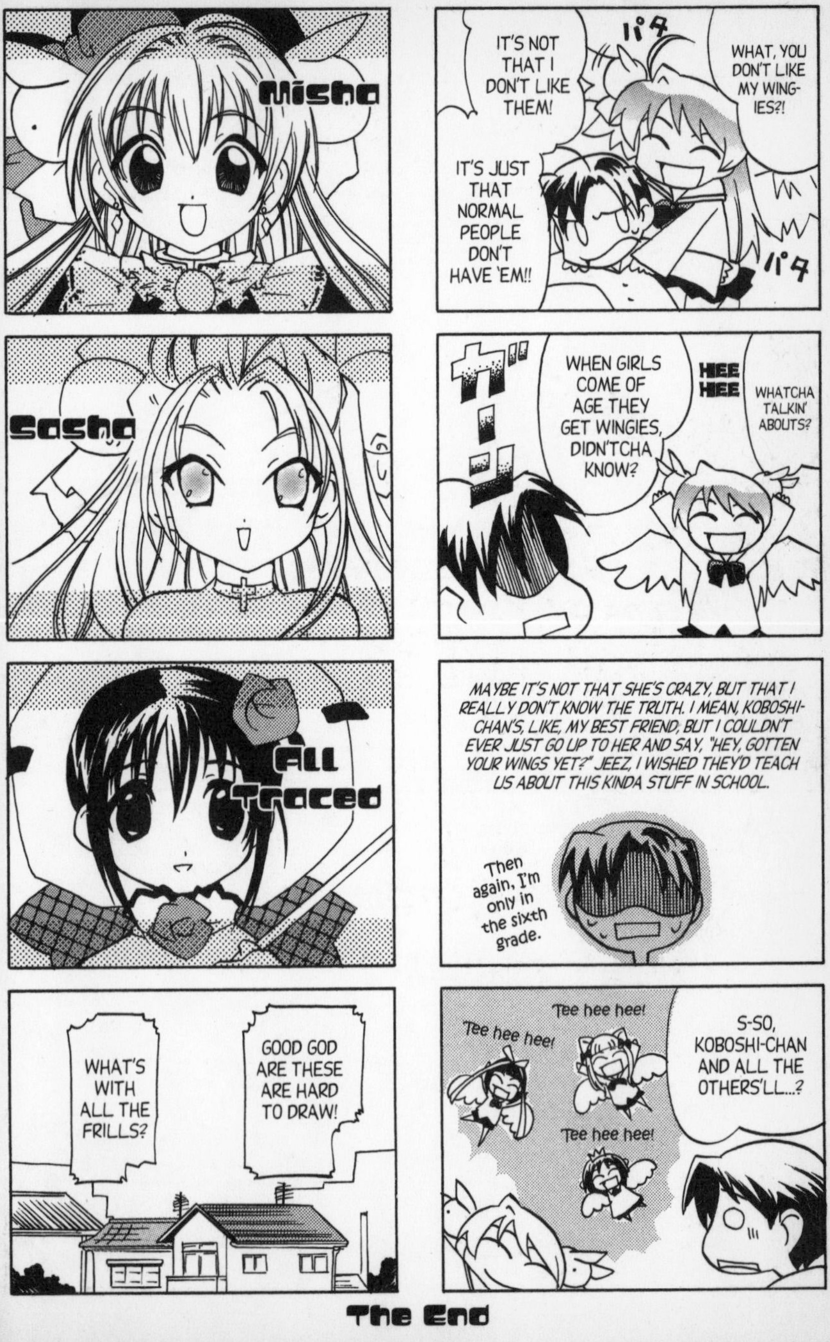
WHAT, YOU DON'T LIKE MY WINGIES?!
パタ
IT'S NOT THAT I DON'T LIKE THEM!
IT'S JUST THAT NORMAL PEOPLE DON'T HAVE 'EM!!
パタ
WHATCHA TALKIN' ABOUTS?
HEE HEE
WHEN GIRLS COME OF AGE THEY GET WINGIES, DIDN'TCHA KNOW?
ガーン
MAYBE IT'S NOT THAT SHE'S CRAZY, BUT THAT I REALLY DON'T KNOW THE TRUTH. I MEAN, KOBOSHI-CHAN'S, LIKE, MY BEST FRIEND, BUT I COULDN'T EVER JUST GO UP TO HER AND SAY, "HEY, GOTTEN YOUR WINGS YET?" JEEZ, I WISHED THEY'D TEACH US ABOUT THIS KINDA STUFF IN SCHOOL.
Then again, I'm only in the sixth grade.
S-SO, KOBOSHI-CHAN AND ALL THE OTHERS'LL...?
Tee hee hee!
Tee hee hee!
Tee hee hee!
Misha
Sasha
All Traced
GOOD GOD ARE THESE ARE HARD TO DRAW!
WHAT'S WITH ALL THE FRILLS?
The End

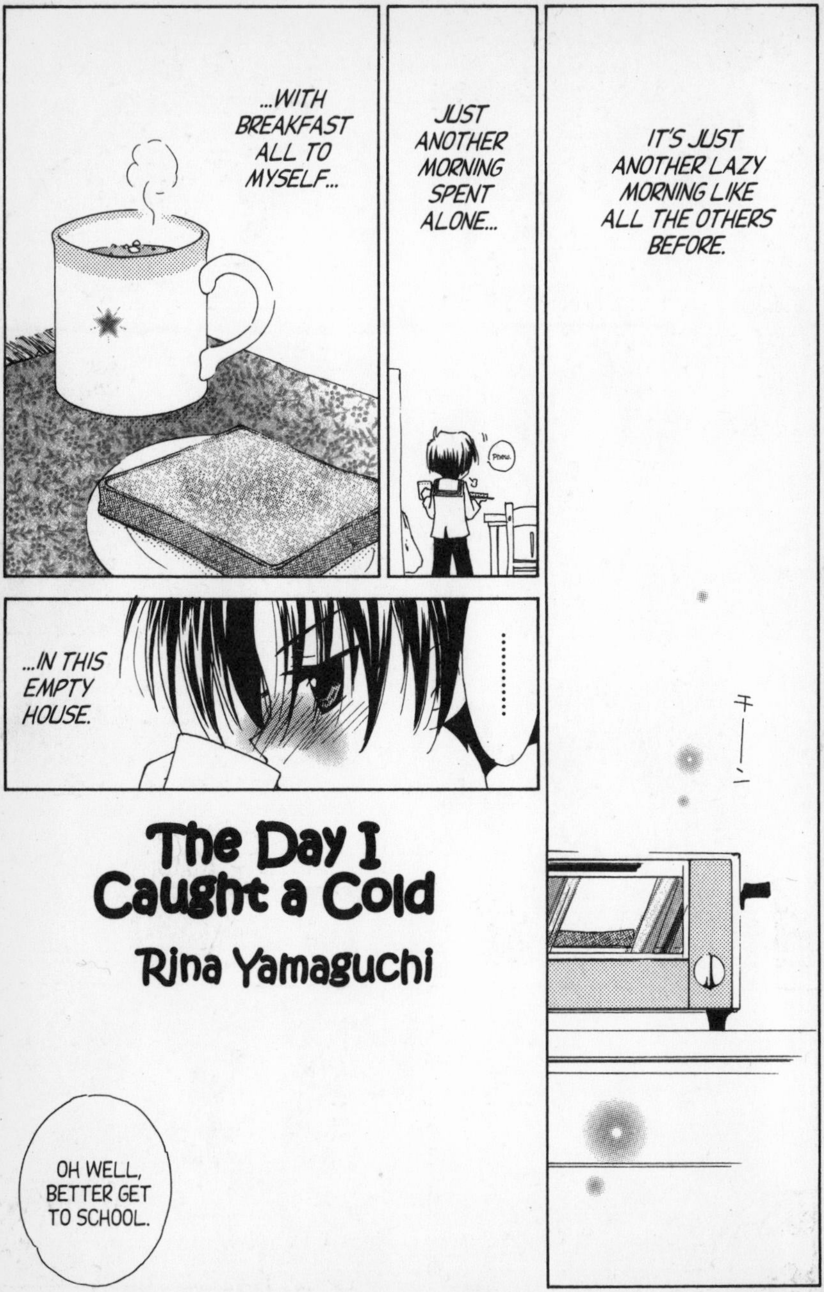
IT'S JUST ANOTHER LAZY MORNING LIKE ALL THE OTHERS BEFORE.
チーン
JUST ANOTHER MORNING SPENT ALONE...
Phew.
...WITH BREAKFAST ALL TO MYSELF...
....
...IN THIS EMPTY HOUSE.
The Day I Caught a Cold
Rina Yamaguchi
OH WELL, BETTER GET TO SCHOOL.

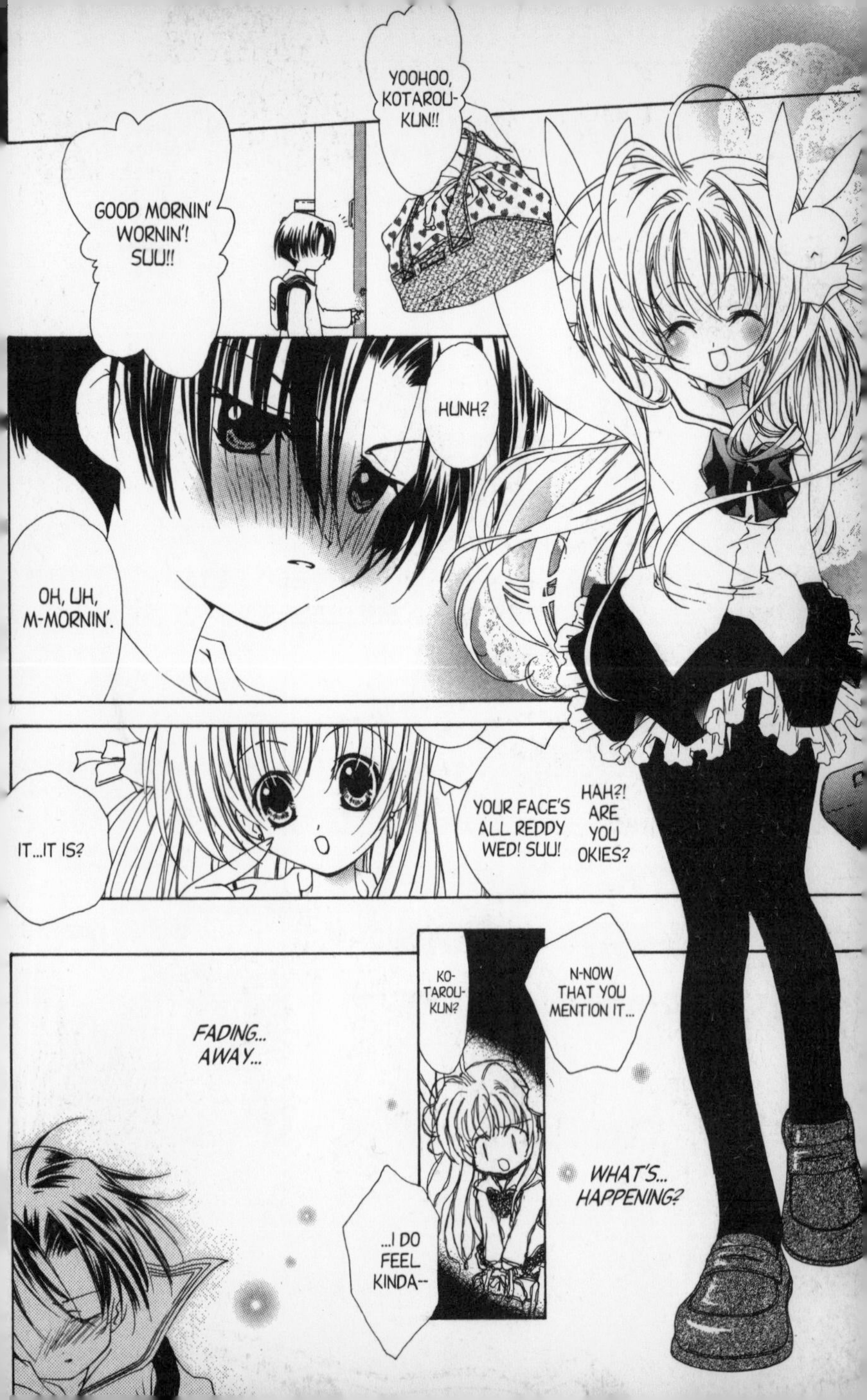
YOOHOO, KOTAROU-KUN!!
GOOD MORNIN' WORNIN'! SUU!!
HUNH?
OH, UH, M-MORNIN'.
HAH?! ARE YOU OKIES?
YOUR FACE'S ALL REDDY WED! SUU!
IT...IT IS?
KO-TAROU-KUN?
N-NOW THAT YOU MENTION IT...
...I DO FEEL KINDA--
WHAT'S... HAPPENING?
FADING... AWAY...

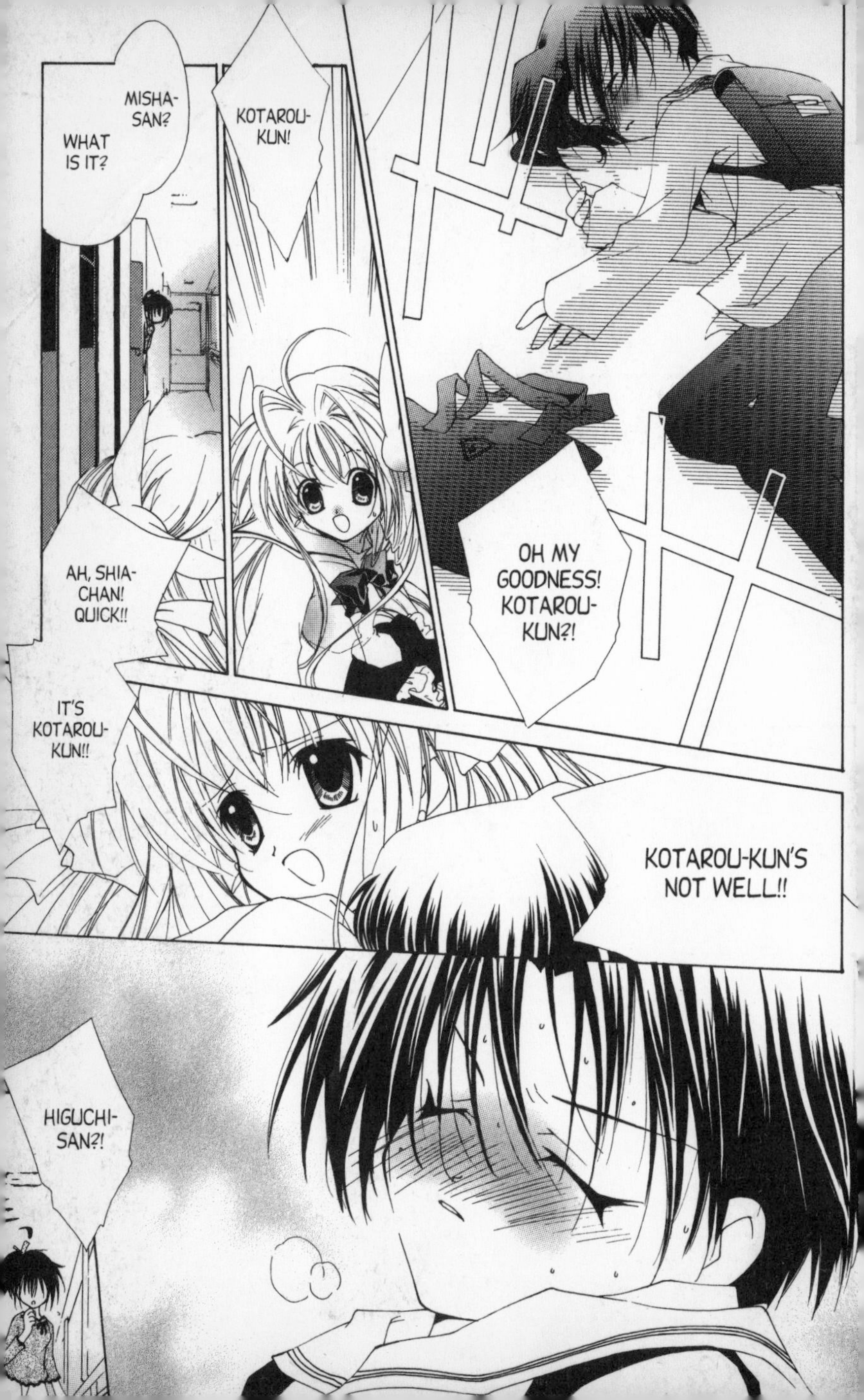
OH MY GOODNESS! KOTAROU-KUN?!
KOTAROU-KUN!
MISHA-SAN? WHAT IS IT?
AH, SHIA-CHAN! QUICK!!
IT'S KOTAROU-KUN!!
KOTAROU-KUN'S NOT WELL!!
HIGUCHI-SAN?!

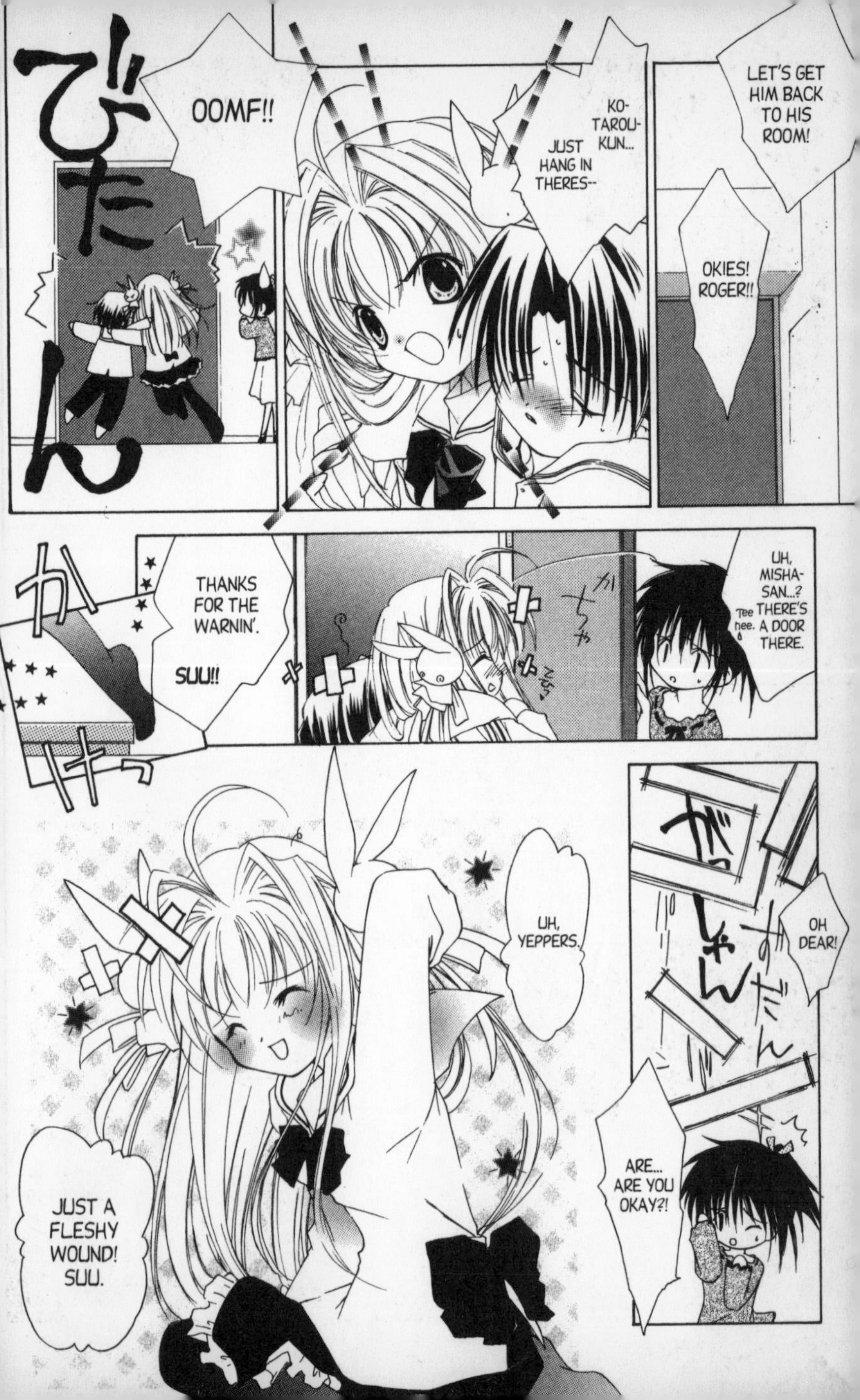
LET'S GET HIM BACK TO HIS ROOM!
OKIES! ROGER!!
KO-TAROU-KUN...
JUST HANG IN THERES--
OOMF!!
びたん
UH, MISHA-SAN...? THERE'S A DOOR THERE.
Tee hee.
THANKS FOR THE WARNIN'.
SUU!!
OH DEAR!
ARE... ARE YOU OKAY?!
UH, YEPPERS.
JUST A FLESHY WOUND! SUU.

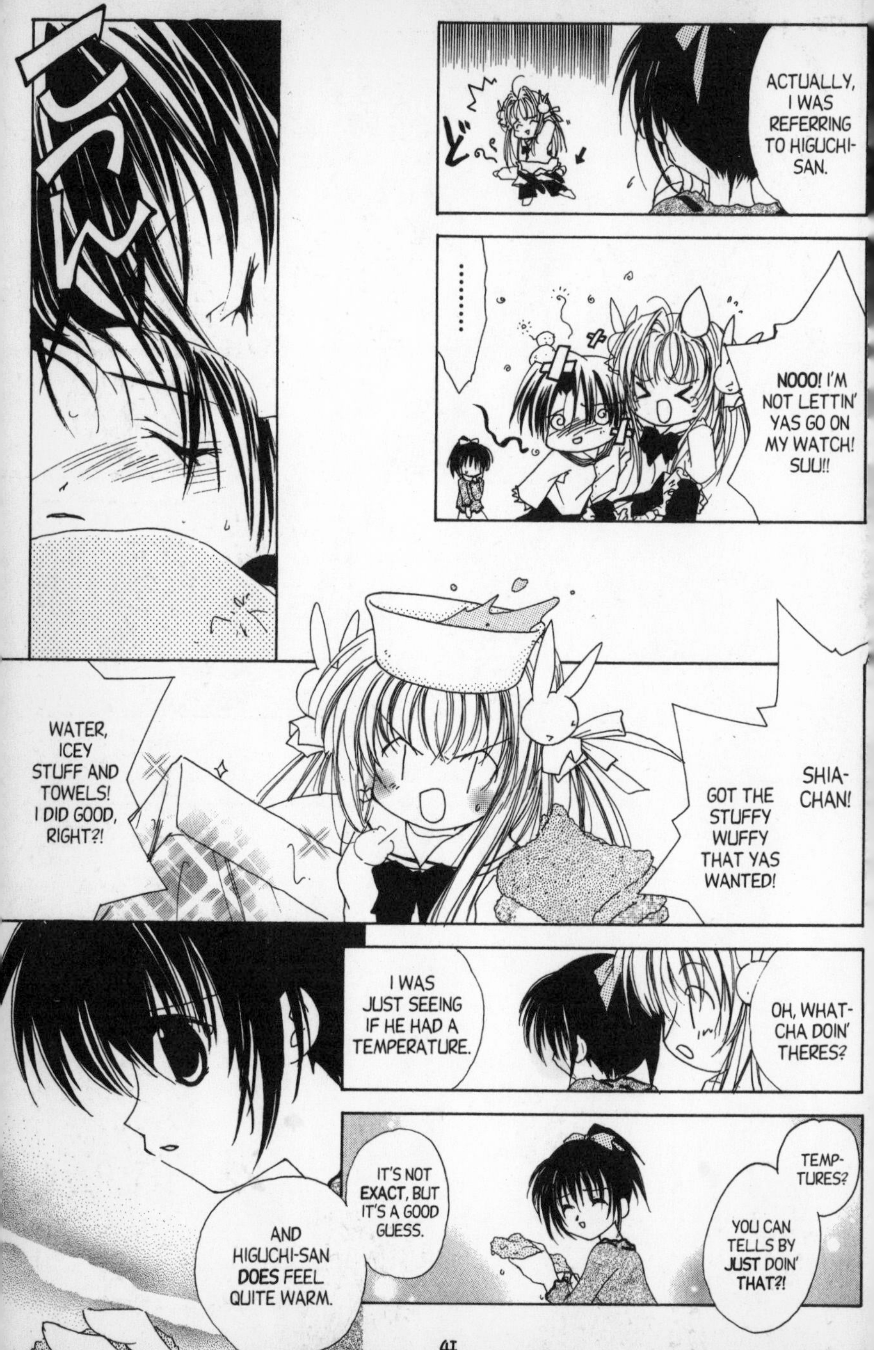
ACTUALLY, I WAS REFERRING TO HIGUCHI-SAN.
ど
NOOO! I'M NOT LETTIN' YAS GO ON MY WATCH! SUU!!
......
こん
SHIA-CHAN!
GOT THE STUFFY WUFFY THAT YAS WANTED!
WATER, ICEY STUFF AND TOWELS! I DID GOOD, RIGHT?!
OH, WHAT-CHA DOIN' THERES?
I WAS JUST SEEING IF HE HAD A TEMPERATURE.
TEMP-TURES?
YOU CAN TELLS BY JUST DOIN' THAT?!
IT'S NOT EXACT, BUT IT'S A GOOD GUESS.
AND HIGUCHI-SAN DOES FEEL QUITE WARM.

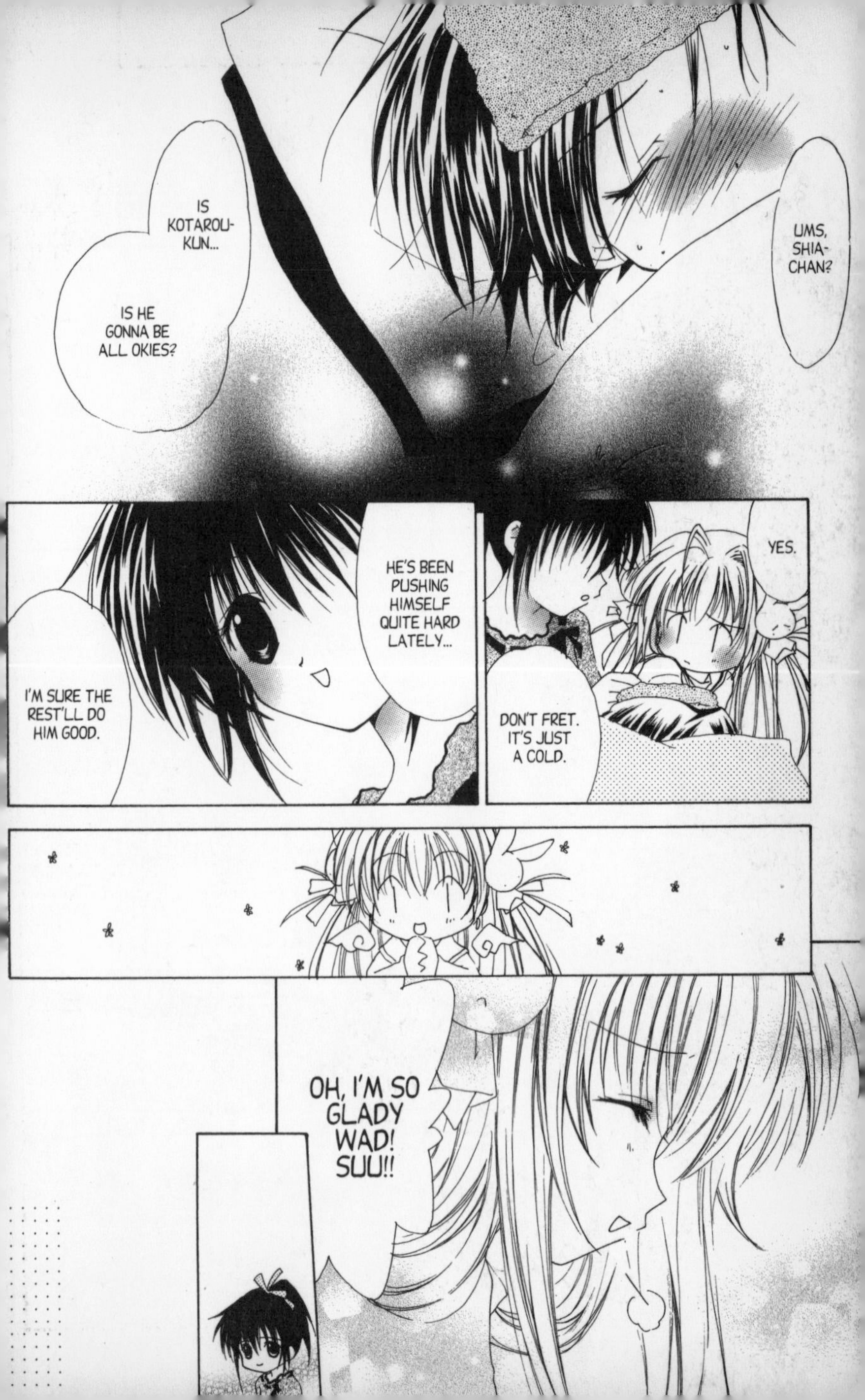
UMS, SHIA-CHAN?
IS KOTAROU-KUN...
IS HE GONNA BE ALL OKIES?
YES.
DON'T FRET. IT'S JUST A COLD.
HE'S BEEN PUSHING HIMSELF QUITE HARD LATELY...
I'M SURE THE REST'LL DO HIM GOOD.
OH, I'M SO GLADY WAD! SUU!!

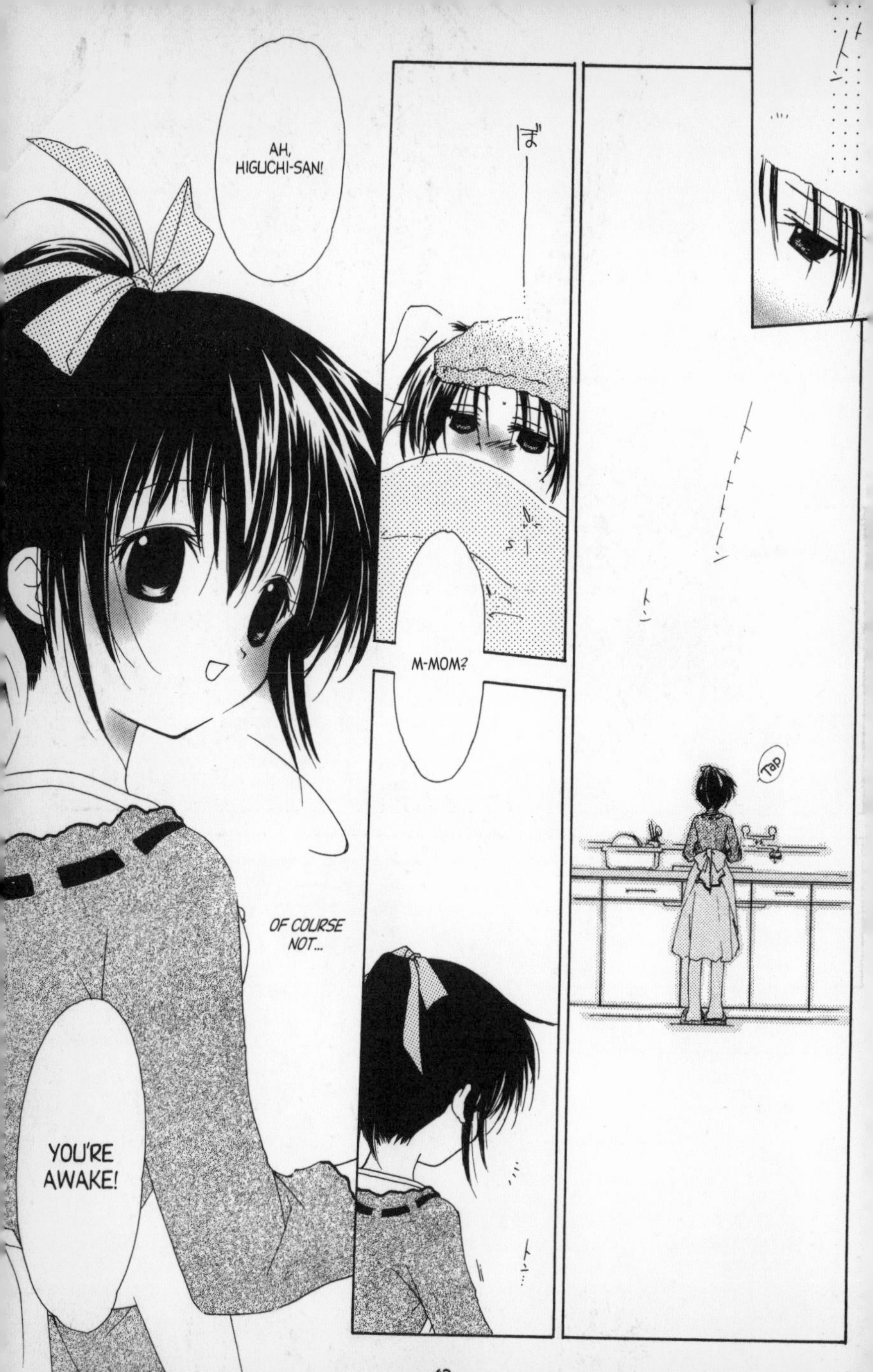
Tap
ぼ
M-MOM?
OF COURSE NOT...
AH, HIGUCHI-SAN!
YOU'RE AWAKE!

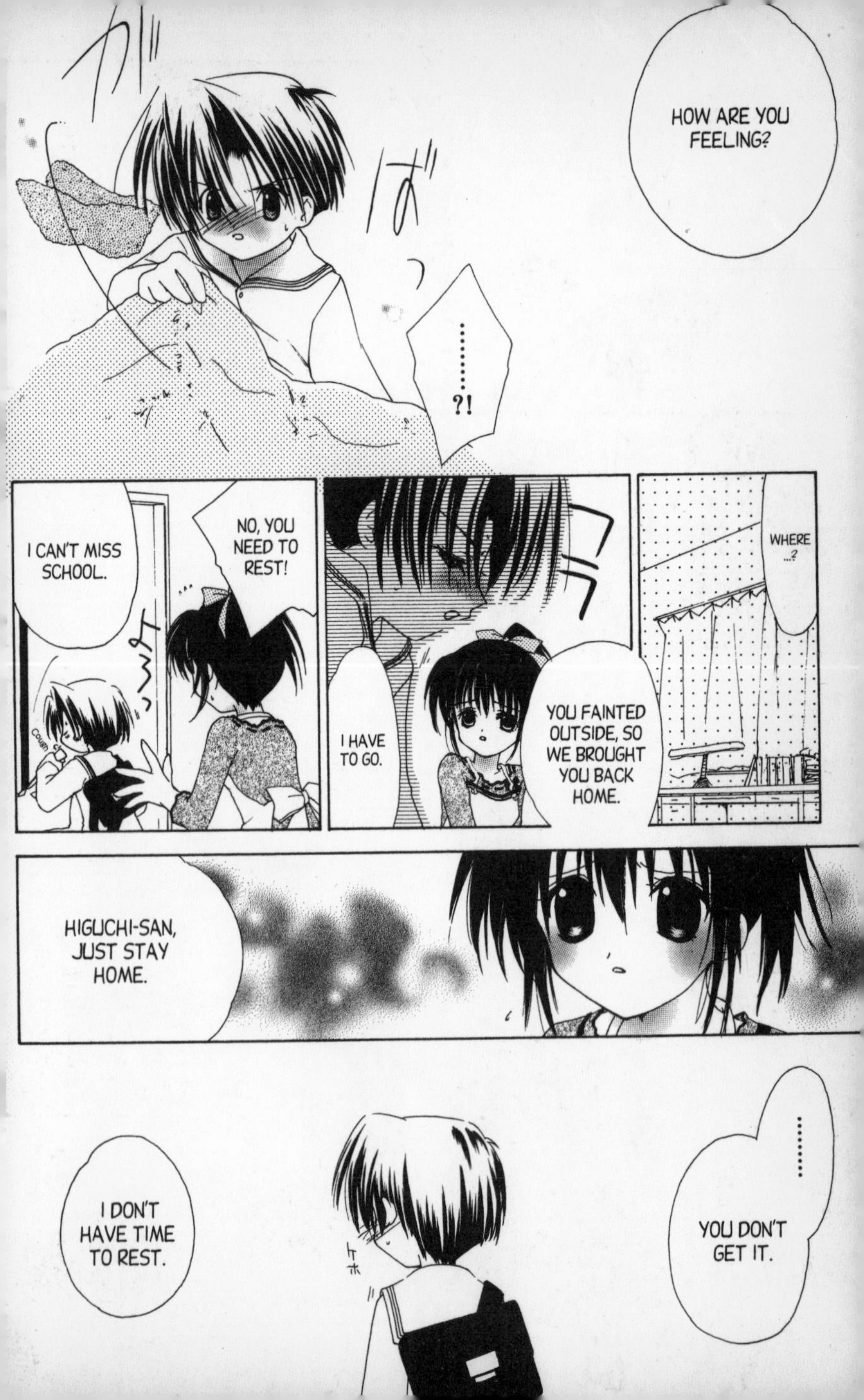
HOW ARE YOU FEELING?
......?!
WHERE ...?
YOU FAINTED OUTSIDE, SO WE BROUGHT YOU BACK HOME.
I HAVE TO GO.
NO, YOU NEED TO REST!
I CAN'T MISS SCHOOL.
COUGH
HIGUCHI-SAN, JUST STAY HOME.
......
YOU DON'T GET IT.
I DON'T HAVE TIME TO REST.

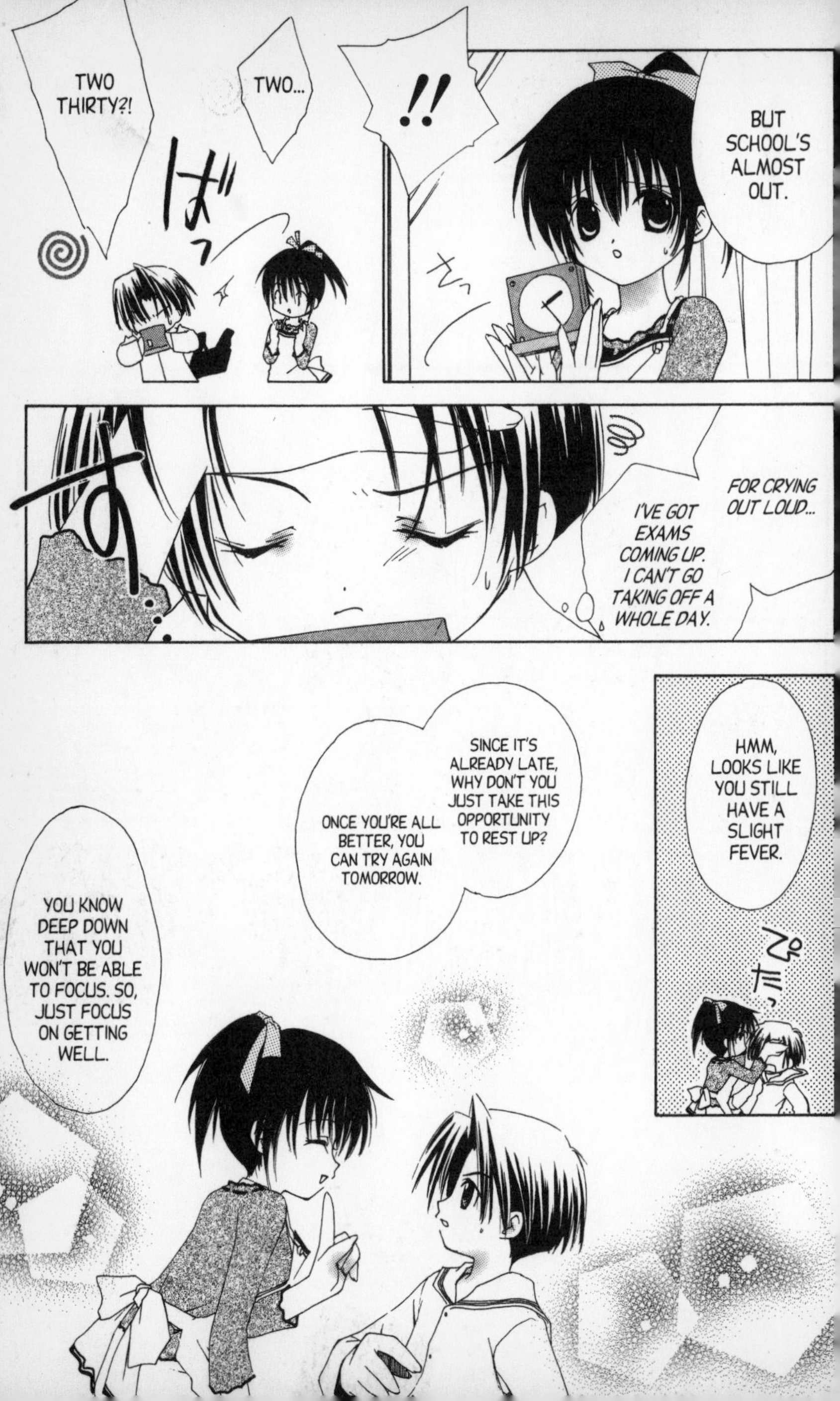
BUT SCHOOL'S ALMOST OUT.
!!
TWO...
TWO THIRTY?!
ばっ
FOR CRYING OUT LOUD...
I'VE GOT EXAMS COMING UP. I CAN'T GO TAKING OFF A WHOLE DAY.
HMM, LOOKS LIKE YOU STILL HAVE A SLIGHT FEVER.
SINCE IT'S ALREADY LATE, WHY DON'T YOU JUST TAKE THIS OPPORTUNITY TO REST UP?
ONCE YOU'RE ALL BETTER, YOU CAN TRY AGAIN TOMORROW.
YOU KNOW DEEP DOWN THAT YOU WON'T BE ABLE TO FOCUS. SO, JUST FOCUS ON GETTING WELL.

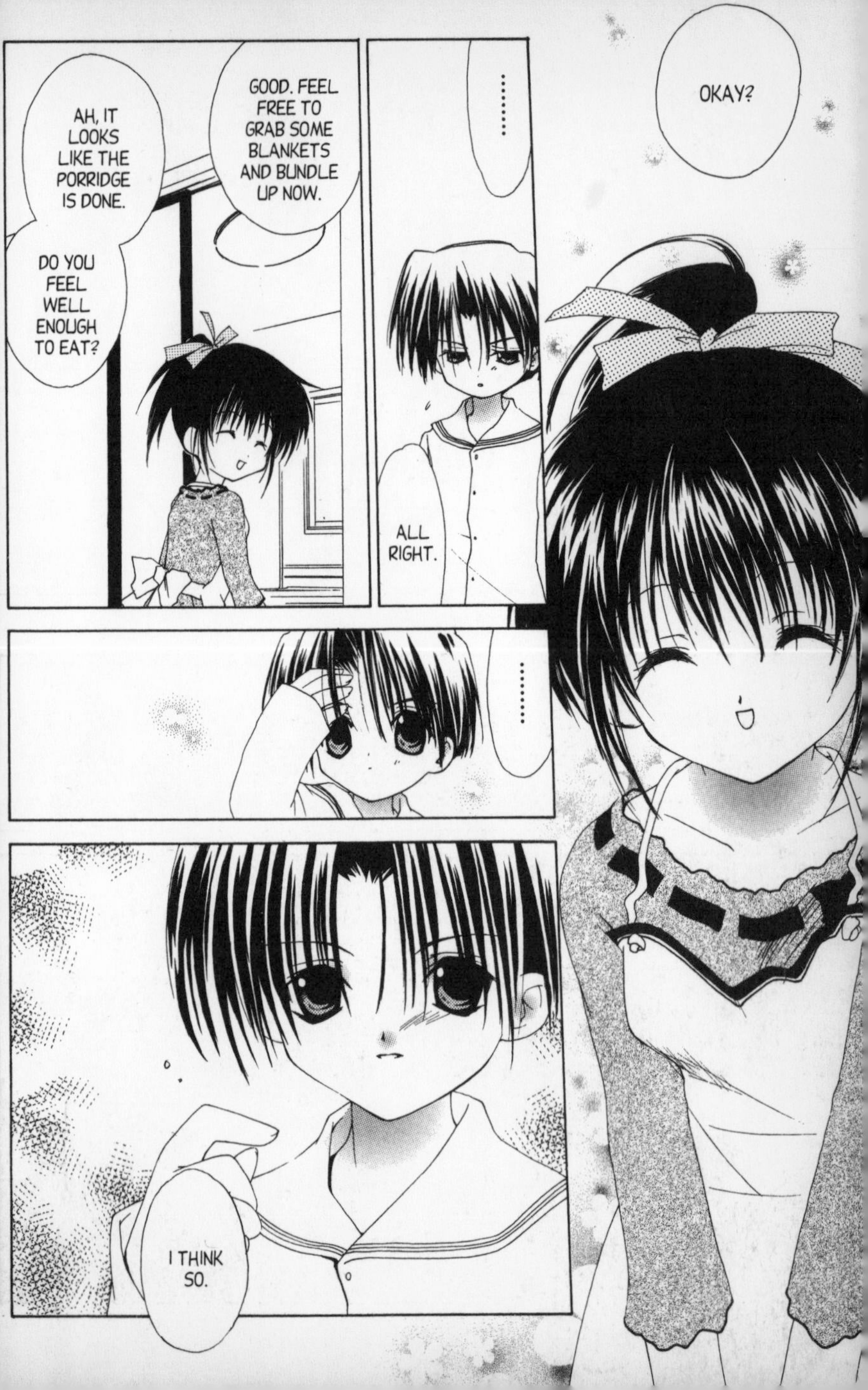

OKAY?
......
ALL RIGHT.
GOOD. FEEL FREE TO GRAB SOME BLANKETS AND BUNDLE UP NOW.
AH, IT LOOKS LIKE THE PORRIDGE IS DONE.
DO YOU FEEL WELL ENOUGH TO EAT?
......
I THINK SO.

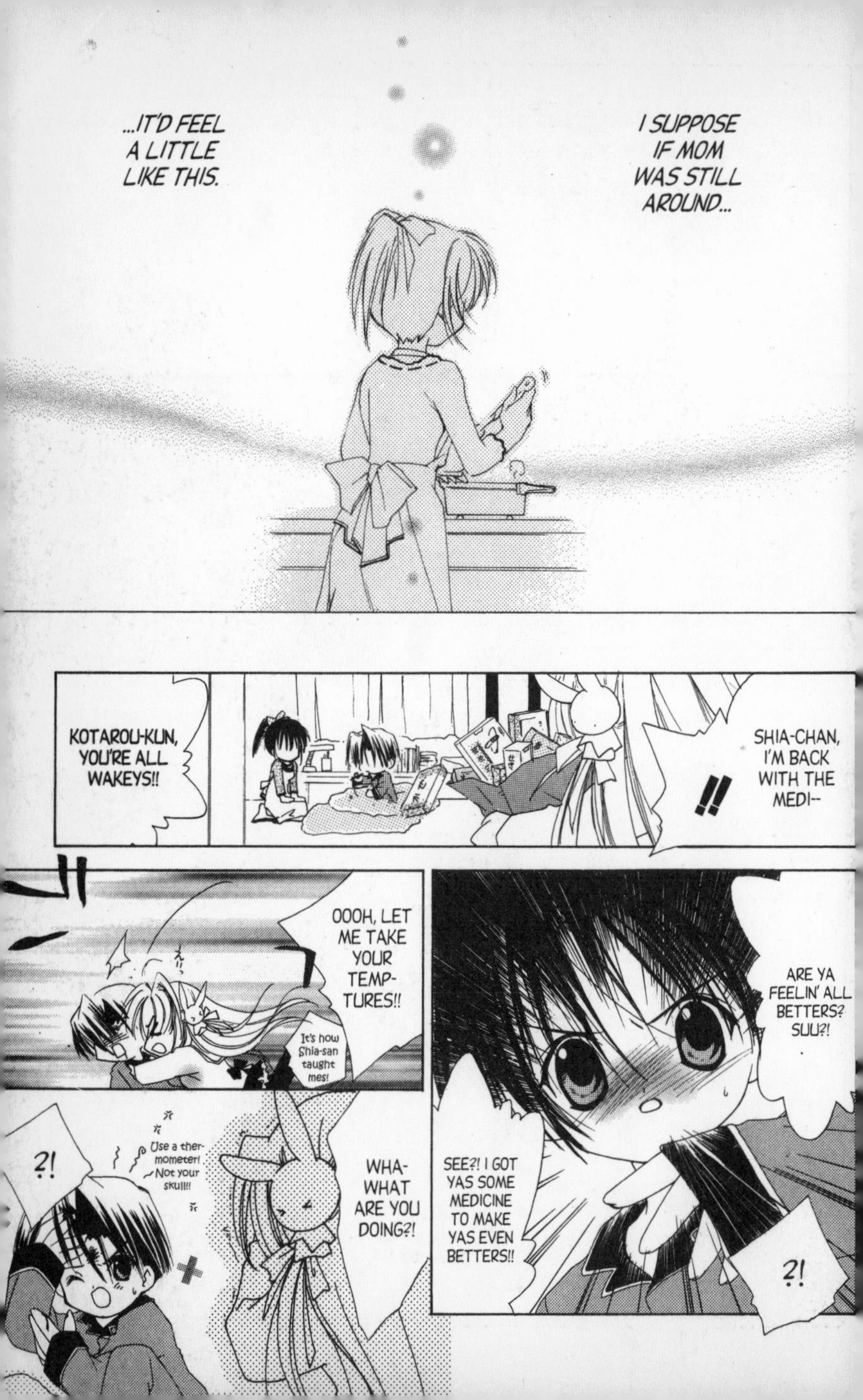
I SUPPOSE IF MOM WAS STILL AROUND...
...IT'D FEEL A LITTLE LIKE THIS.
SHIA-CHAN, I'M BACK WITH THE MEDI--
!!
KOTAROU-KUN, YOU'RE ALL WAKEYS!!
ARE YA FEELIN' ALL BETTERS? SUU?!
SEE?! I GOT YAS SOME MEDICINE TO MAKE YAS EVEN BETTERS!!
?!
OOOH, LET ME TAKE YOUR TEMP-TURES!!
It's how Shia-san taught mes!
WHA-WHAT ARE YOU DOING?!
Use a ther-mometer! Not your skull!!
?!

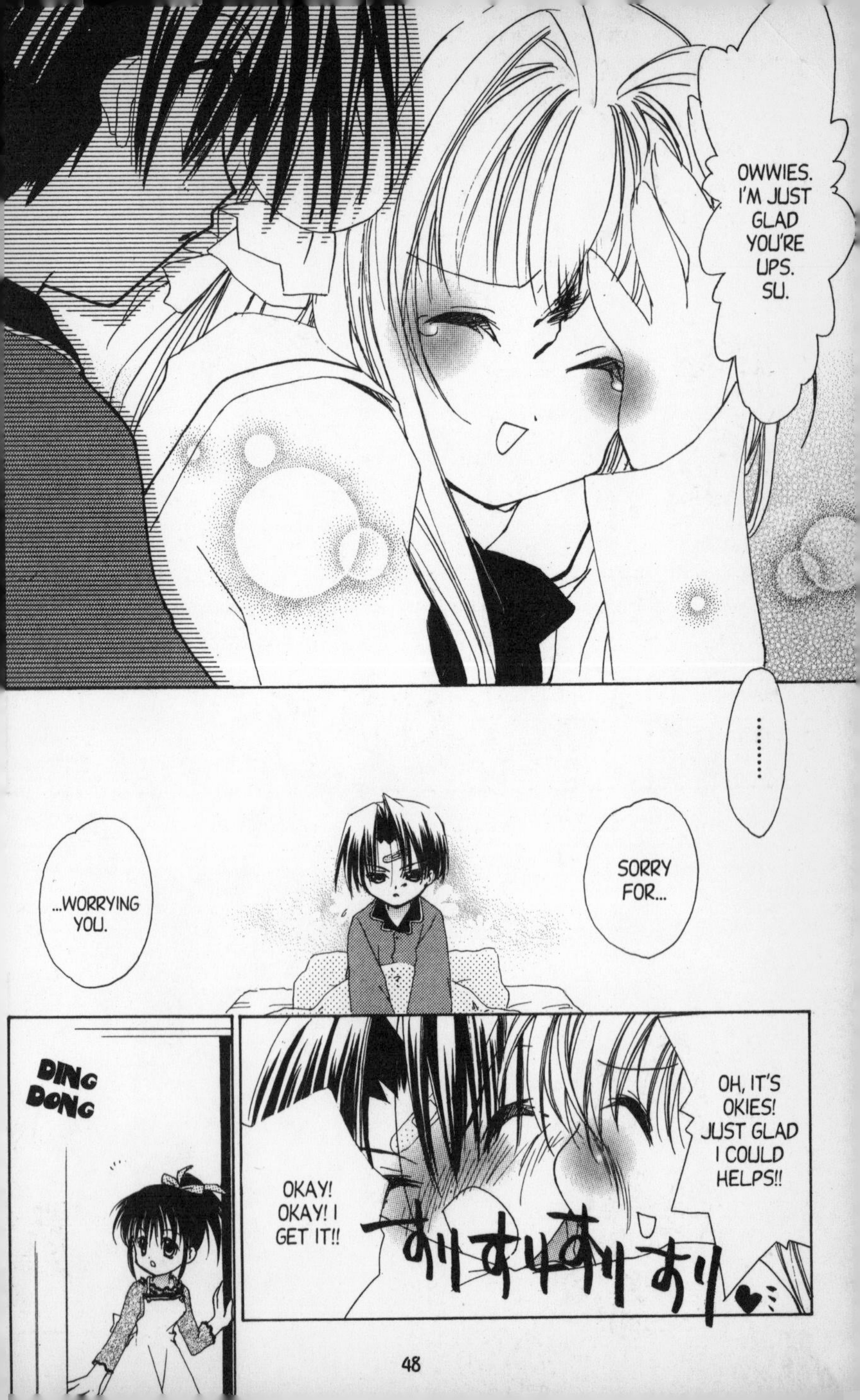
OWWIES. I'M JUST GLAD YOU'RE UPS. SU.
......
SORRY FOR...
...WORRYING YOU.
OH, IT'S OKIES! JUST GLAD I COULD HELPS!!
OKAY! OKAY! I GET IT!!
すりすりすりすり
DING DONG

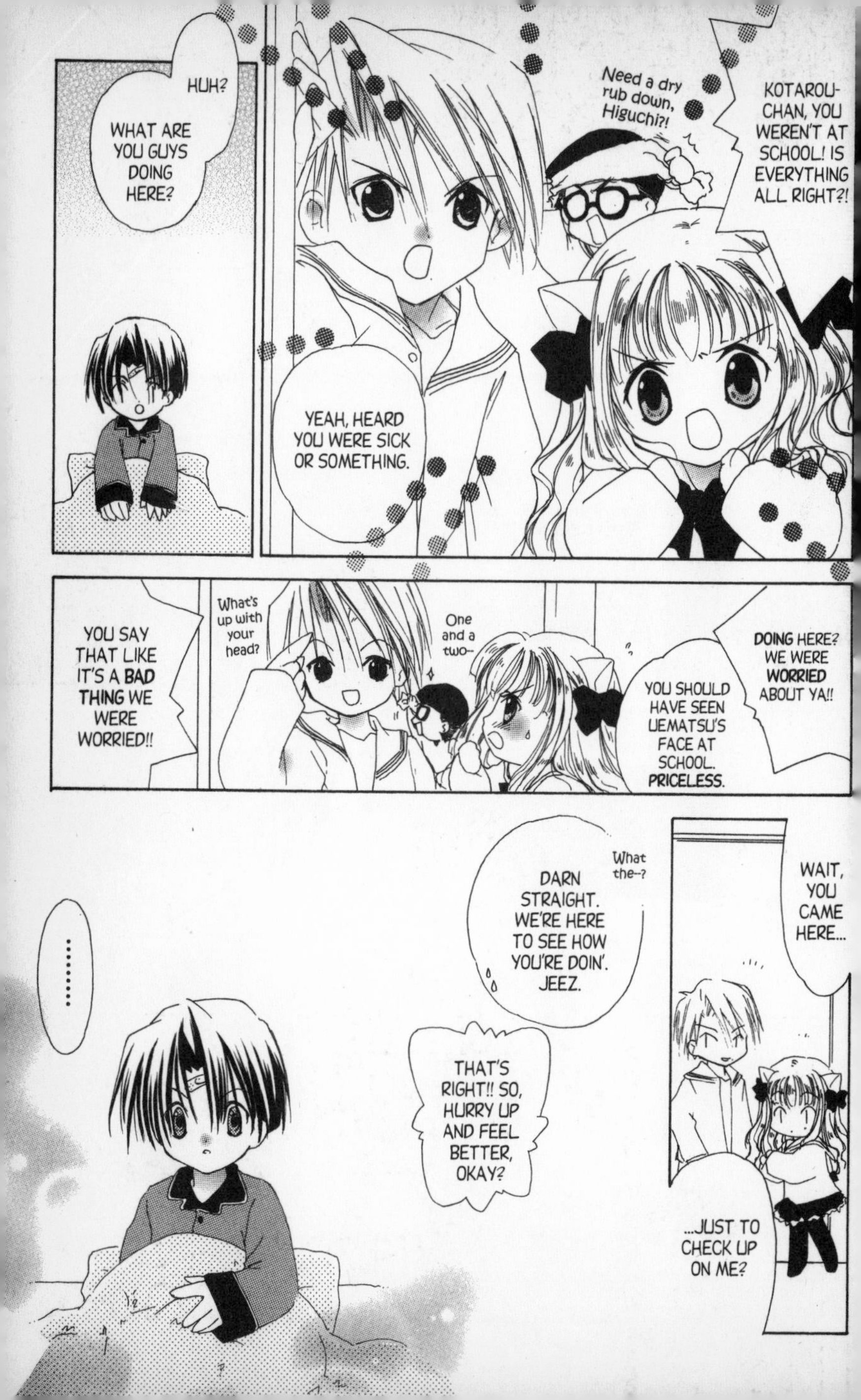
KOTAROU-CHAN, YOU WEREN'T AT SCHOOL! IS EVERYTHING ALL RIGHT?!
Need a dry rub down, Higuchi?!
YEAH, HEARD YOU WERE SICK OR SOMETHING.
HUH?
WHAT ARE YOU GUYS DOING HERE?
DOING HERE? WE WERE WORRIED ABOUT YA!!
YOU SHOULD HAVE SEEN UEMATSU'S FACE AT SCHOOL. PRICELESS.
One and a two--
What's up with your head?
YOU SAY THAT LIKE IT'S A BAD THING WE WERE WORRIED!!
WAIT, YOU CAME HERE...
...JUST TO CHECK UP ON ME?
What the--?
DARN STRAIGHT. WE'RE HERE TO SEE HOW YOU'RE DOIN'. JEEZ.
THAT'S RIGHT!! SO, HURRY UP AND FEEL BETTER, OKAY?
....

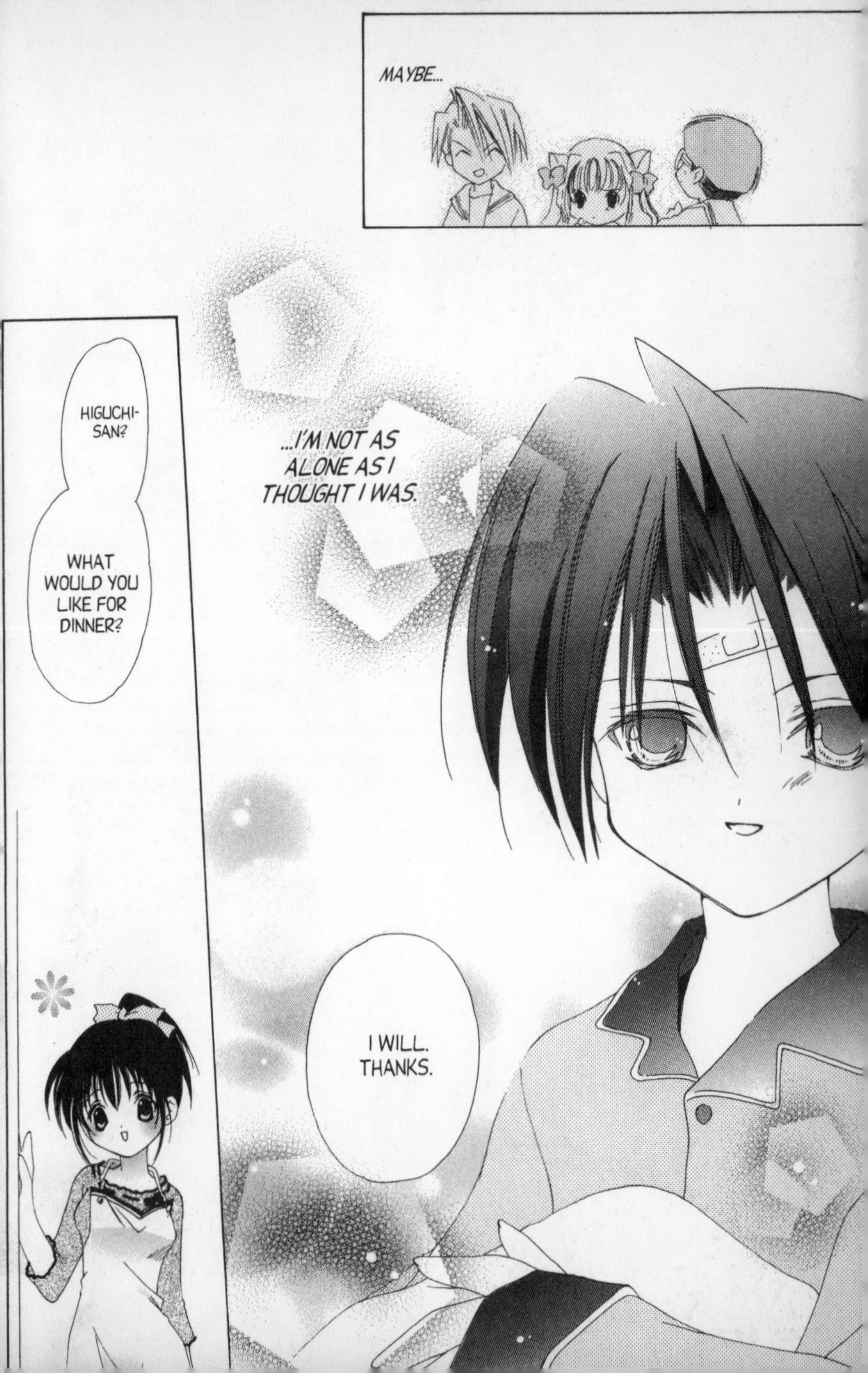
MAYBE...
...I'M NOT AS ALONE AS I THOUGHT I WAS.
I WILL. THANKS.
HIGUCHI-SAN?
WHAT WOULD YOU LIKE FOR DINNER?

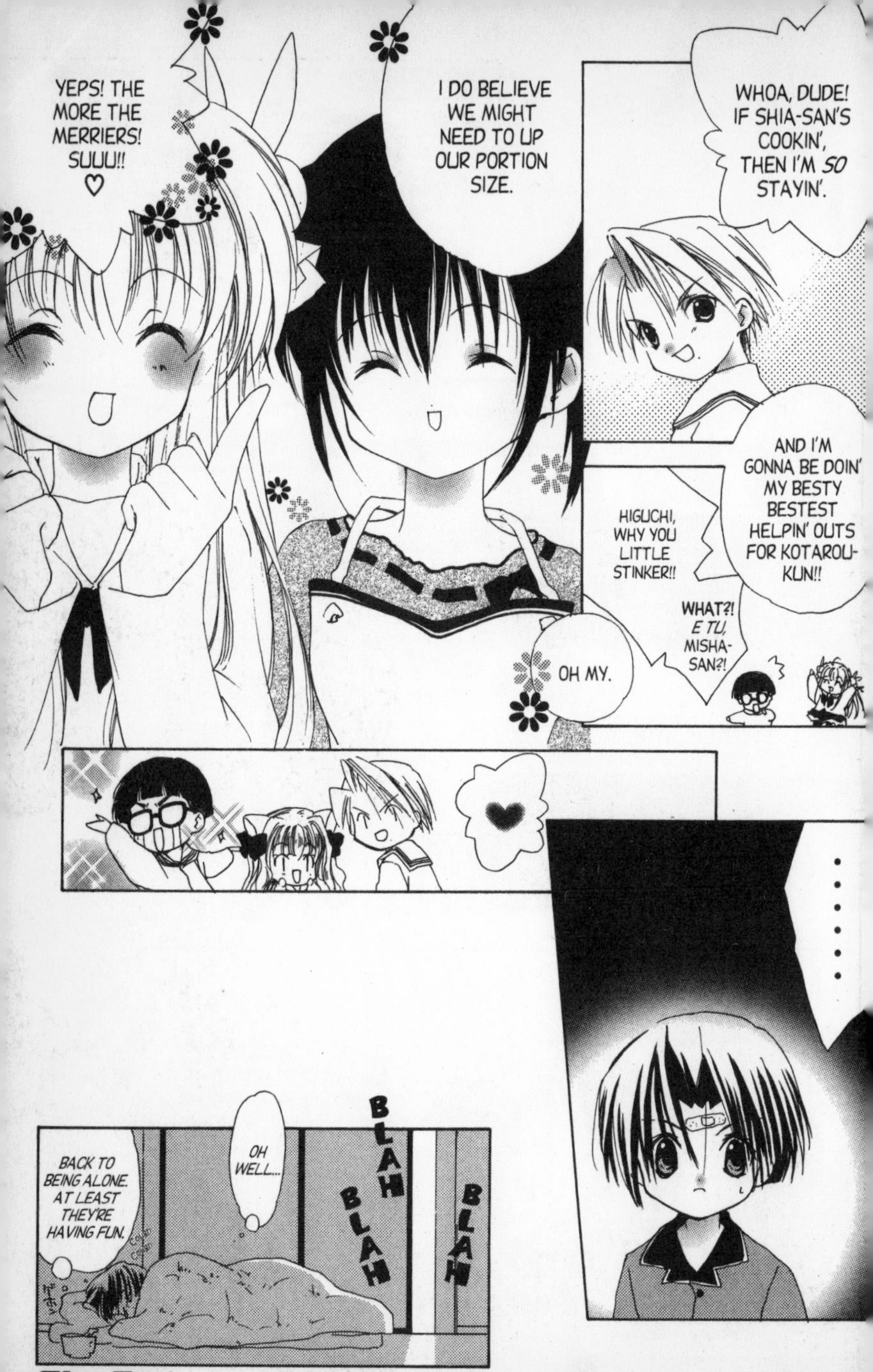
WHOA, DUDE! IF SHIA-SAN'S COOKIN', THEN I'M *SO* STAYIN'.
AND I'M GONNA BE DOIN' MY BESTY BESTEST HELPIN' OUTS FOR KOTAROU-KUN!!
HIGUCHI, WHY YOU LITTLE STINKER!!
WHAT?! *E TU*, MISHA-SAN?!
OH MY.
I DO BELIEVE WE MIGHT NEED TO UP OUR PORTION SIZE.
YEPS! THE MORE THE MERRIERS! SUUU!! ♡
• • • • • •
BLAH
BLAH
OH WELL...
BLAH
BACK TO BEING ALONE. AT LEAST THEY'RE HAVING FUN.

The End

I had a lot of fun drawing this manga and I even got to draw the insert pictures for the novels. Check them out if you get the chance.

Rina Yamaguchi

▶ P.37

Rina Yamaguchi

Writer's Talk

◀ P.53

Hiroshi Ueda

☆ I decided to put an Ueda-tique touch on Dai-chan and feature him in this story. Hope it works out for everyone. It was great to have the opportunity to draw all the other characters too. ♪

Hiroshi Ueda

↳ Please visit my Web site:
http://uedaman.hoops.ne.jp/

How to Help Out

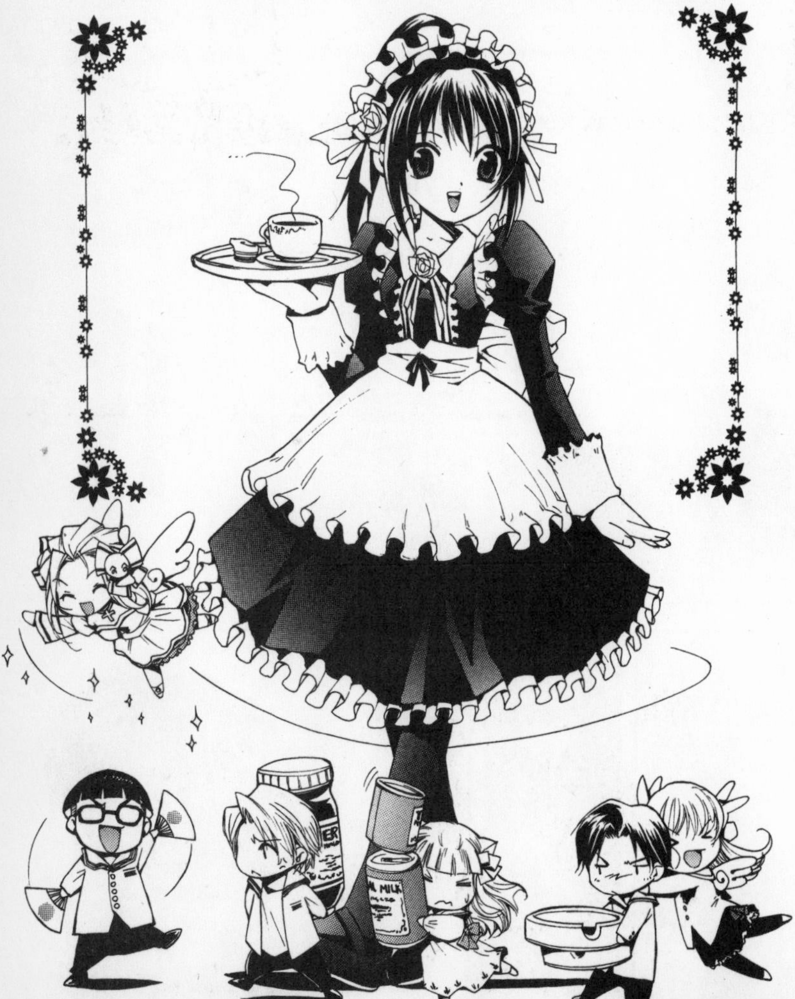

Hiroshi Ueda

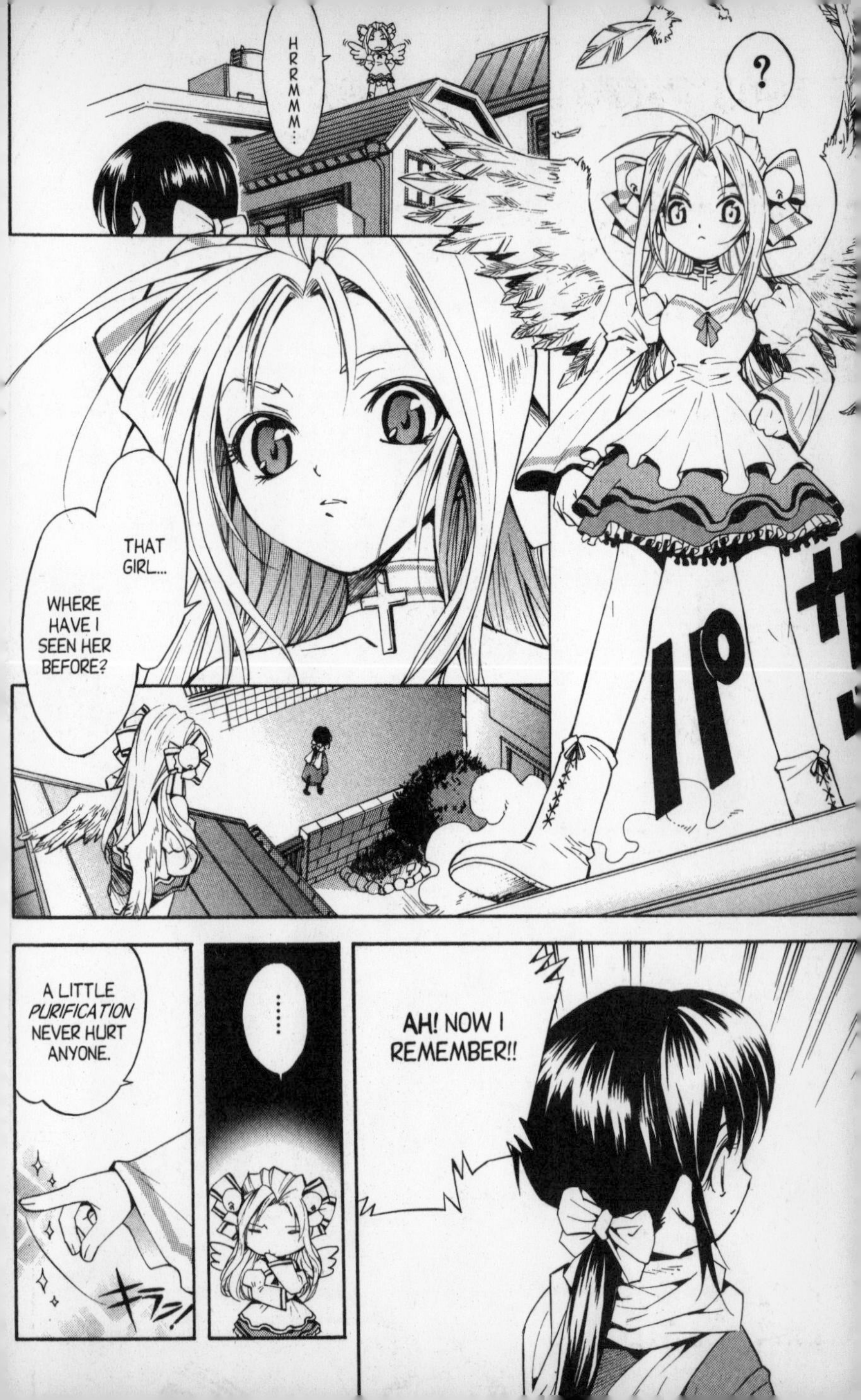
?
HRRMMM...
THAT GIRL...
WHERE HAVE I SEEN HER BEFORE?
AH! NOW I REMEMBER!!
......
A LITTLE *PURIFICATION* NEVER HURT ANYONE.

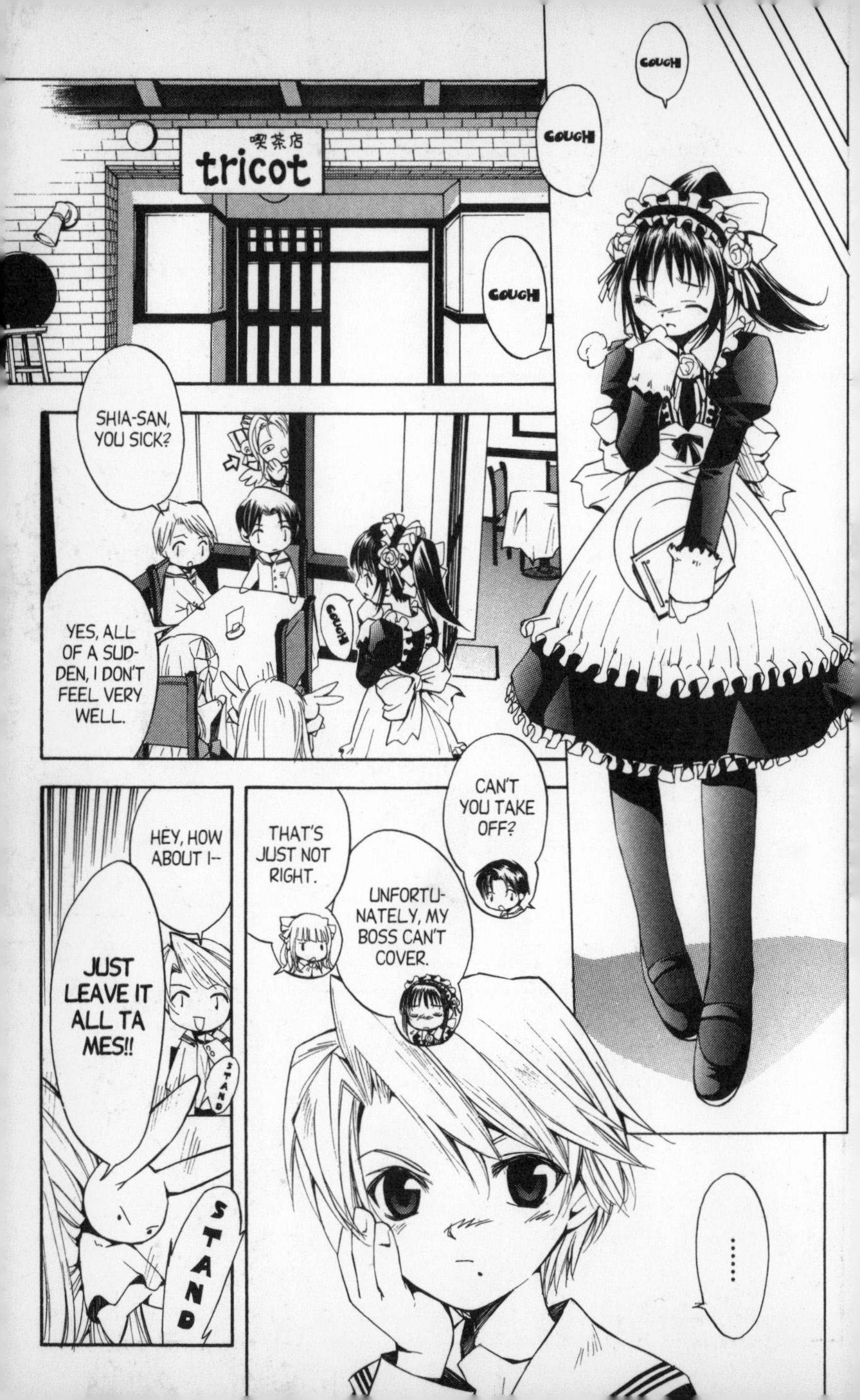
COUGH
COUGH
COUGH
喫茶店
tricot
SHIA-SAN, YOU SICK?
COUGH
YES, ALL OF A SUDDEN, I DON'T FEEL VERY WELL.
......
CAN'T YOU TAKE OFF?
THAT'S JUST NOT RIGHT.
UNFORTUNATELY, MY BOSS CAN'T COVER.
HEY, HOW ABOUT I--
JUST LEAVE IT ALL TA MES!!
STAND
STAND

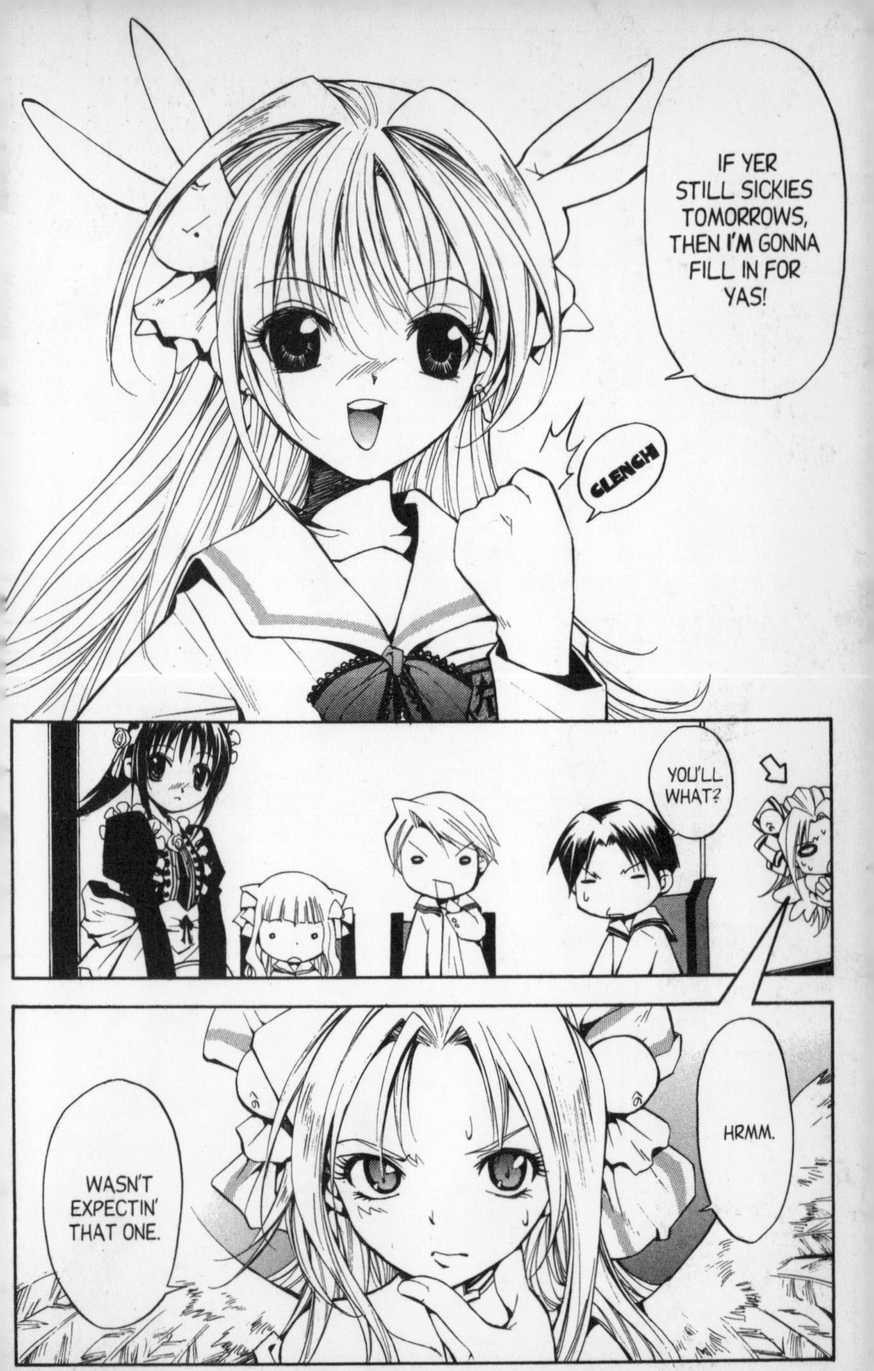
IF YER STILL SICKIES TOMORROWS, THEN I'M GONNA FILL IN FOR YAS!
CLENCH
YOU'LL WHAT?
HRMM.
WASN'T EXPECTIN' THAT ONE.

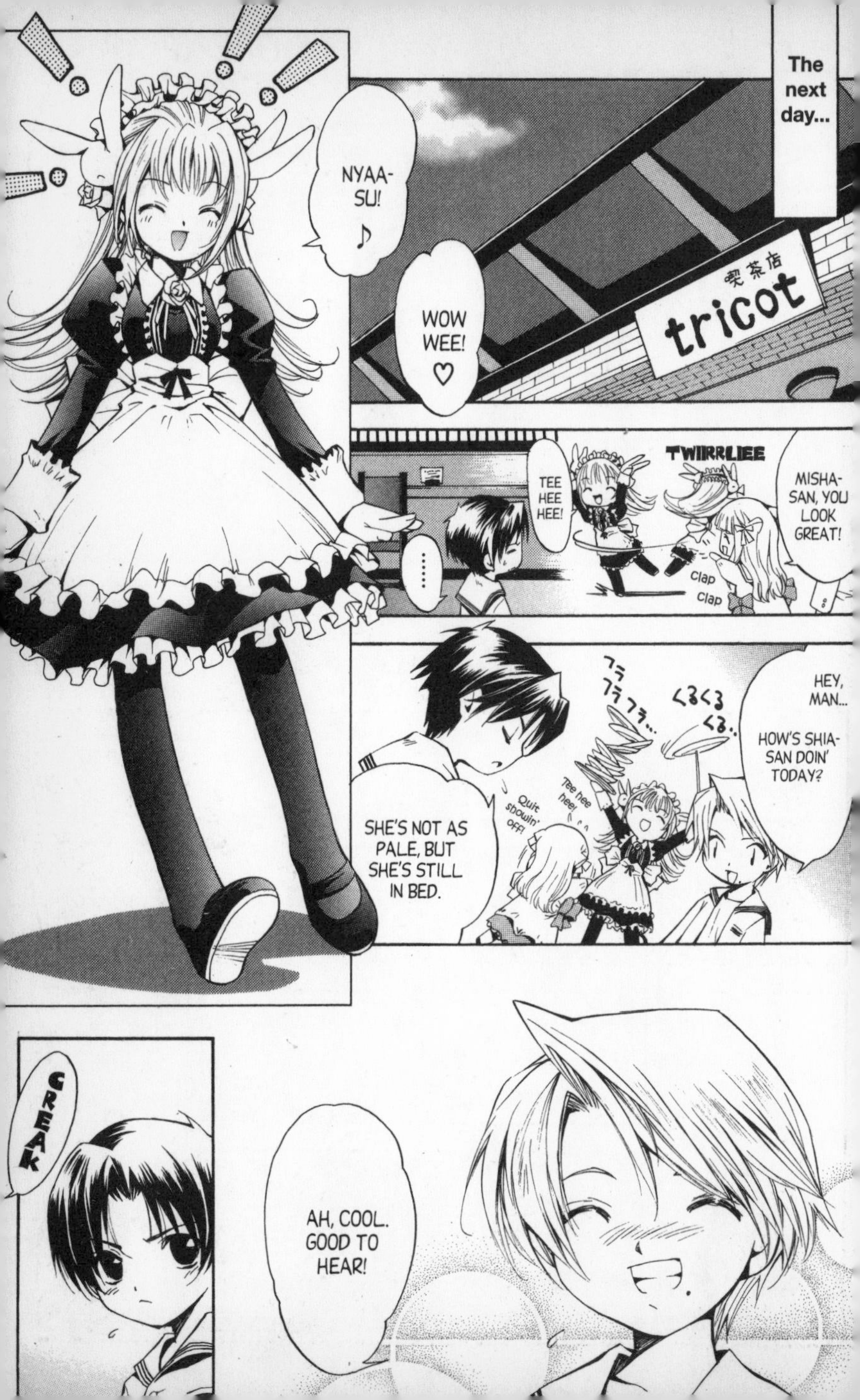
The next day...
喫茶店
tricot
MISHA-SAN, YOU LOOK GREAT!
TWIRRLIEE
Clap
Clap
TEE HEE HEE!
......
HEY, MAN...
HOW'S SHIA-SAN DOIN' TODAY?
くるくるくる...
フラフラフラ...
Tee hee hee!
Quit showin' off!
SHE'S NOT AS PALE, BUT SHE'S STILL IN BED.
NYAA-SU! ♪
WOW WEE! ♡
AH, COOL. GOOD TO HEAR!
CREAK

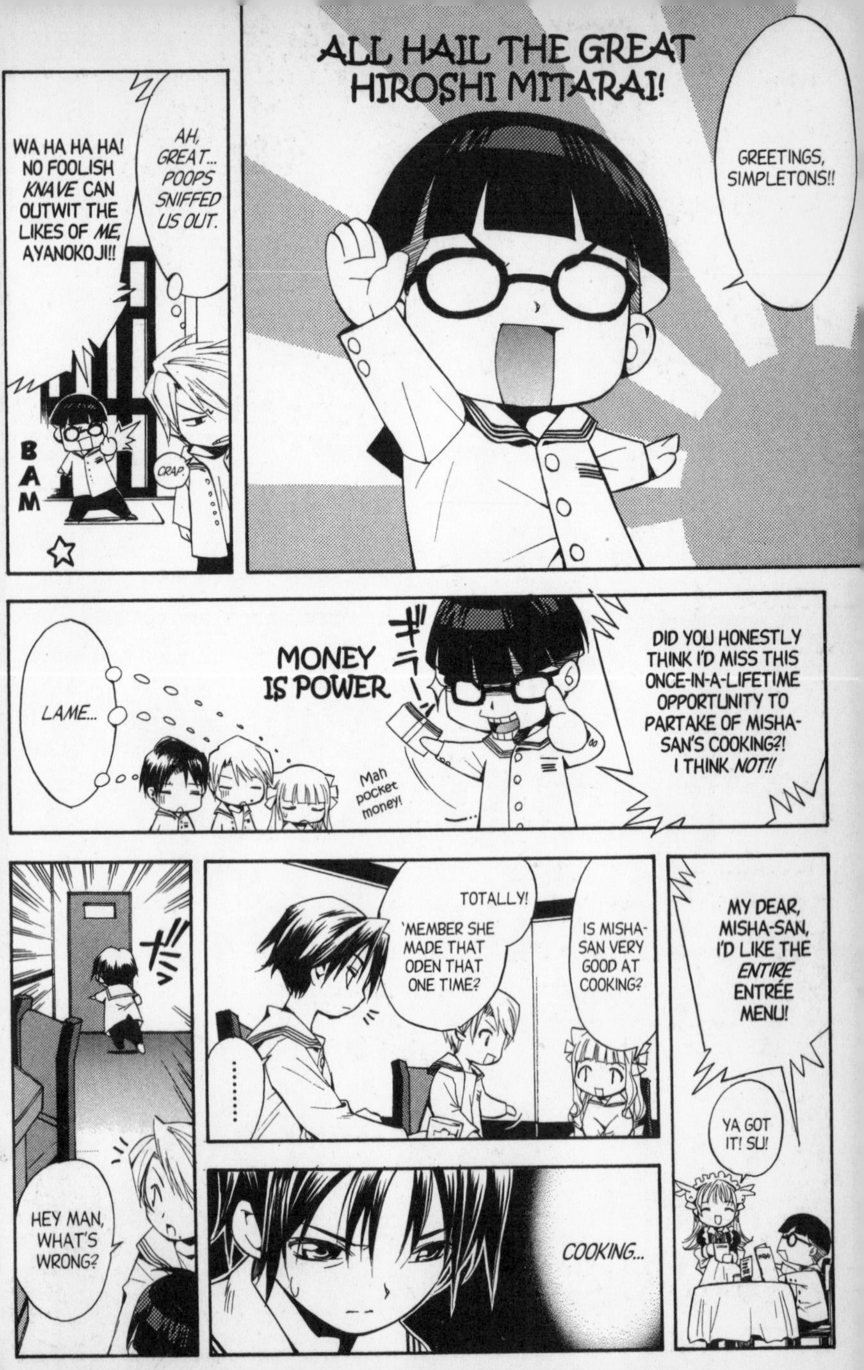

ALL HAIL THE GREAT HIROSHI MITARAI!
GREETINGS, SIMPLETONS!!
AH, GREAT... POOPS SNIFFED US OUT.
WA HA HA HA! NO FOOLISH *KNAVE* CAN OUTWIT THE LIKES OF *ME*, AYANOKOJI!!
CRAP.
BAM
DID YOU HONESTLY THINK I'D MISS THIS ONCE-IN-A-LIFETIME OPPORTUNITY TO PARTAKE OF MISHA-SAN'S COOKING?! I THINK *NOT!!*
MONEY IS POWER
Mah pocket money!
LAME...
MY DEAR, MISHA-SAN, I'D LIKE THE *ENTIRE* ENTRÉE MENU!
YA GOT IT! SU!
IS MISHA-SAN VERY GOOD AT COOKING?
TOTALLY! 'MEMBER SHE MADE THAT ODEN THAT ONE TIME?
....
COOKING...
HEY MAN, WHAT'S WRONG?

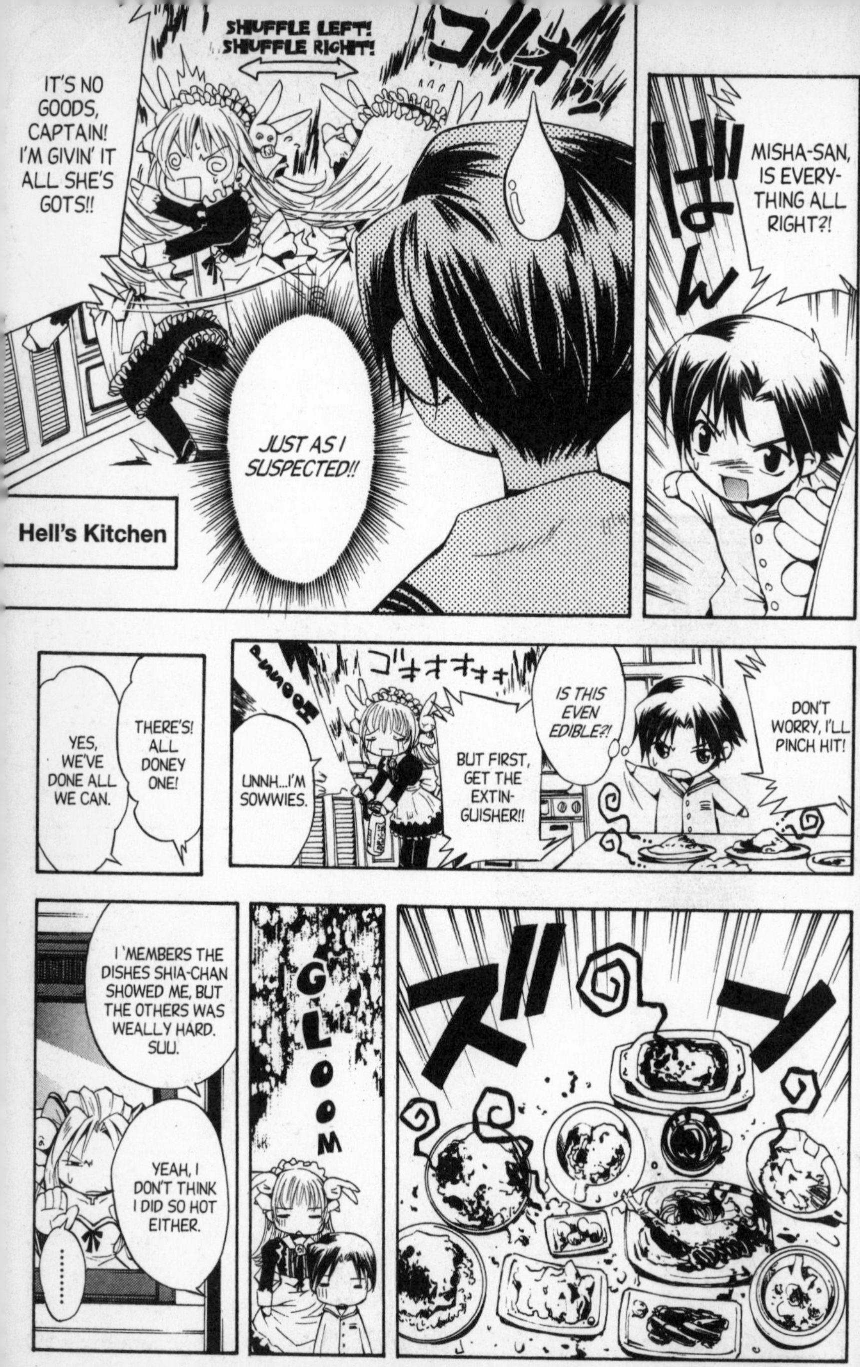
MISHA-SAN, IS EVERYTHING ALL RIGHT?!
SHUFFLE LEFT! SHUFFLE RIGHT!
JUST AS I SUSPECTED!!
IT'S NO GOODS, CAPTAIN! I'M GIVIN' IT ALL SHE'S GOTS!!
Hell's Kitchen
DON'T WORRY, I'LL PINCH HIT!
IS THIS EVEN EDIBLE?!
BUT FIRST, GET THE EXTINGUISHER!!
UNNH...I'M SOWWIES.
THERE'S! ALL DONEY ONE!
YES, WE'VE DONE ALL WE CAN.
GLOOOM
I 'MEMBERS THE DISHES SHIA-CHAN SHOWED ME, BUT THE OTHERS WAS WEALLY HARD. SUU.
YEAH, I DON'T THINK I DID SO HOT EITHER.
......

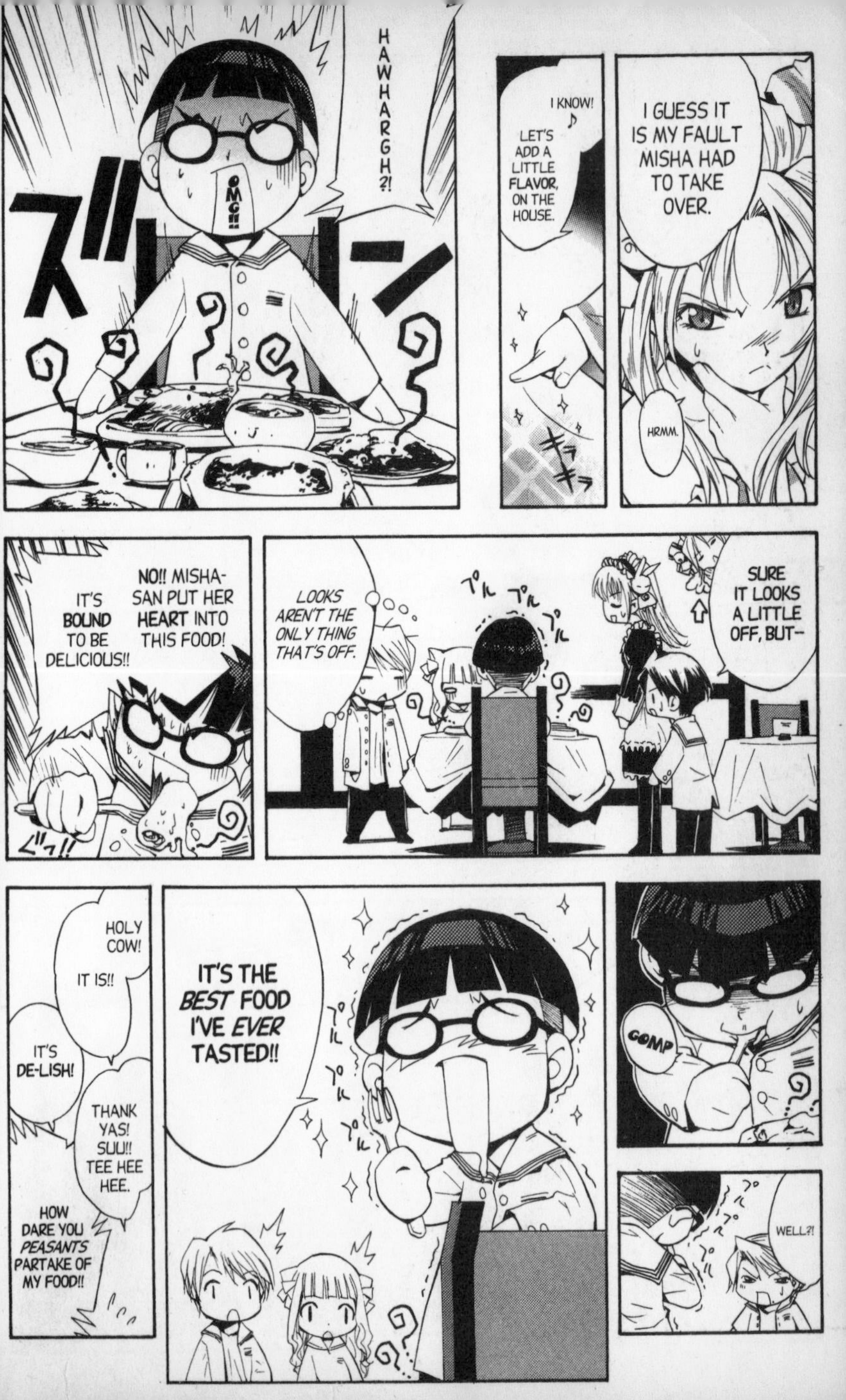
I GUESS IT IS MY FAULT MISHA HAD TO TAKE OVER.
HRMM.
I KNOW! ♪
LET'S ADD A LITTLE FLAVOR, ON THE HOUSE.
HAWHARGH?!
OMG!!
SURE IT LOOKS A LITTLE OFF, BUT--
LOOKS AREN'T THE ONLY THING THAT'S OFF.
NO!! MISHA-SAN PUT HER HEART INTO THIS FOOD!
IT'S BOUND TO BE DELICIOUS!!
GOMP
WELL?!
IT'S THE BEST FOOD I'VE EVER TASTED!!
HOLY COW!
IT IS!!
IT'S DE-LISH!
THANK YAS! SUU!! TEE HEE HEE.
HOW DARE YOU PEASANTS PARTAKE OF MY FOOD!!

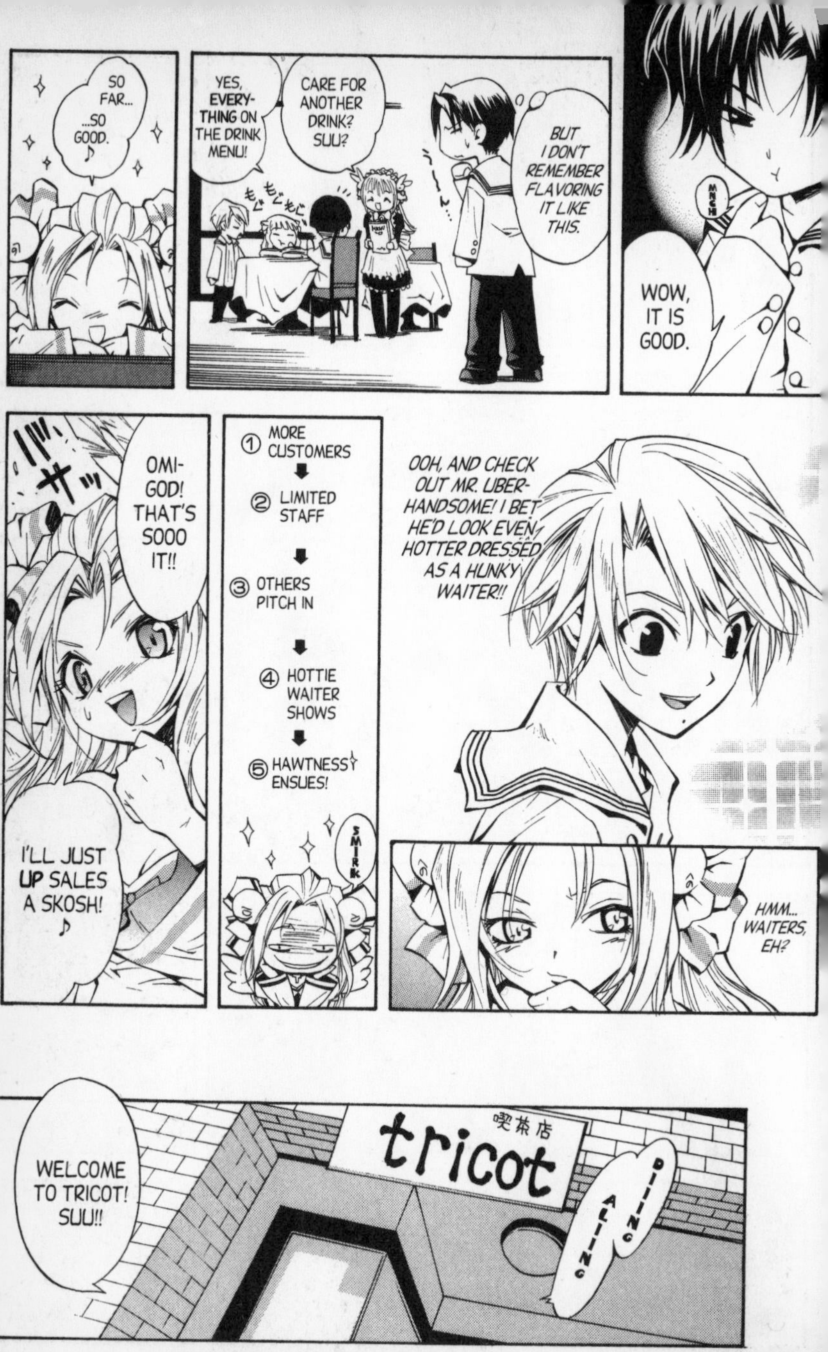
MNCH
WOW, IT IS GOOD.
BUT I DON'T REMEMBER FLAVORING IT LIKE THIS.
CARE FOR ANOTHER DRINK? SUU?
YES, EVERYTHING ON THE DRINK MENU!
SO FAR... ...SO GOOD. ♪
OOH, AND CHECK OUT MR. UBER-HANDSOME! I BET HE'D LOOK EVEN HOTTER DRESSED AS A HUNKY WAITER!!
HMM... WAITERS, EH?
① MORE CUSTOMERS
② LIMITED STAFF
③ OTHERS PITCH IN
④ HOTTIE WAITER SHOWS
⑤ HAWTNESS ENSUES!
SMIRK
OMI-GOD! THAT'S SOOO IT!!
I'LL JUST UP SALES A SKOSH! ♪
喫茶店 tricot
DIIING ALING
WELCOME TO TRICOT! SUU!!

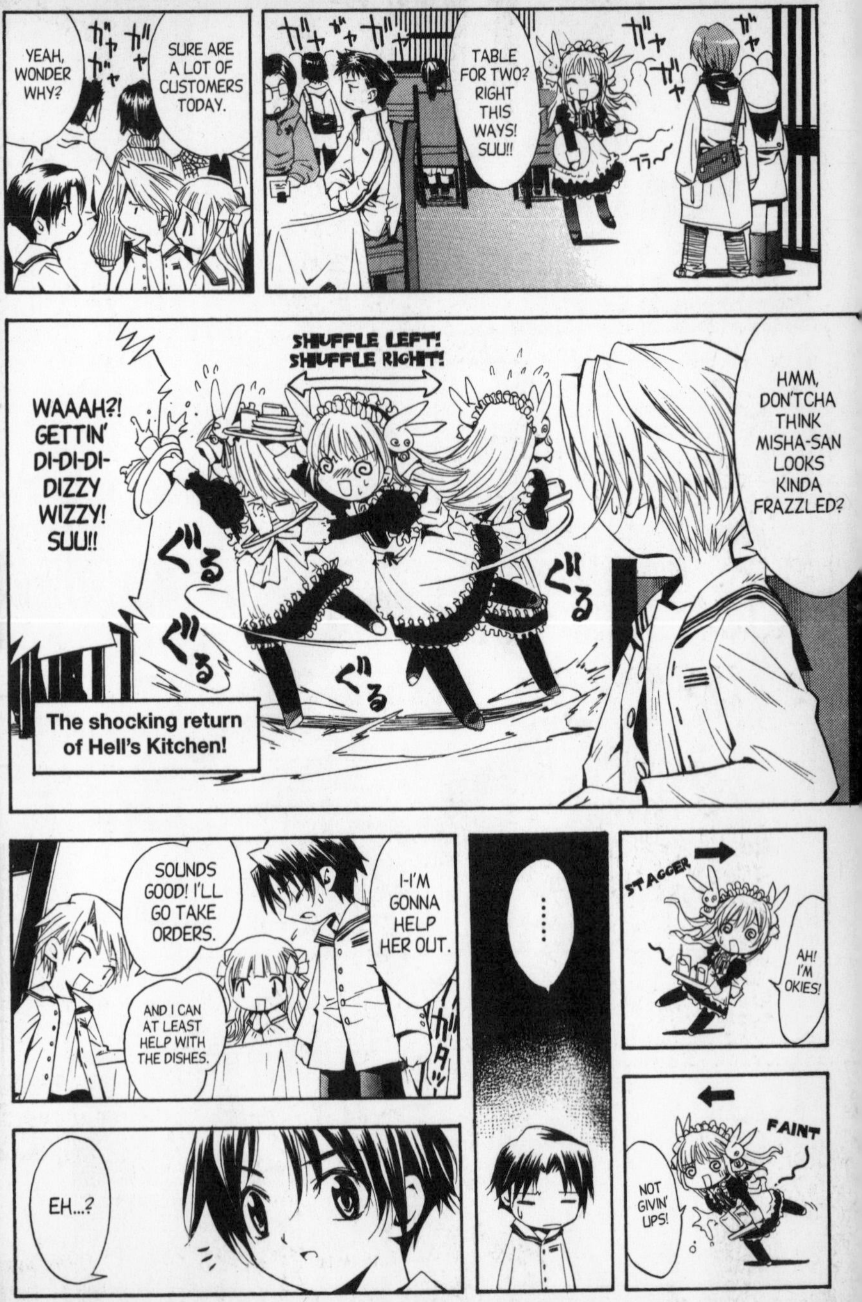
TABLE FOR TWO? RIGHT THIS WAYS! SUU!!
ガヤガヤ
フラ~
SURE ARE A LOT OF CUSTOMERS TODAY.
YEAH, WONDER WHY?
HMM, DON'TCHA THINK MISHA-SAN LOOKS KINDA FRAZZLED?
SHUFFLE LEFT! SHUFFLE RIGHT!
WAAAH?! GETTIN' DI-DI-DI-DIZZY WIZZY! SUU!!
ぐる ぐる ぐる ぐる
The shocking return of Hell's Kitchen!
STAGGER
AH! I'M OKIES!
FAINT
NOT GIVIN' UPS!
......
I-I'M GONNA HELP HER OUT.
SOUNDS GOOD! I'LL GO TAKE ORDERS.
AND I CAN AT LEAST HELP WITH THE DISHES.
EH...?

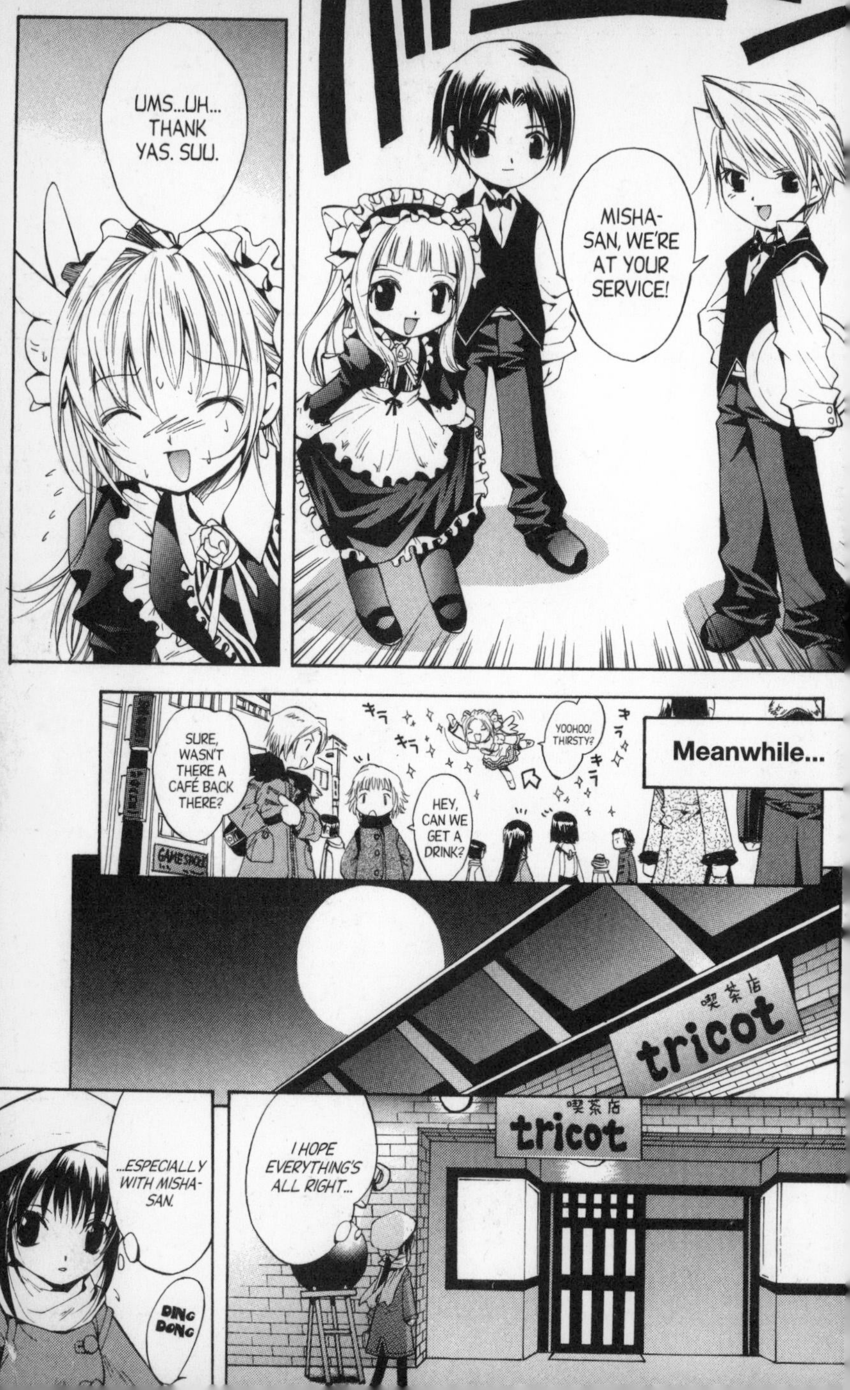
MISHA-SAN, WE'RE AT YOUR SERVICE!
UMS...UH... THANK YAS. SUU.
Meanwhile...
YOOHOO! THIRSTY?
HEY, CAN WE GET A DRINK?
SURE, WASN'T THERE A CAFÉ BACK THERE?
喫茶店
tricot
喫茶店
tricot
I HOPE EVERYTHING'S ALL RIGHT...
...ESPECIALLY WITH MISHA-SAN.
DING DONG

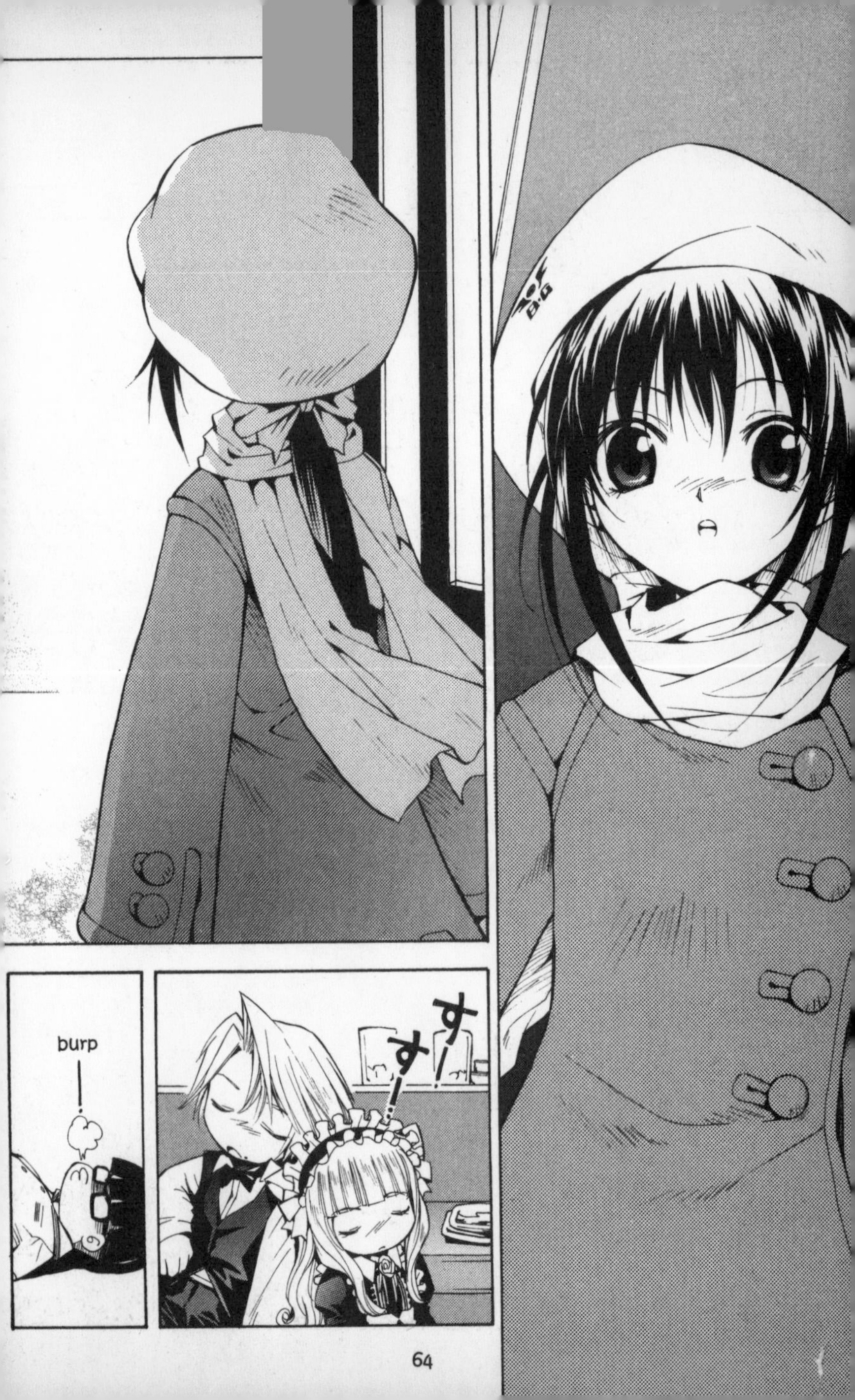
す！
すー…
burp

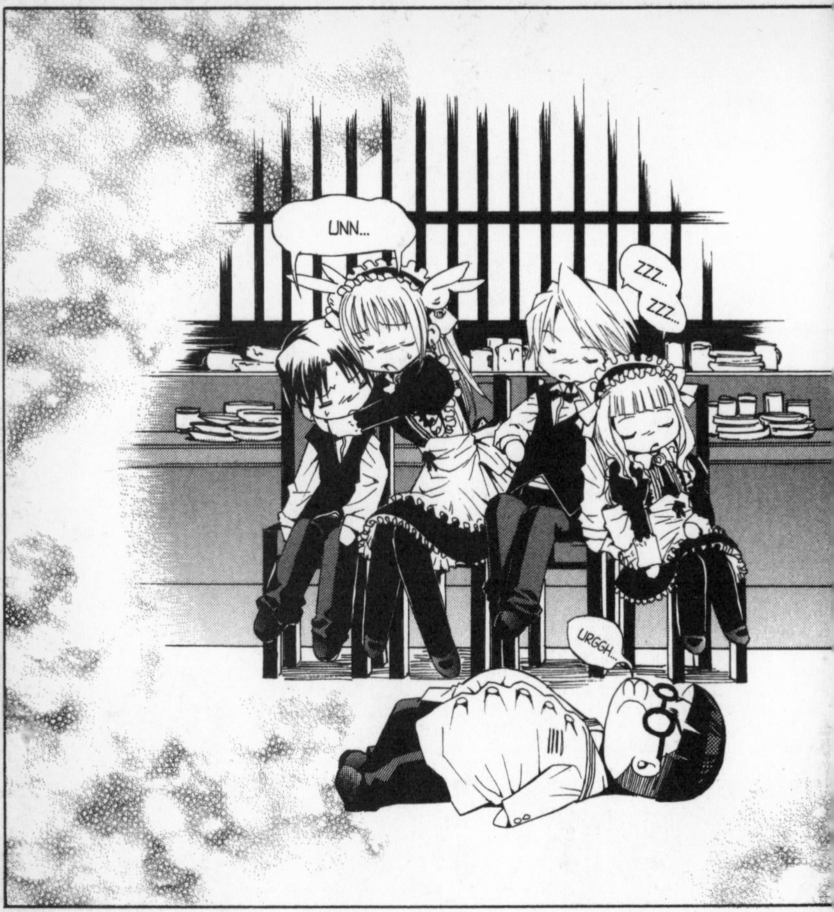
UNN...
ZZZ... ZZZ...
URGGH...

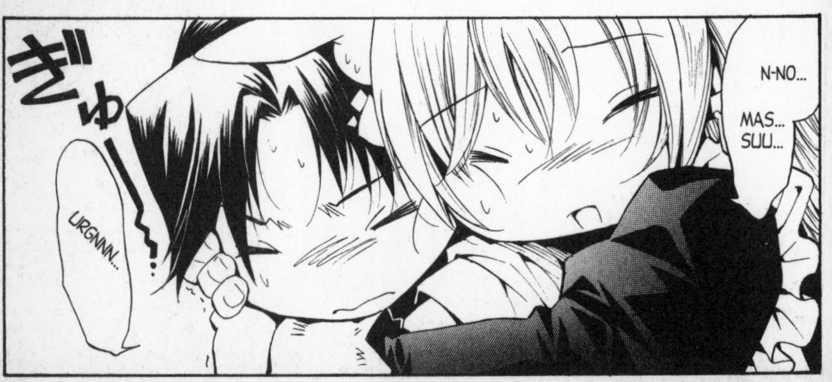
N-NO... MAS... SUU...
ぎゅー
URGNNN...

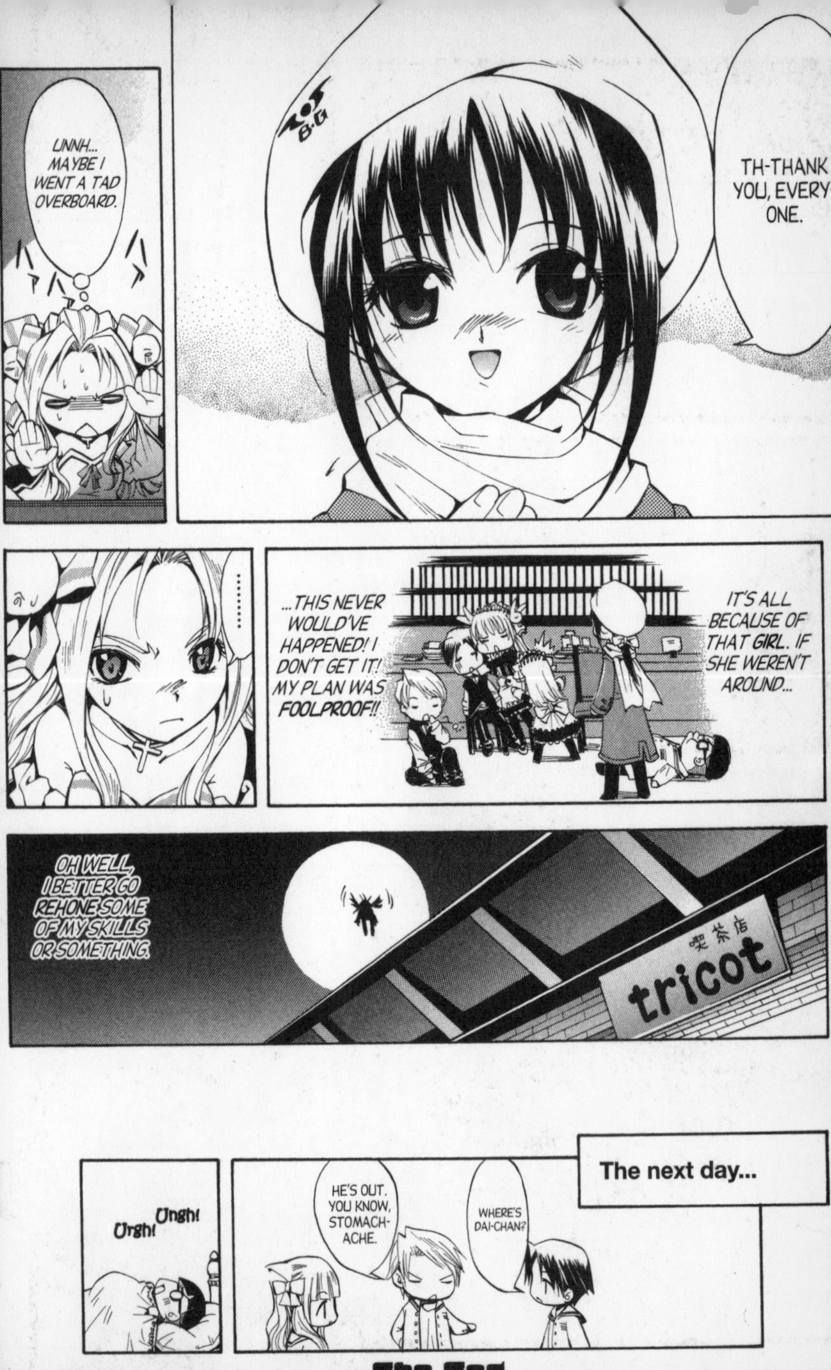
TH-THANK YOU, EVERY-ONE.
UNNH... MAYBE I WENT A TAD OVERBOARD.
IT'S ALL BECAUSE OF THAT GIRL. IF SHE WEREN'T AROUND...
...THIS NEVER WOULD'VE HAPPENED! I DON'T GET IT! MY PLAN WAS FOOLPROOF!!
......
OH WELL, I BETTER GO REHONE SOME OF MY SKILLS OR SOMETHING.
喫茶店
tricot
The next day...
WHERE'S DAI-CHAN?
HE'S OUT. YOU KNOW, STOMACH-ACHE.
Ungh!
Urgh!

The End

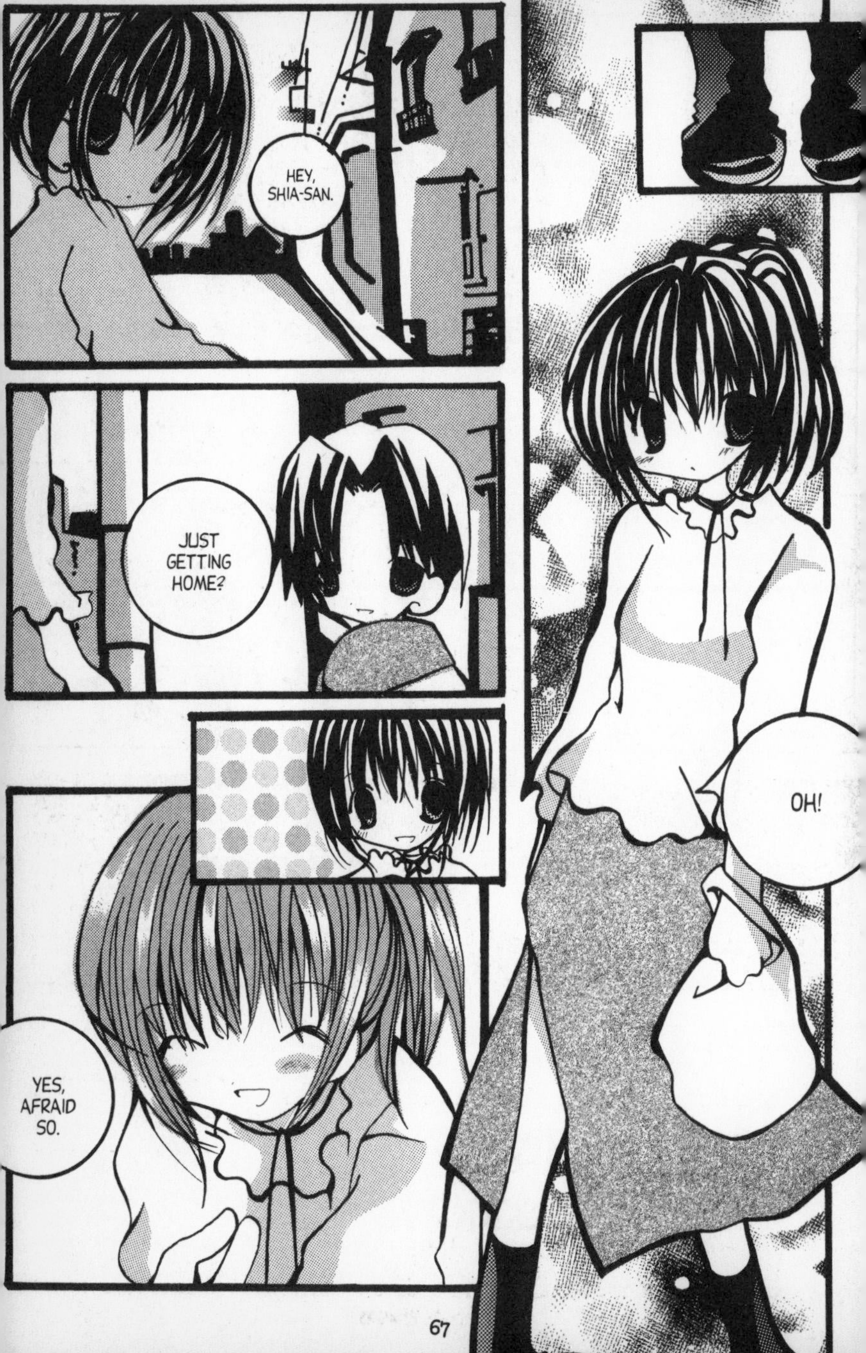
OH!
HEY, SHIA-SAN.
JUST GETTING HOME?
YES, AFRAID SO.

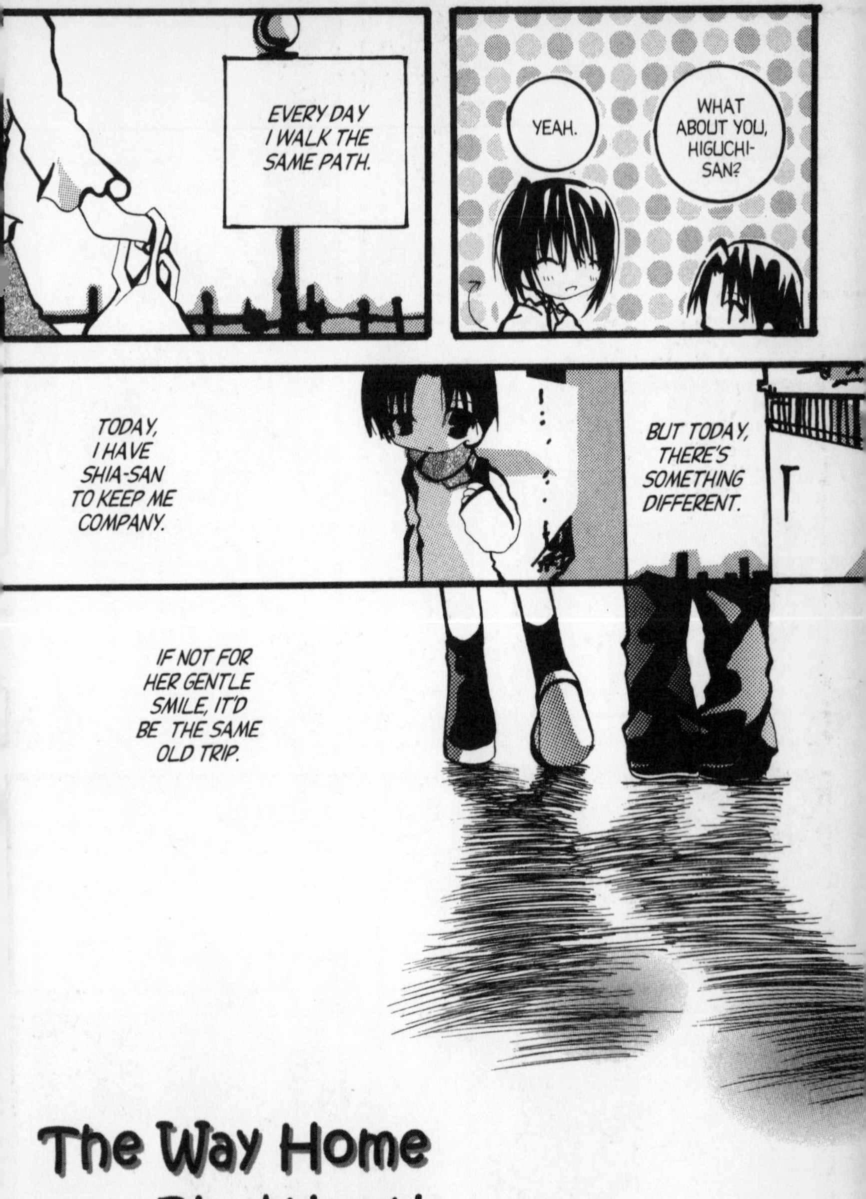
WHAT ABOUT YOU, HIGUCHI-SAN?
YEAH.
EVERY DAY I WALK THE SAME PATH.
BUT TODAY, THERE'S SOMETHING DIFFERENT.
TODAY, I HAVE SHIA-SAN TO KEEP ME COMPANY.
IF NOT FOR HER GENTLE SMILE, IT'D BE THE SAME OLD TRIP.

The Way Home

Rju Akitsuki

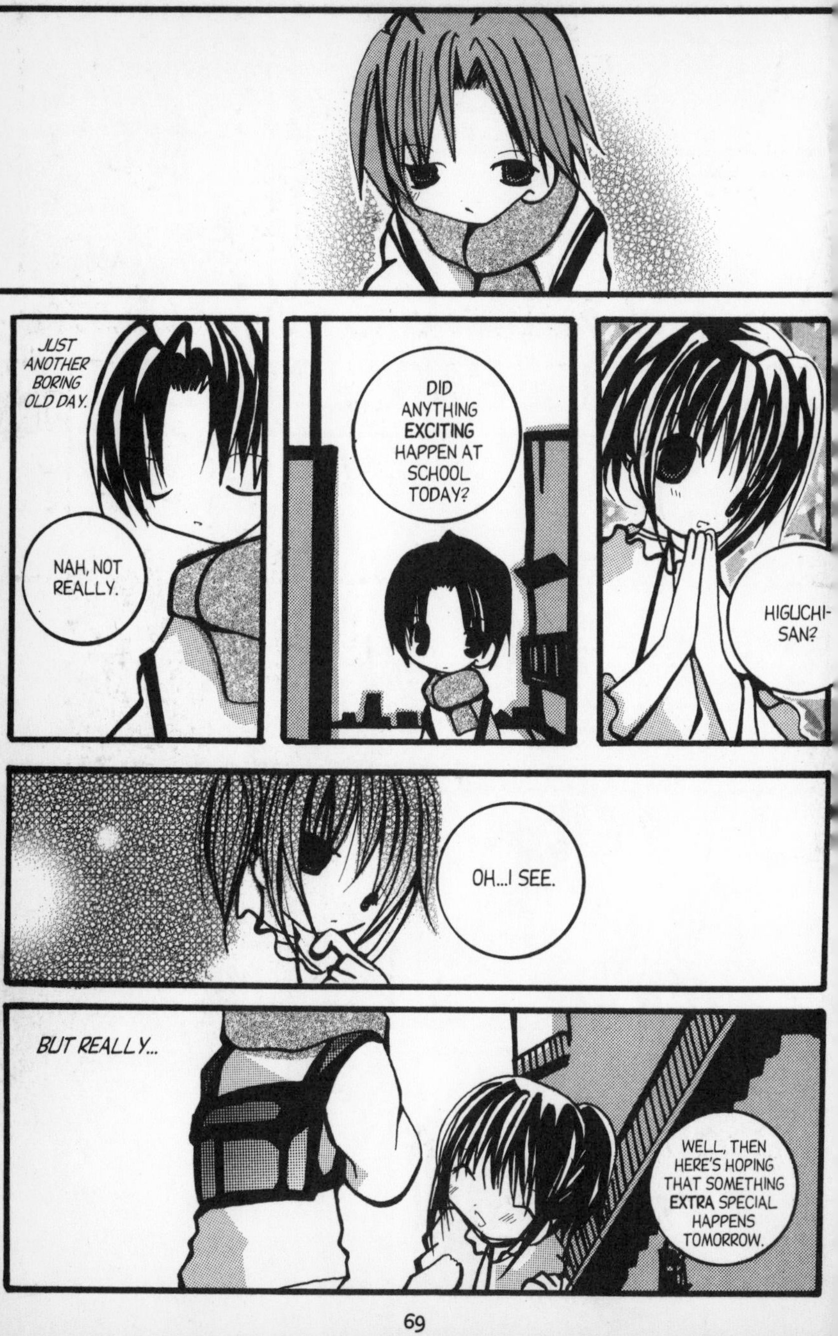
HIGUCHI-SAN?
DID ANYTHING EXCITING HAPPEN AT SCHOOL TODAY?
JUST ANOTHER BORING OLD DAY.
NAH, NOT REALLY.
OH...I SEE.
WELL, THEN HERE'S HOPING THAT SOMETHING EXTRA SPECIAL HAPPENS TOMORROW.
BUT REALLY...

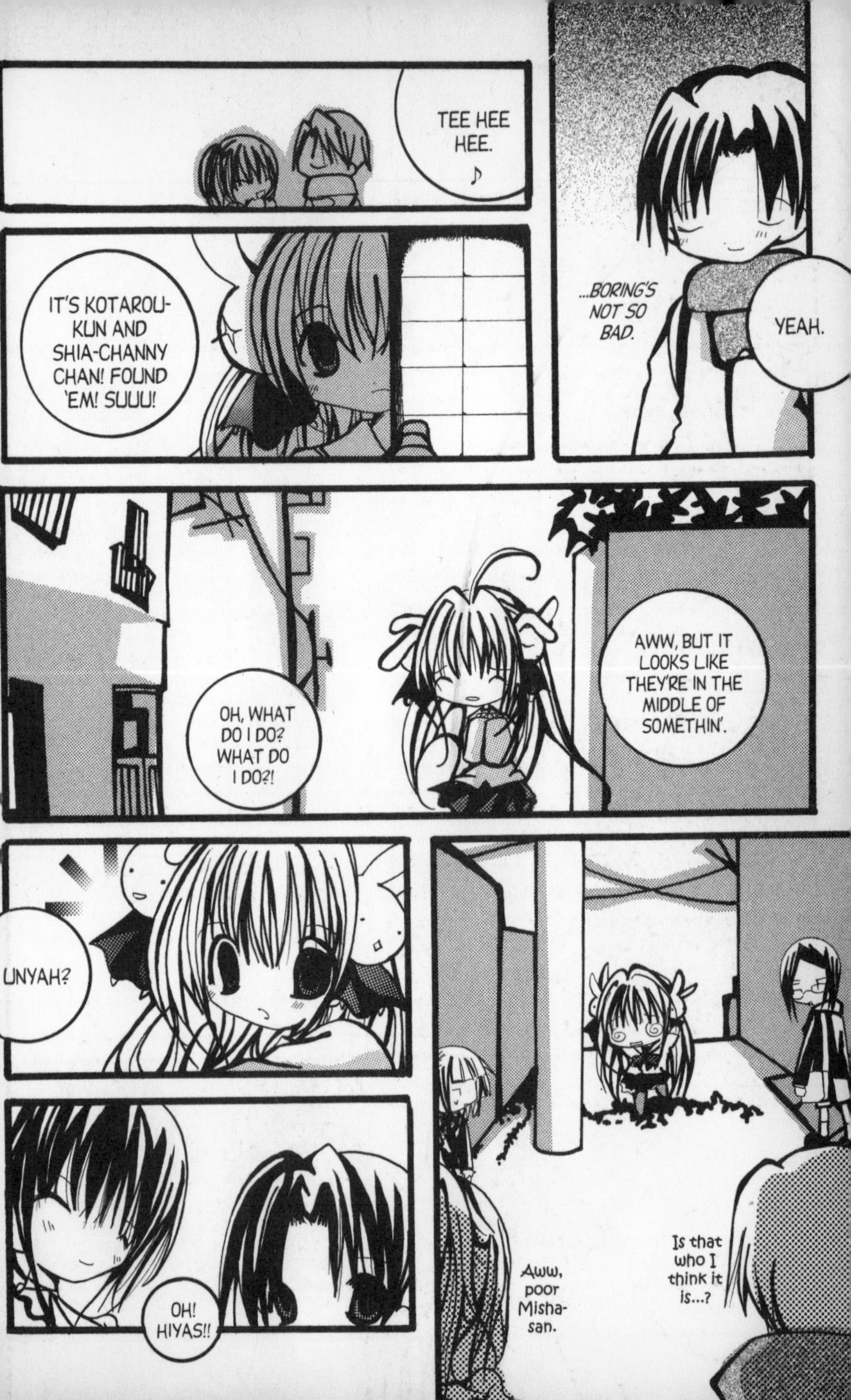
YEAH.
...BORING'S NOT SO BAD.
TEE HEE HEE. ♪
IT'S KOTAROU-KUN AND SHIA-CHANNY CHAN! FOUND 'EM! SUUU!
AWW, BUT IT LOOKS LIKE THEY'RE IN THE MIDDLE OF SOMETHIN'.
OH, WHAT DO I DO? WHAT DO I DO?!
Is that who I think it is...?
Aww, poor Misha-san.
UNYAH?
OH! HIYAS!!

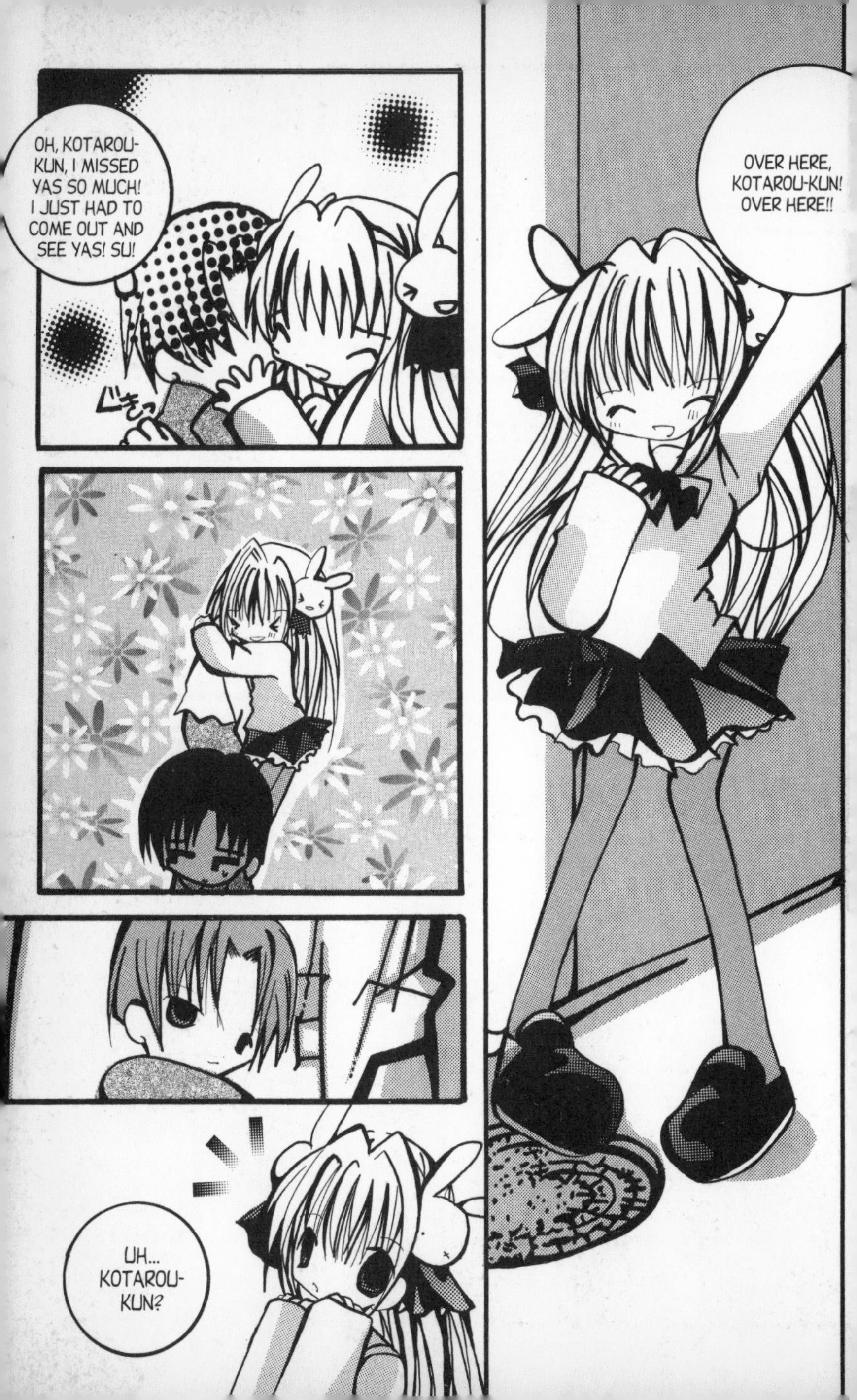
OVER HERE, KOTAROU-KUN! OVER HERE!!
OH, KOTAROU-KUN, I MISSED YAS SO MUCH! I JUST HAD TO COME OUT AND SEE YAS! SU!
UH... KOTAROU-KUN?

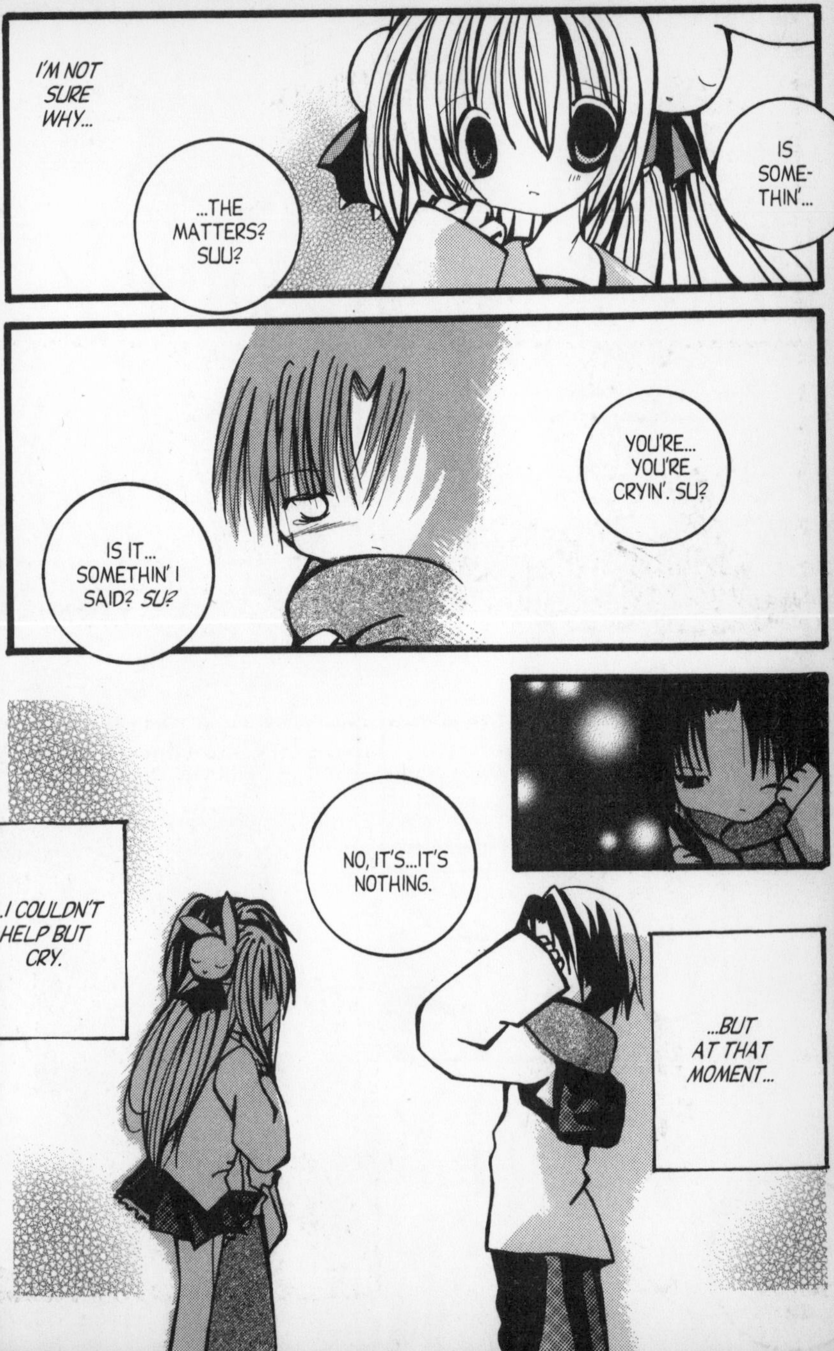
IS SOME-THIN'...
...THE MATTERS? SUU?
I'M NOT SURE WHY...
YOU'RE... YOU'RE CRYIN'. SU?
IS IT... SOMETHIN' I SAID? SU?
NO, IT'S...IT'S NOTHING.
...BUT AT THAT MOMENT...
...I COULDN'T HELP BUT CRY.

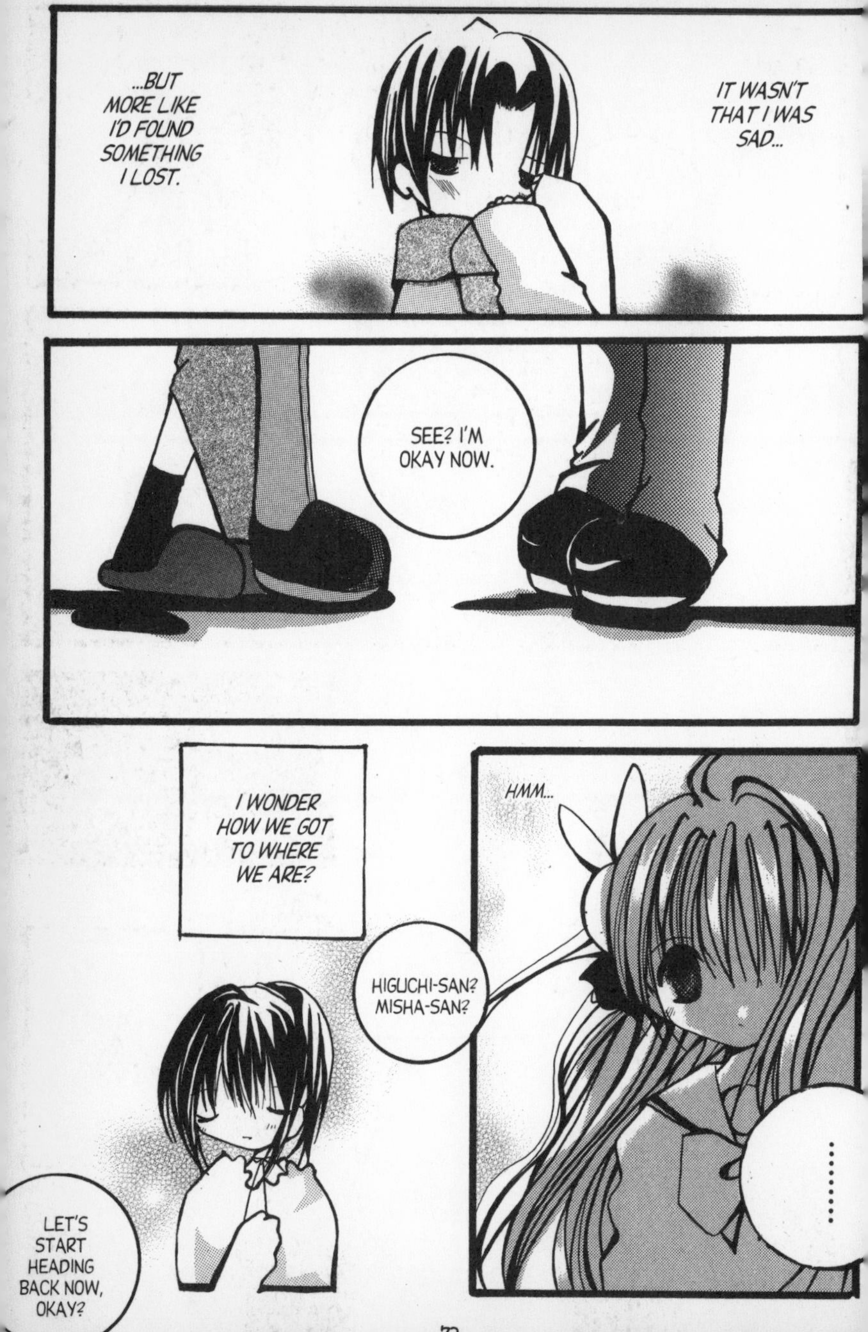
IT WASN'T THAT I WAS SAD...
...BUT MORE LIKE I'D FOUND SOMETHING I LOST.
SEE? I'M OKAY NOW.
HMM...
HIGUCHI-SAN? MISHA-SAN?
......
I WONDER HOW WE GOT TO WHERE WE ARE?
LET'S START HEADING BACK NOW, OKAY?

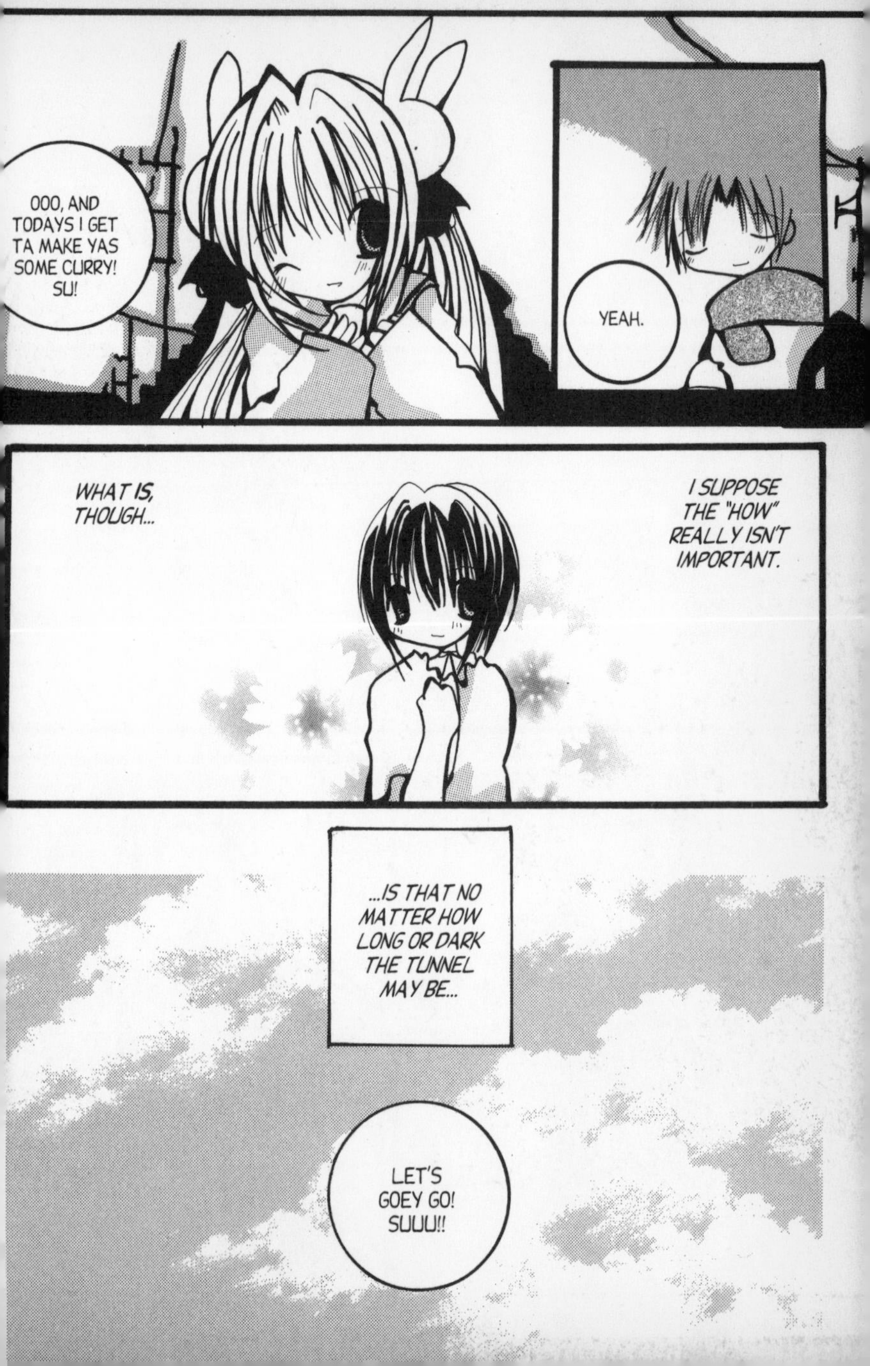
YEAH.
OOO, AND TODAYS I GET TA MAKE YAS SOME CURRY! SU!
I SUPPOSE THE "HOW" REALLY ISN'T IMPORTANT.
WHAT IS, THOUGH...
...IS THAT NO MATTER HOW LONG OR DARK THE TUNNEL MAY BE...
LET'S GOEY GO! SUUU!!

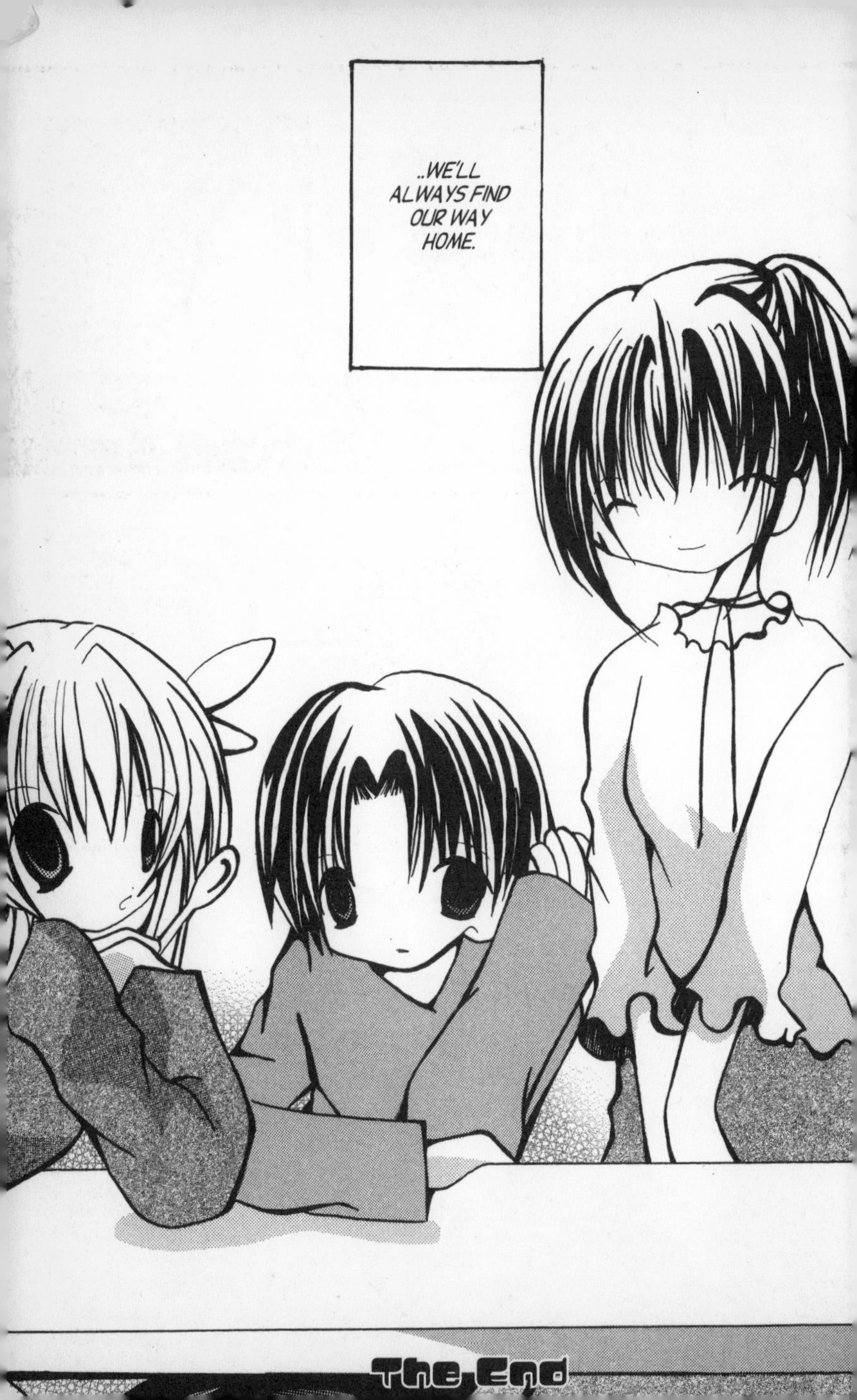
..WE'LL ALWAYS FIND OUR WAY HOME.
The End

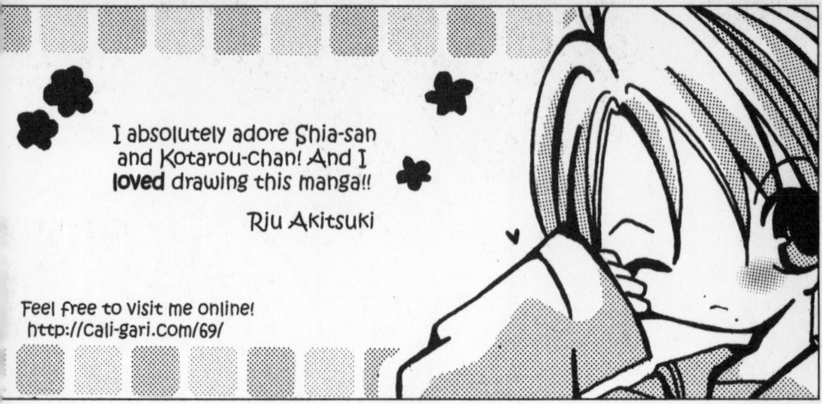
I absolutely adore Shia-san and Kotarou-chan! And I **loved** drawing this manga!!
Riu Akitsuki
Feel free to visit me online!
http://cali-gari.com/69/

▶ P.67

Riu Akitsuki

Writer's Talk

◀ P.77

Mahide Ooya

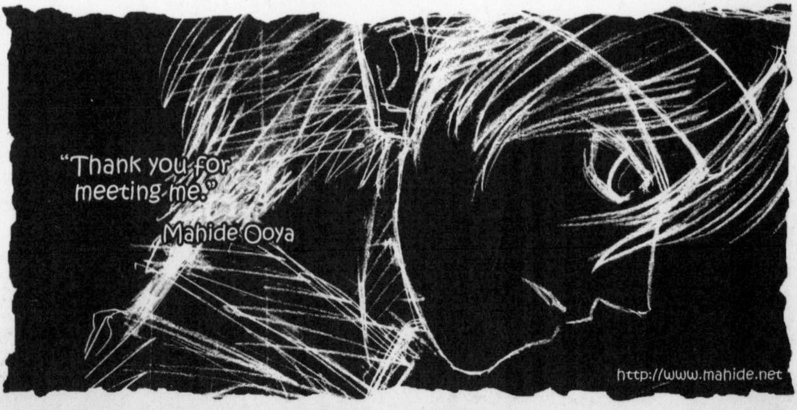
"Thank you for meeting me."
Mahide Ooya
http://www.mahide.net

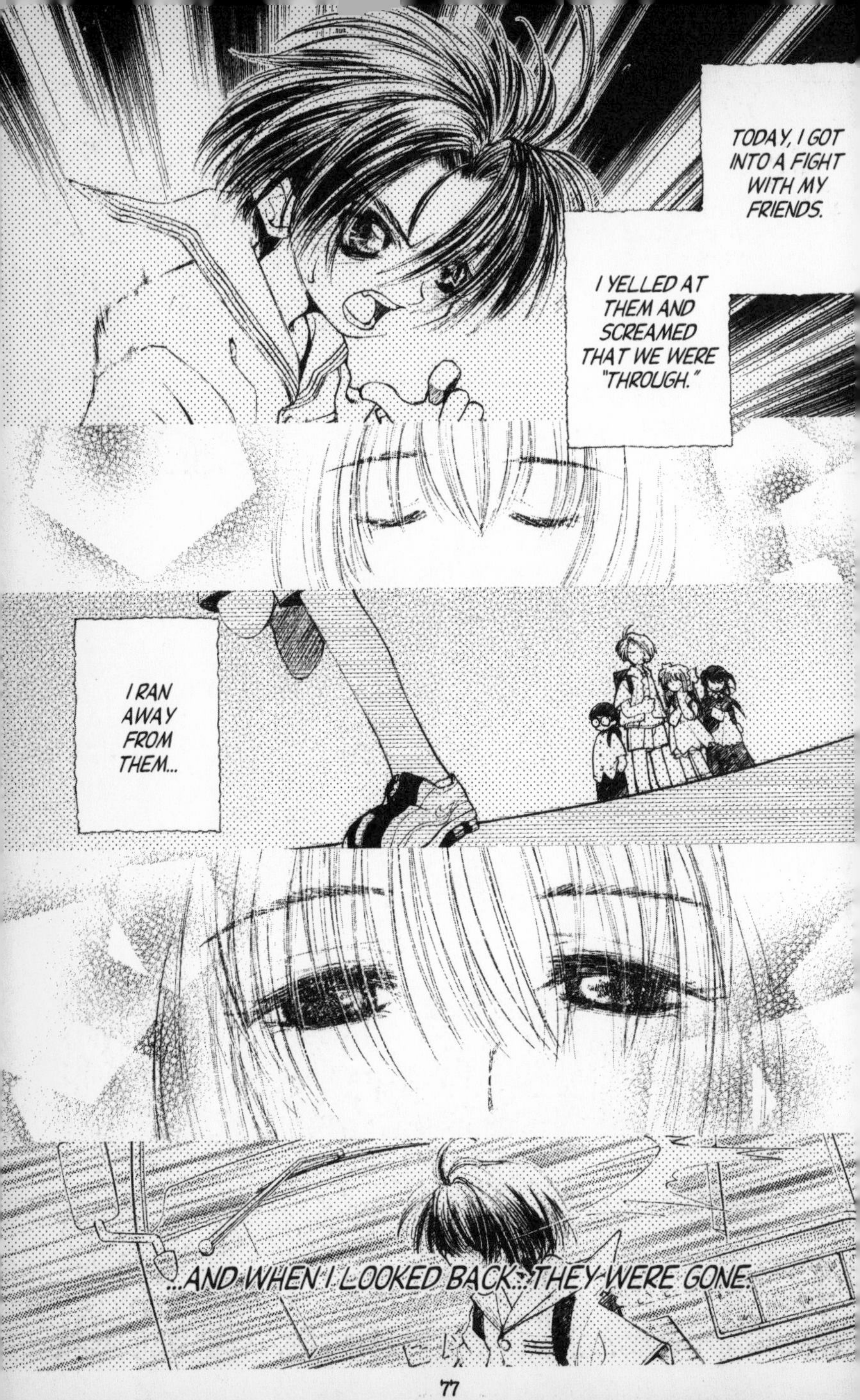
TODAY, I GOT INTO A FIGHT WITH MY FRIENDS.
I YELLED AT THEM AND SCREAMED THAT WE WERE "THROUGH."
I RAN AWAY FROM THEM...
...AND WHEN I LOOKED BACK... THEY WERE GONE.

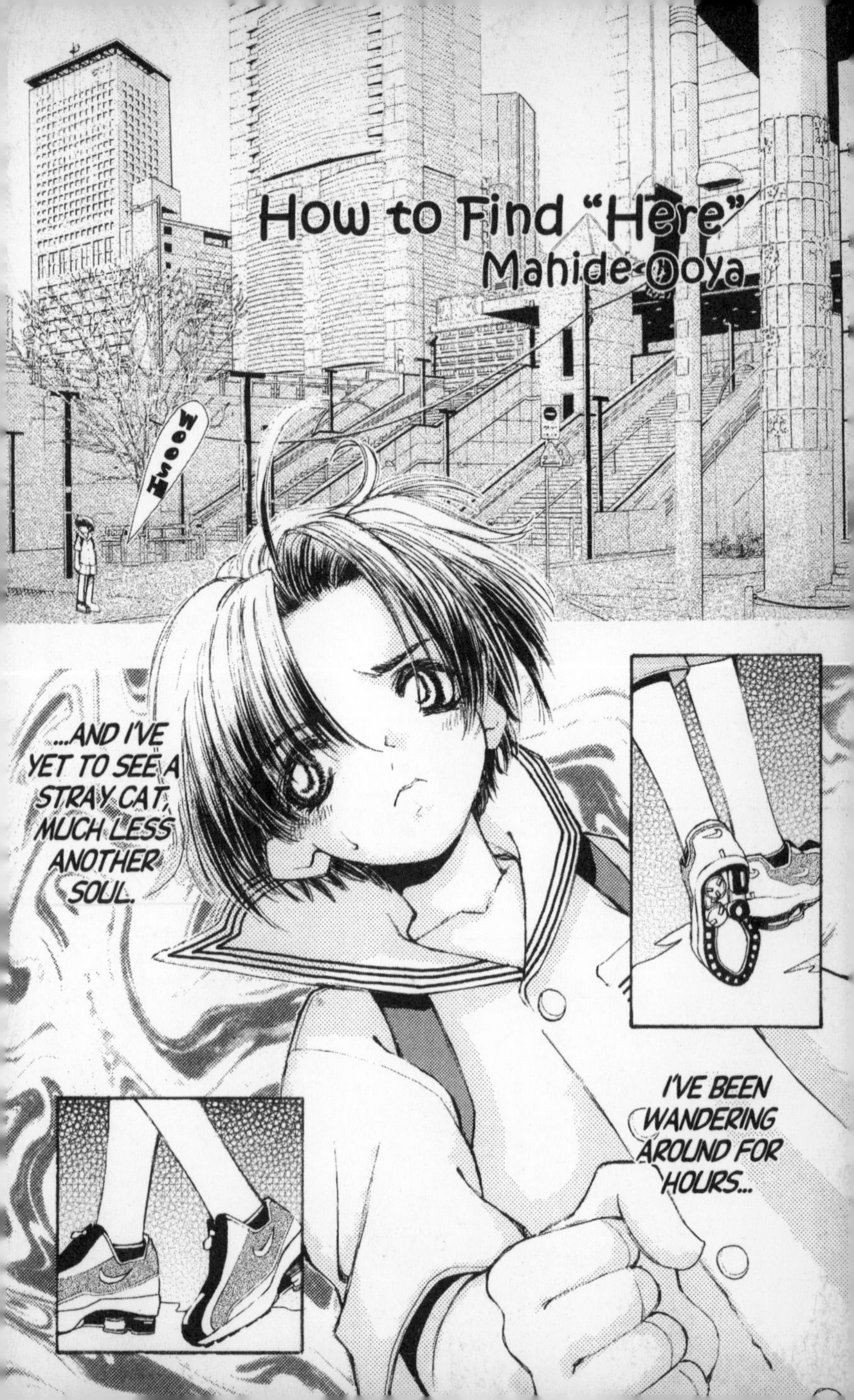
How to Find "Here"
Mahide Ooya
WOOSH
I'VE BEEN WANDERING AROUND FOR HOURS...
...AND I'VE YET TO SEE A STRAY CAT, MUCH LESS ANOTHER SOUL.

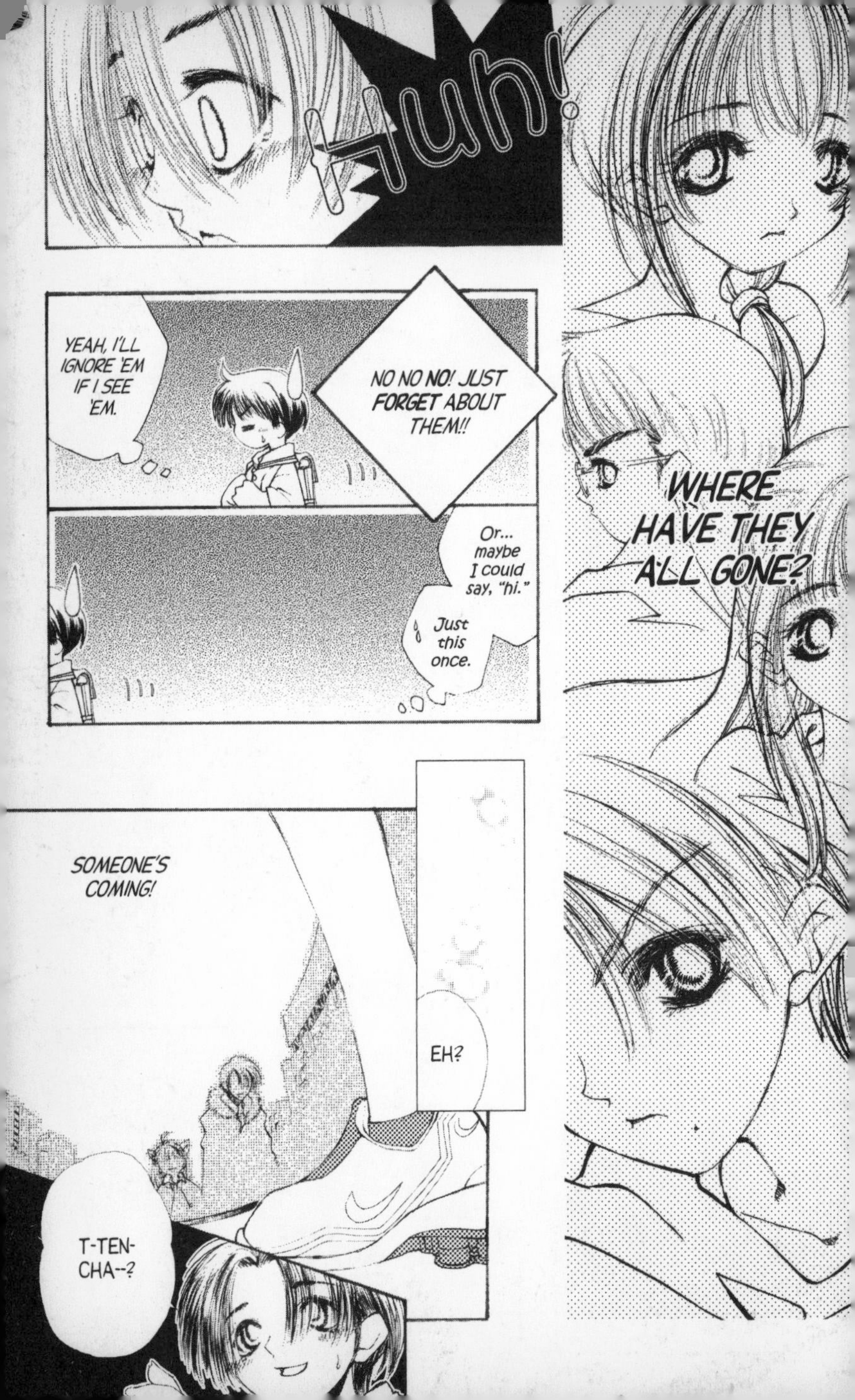
WHERE HAVE THEY ALL GONE?
HUH!
NO NO NO! JUST FORGET ABOUT THEM!!
YEAH, I'LL IGNORE 'EM IF I SEE 'EM.
Or... maybe I could say, "hi."
Just this once.
EH?
SOMEONE'S COMING!
T-TEN-CHA--?

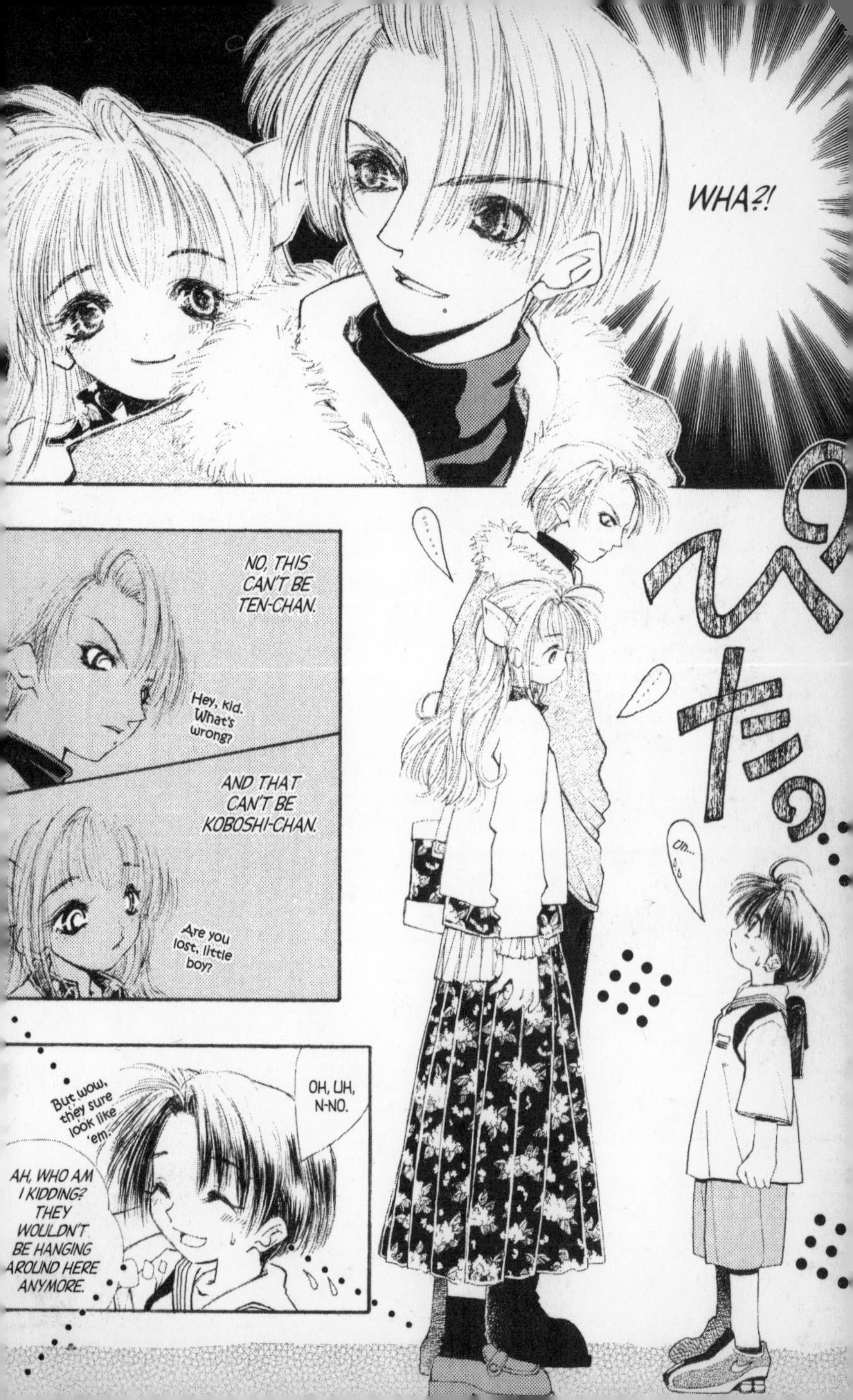
WHA?!
ぺたっ
Uh...
NO, THIS CAN'T BE TEN-CHAN.
Hey, kid. What's wrong?
AND THAT CAN'T BE KOBOSHI-CHAN.
Are you lost, little boy?
OH, UH, N-NO.
But wow, they sure look like 'em.
AH, WHO AM I KIDDING? THEY WOULDN'T BE HANGING AROUND HERE ANYMORE.

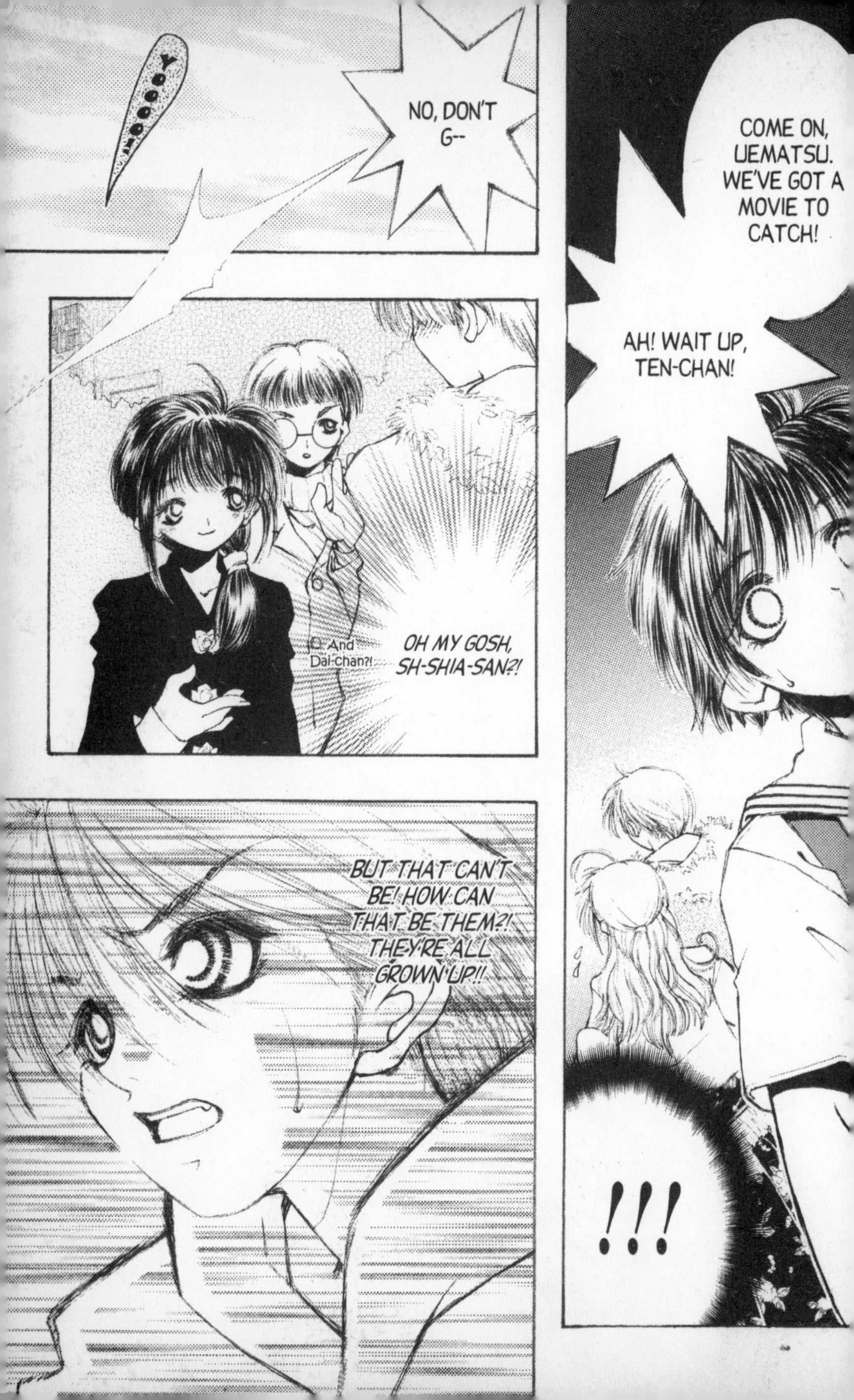
COME ON, UEMATSU. WE'VE GOT A MOVIE TO CATCH!
AH! WAIT UP, TEN-CHAN!
!!!
YOOOO!
NO, DON'T G--
OH MY GOSH, SH-SHIA-SAN?!
And Dai-chan?!
BUT THAT CAN'T BE! HOW CAN THAT BE THEM?! THEY'RE ALL GROWN UP!!

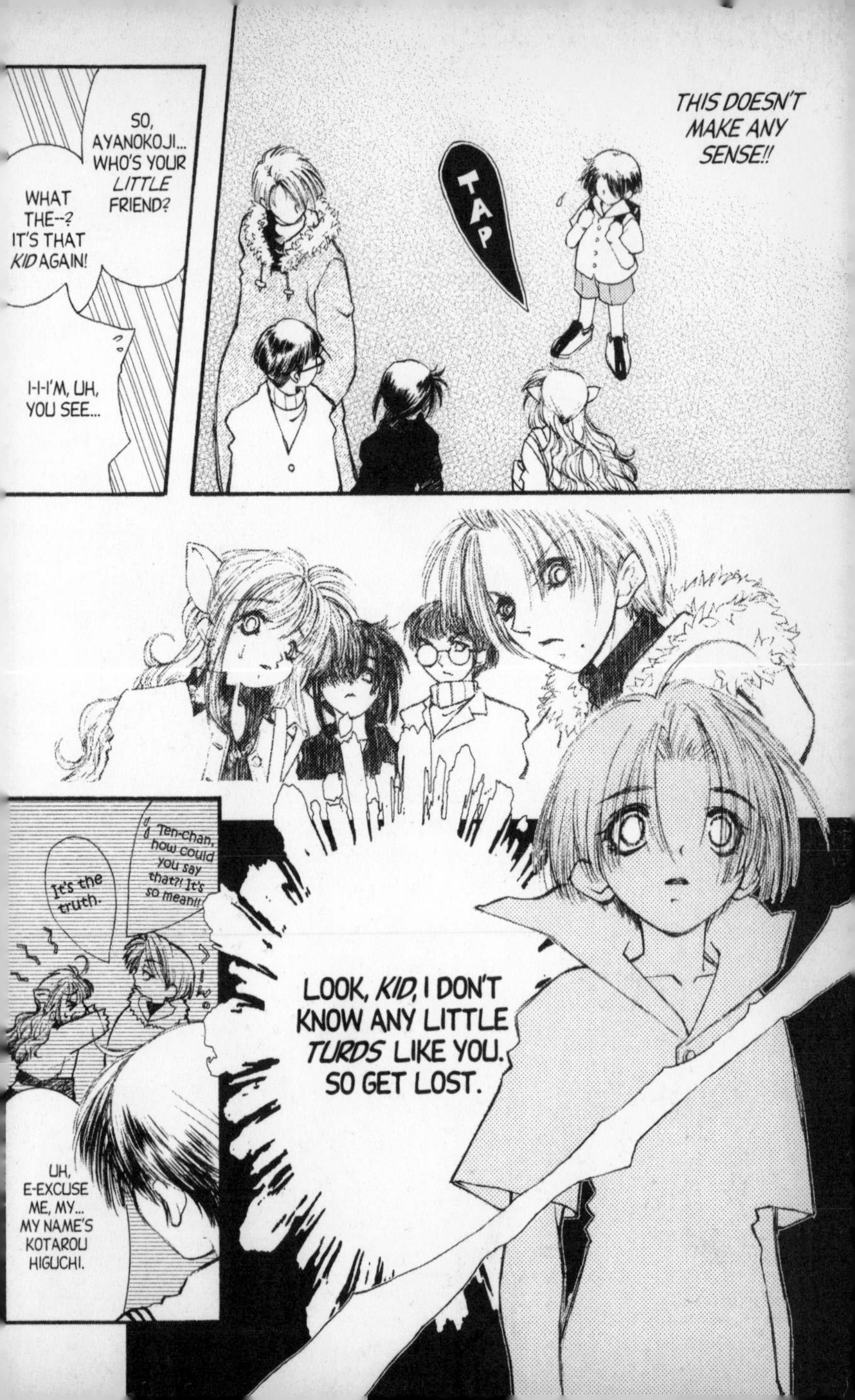
THIS DOESN'T MAKE ANY SENSE!!
TAP
SO, AYANOKOJI... WHO'S YOUR *LITTLE* FRIEND?
WHAT THE--? IT'S THAT *KID* AGAIN!
I-I-I'M, UH, YOU SEE...
LOOK, *KID*, I DON'T KNOW ANY LITTLE *TURDS* LIKE YOU. SO GET LOST.
Ten-chan, how could you say that?! It's so mean!!
It's the truth.
UH, E-EXCUSE ME, MY... MY NAME'S KOTAROU HIGUCHI.

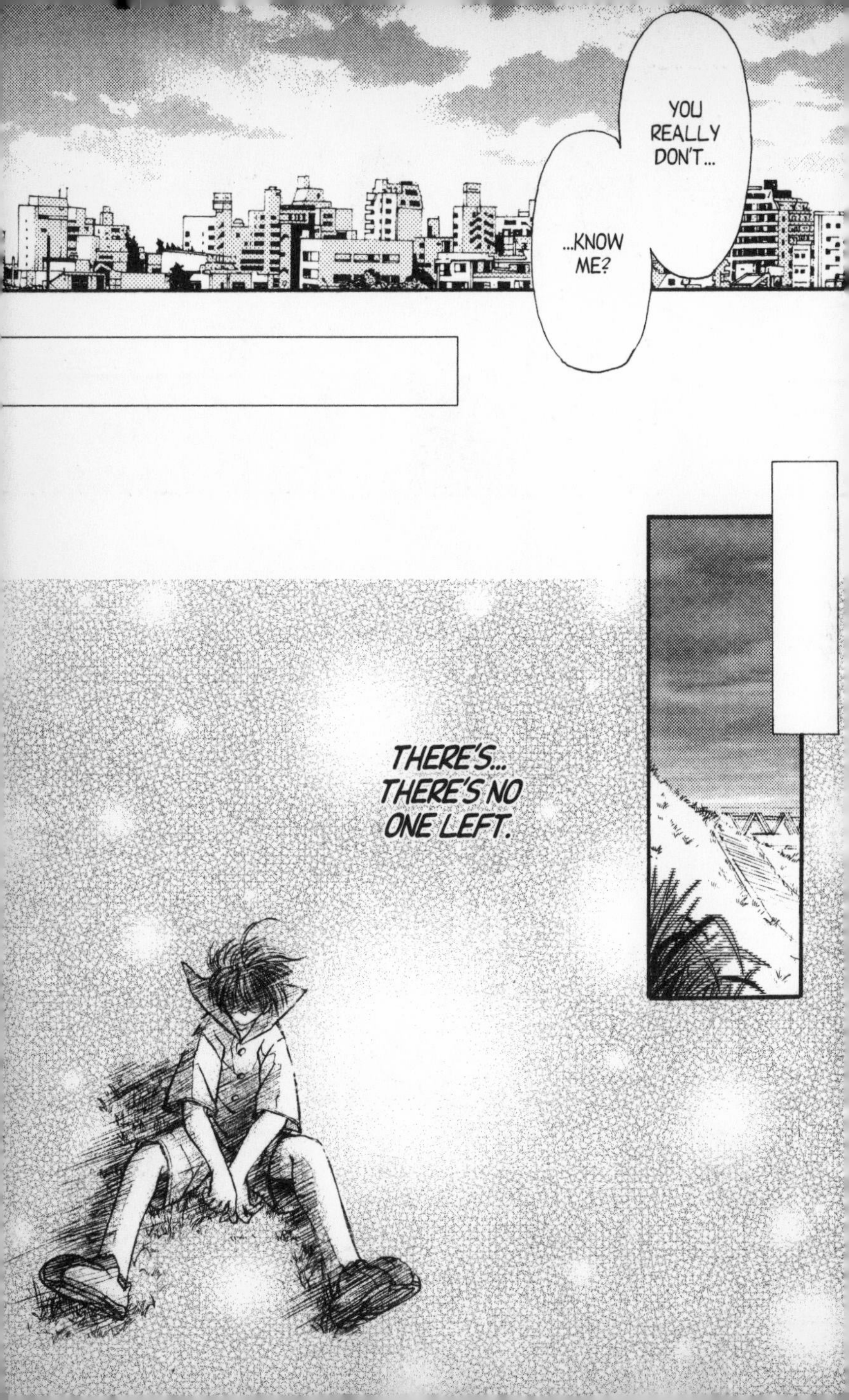
YOU REALLY DON'T...
...KNOW ME?
THERE'S... THERE'S NO ONE LEFT.

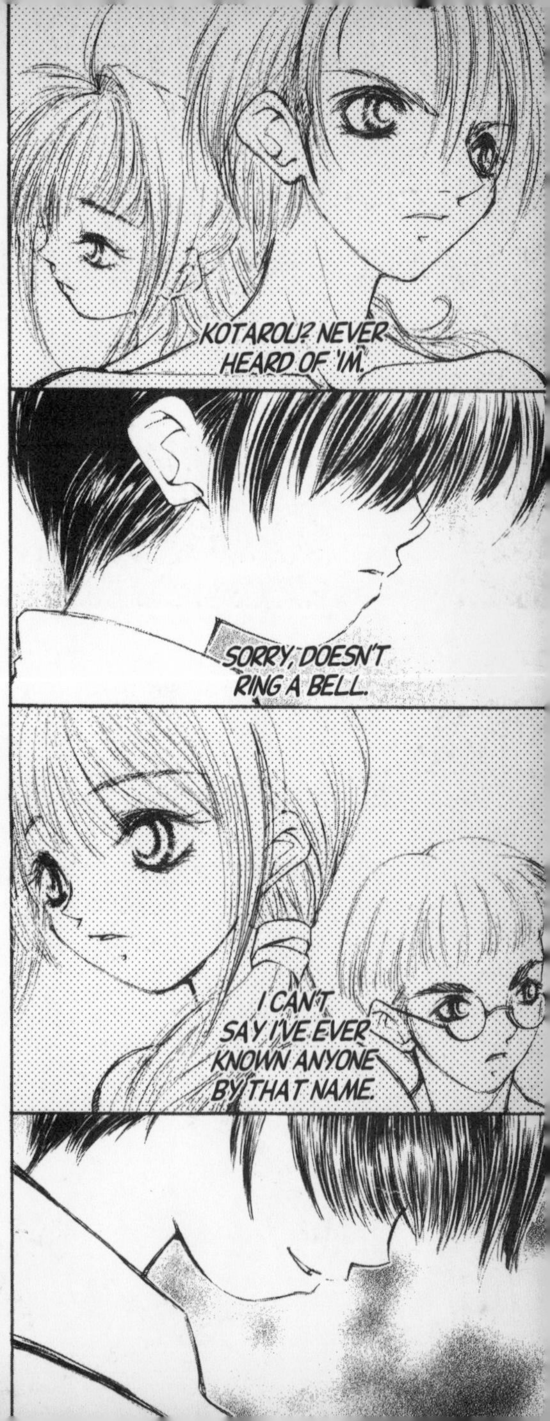
KOTAROU? NEVER HEARD OF 'IM.
SORRY, DOESN'T RING A BELL.
I CAN'T SAY I'VE EVER KNOWN ANYONE BY THAT NAME.

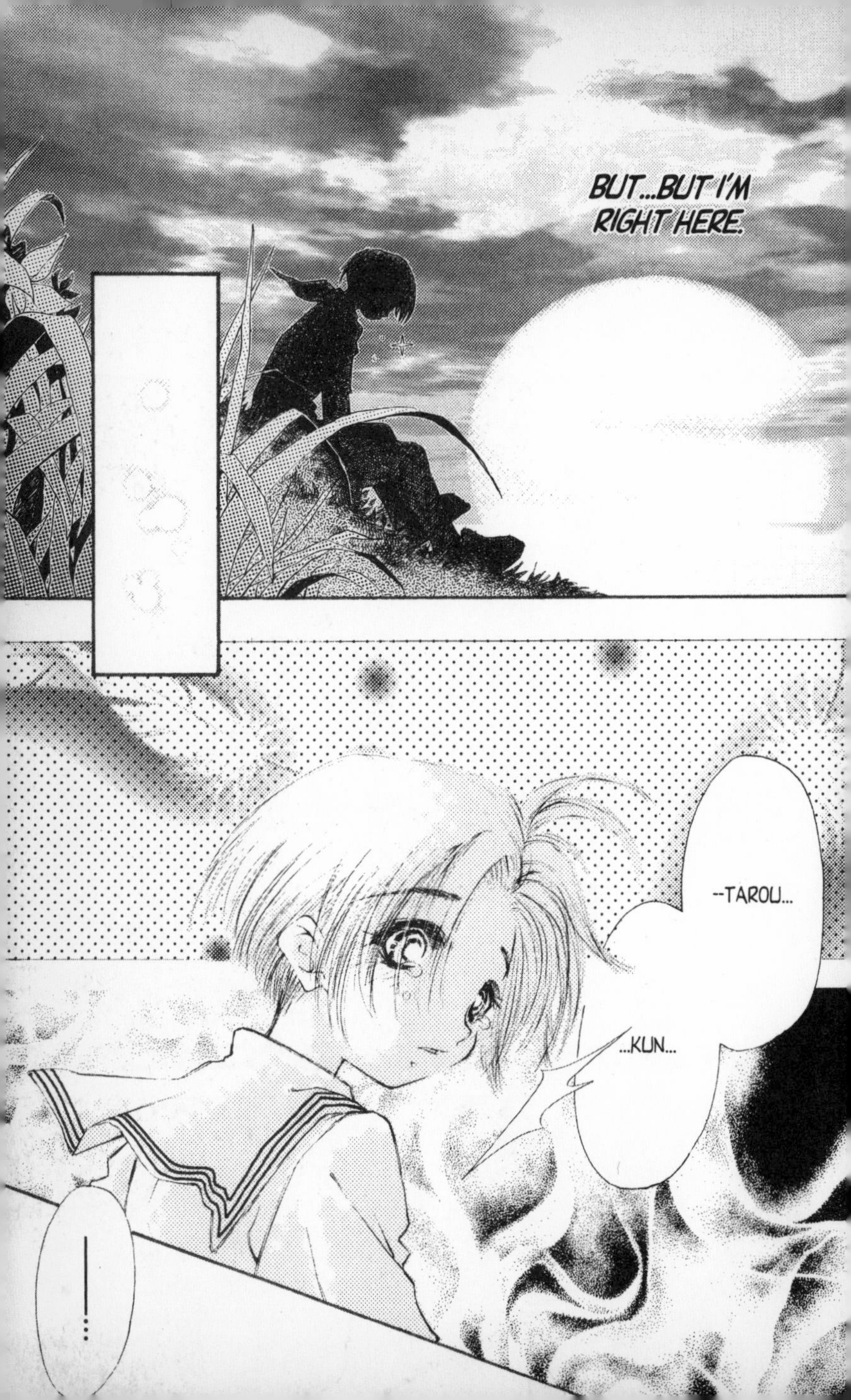
BUT...BUT I'M RIGHT HERE.
--TAROU...
...KUN...
......

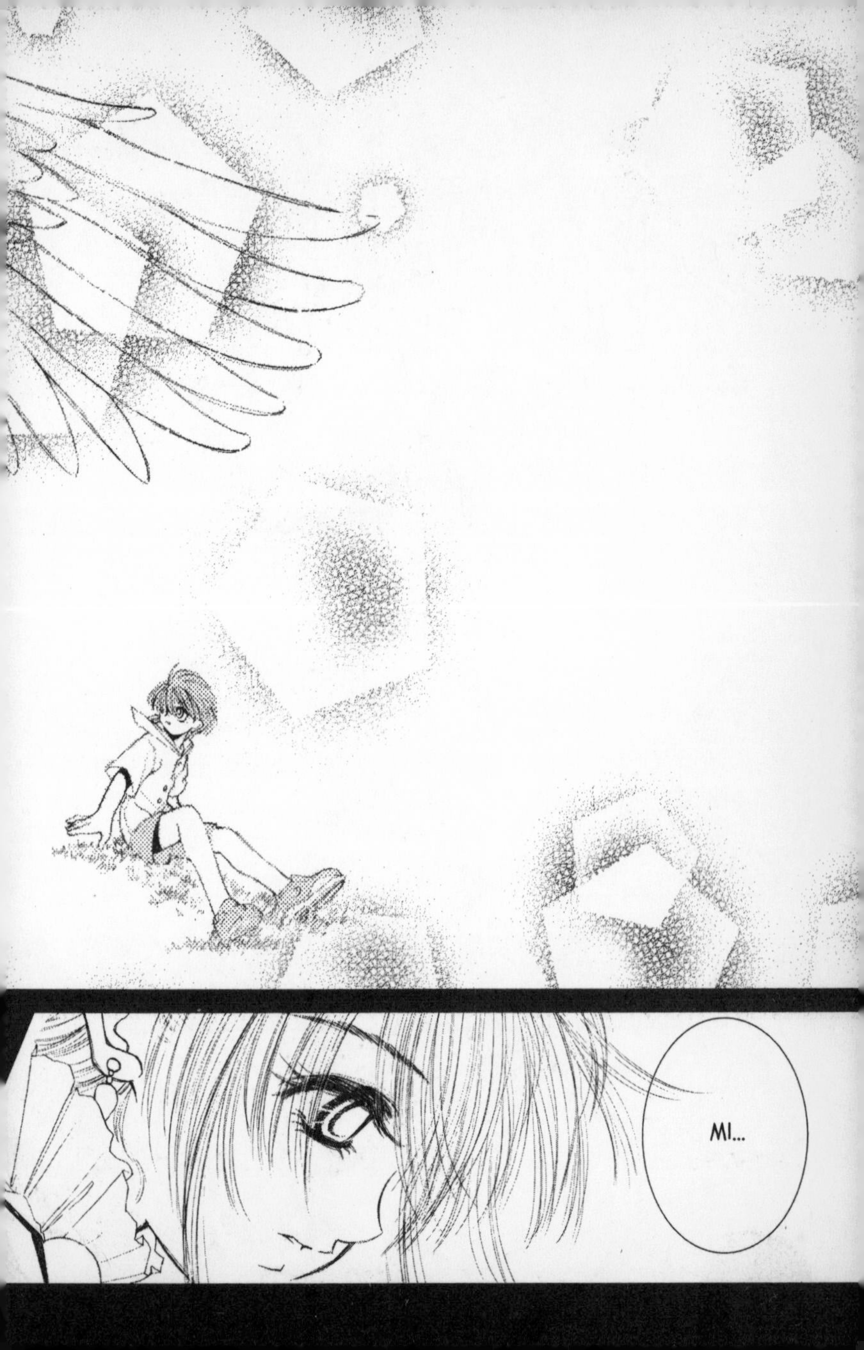
MI...

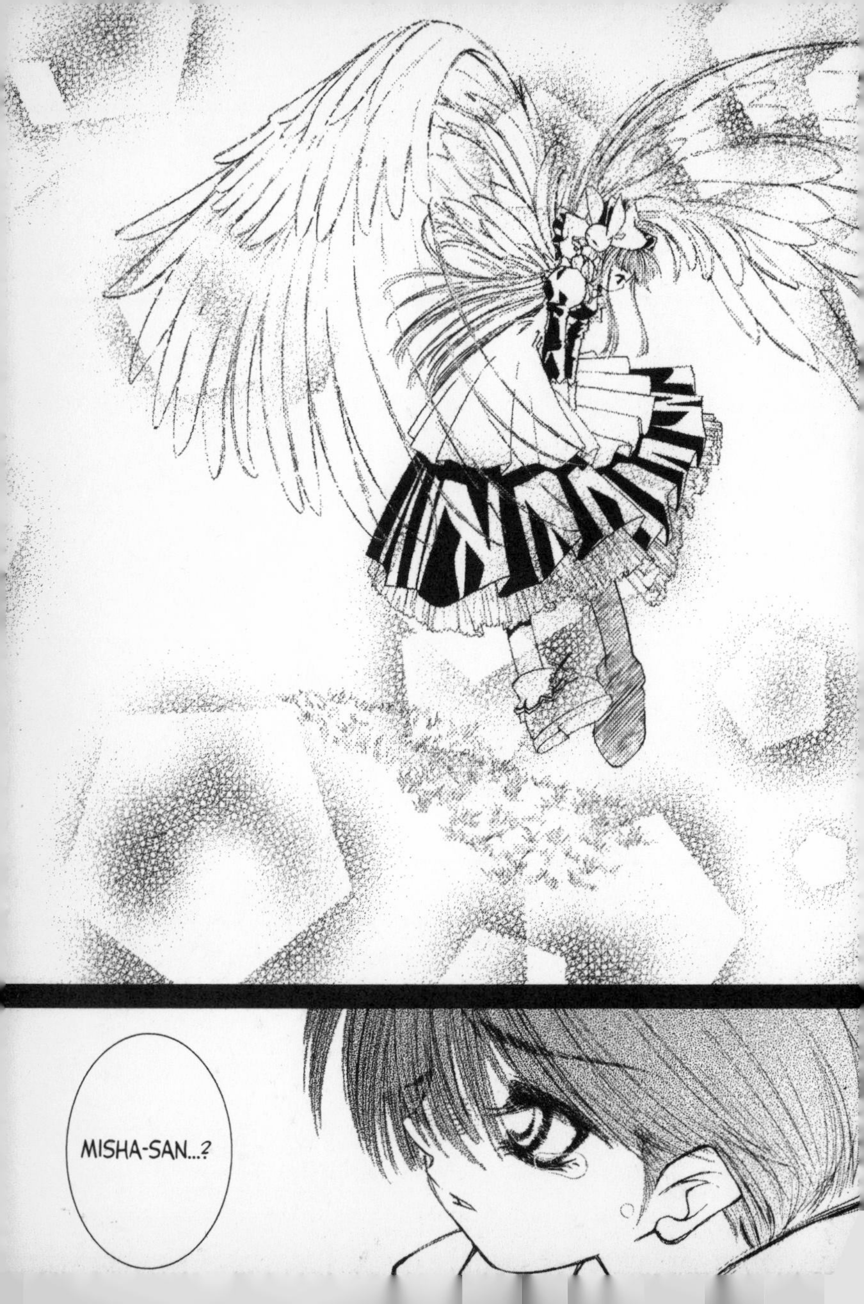
MISHA-SAN...?

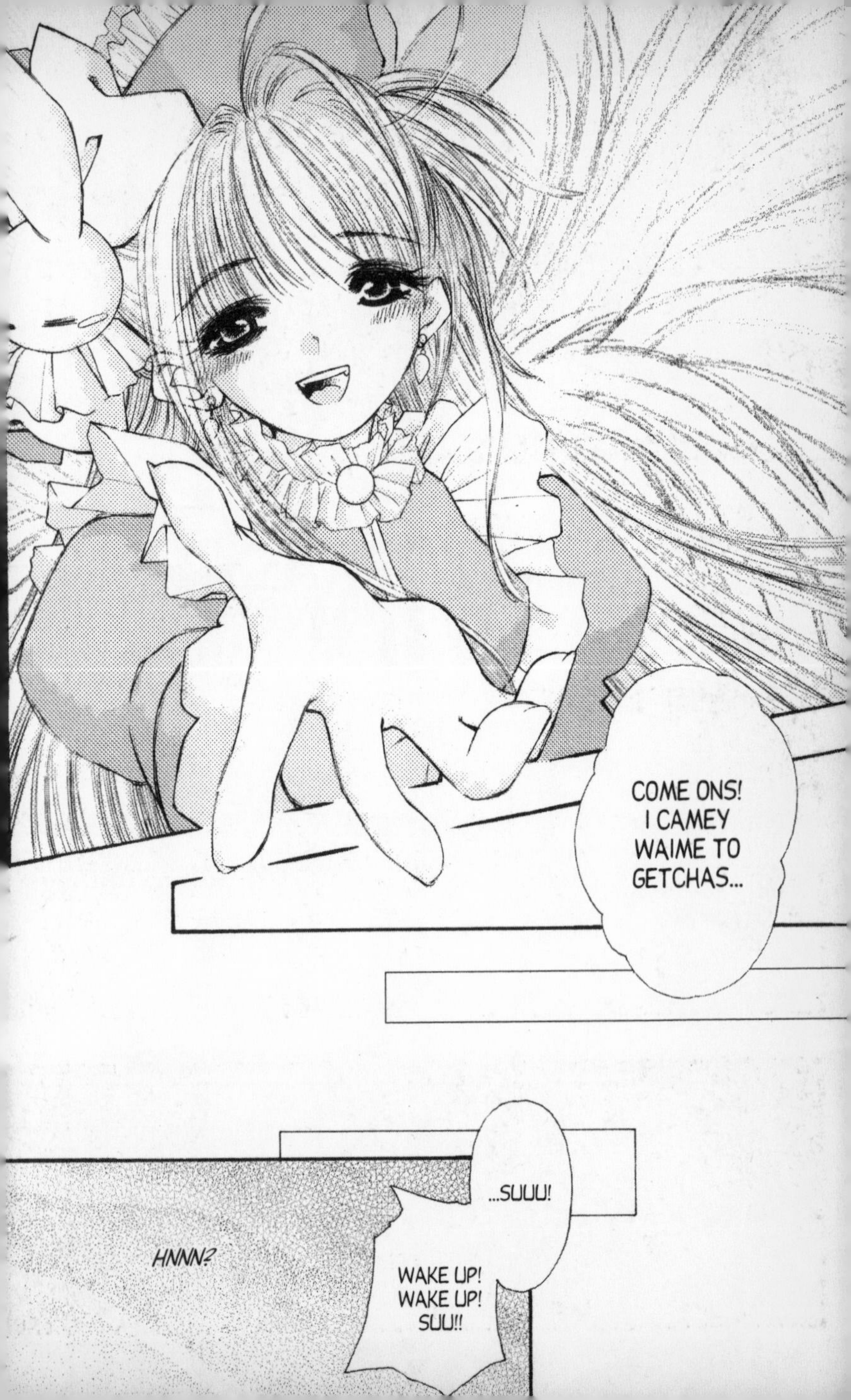
COME ONS! I CAMEY WAIME TO GETCHAS...
...SUUU!
WAKE UP! WAKE UP! SUU!!
HNNN?

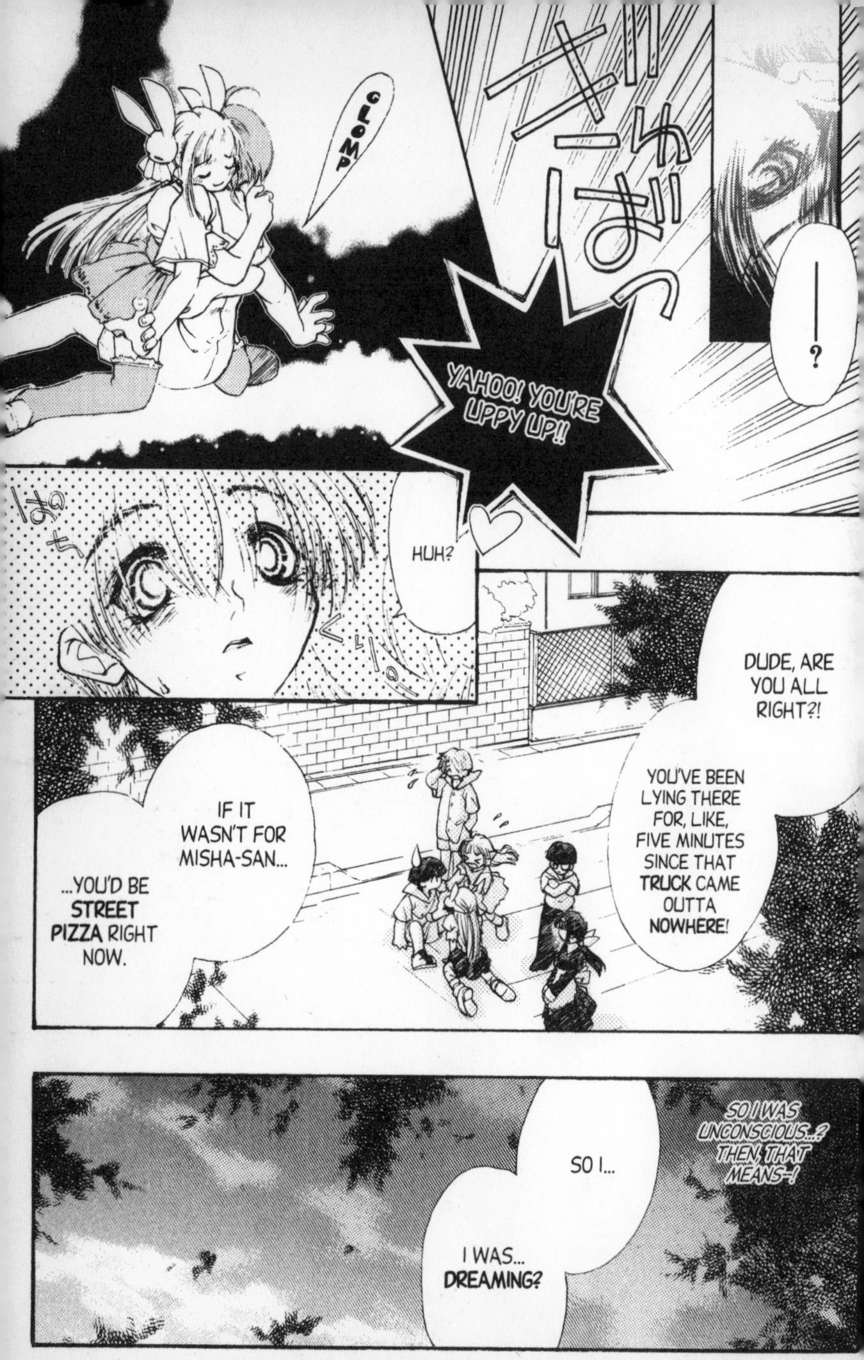
—?
YAHOO! YOU'RE UPPY UP!!
GLOMP
HUH?
DUDE, ARE YOU ALL RIGHT?!
YOU'VE BEEN LYING THERE FOR, LIKE, FIVE MINUTES SINCE THAT TRUCK CAME OUTTA NOWHERE!
IF IT WASN'T FOR MISHA-SAN...
...YOU'D BE STREET PIZZA RIGHT NOW.
SO I WAS UNCONSCIOUS...? THEN, THAT MEANS—!
SO I...
I WAS... DREAMING?

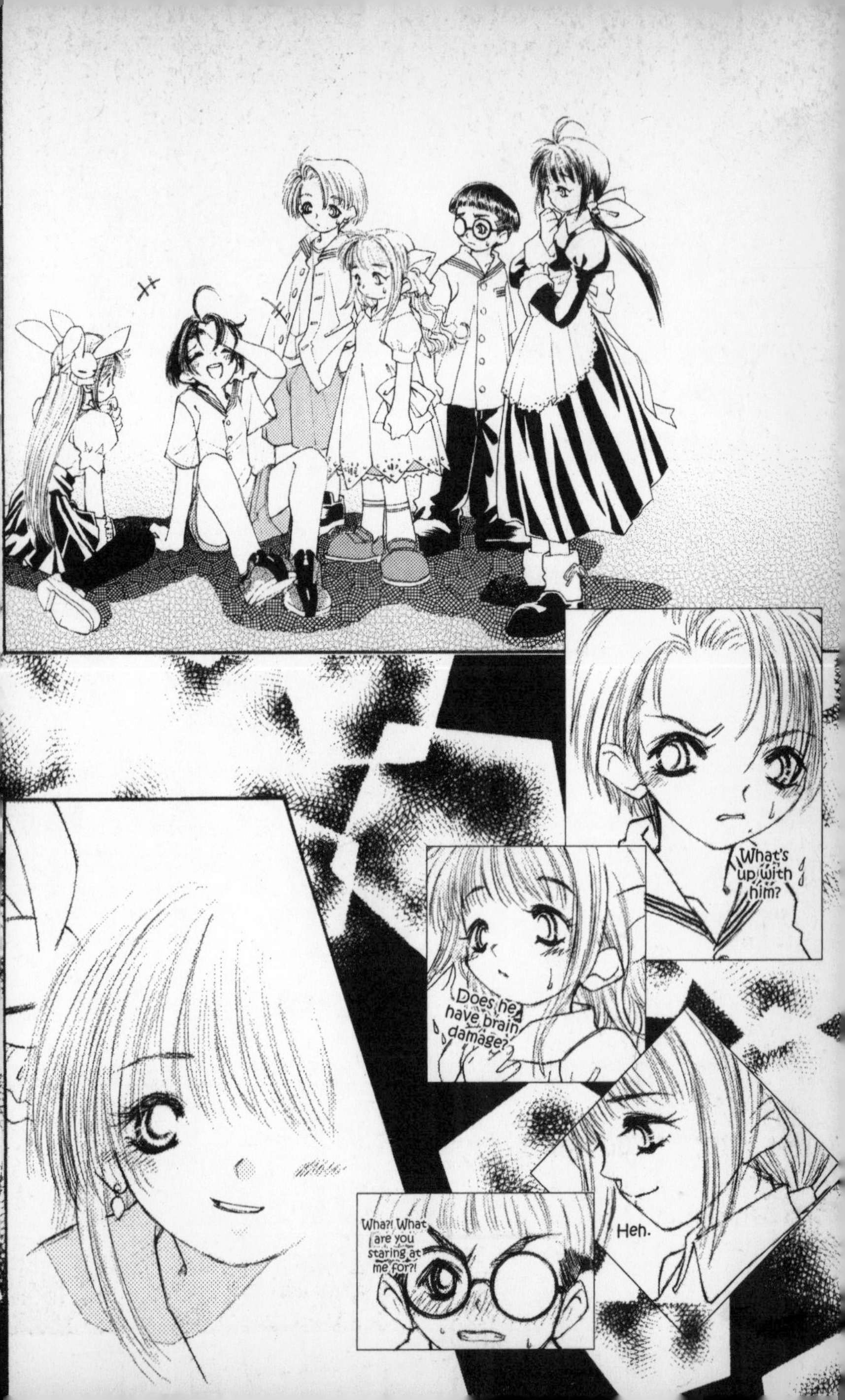
What's up with him?
Does he have brain damage?
Heh.
What?! What are you staring at me for?!

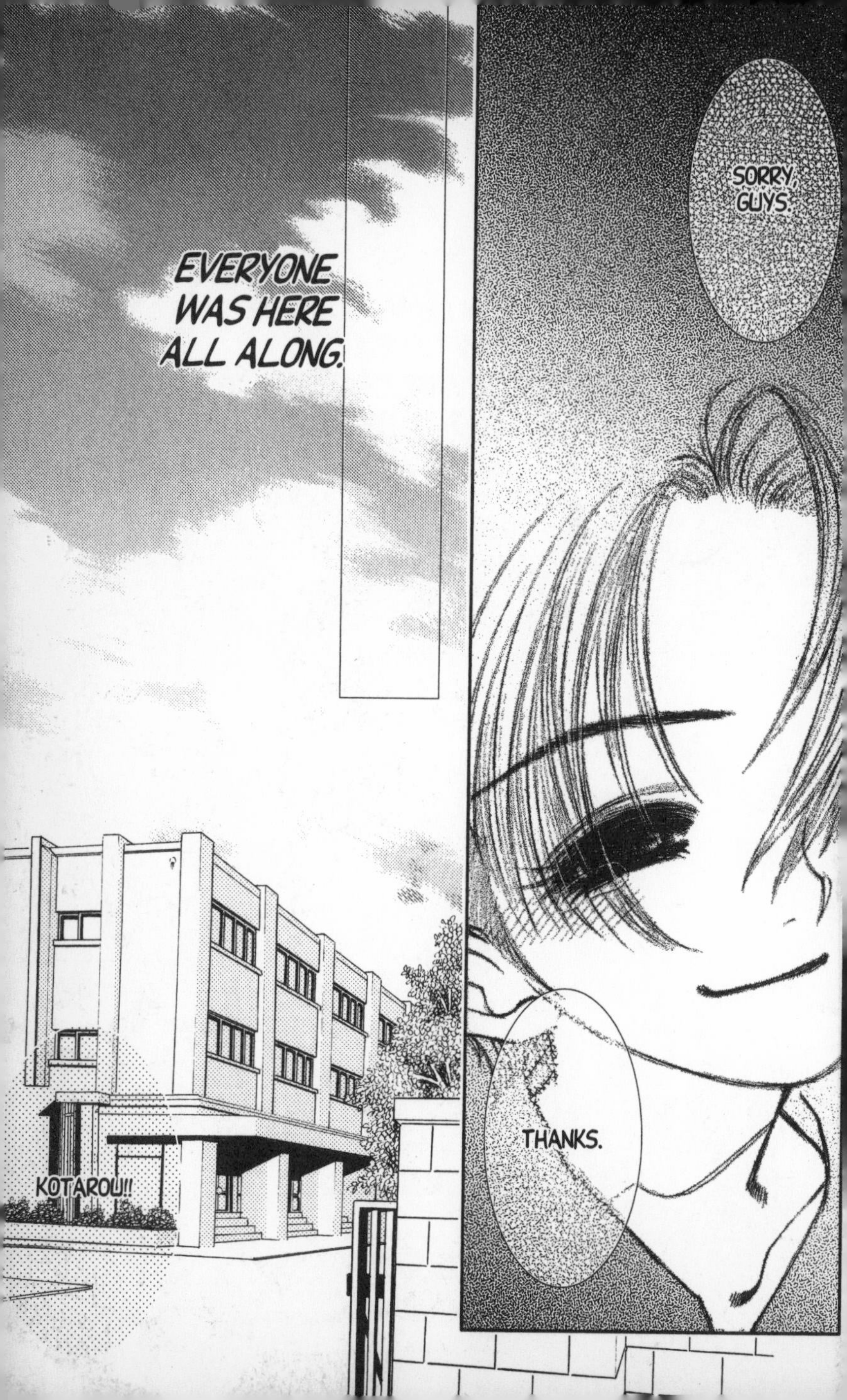
SORRY, GUYS.
THANKS.
EVERYONE WAS HERE ALL ALONG.
KOTAROU!!

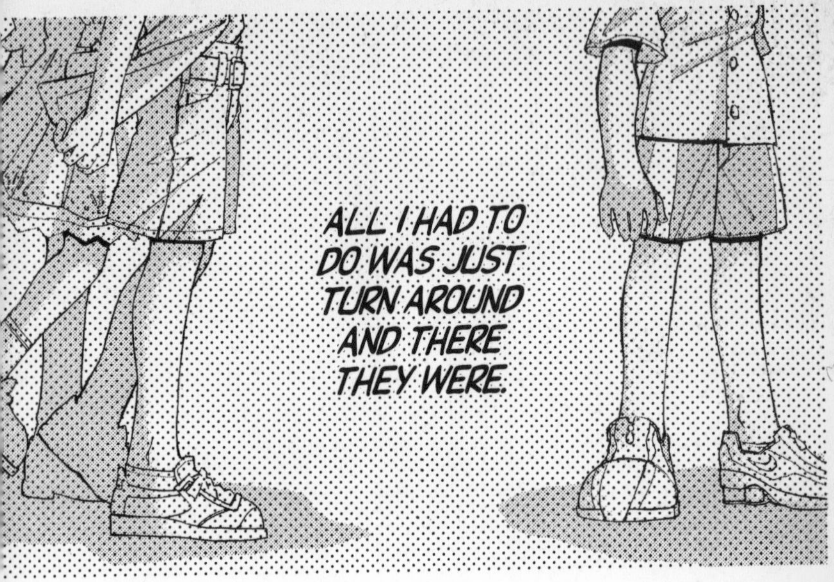
ALL I HAD TO DO WAS JUST TURN AROUND AND THERE THEY WERE.

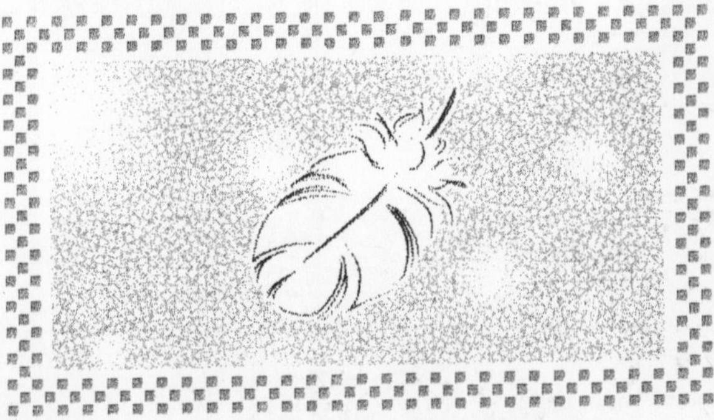

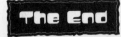

The End

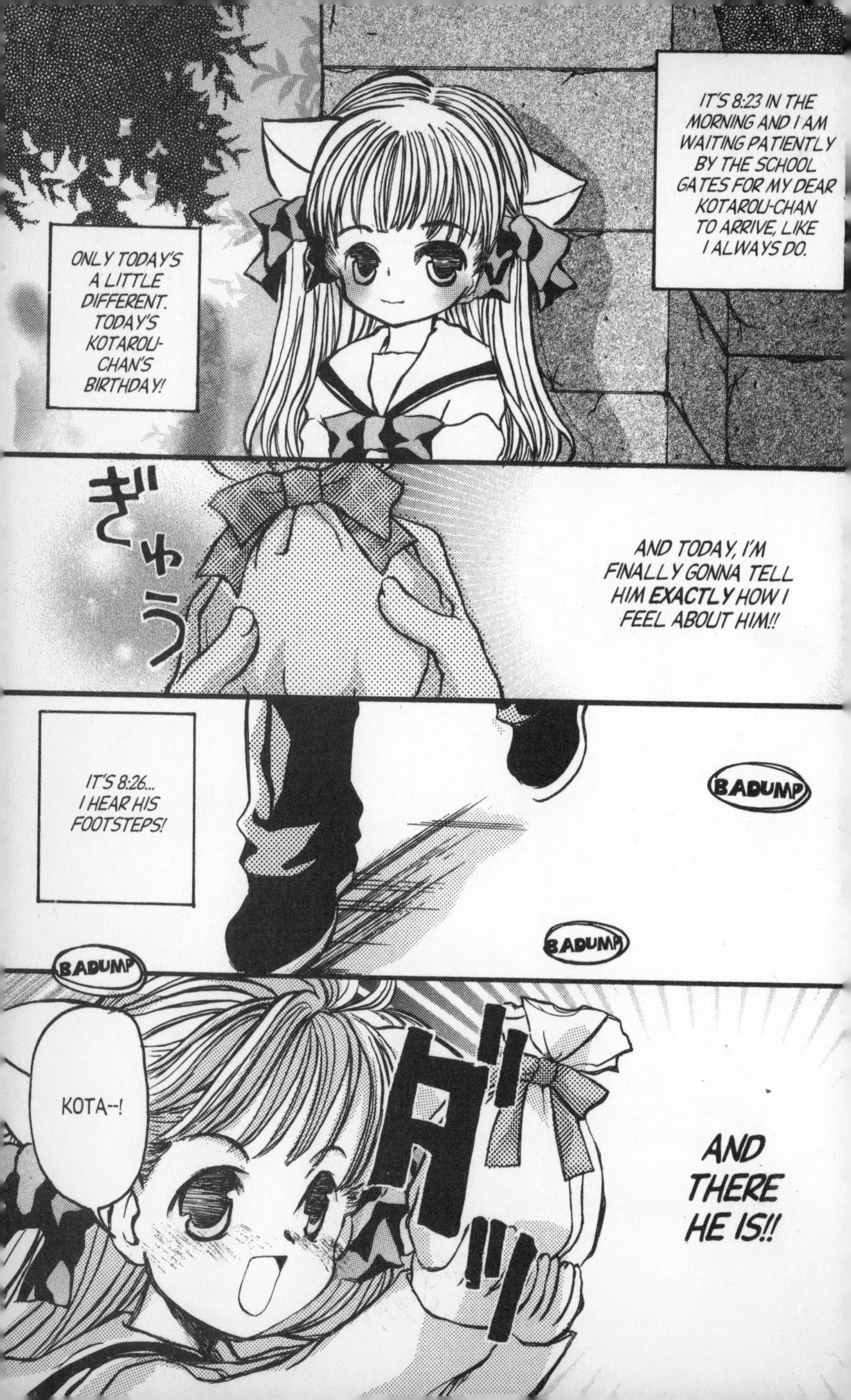
IT'S 8:23 IN THE MORNING AND I AM WAITING PATIENTLY BY THE SCHOOL GATES FOR MY DEAR KOTAROU-CHAN TO ARRIVE, LIKE I ALWAYS DO.
ONLY TODAY'S A LITTLE DIFFERENT. TODAY'S KOTAROU-CHAN'S BIRTHDAY!
AND TODAY, I'M FINALLY GONNA TELL HIM EXACTLY HOW I FEEL ABOUT HIM!!
ぎゅう
BADUMP
IT'S 8:26... I HEAR HIS FOOTSTEPS!
BADUMP
BADUMP
AND THERE HE IS!!
ガッ
KOTA--!

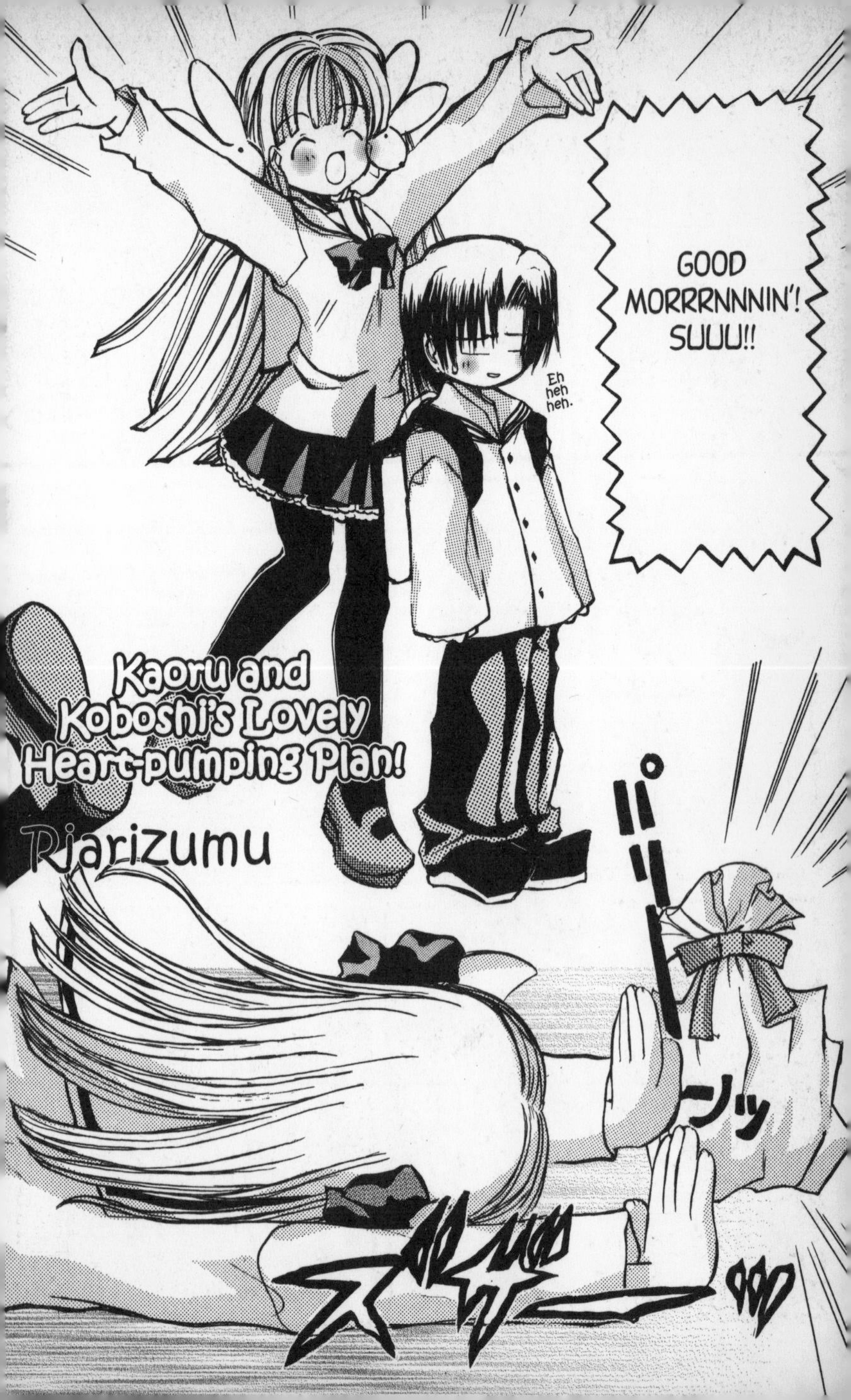
GOOD MORRRNNNIN'! SUUU!!
Eh heh heh.
Kaoru and Koboshi's Lovely Heart-pumping Plan!
Rjarizumu

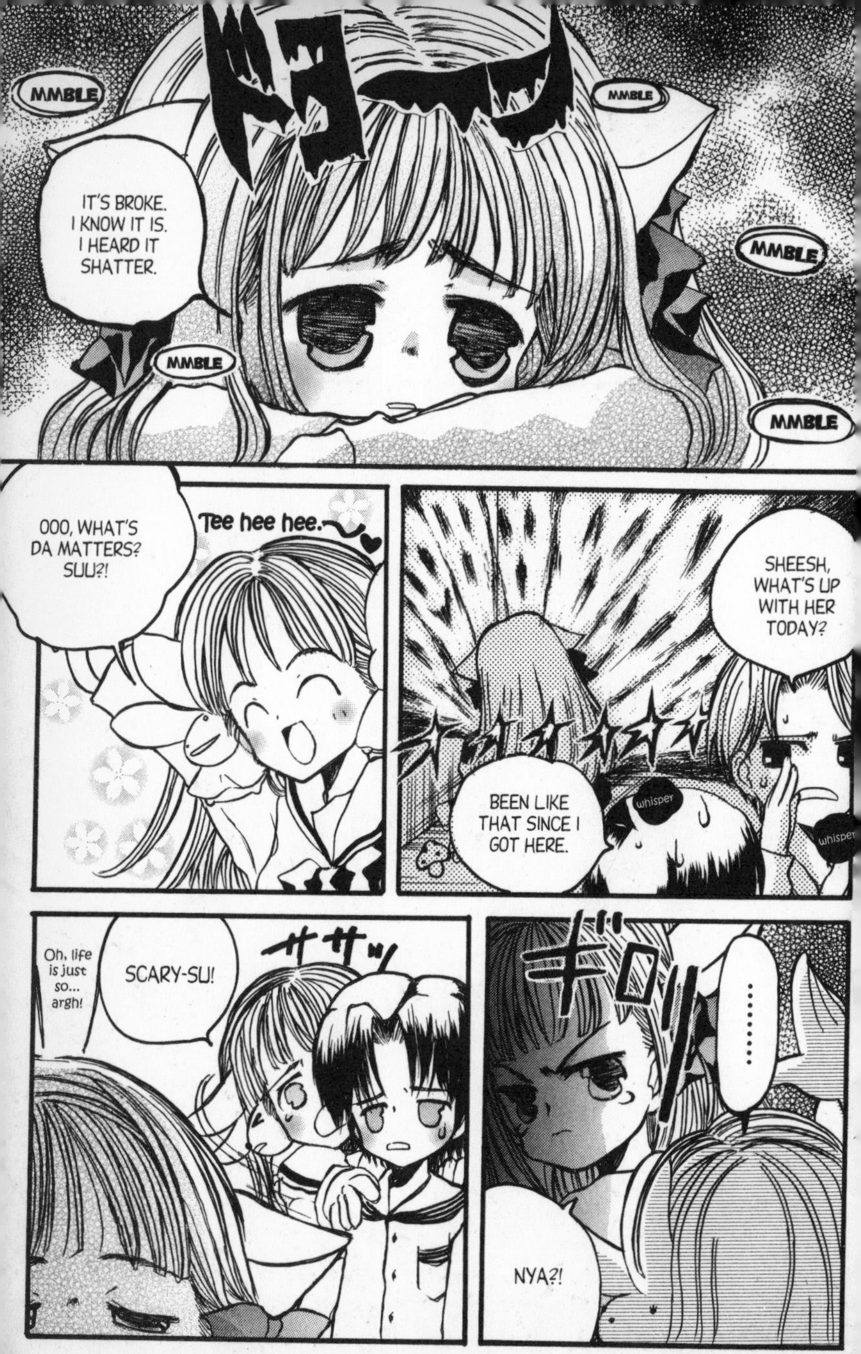
MMBLE
MMBLE
IT'S BROKE. I KNOW IT IS. I HEARD IT SHATTER.
MMBLE
MMBLE
MMBLE
SHEESH, WHAT'S UP WITH HER TODAY?
whisper
BEEN LIKE THAT SINCE I GOT HERE.
whisper
Tee hee hee.
OOO, WHAT'S DA MATTERS? SUU?!
....
NYA?!
SCARY-SU!
Oh, life is just so... argh!

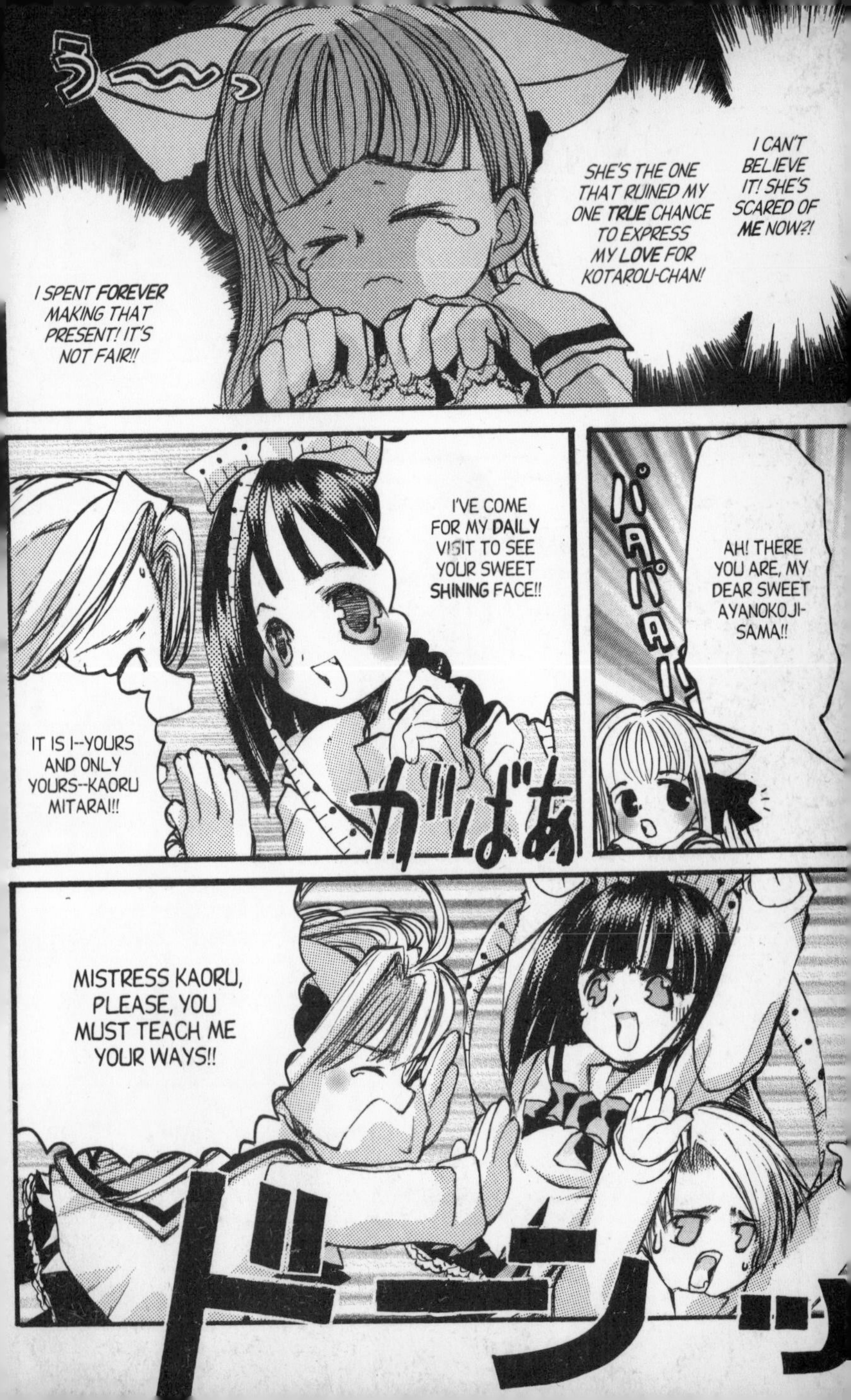
I CAN'T BELIEVE IT! SHE'S SCARED OF ME NOW?!
SHE'S THE ONE THAT RUINED MY ONE TRUE CHANCE TO EXPRESS MY LOVE FOR KOTAROU-CHAN!
I SPENT FOREVER MAKING THAT PRESENT! IT'S NOT FAIR!!
AH! THERE YOU ARE, MY DEAR SWEET AYANOKOJI-SAMA!!
I'VE COME FOR MY DAILY VISIT TO SEE YOUR SWEET SHINING FACE!!
IT IS I--YOURS AND ONLY YOURS--KAORU MITARAI!!
がばあ
MISTRESS KAORU, PLEASE, YOU MUST TEACH ME YOUR WAYS!!

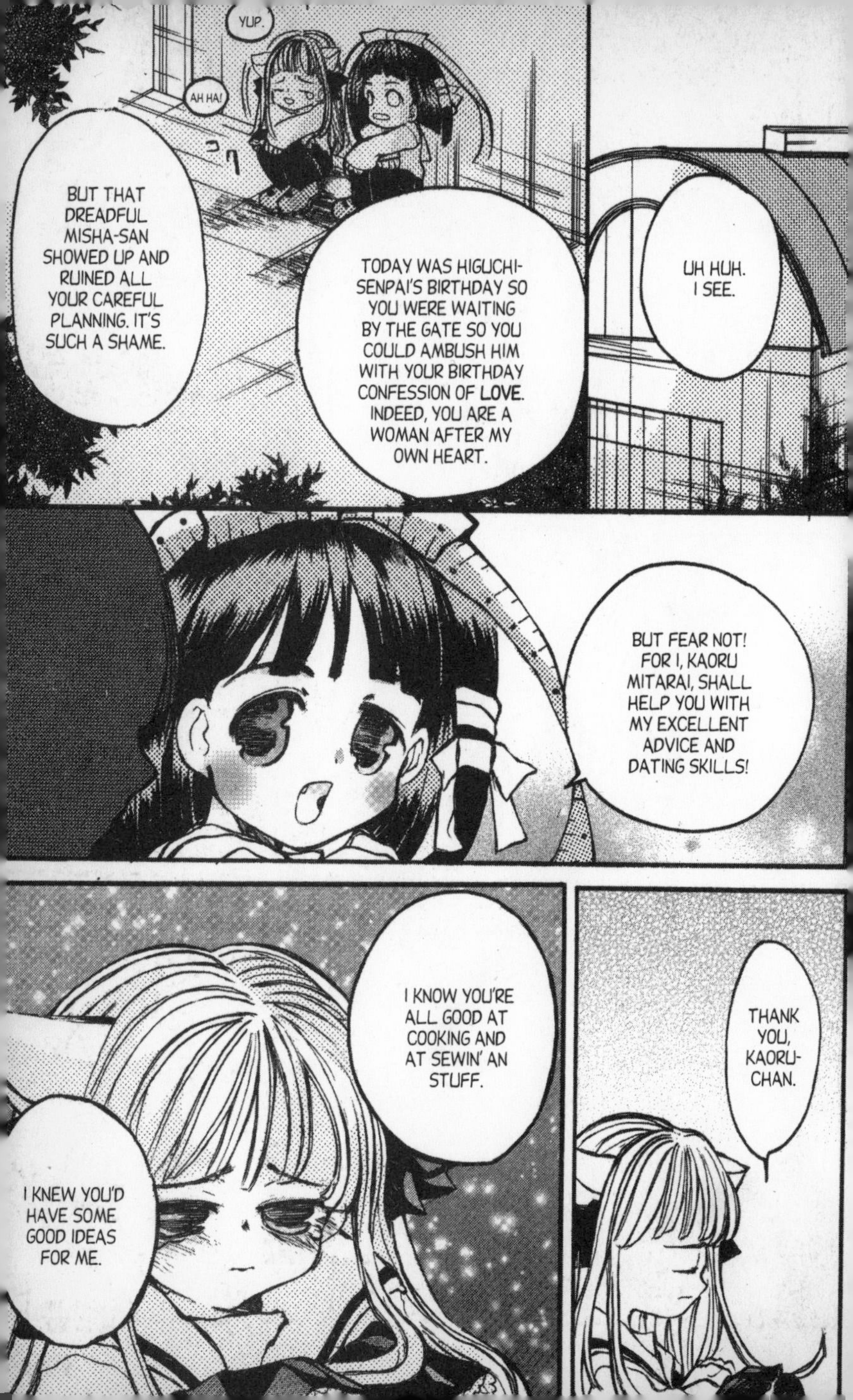
UH HUH. I SEE.
TODAY WAS HIGUCHI-SENPAI'S BIRTHDAY SO YOU WERE WAITING BY THE GATE SO YOU COULD AMBUSH HIM WITH YOUR BIRTHDAY CONFESSION OF **LOVE**. INDEED, YOU ARE A WOMAN AFTER MY OWN HEART.
YUP.
AH HA!
BUT THAT DREADFUL MISHA-SAN SHOWED UP AND RUINED ALL YOUR CAREFUL PLANNING. IT'S SUCH A SHAME.
BUT FEAR NOT! FOR I, KAORU MITARAI, SHALL HELP YOU WITH MY EXCELLENT ADVICE AND DATING SKILLS!
THANK YOU, KAORU-CHAN.
I KNOW YOU'RE ALL GOOD AT COOKING AND AT SEWIN' AN STUFF.
I KNEW YOU'D HAVE SOME GOOD IDEAS FOR ME.

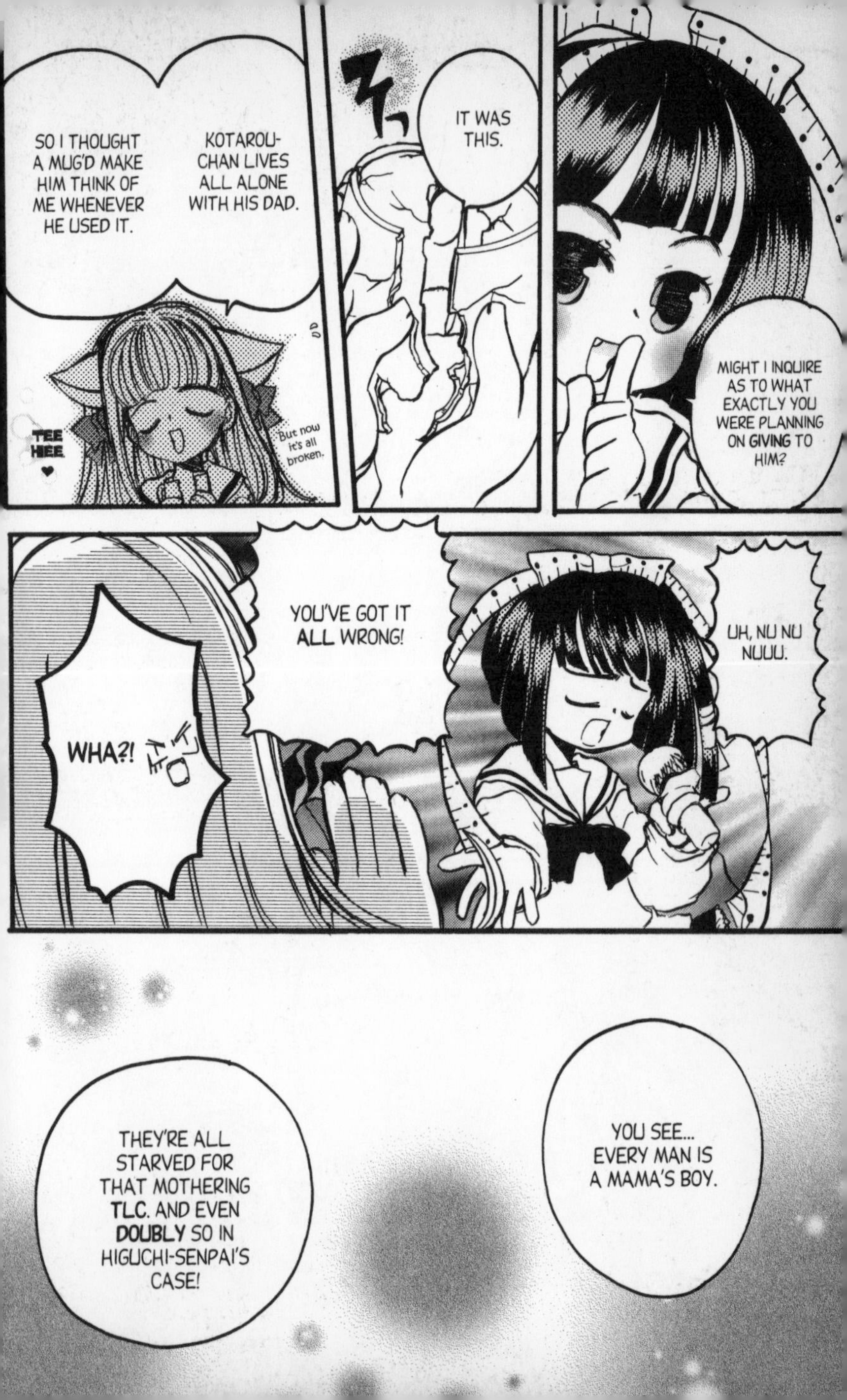
MIGHT I INQUIRE AS TO WHAT EXACTLY YOU WERE PLANNING ON GIVING TO HIM?
IT WAS THIS.
KOTAROU-CHAN LIVES ALL ALONE WITH HIS DAD.
SO I THOUGHT A MUG'D MAKE HIM THINK OF ME WHENEVER HE USED IT.
TEE HEE ♥
But now it's all broken.
UH, NU NU NUUU.
YOU'VE GOT IT ALL WRONG!
WHA?!
YOU SEE... EVERY MAN IS A MAMA'S BOY.
THEY'RE ALL STARVED FOR THAT MOTHERING TLC. AND EVEN DOUBLY SO IN HIGUCHI-SENPAI'S CASE!

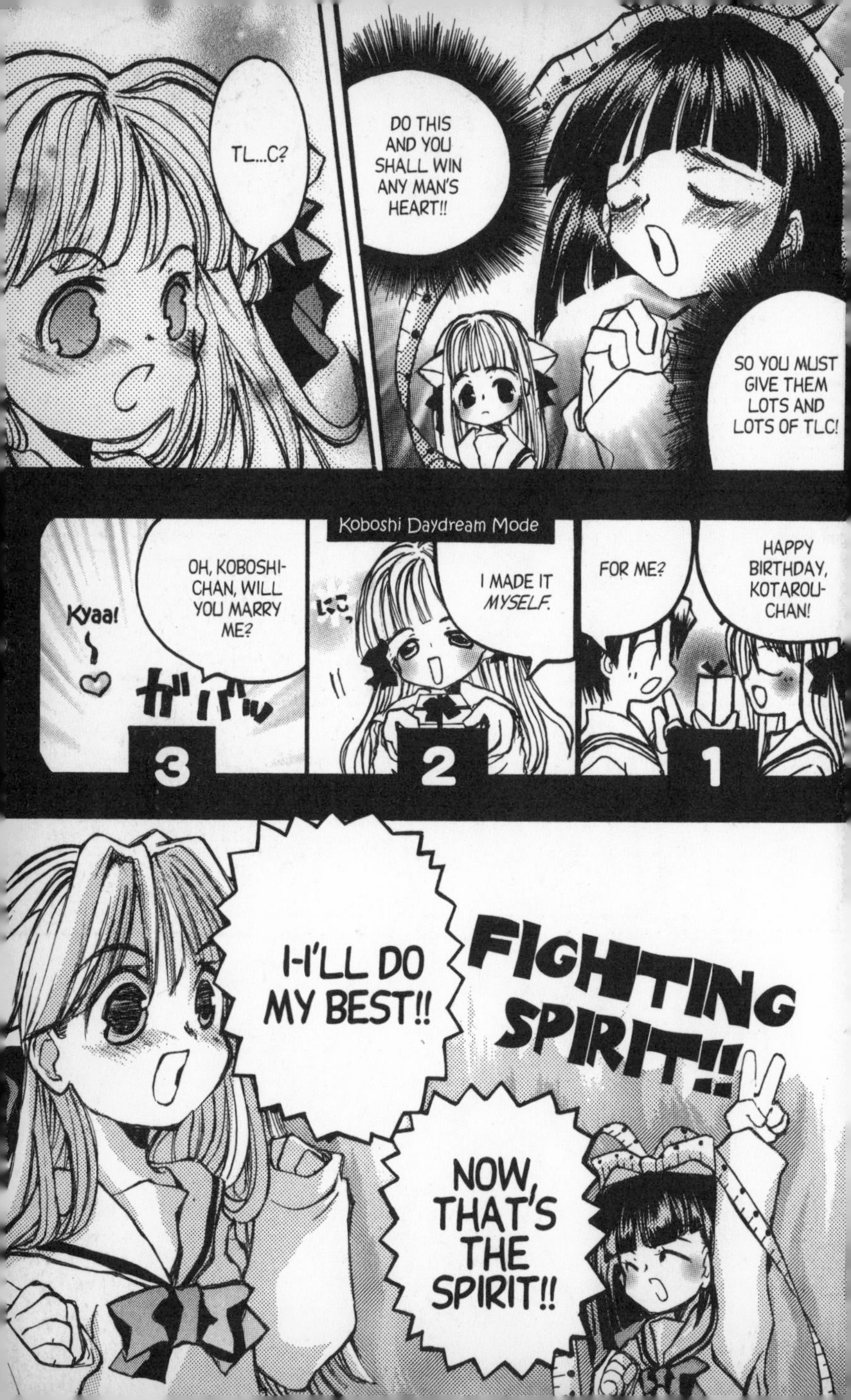
DO THIS AND YOU SHALL WIN ANY MAN'S HEART!!
SO YOU MUST GIVE THEM LOTS AND LOTS OF TLC!
TL...C?
Koboshi Daydream Mode
HAPPY BIRTHDAY, KOTAROU-CHAN!
FOR ME?
I MADE IT *MYSELF*.
OH, KOBOSHI-CHAN, WILL YOU MARRY ME?
Kyaa!
3
2
1
FIGHTING SPIRIT!!
I-I'LL DO MY BEST!!
NOW, THAT'S THE SPIRIT!!

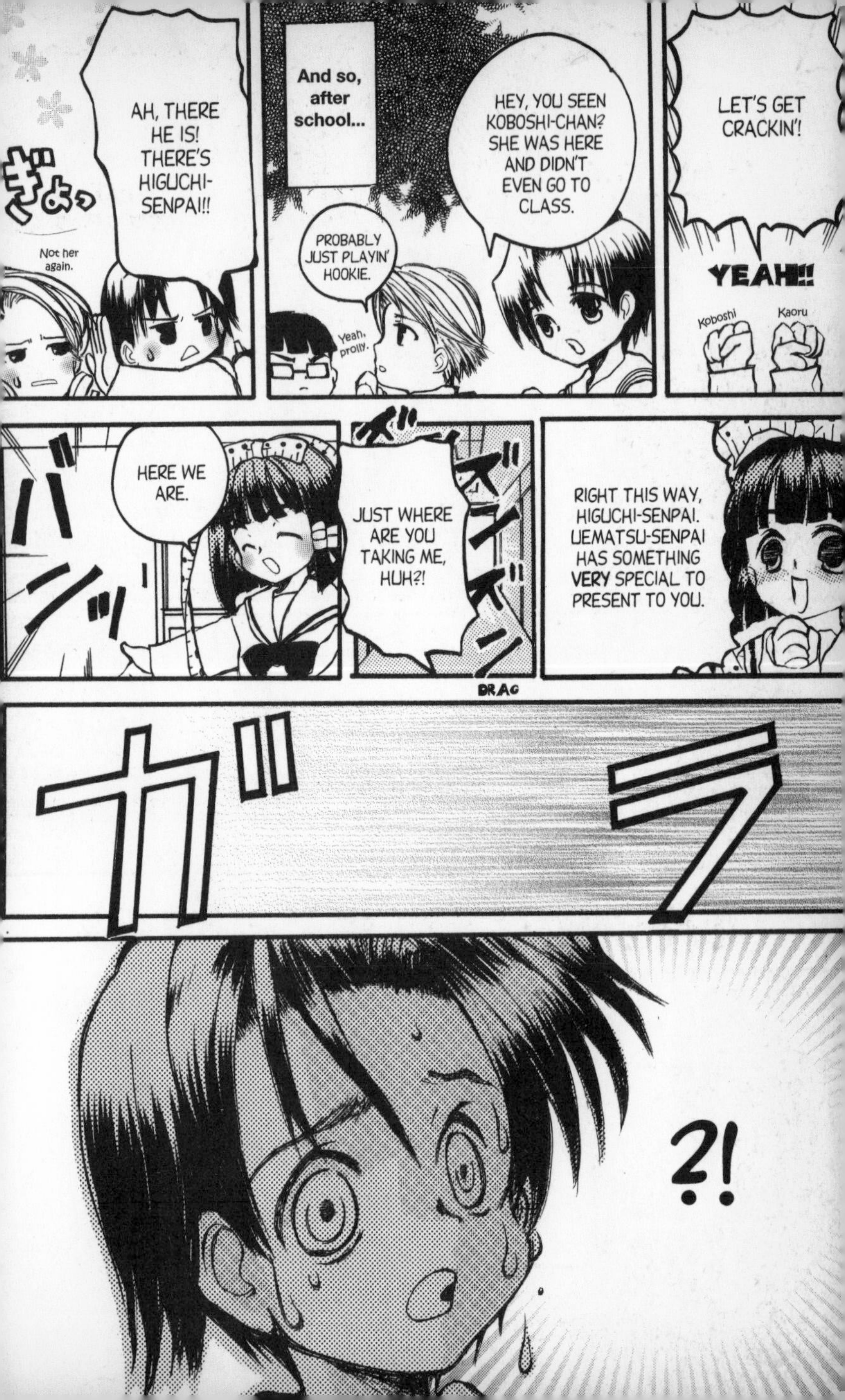
LET'S GET CRACKIN'!
YEAH!!
Koboshi
Kaoru
And so, after school...
HEY, YOU SEEN KOBOSHI-CHAN? SHE WAS HERE AND DIDN'T EVEN GO TO CLASS.
PROBABLY JUST PLAYIN' HOOKIE.
Yeah, prolly.
AH, THERE HE IS! THERE'S HIGUCHI-SENPAI!!
ぎょっ
Not her again.
RIGHT THIS WAY, HIGUCHI-SENPAI. UEMATSU-SENPAI HAS SOMETHING VERY SPECIAL TO PRESENT TO YOU.
JUST WHERE ARE YOU TAKING ME, HUH?!
DRAG
HERE WE ARE.
バンッ
ガラ
?!

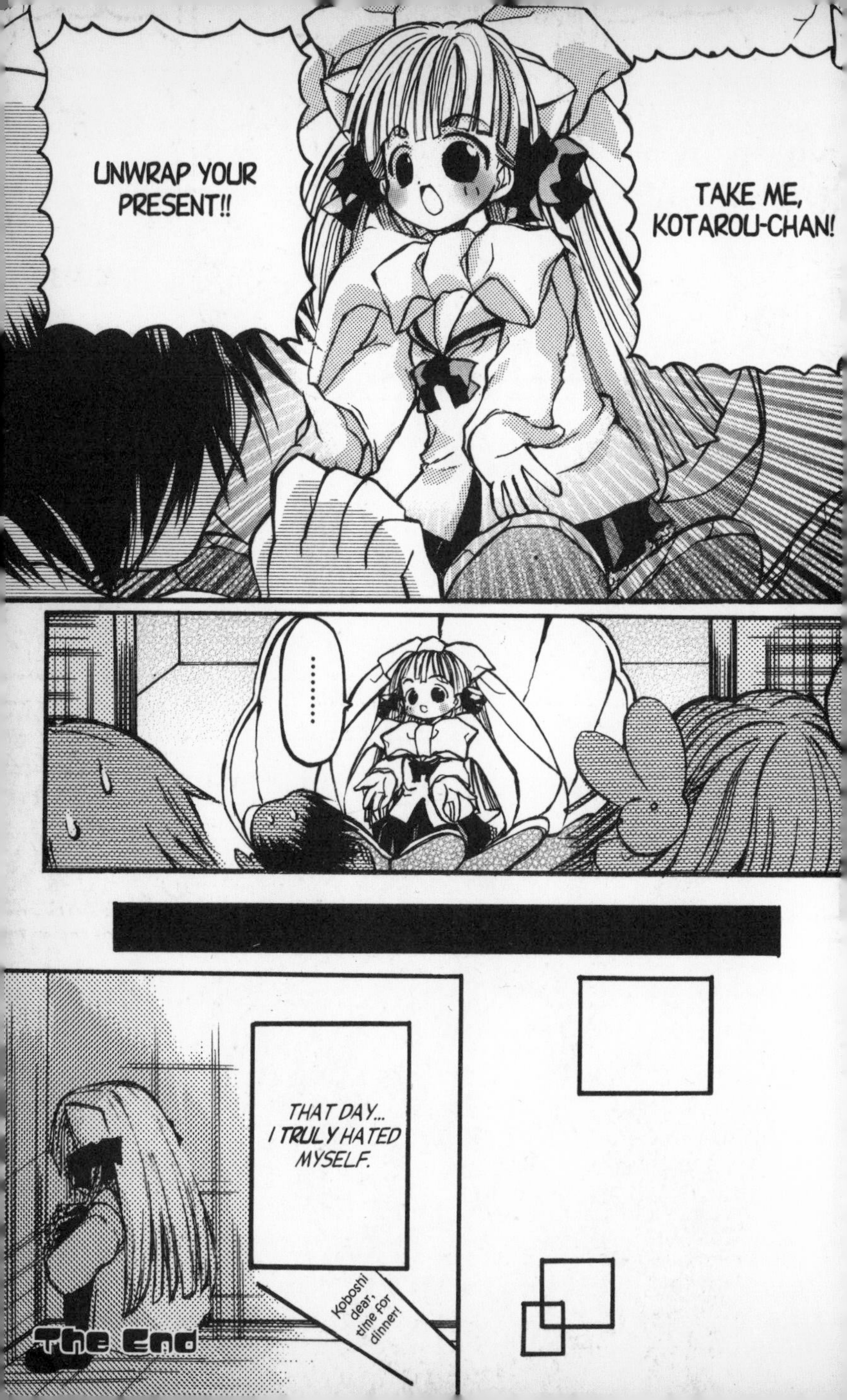
TAKE ME, KOTAROU-CHAN!
UNWRAP YOUR PRESENT!!
....
THAT DAY... I TRULY HATED MYSELF.
Koboshi dear, time for dinner!
The End

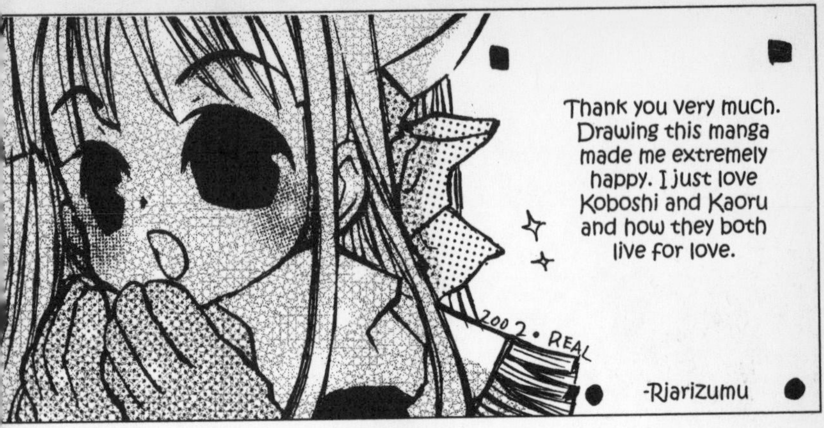
Thank you very much. Drawing this manga made me extremely happy. I just love Koboshi and Kaoru and how they both live for love.
2002 • REAL
-Rjarizumu

P.93
Riarizumu

Writer's Talk

P.103
Chimachi Kawarafuji

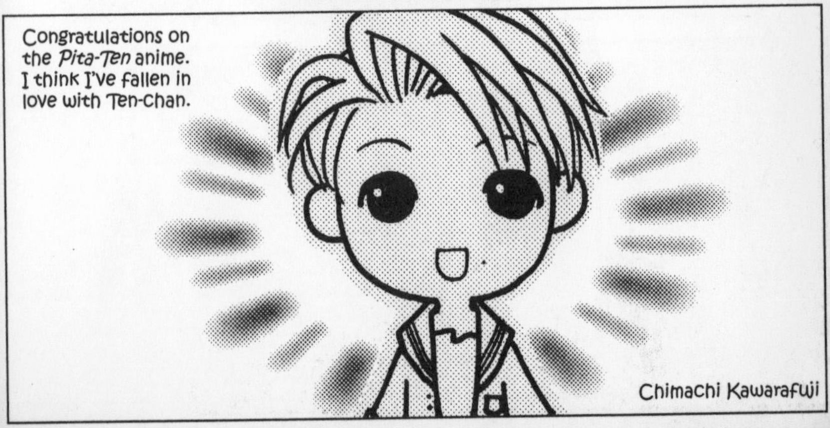
Congratulations on the *Pita-Ten* anime. I think I've fallen in love with Ten-Chan.
Chimachi Kawarafuji

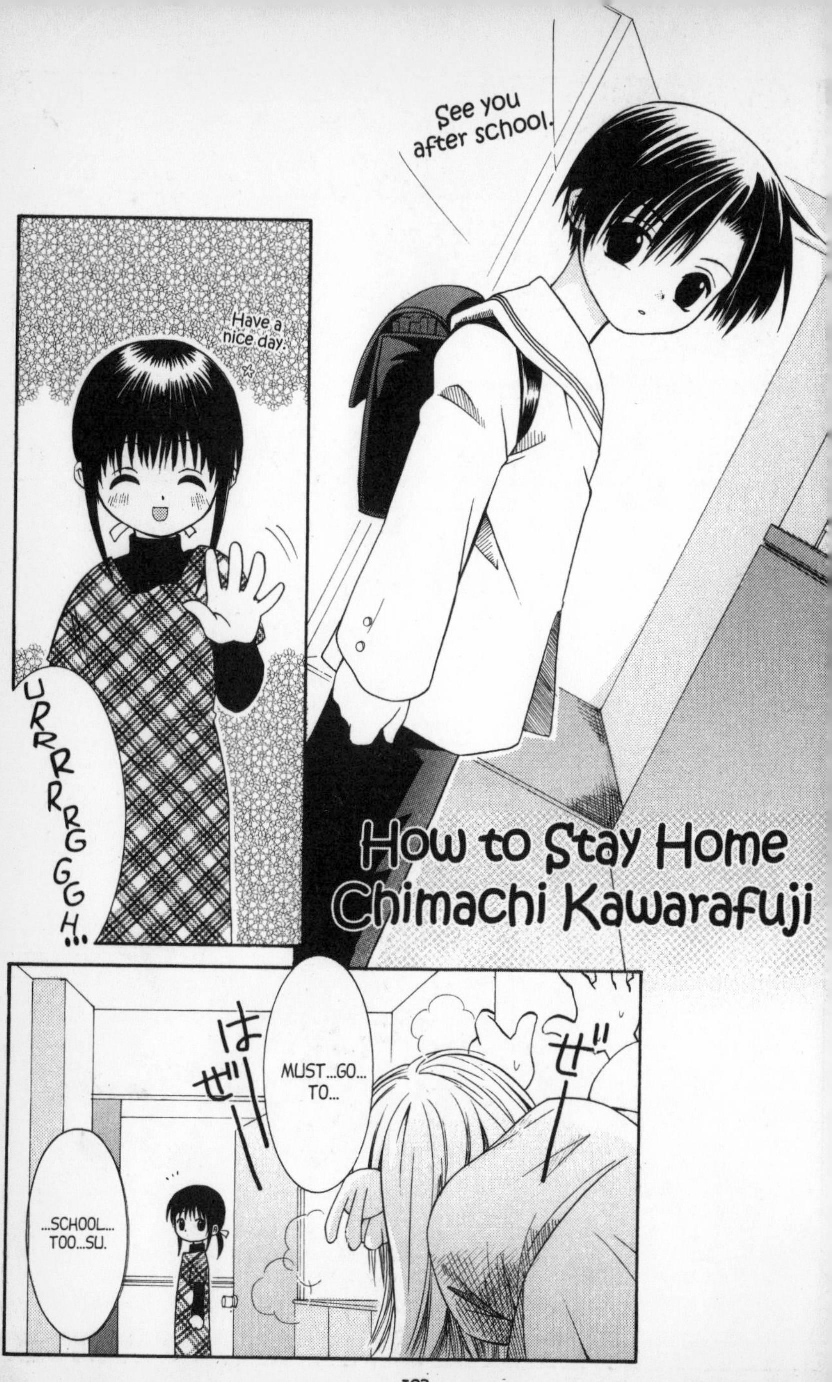

See you after school.
How to Stay Home
Chimachi Kawarafuji
Have a nice day. ☆
URRRRRGGGH..
ぜー
MUST...GO... TO...
はぜー
...SCHOOL... TOO...SU.

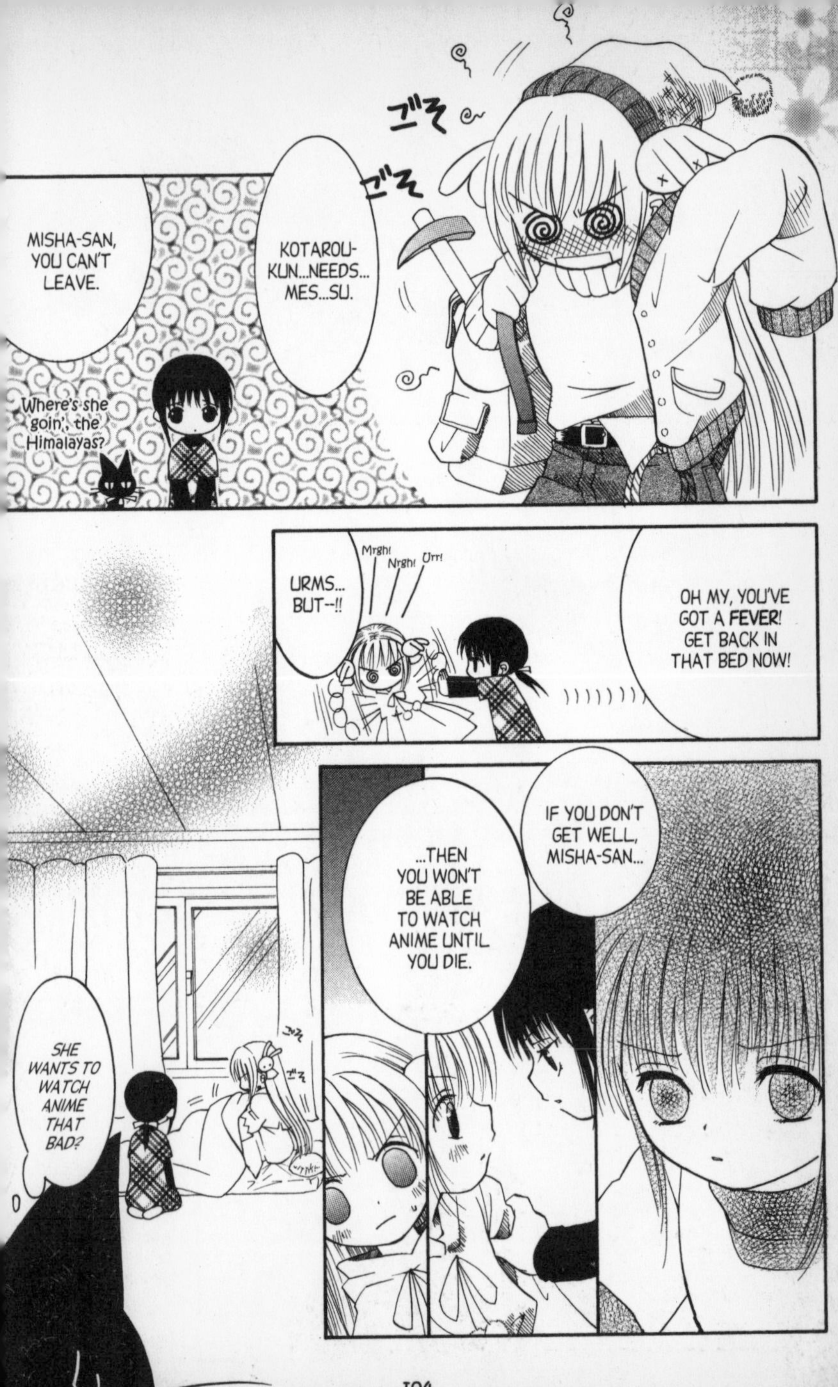
KOTAROU-KUN...NEEDS... MES...SU.
MISHA-SAN, YOU CAN'T LEAVE.
Where's she goin', the Himalayas?
OH MY, YOU'VE GOT A **FEVER**! GET BACK IN THAT BED NOW!
URMS... BUT--!!
Mrgh! Nrgh! Urr!
IF YOU DON'T GET WELL, MISHA-SAN...
...THEN YOU WON'T BE ABLE TO WATCH ANIME UNTIL YOU DIE.
SHE WANTS TO WATCH ANIME THAT BAD?

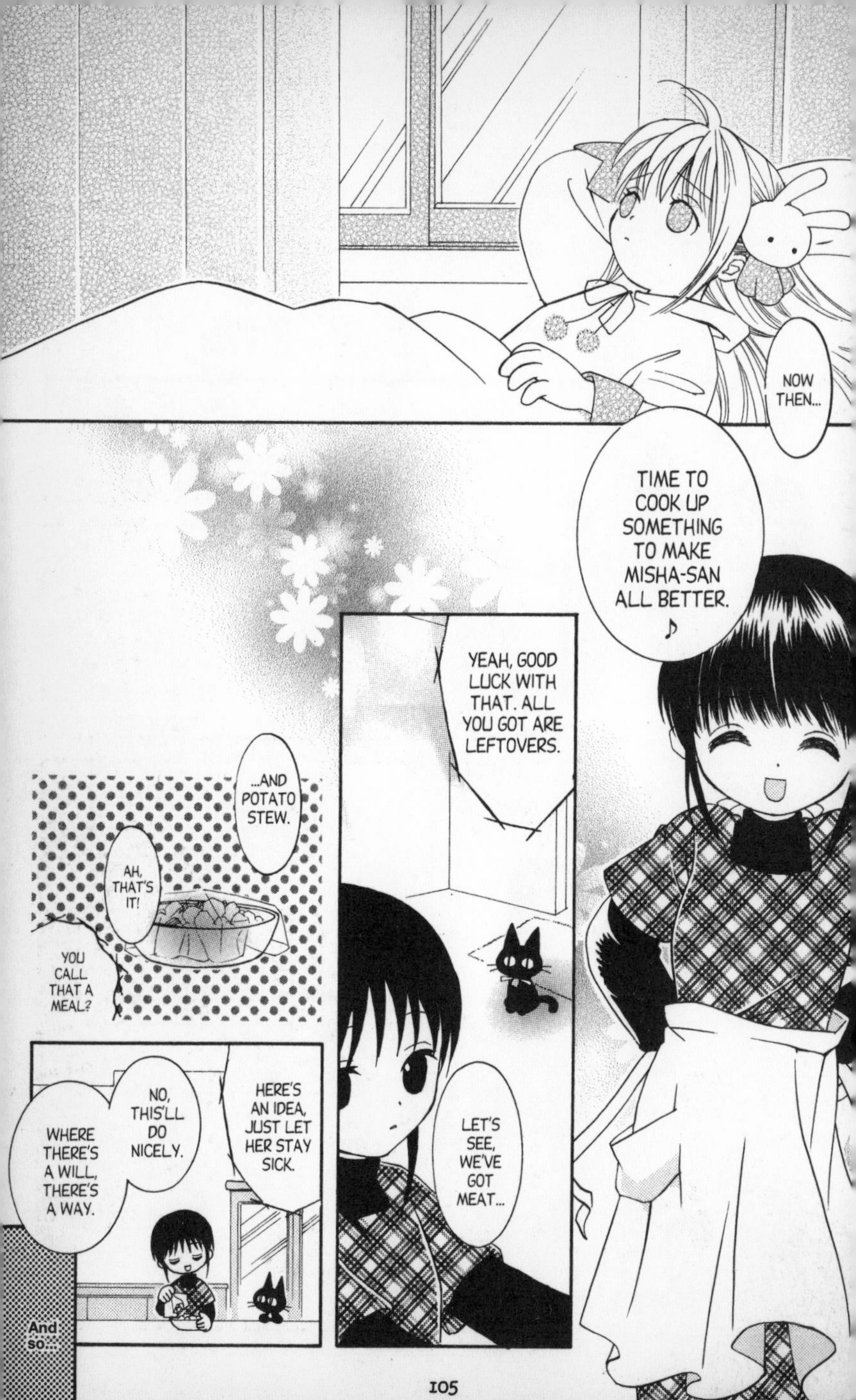
NOW THEN...
TIME TO COOK UP SOMETHING TO MAKE MISHA-SAN ALL BETTER. ♪
YEAH, GOOD LUCK WITH THAT. ALL YOU GOT ARE LEFTOVERS.
LET'S SEE, WE'VE GOT MEAT...
...AND POTATO STEW.
AH, THAT'S IT!
YOU CALL THAT A MEAL?
HERE'S AN IDEA, JUST LET HER STAY SICK.
NO, THIS'LL DO NICELY.
WHERE THERE'S A WILL, THERE'S A WAY.
And so...

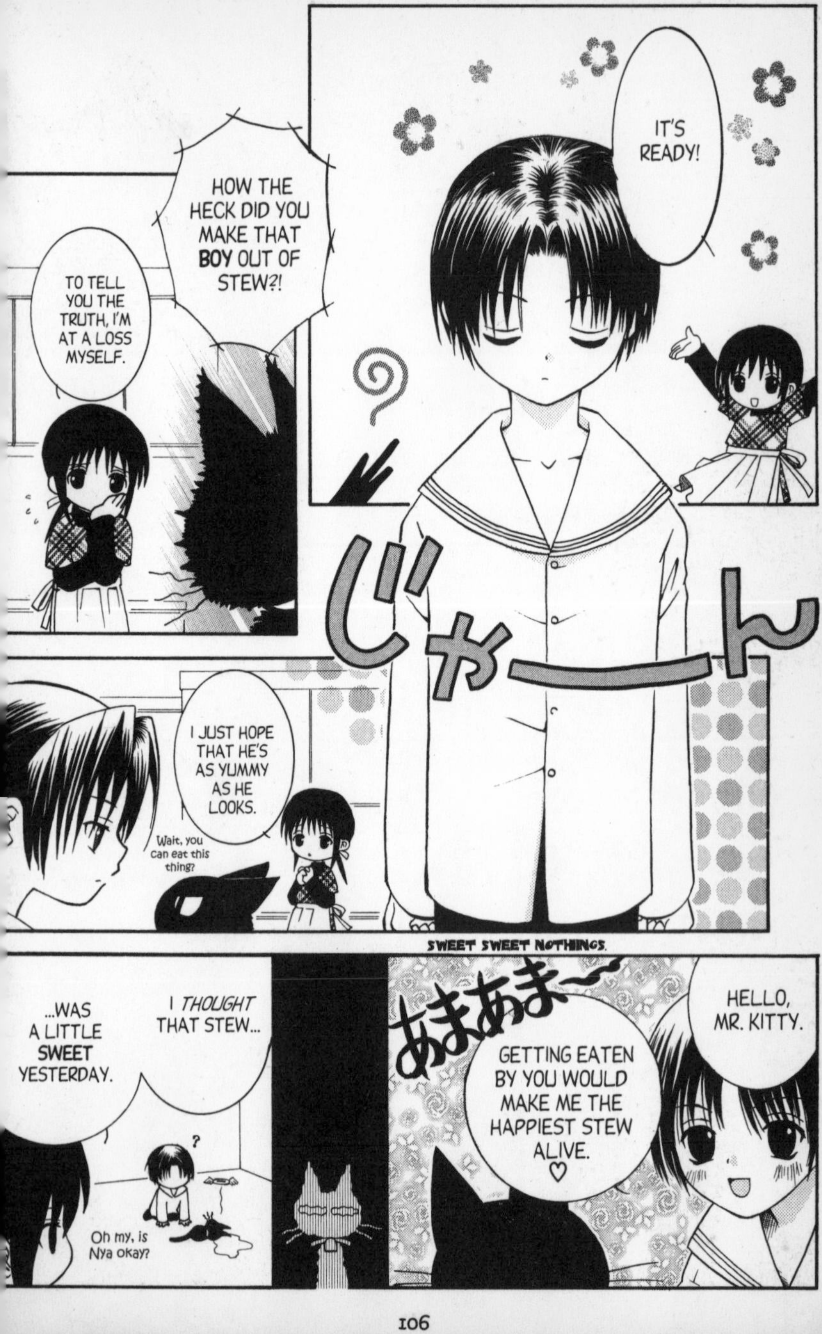
IT'S READY!
じゃーん
HOW THE HECK DID YOU MAKE THAT BOY OUT OF STEW?!
TO TELL YOU THE TRUTH, I'M AT A LOSS MYSELF.
I JUST HOPE THAT HE'S AS YUMMY AS HE LOOKS.
Wait, you can eat this thing?
SWEET SWEET NOTHINGS.
HELLO, MR. KITTY.
あまあま〜
GETTING EATEN BY YOU WOULD MAKE ME THE HAPPIEST STEW ALIVE. ♡
I THOUGHT THAT STEW...
...WAS A LITTLE SWEET YESTERDAY.
Oh my, is Nya okay?

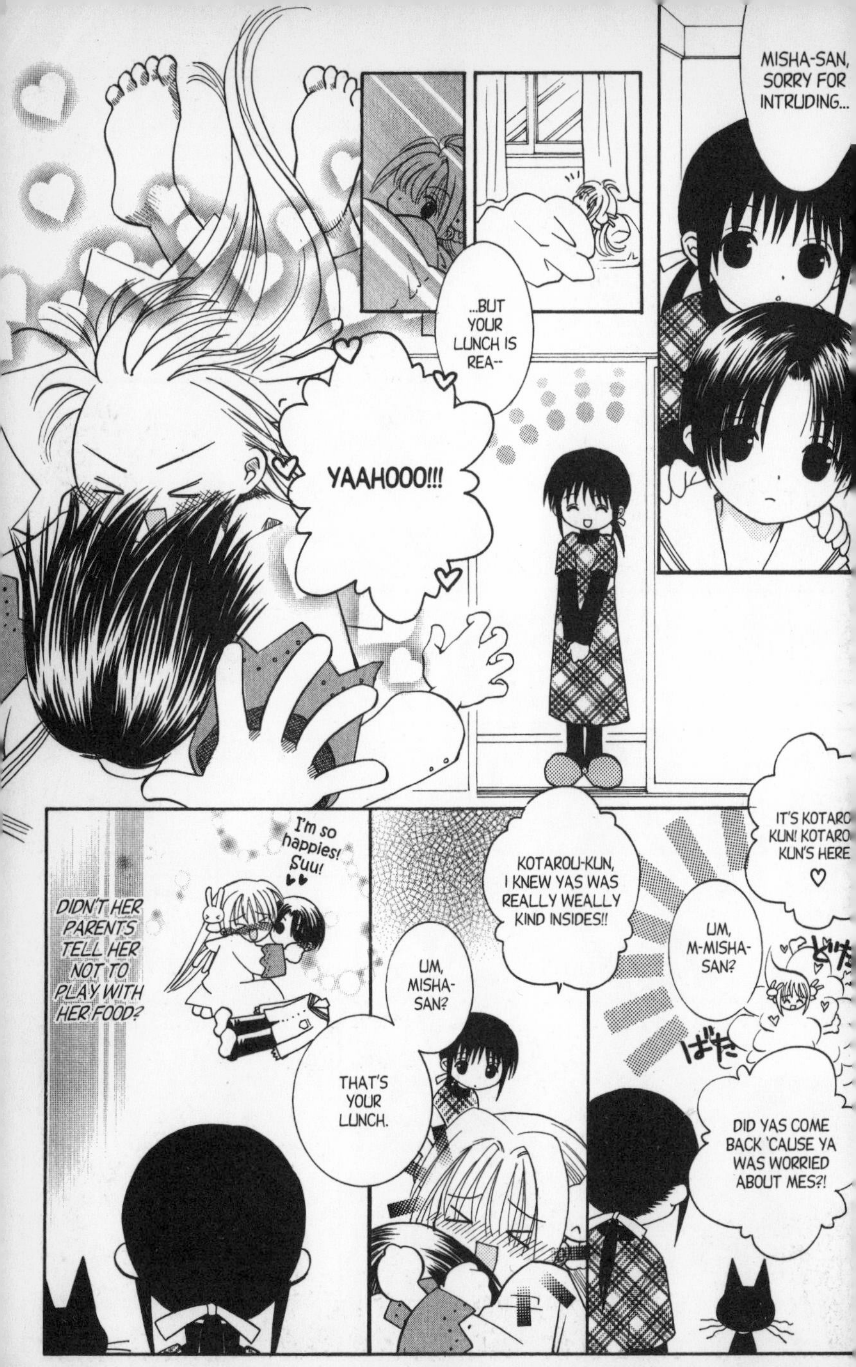
MISHA-SAN, SORRY FOR INTRUDING...
...BUT YOUR LUNCH IS REA--
YAAHOOO!!!
IT'S KOTARO KUN! KOTARO KUN'S HERE ♡
UM, M-MISHA-SAN?
ばた
DID YAS COME BACK 'CAUSE YA WAS WORRIED ABOUT MES?!
KOTAROU-KUN, I KNEW YAS WAS REALLY WEALLY KIND INSIDES!!
UM, MISHA-SAN?
THAT'S YOUR LUNCH.
I'm so happies! Suu!
DIDN'T HER PARENTS TELL HER NOT TO PLAY WITH HER FOOD?

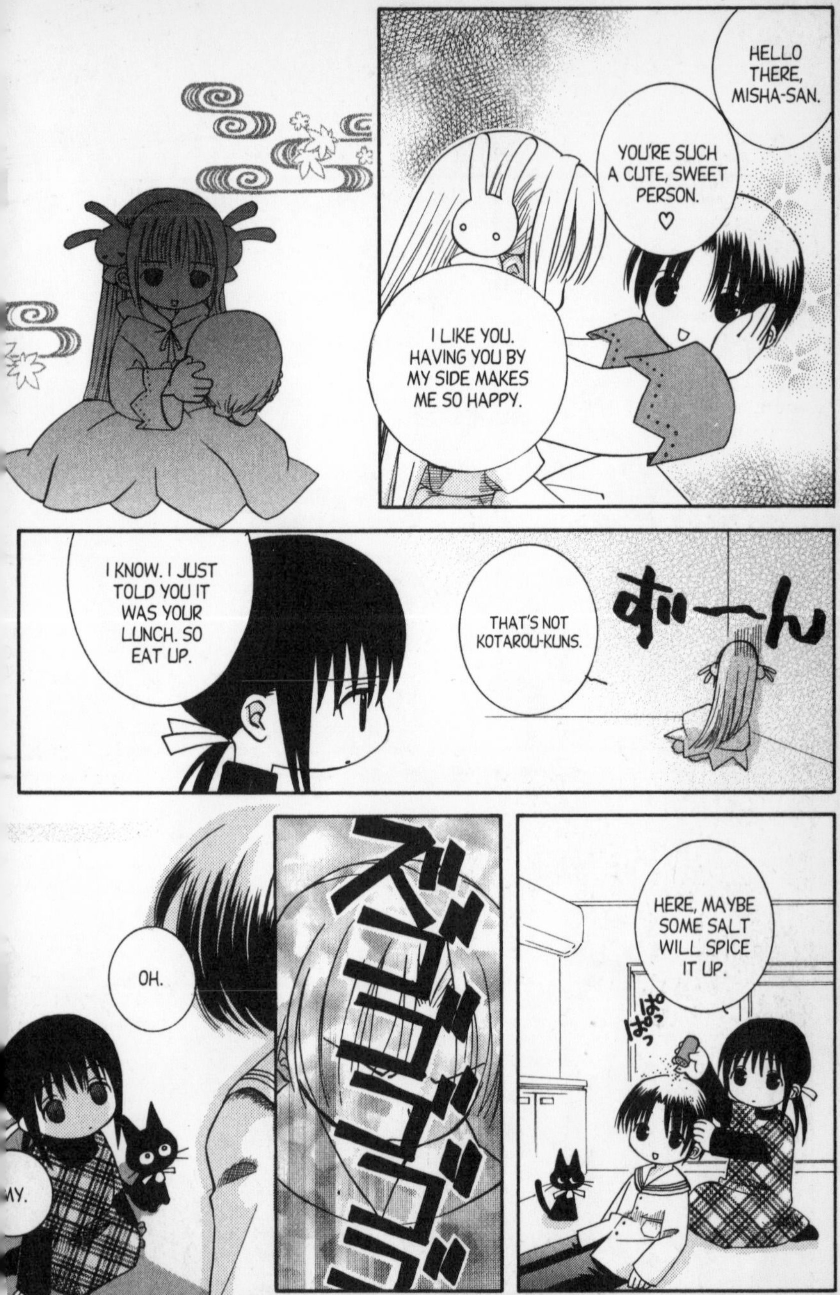
HELLO THERE, MISHA-SAN.
YOU'RE SUCH A CUTE, SWEET PERSON. ♡
I LIKE YOU. HAVING YOU BY MY SIDE MAKES ME SO HAPPY.
ずーーん
THAT'S NOT KOTAROU-KUNS.
I KNOW. I JUST TOLD YOU IT WAS YOUR LUNCH. SO EAT UP.
HERE, MAYBE SOME SALT WILL SPICE IT UP.
ぱっぱっ
OH.
MY.

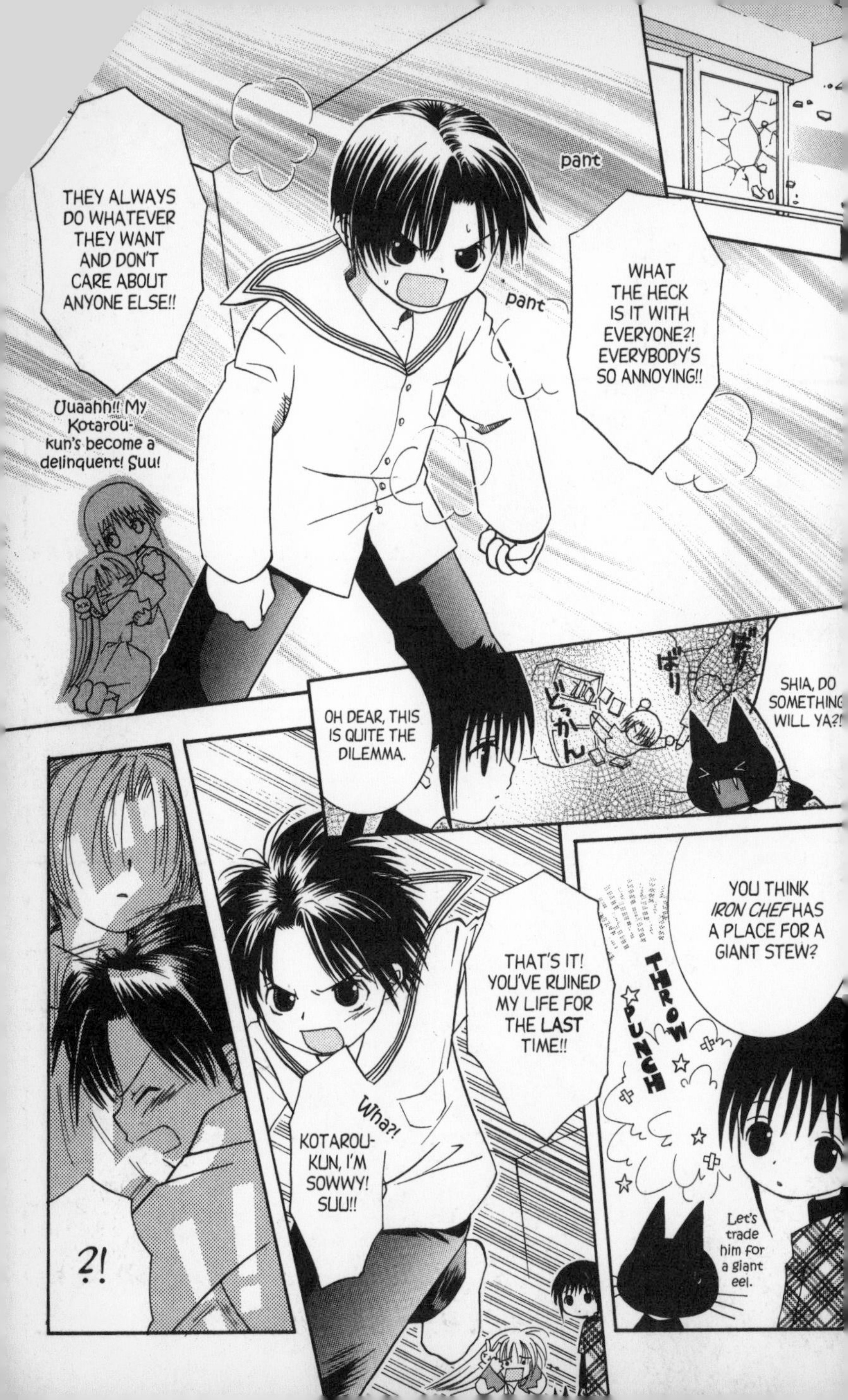
pant
WHAT THE HECK IS IT WITH EVERYONE?! EVERYBODY'S SO ANNOYING!!
pant
THEY ALWAYS DO WHATEVER THEY WANT AND DON'T CARE ABOUT ANYONE ELSE!!
Uuaahh!! My Kotarou-kun's become a delinquent! Suu!
SHIA, DO SOMETHING WILL YA?!
ばり
ばり
どっかん
OH DEAR, THIS IS QUITE THE DILEMMA.
YOU THINK *IRON CHEF* HAS A PLACE FOR A GIANT STEW?
THROW
PUNCH
Let's trade him for a giant eel.
THAT'S IT! YOU'VE RUINED MY LIFE FOR THE LAST TIME!!
Wha?!
KOTAROU-KUN, I'M SOWWY! SUU!!
?!

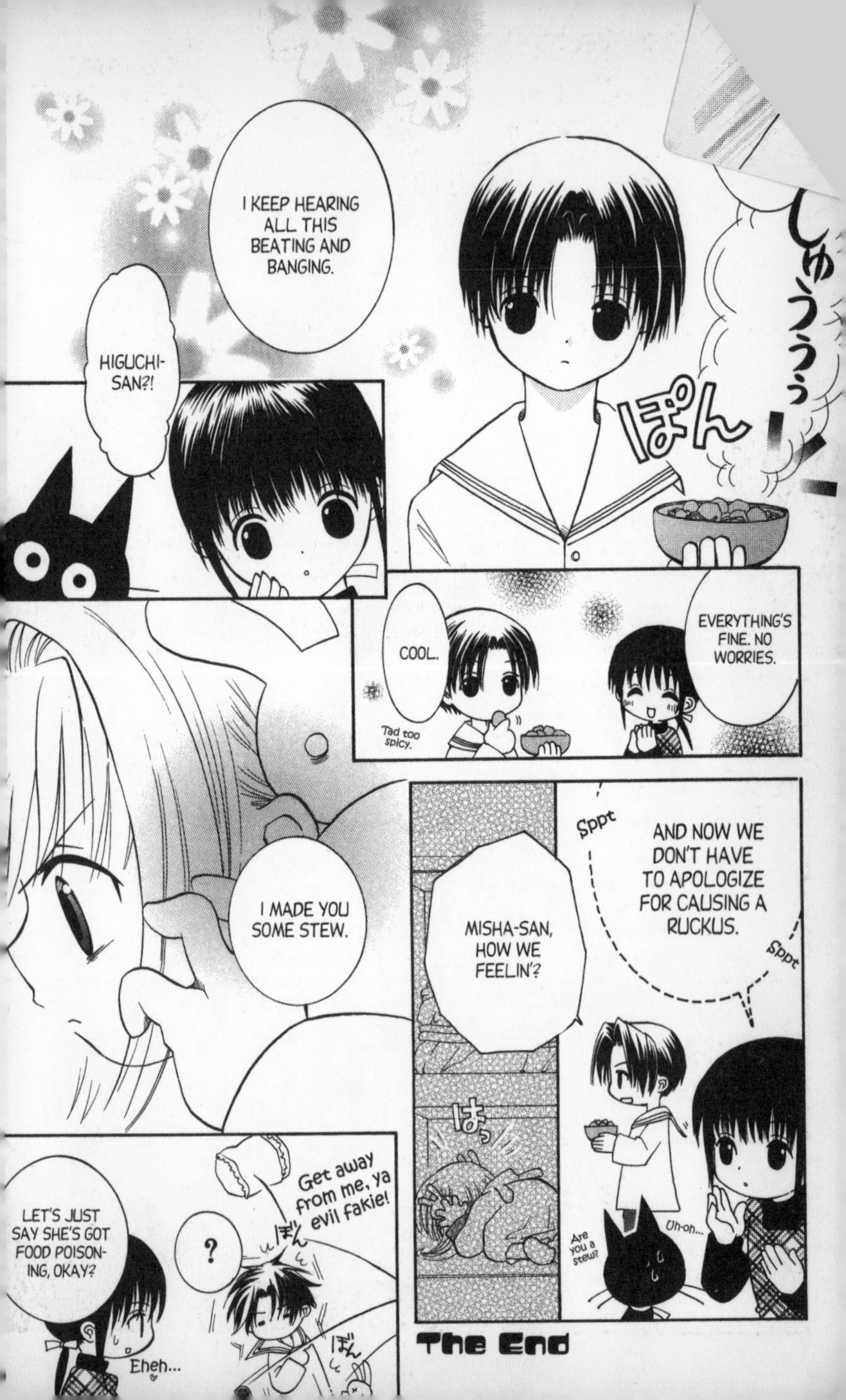
しゅううう
ぽん
I KEEP HEARING ALL THIS BEATING AND BANGING.
HIGUCHI-SAN?!
EVERYTHING'S FINE. NO WORRIES.
COOL.
Tad too spicy.
I MADE YOU SOME STEW.
Sppt
AND NOW WE DON'T HAVE TO APOLOGIZE FOR CAUSING A RUCKUS.
Sppt
MISHA-SAN, HOW WE FEELIN'?
はっ
Uh-oh...
Are you a stew?
Get away from me, ya evil fakie!
ぼん
?
LET'S JUST SAY SHE'S GOT FOOD POISONING, OKAY?
Eheh...
ぼん
The End

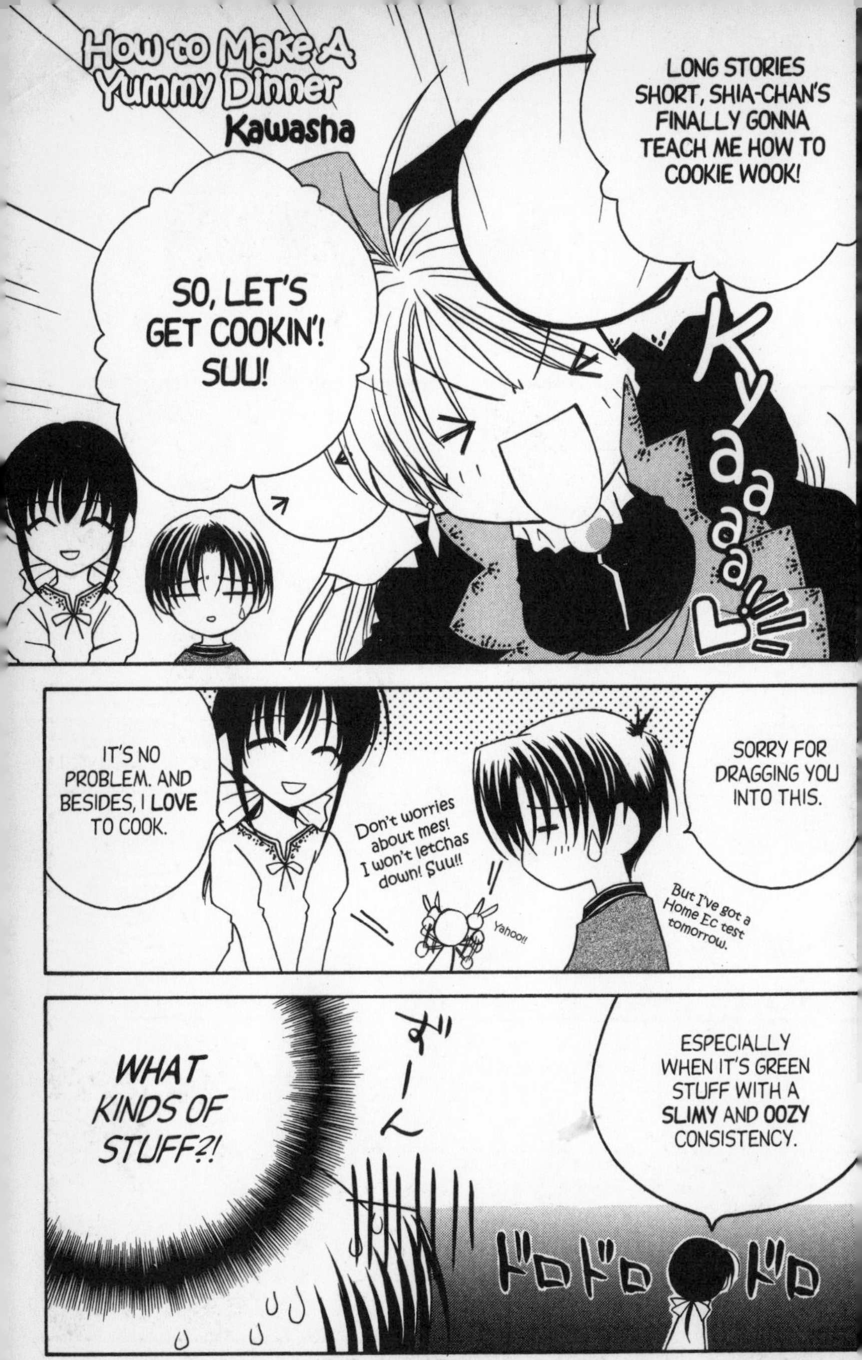
How to Make A Yummy Dinner
Kawasha
LONG STORIES SHORT, SHIA-CHAN'S FINALLY GONNA TEACH ME HOW TO COOKIE WOOK!
SO, LET'S GET COOKIN'! SUU!
Kyaaaaa!!
SORRY FOR DRAGGING YOU INTO THIS.
But I've got a Home Ec test tomorrow.
Don't worries about mes! I won't letchas down! Suu!!
Yahoo!!
IT'S NO PROBLEM. AND BESIDES, I LOVE TO COOK.
ESPECIALLY WHEN IT'S GREEN STUFF WITH A SLIMY AND OOZY CONSISTENCY.
ドロドロ ドロ
ずーん
WHAT KINDS OF STUFF?!

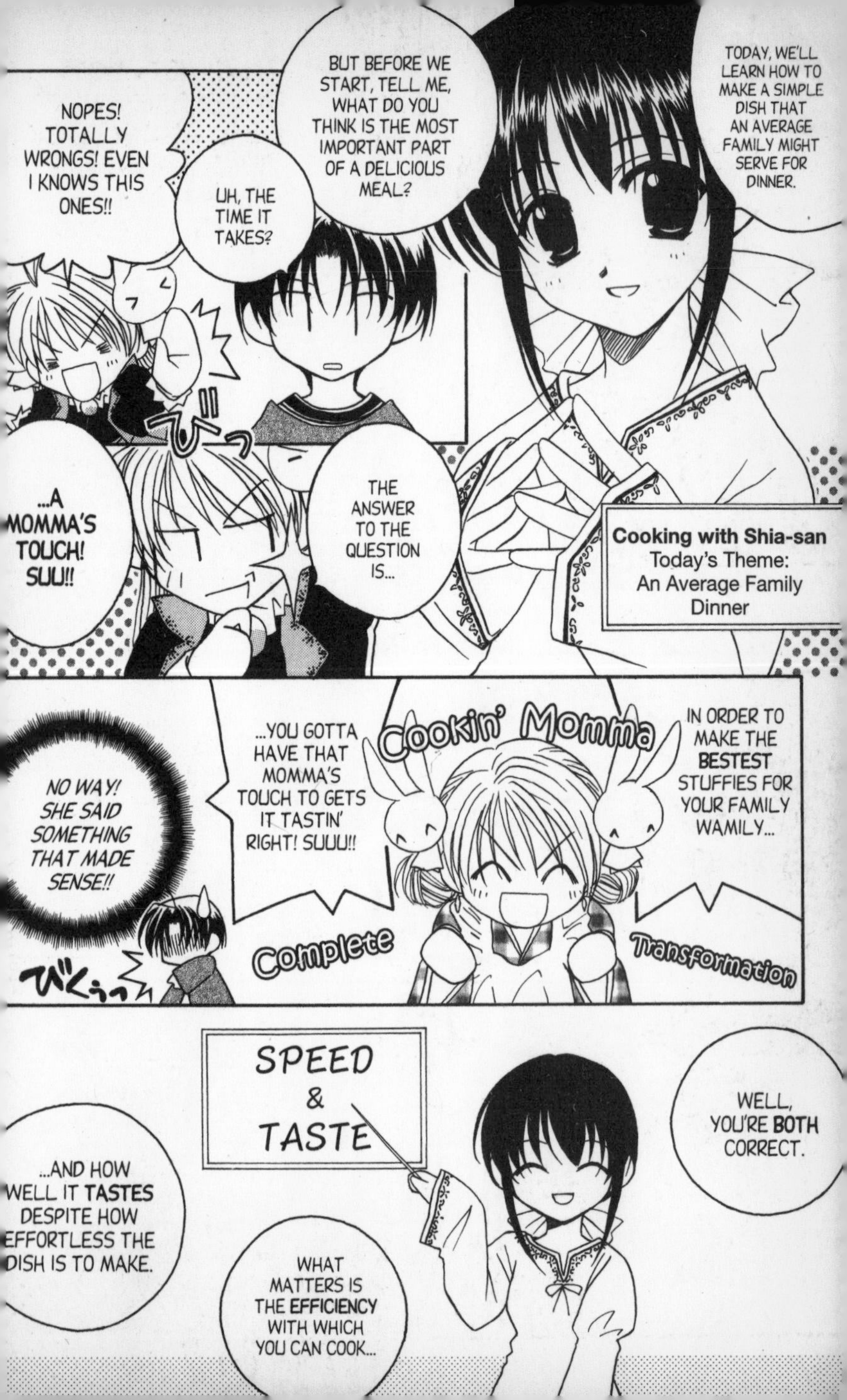

Cooking with Shia-san
Today's Theme: An Average Family Dinner
TODAY, WE'LL LEARN HOW TO MAKE A SIMPLE DISH THAT AN AVERAGE FAMILY MIGHT SERVE FOR DINNER.
BUT BEFORE WE START, TELL ME, WHAT DO YOU THINK IS THE MOST IMPORTANT PART OF A DELICIOUS MEAL?
UH, THE TIME IT TAKES?
NOPES! TOTALLY WRONGS! EVEN I KNOWS THIS ONES!!
びっ
THE ANSWER TO THE QUESTION IS...
...A MOMMA'S TOUCH! SUU!!
IN ORDER TO MAKE THE BESTEST STUFFIES FOR YOUR FAMILY WAMILY...
Cookin' Momma
...YOU GOTTA HAVE THAT MOMMA'S TOUCH TO GETS IT TASTIN' RIGHT! SUUU!!
Complete
Transformation
NO WAY! SHE SAID SOMETHING THAT MADE SENSE!!
びくっ
WELL, YOU'RE BOTH CORRECT.
SPEED & TASTE
WHAT MATTERS IS THE EFFICIENCY WITH WHICH YOU CAN COOK...
...AND HOW WELL IT TASTES DESPITE HOW EFFORTLESS THE DISH IS TO MAKE.

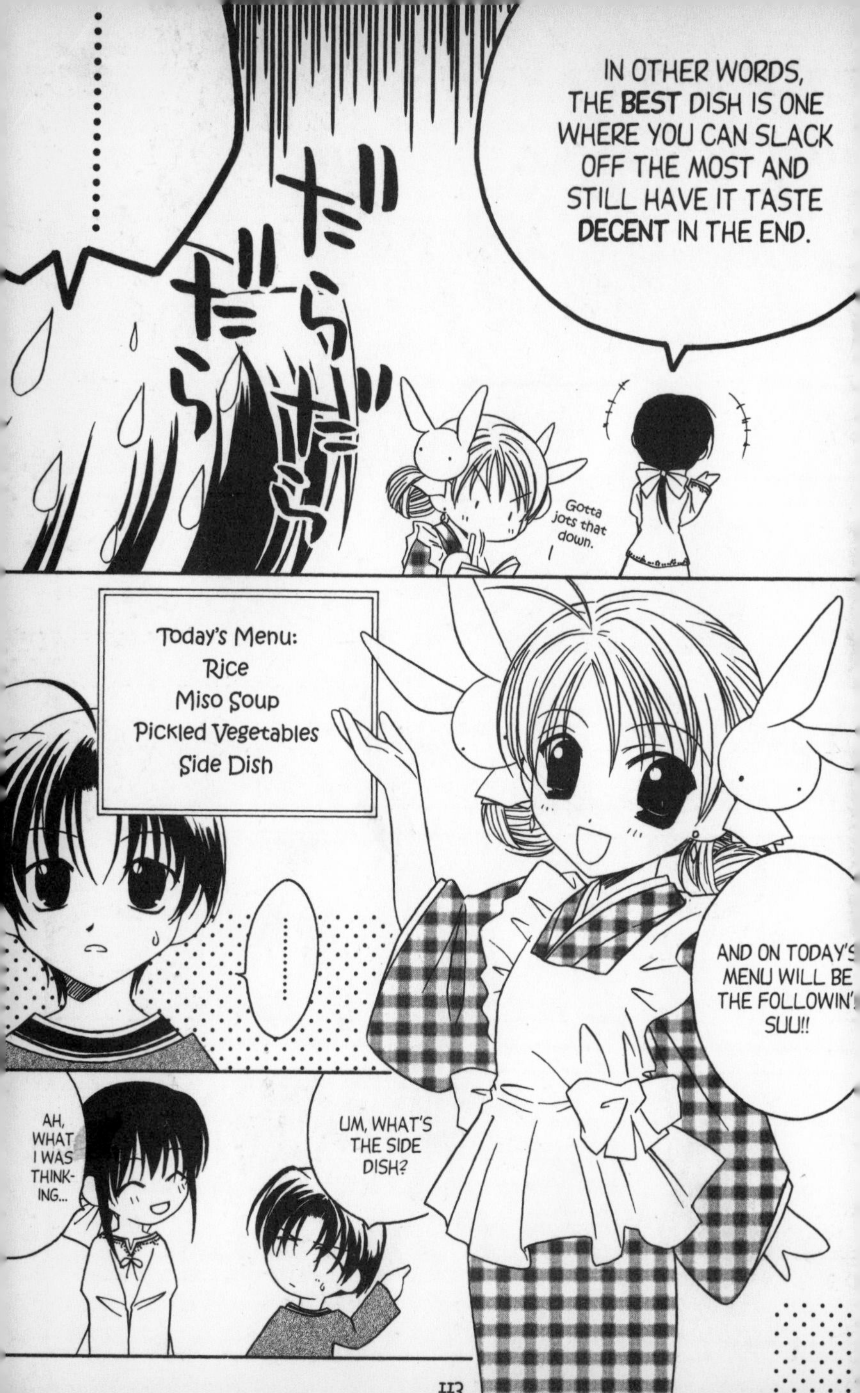

IN OTHER WORDS, THE **BEST** DISH IS ONE WHERE YOU CAN SLACK OFF THE MOST AND STILL HAVE IT TASTE **DECENT** IN THE END.
Gotta jots that down.
だらだら
......
AND ON TODAY'S MENU WILL BE THE FOLLOWIN', SUU!!
Today's Menu:
Rice
Miso Soup
Pickled Vegetables
Side Dish
......
UM, WHAT'S THE SIDE DISH?
AH, WHAT I WAS THINK-ING...

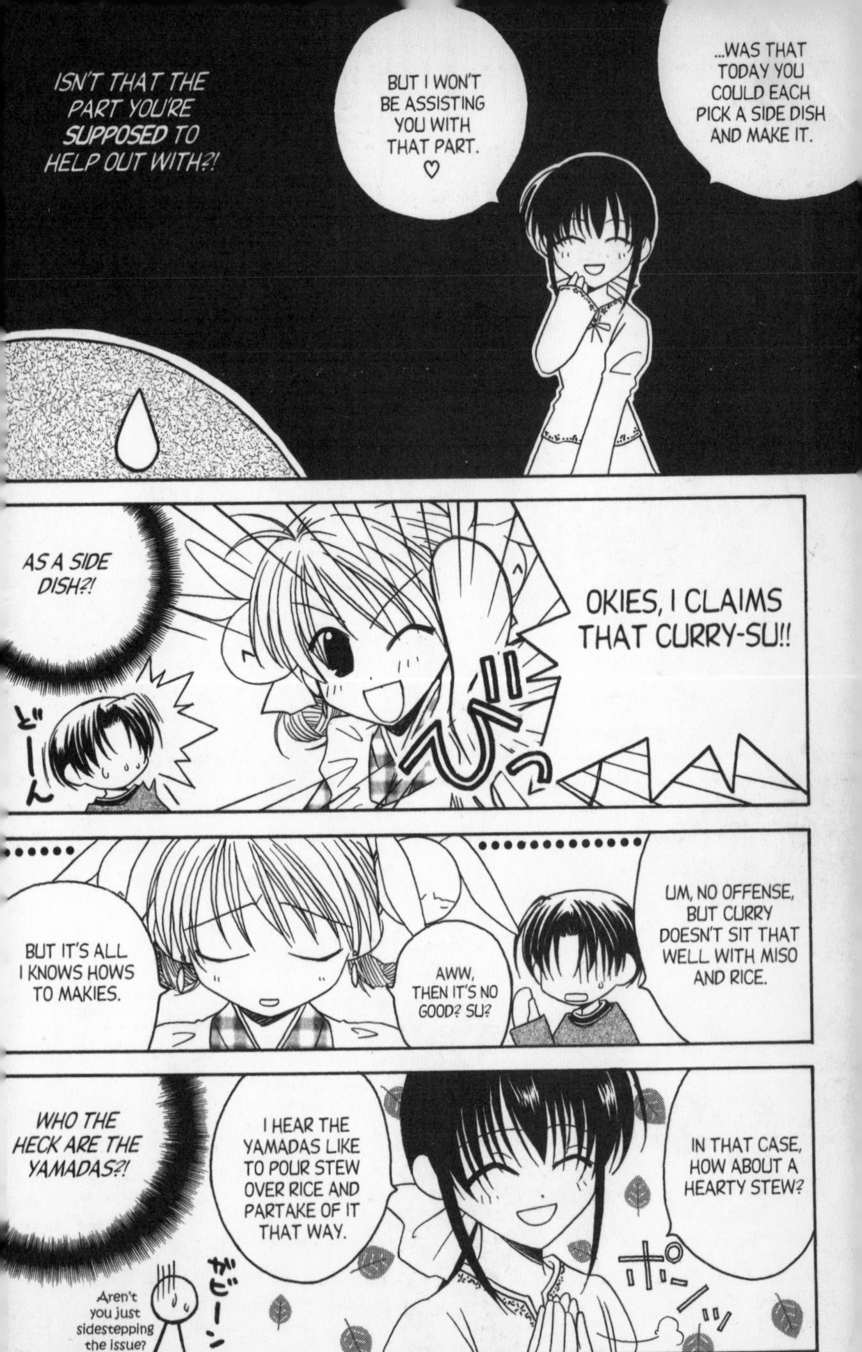
...WAS THAT TODAY YOU COULD EACH PICK A SIDE DISH AND MAKE IT.
BUT I WON'T BE ASSISTING YOU WITH THAT PART. ♡
ISN'T THAT THE PART YOU'RE SUPPOSED TO HELP OUT WITH?!
OKIES, I CLAIMS THAT CURRY-SU!!
AS A SIDE DISH?!
どーん
......
UM, NO OFFENSE, BUT CURRY DOESN'T SIT THAT WELL WITH MISO AND RICE.
AWW, THEN IT'S NO GOOD? SU?
BUT IT'S ALL I KNOWS HOWS TO MAKIES.
.....
IN THAT CASE, HOW ABOUT A HEARTY STEW?
I HEAR THE YAMADAS LIKE TO POUR STEW OVER RICE AND PARTAKE OF IT THAT WAY.
WHO THE HECK ARE THE YAMADAS?!
Aren't you just sidestepping the issue?

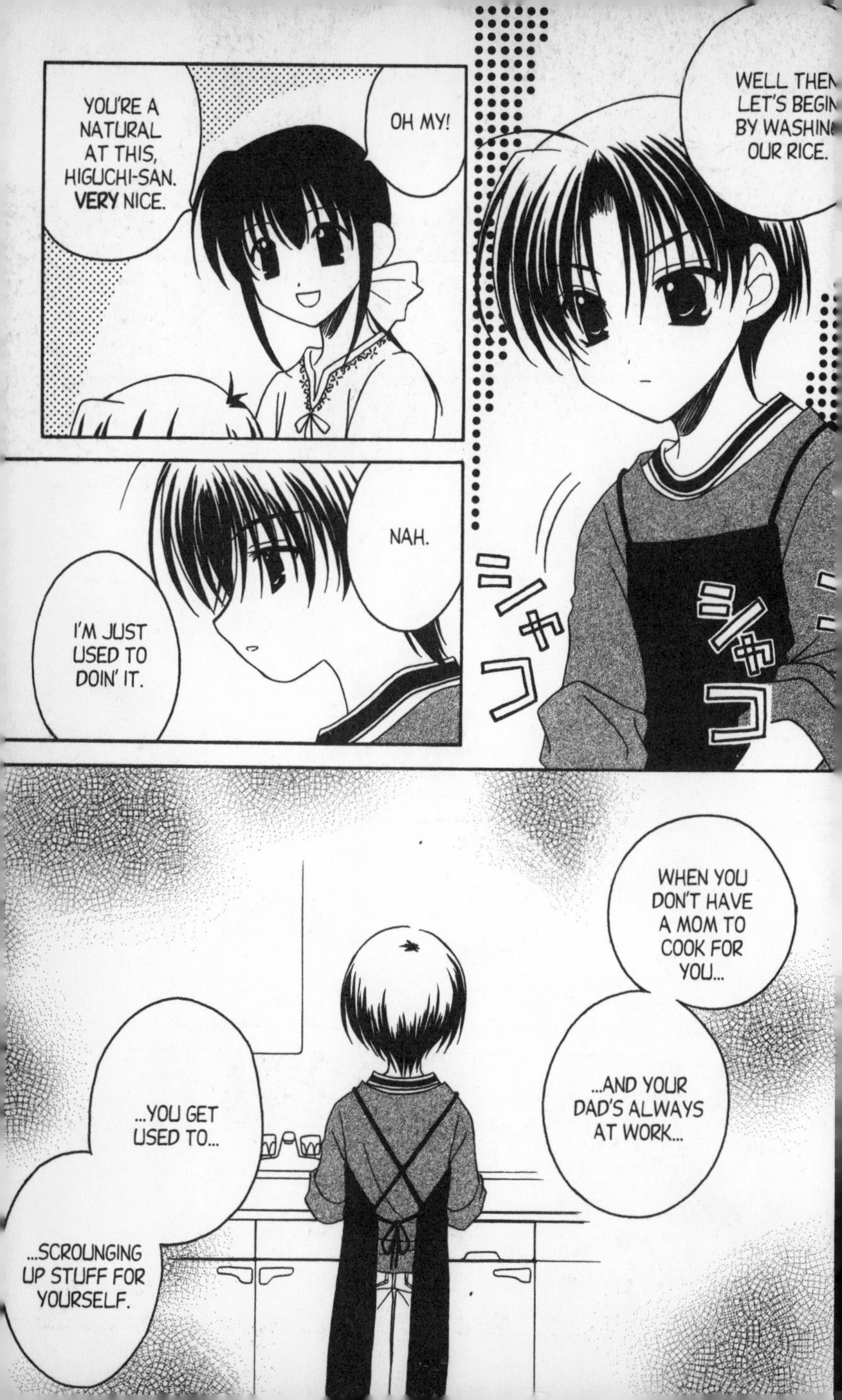
WELL THEN LET'S BEGIN BY WASHING OUR RICE.
シャコ
シャコ
OH MY!
YOU'RE A NATURAL AT THIS, HIGUCHI-SAN. **VERY** NICE.
NAH.
I'M JUST USED TO DOIN' IT.
WHEN YOU DON'T HAVE A MOM TO COOK FOR YOU...
...AND YOUR DAD'S ALWAYS AT WORK...
...YOU GET USED TO...
...SCROUNGING UP STUFF FOR YOURSELF.

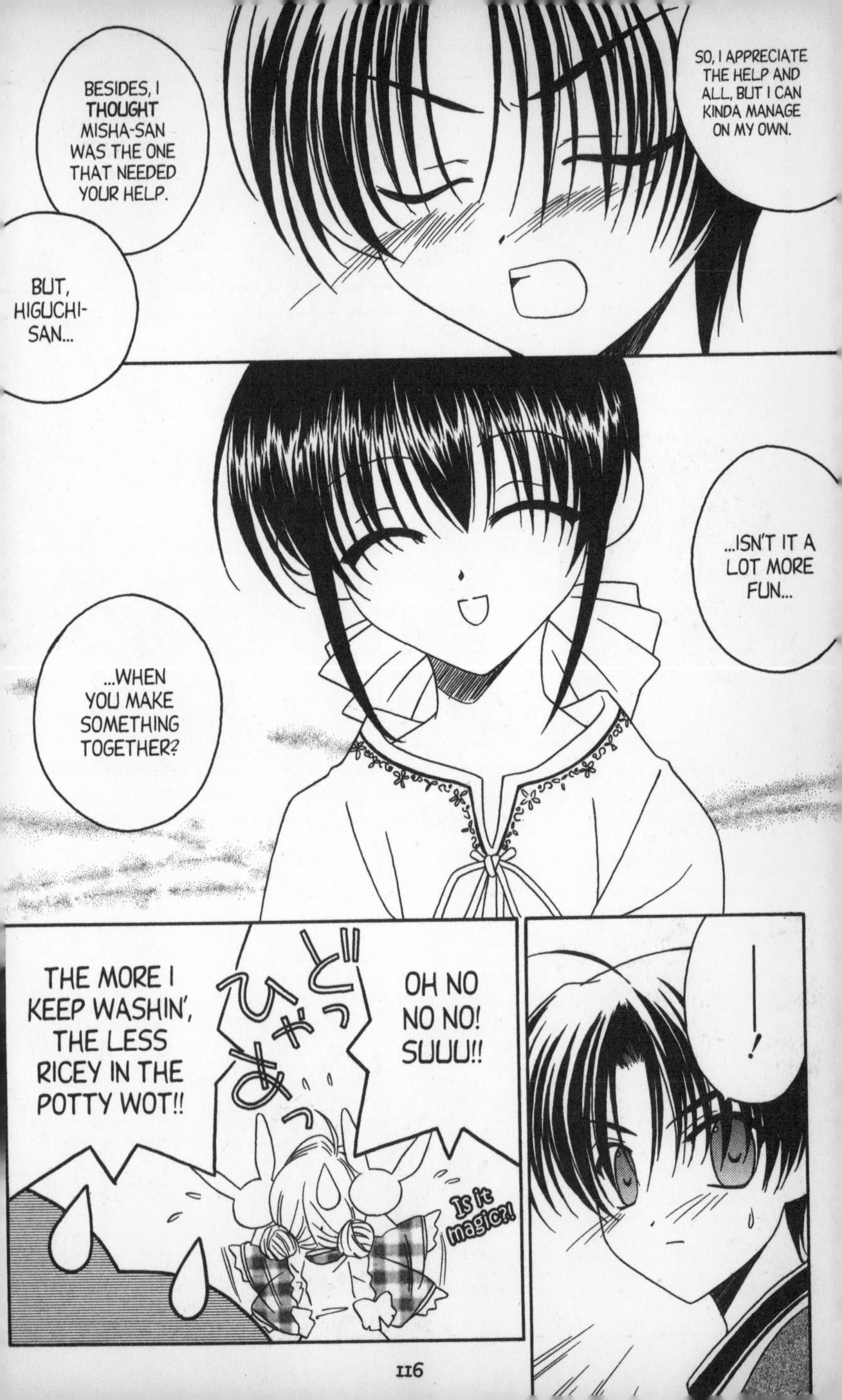
SO, I APPRECIATE THE HELP AND ALL, BUT I CAN KINDA MANAGE ON MY OWN.
BESIDES, I THOUGHT MISHA-SAN WAS THE ONE THAT NEEDED YOUR HELP.
BUT, HIGUCHI-SAN...
...ISN'T IT A LOT MORE FUN...
...WHEN YOU MAKE SOMETHING TOGETHER?
!
OH NO NO NO! SUUU!!
どっ
ひゃあっ
THE MORE I KEEP WASHIN', THE LESS RICEY IN THE POTTY WOT!!
Is it magic?!

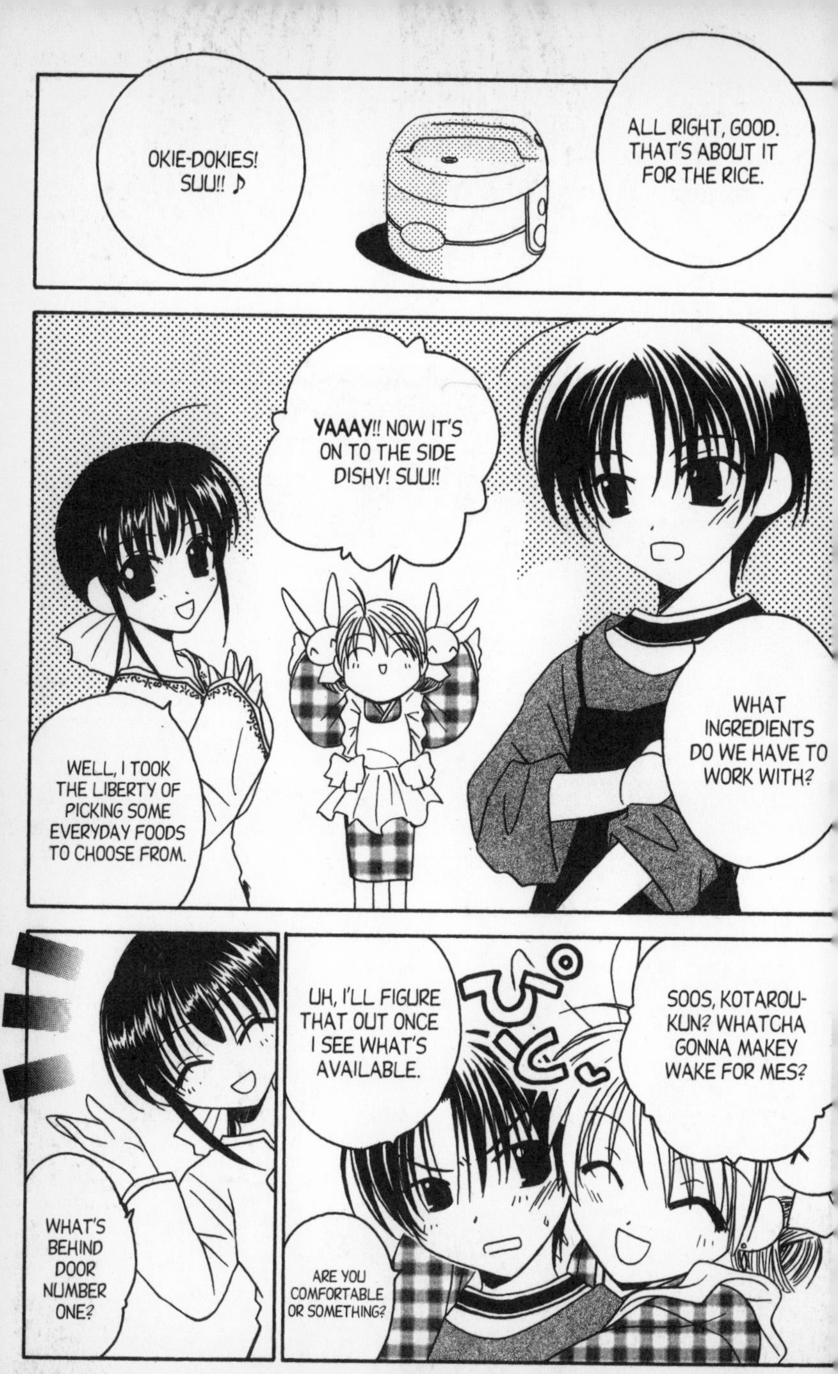

ALL RIGHT, GOOD. THAT'S ABOUT IT FOR THE RICE.
OKIE-DOKIES! SUU!! ♪
YAAAY!! NOW IT'S ON TO THE SIDE DISHY! SUU!!
WHAT INGREDIENTS DO WE HAVE TO WORK WITH?
WELL, I TOOK THE LIBERTY OF PICKING SOME EVERYDAY FOODS TO CHOOSE FROM.
SOOS, KOTAROU-KUN? WHATCHA GONNA MAKEY WAKE FOR MES?
UH, I'LL FIGURE THAT OUT ONCE I SEE WHAT'S AVAILABLE.
ARE YOU COMFORTABLE OR SOMETHING?
WHAT'S BEHIND DOOR NUMBER ONE?

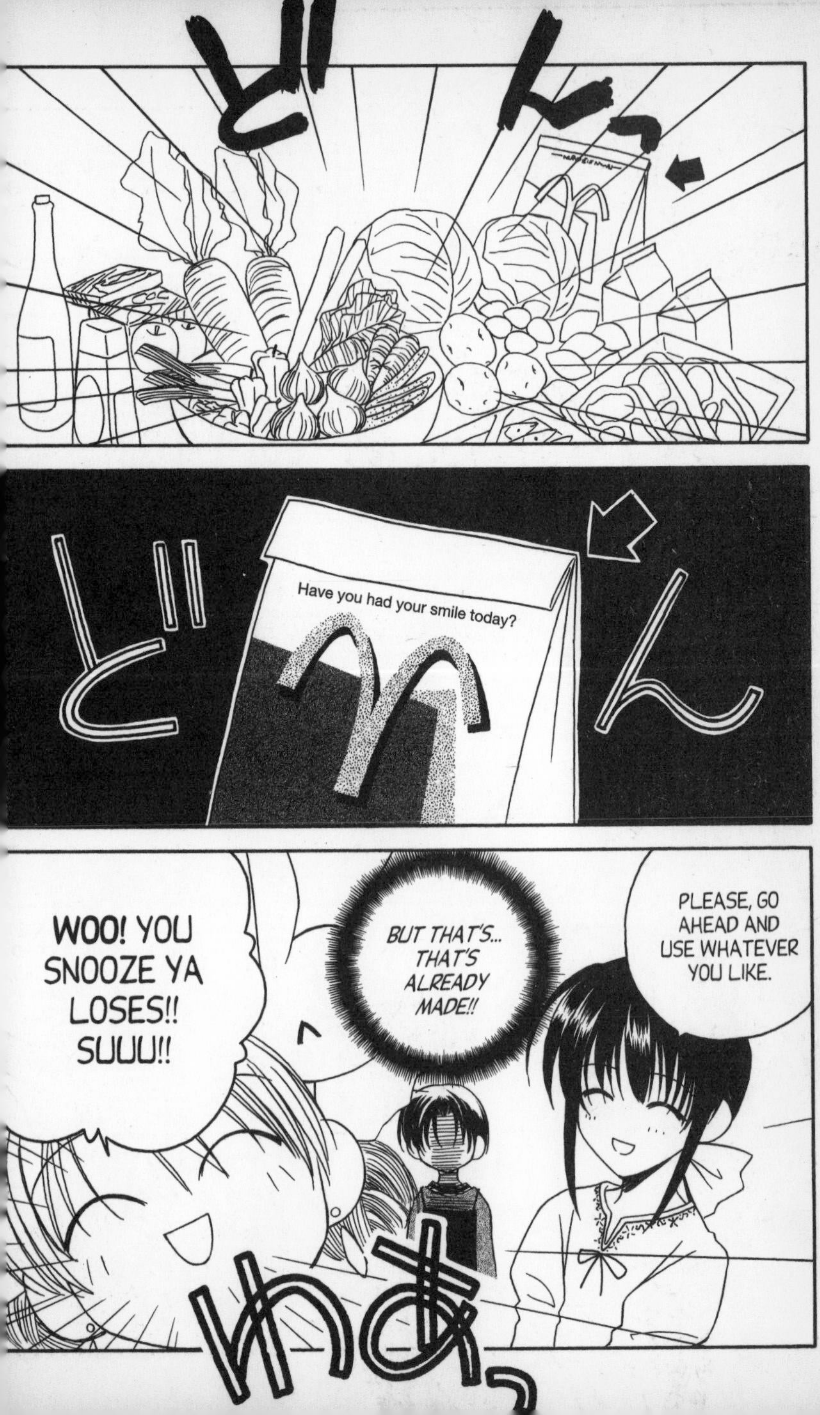
どんっ
どん
Have you had your smile today?
PLEASE, GO AHEAD AND USE WHATEVER YOU LIKE.
BUT THAT'S... THAT'S ALREADY MADE!!
WOO! YOU SNOOZE YA LOSES!! SUUU!!
わあっ

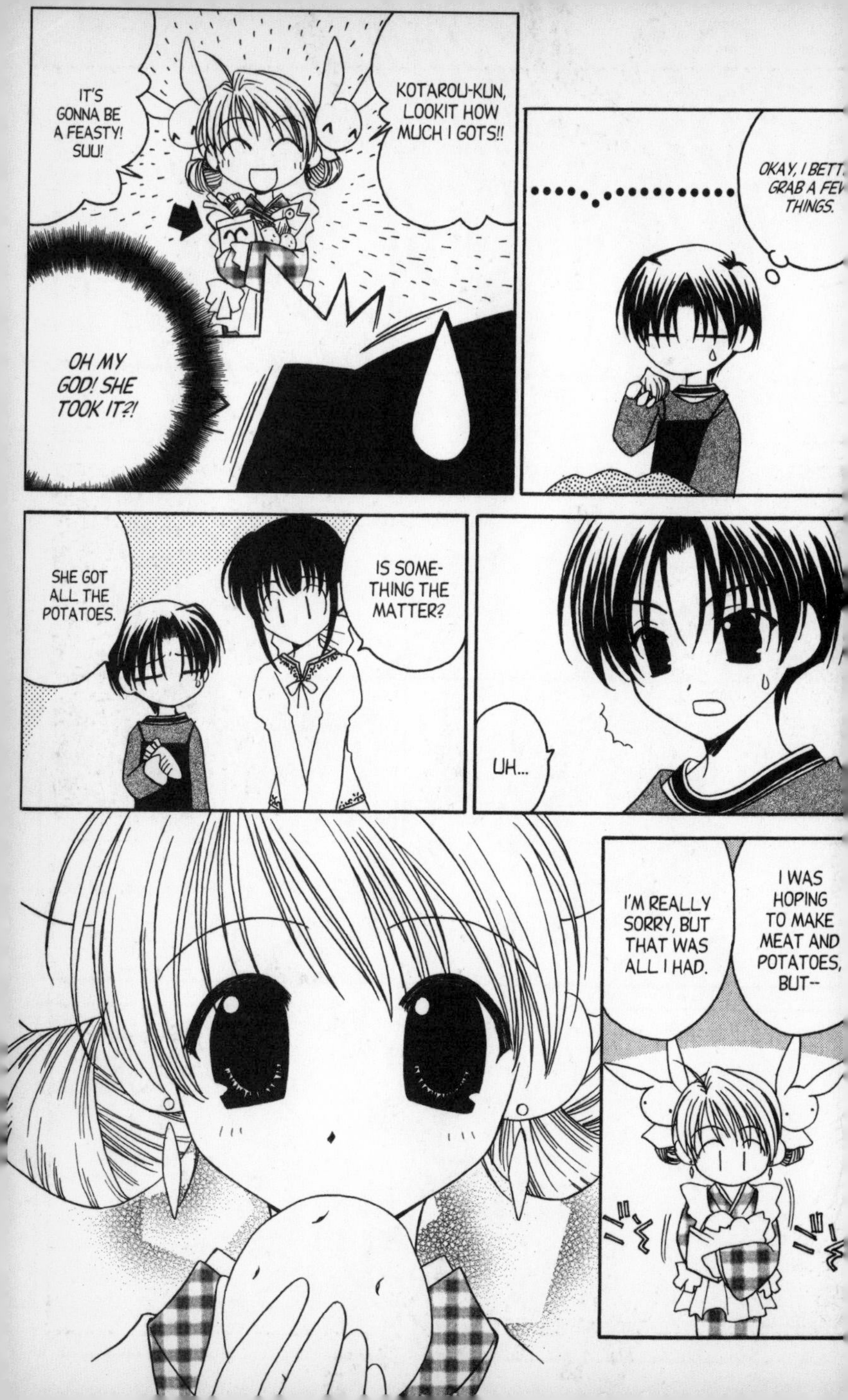
....
OKAY, I BETT GRAB A FE THINGS.
KOTAROU-KUN, LOOKIT HOW MUCH I GOTS!!
IT'S GONNA BE A FEASTY! SUU!
OH MY GOD! SHE TOOK IT?!
UH...
IS SOME-THING THE MATTER?
SHE GOT ALL THE POTATOES.
I WAS HOPING TO MAKE MEAT AND POTATOES, BUT--
I'M REALLY SORRY, BUT THAT WAS ALL I HAD.

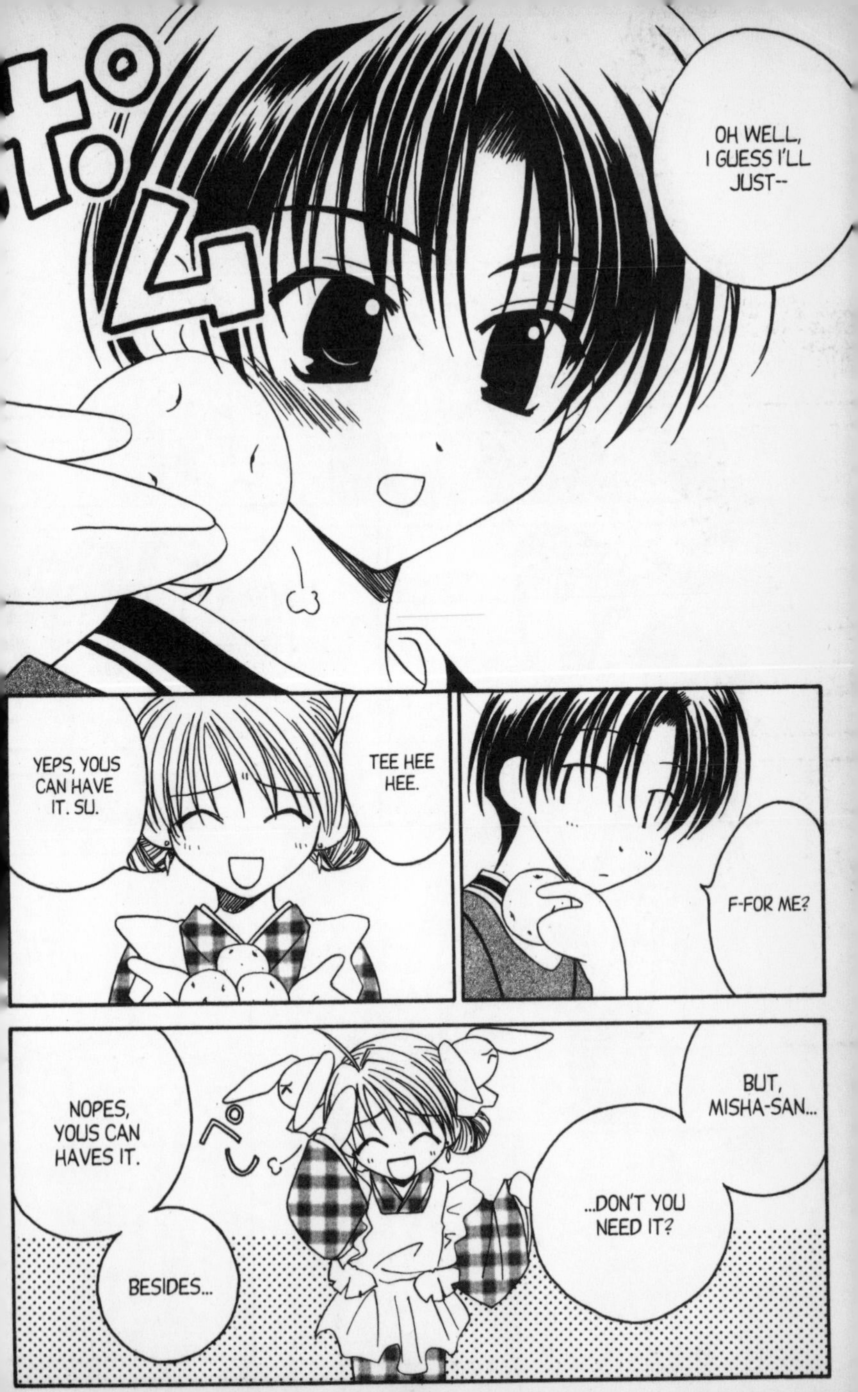
OH WELL, I GUESS I'LL JUST--
F-FOR ME?
TEE HEE HEE.
YEPS, YOUS CAN HAVE IT. SU.
BUT, MISHA-SAN...
...DON'T YOU NEED IT?
NOPES, YOUS CAN HAVES IT.
BESIDES...

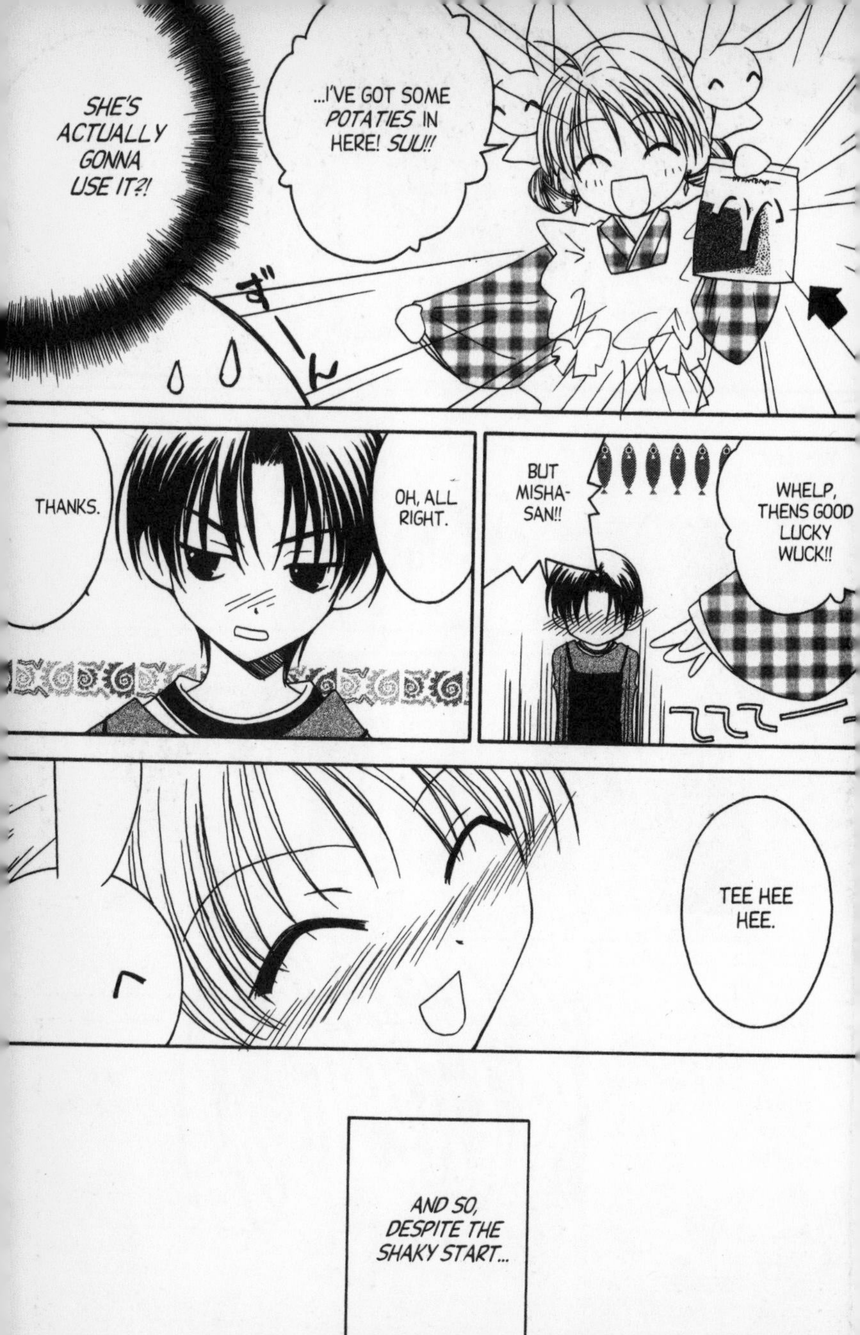
...I'VE GOT SOME POTATIES IN HERE! SUU!!
SHE'S ACTUALLY GONNA USE IT?!
ずーん
WHELP, THENS GOOD LUCKY WUCK!!
BUT MISHA-SAN!!
OH, ALL RIGHT.
THANKS.
TEE HEE HEE.
AND SO, DESPITE THE SHAKY START...

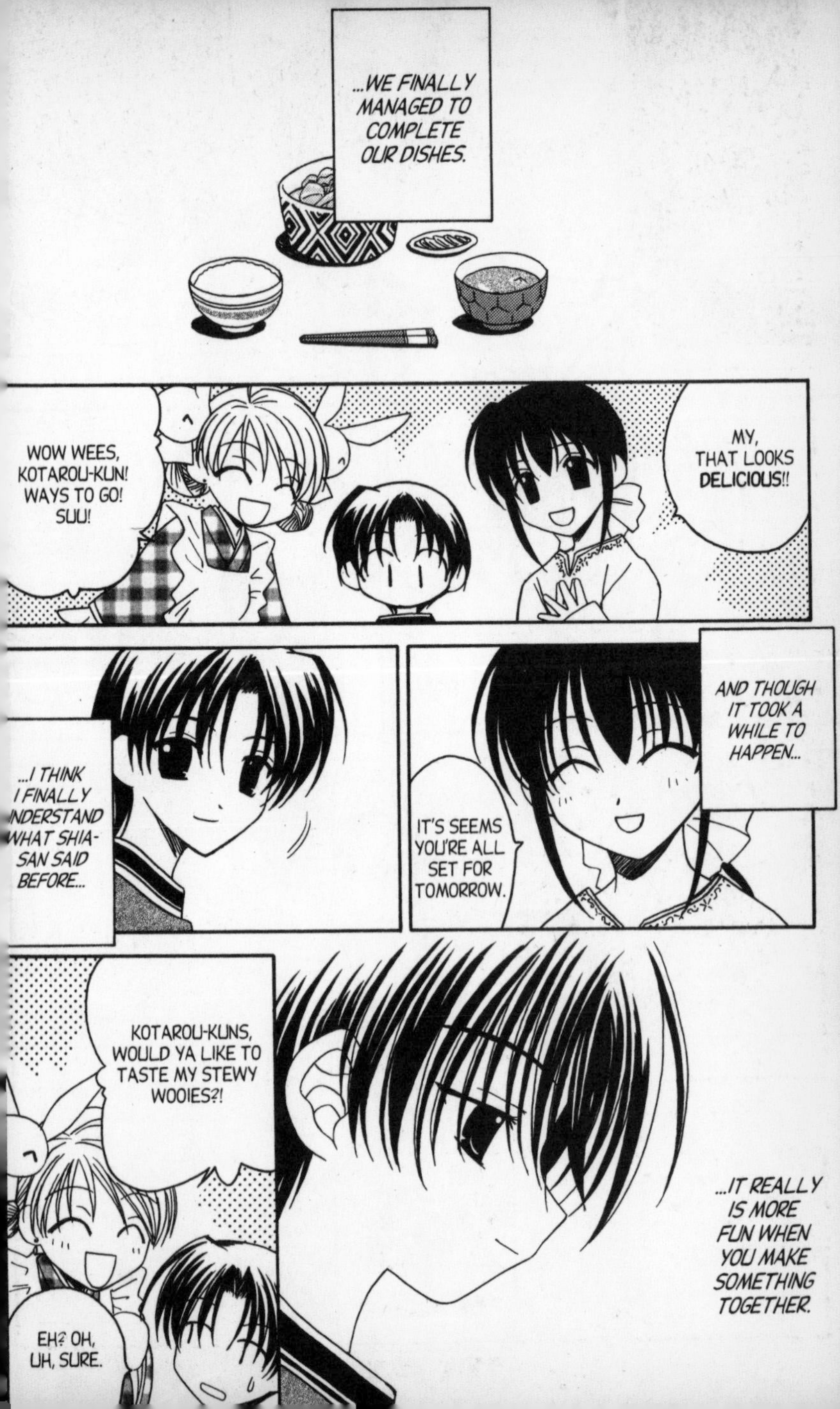
...WE FINALLY MANAGED TO COMPLETE OUR DISHES.
MY, THAT LOOKS DELICIOUS!!
WOW WEES, KOTAROU-KUN! WAYS TO GO! SUU!
AND THOUGH IT TOOK A WHILE TO HAPPEN...
IT'S SEEMS YOU'RE ALL SET FOR TOMORROW.
...I THINK I FINALLY UNDERSTAND WHAT SHIA-SAN SAID BEFORE...
...IT REALLY IS MORE FUN WHEN YOU MAKE SOMETHING TOGETHER.
KOTAROU-KUNS, WOULD YA LIKE TO TASTE MY STEWY WOOIES?!
EH? OH, UH, SURE.

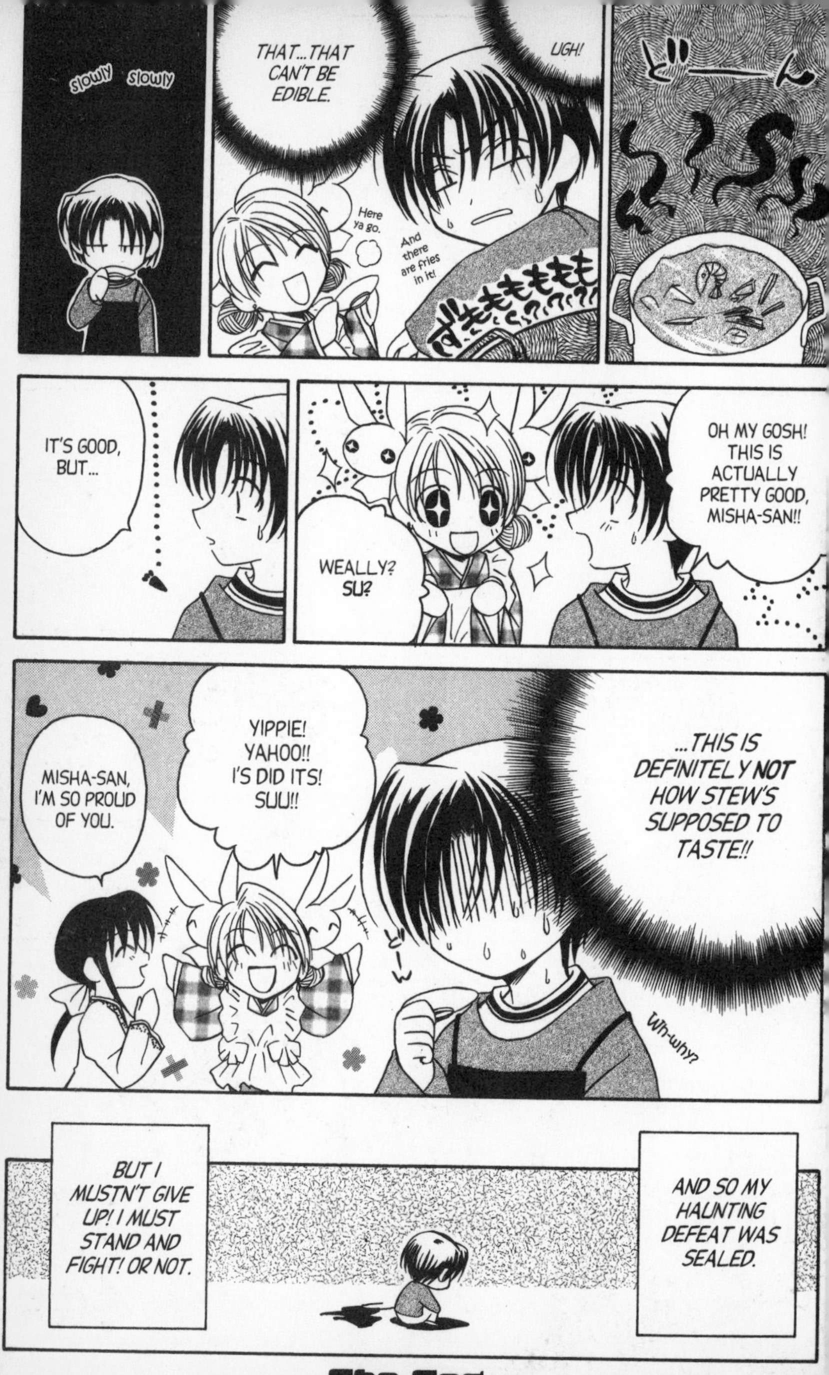
どーーん
UGH!
THAT...THAT CAN'T BE EDIBLE.
Here ya go.
And there are fries in it!
slowly slowly
OH MY GOSH! THIS IS ACTUALLY PRETTY GOOD, MISHA-SAN!!
WEALLY? SU?
IT'S GOOD, BUT...
...THIS IS DEFINITELY NOT HOW STEW'S SUPPOSED TO TASTE!!
Wh-why?
YIPPIE! YAHOO!! I'S DID ITS! SUU!!
MISHA-SAN, I'M SO PROUD OF YOU.
AND SO MY HAUNTING DEFEAT WAS SEALED.
BUT I MUSTN'T GIVE UP! I MUST STAND AND FIGHT! OR NOT.

The End

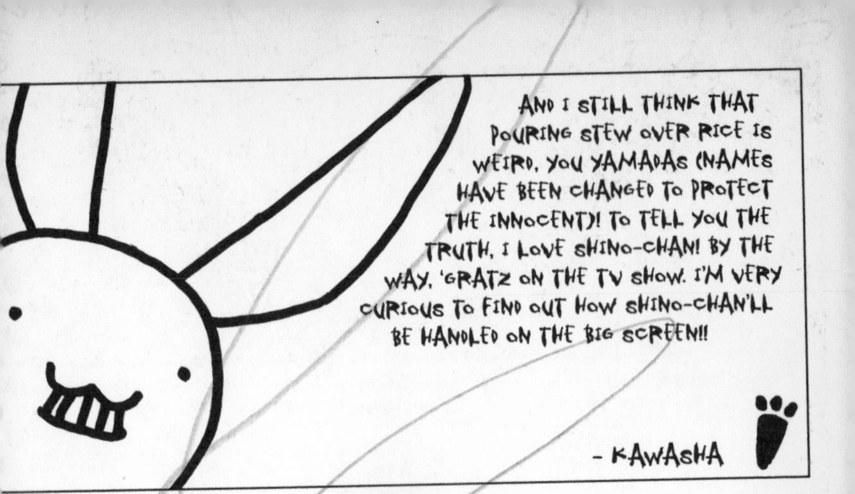

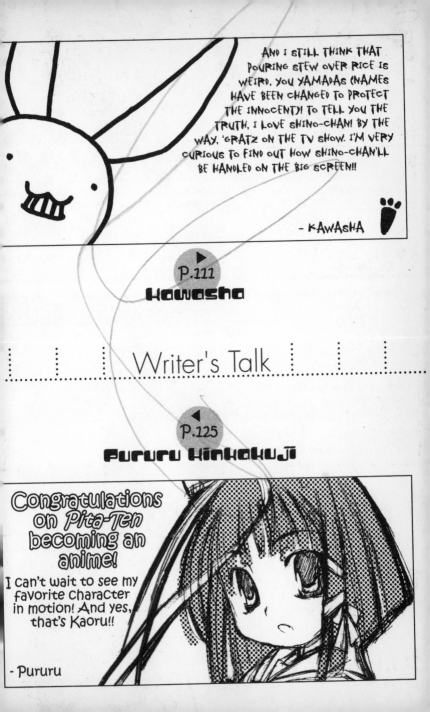

AND I STILL THINK THAT POURING STEW OVER RICE IS WEIRD, YOU YAMADAS (NAMES HAVE BEEN CHANGED TO PROTECT THE INNOCENT)! TO TELL YOU THE TRUTH, I LOVE SHINO-CHAN! BY THE WAY, 'GRATZ ON THE TV SHOW. I'M VERY CURIOUS TO FIND OUT HOW SHINO-CHAN'LL BE HANDLED ON THE BIG SCREEN!!

- KAWASHA

P.111

Kawasha

Writer's Talk

P.125

Pururu Kinkakuji

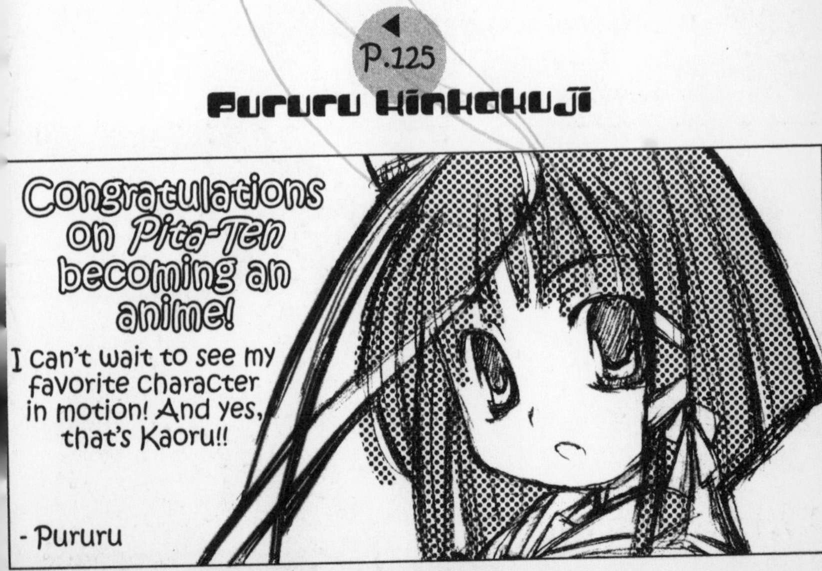

Congratulations on *Pita-Ten* becoming an anime!

I can't wait to see my favorite character in motion! And yes, that's Kaoru!!

- Pururu

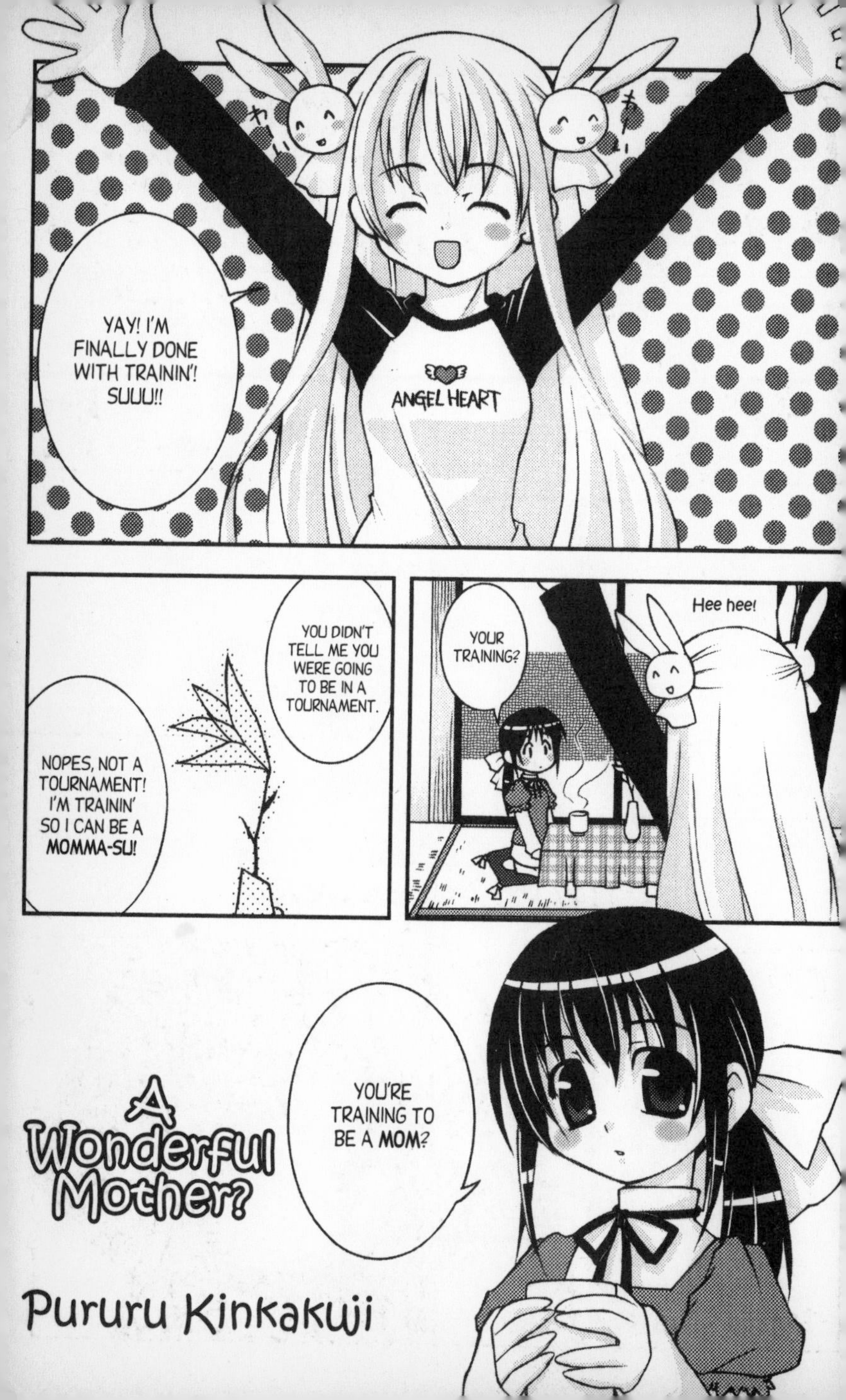
YAY! I'M FINALLY DONE WITH TRAININ'! SUUU!!
ANGEL HEART
YOUR TRAINING?
Hee hee!
YOU DIDN'T TELL ME YOU WERE GOING TO BE IN A TOURNAMENT.
NOPES, NOT A TOURNAMENT! I'M TRAININ' SO I CAN BE A MOMMA-SU!
YOU'RE TRAINING TO BE A MOM?
A Wonderful Mother?
Pururu Kinkakuji

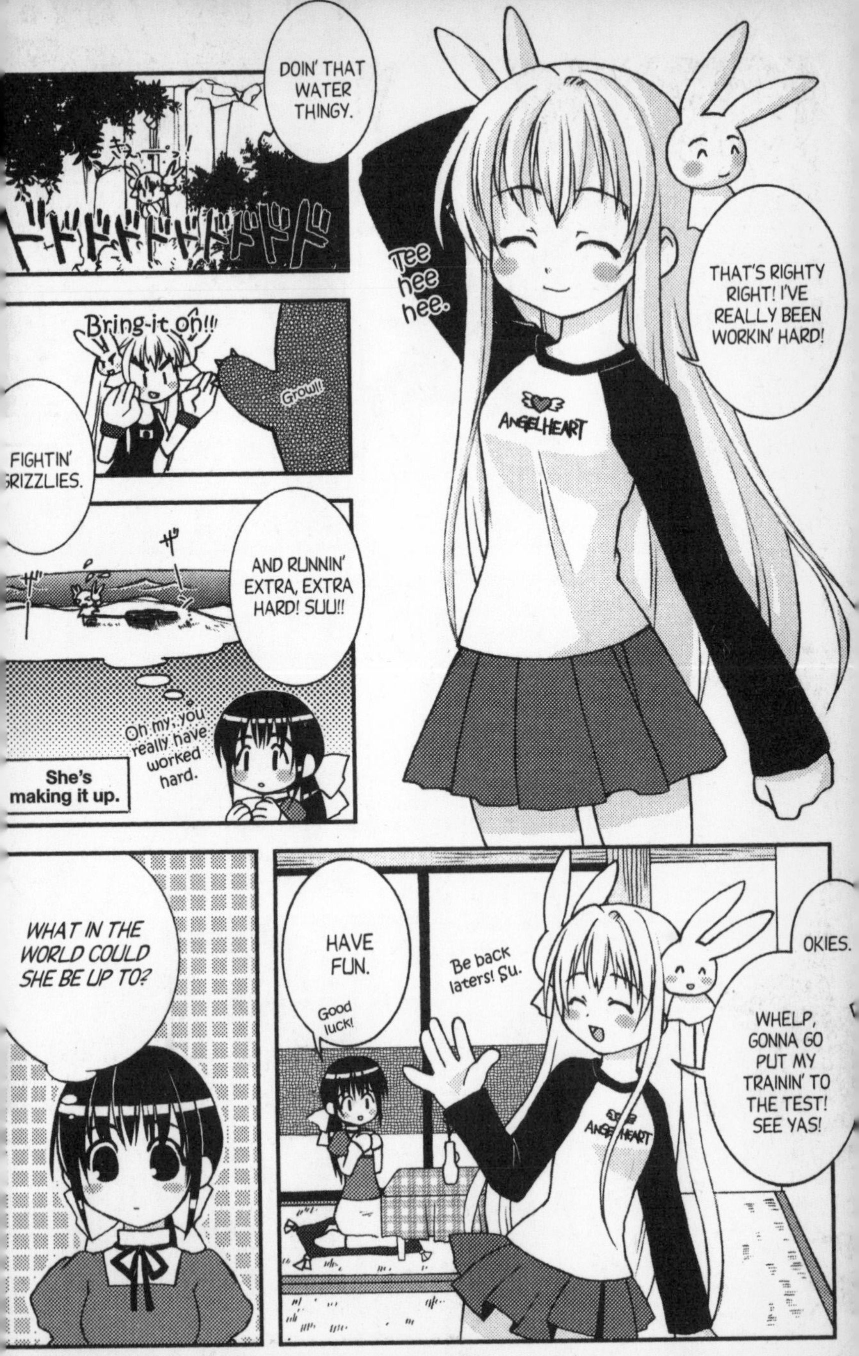

Tee hee hee.
ANGELHEART
THAT'S RIGHTY RIGHT! I'VE REALLY BEEN WORKIN' HARD!
DOIN' THAT WATER THINGY.
Bring-it on!!!
Growl!!
FIGHTIN' GRIZZLIES.
AND RUNNIN' EXTRA, EXTRA HARD! SUU!!
Oh my, you really have worked hard.
She's making it up.
OKIES.
WHELP, GONNA GO PUT MY TRAININ' TO THE TEST! SEE YAS!
ANGELHEART
Be back laters! Su.
HAVE FUN.
Good luck!
WHAT IN THE WORLD COULD SHE BE UP TO?

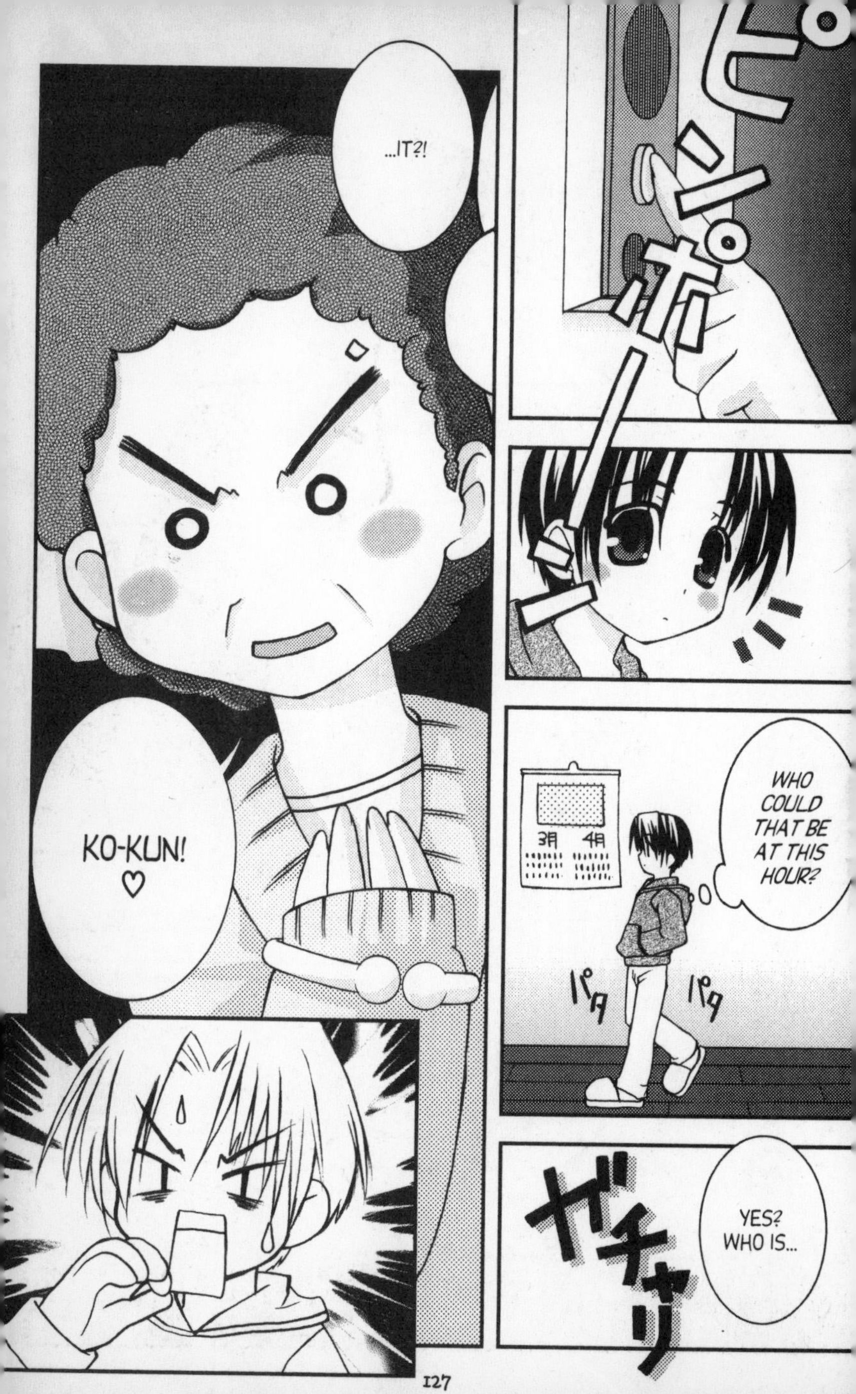
ピンポーン
WHO COULD THAT BE AT THIS HOUR?
パタ パタ
ガチャリ
YES? WHO IS...
...IT?!
KO-KUN! ♡

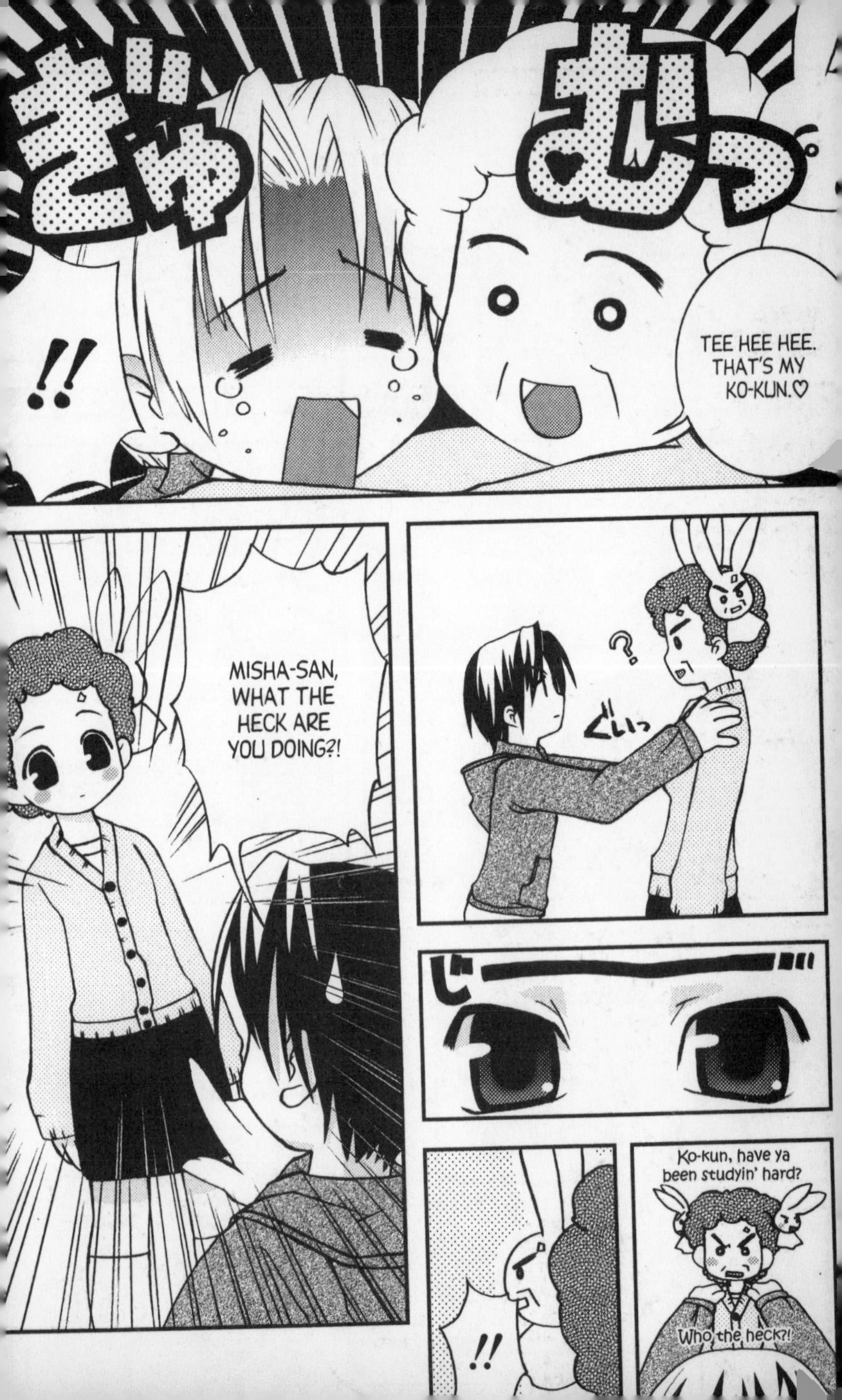

ぎゅむっ
TEE HEE HEE. THAT'S MY KO-KUN.♡
!!
?
ぐいっ
じーーー
Ko-kun, have ya been studyin' hard?
Who the heck?!
!!
MISHA-SAN, WHAT THE HECK ARE YOU DOING?!

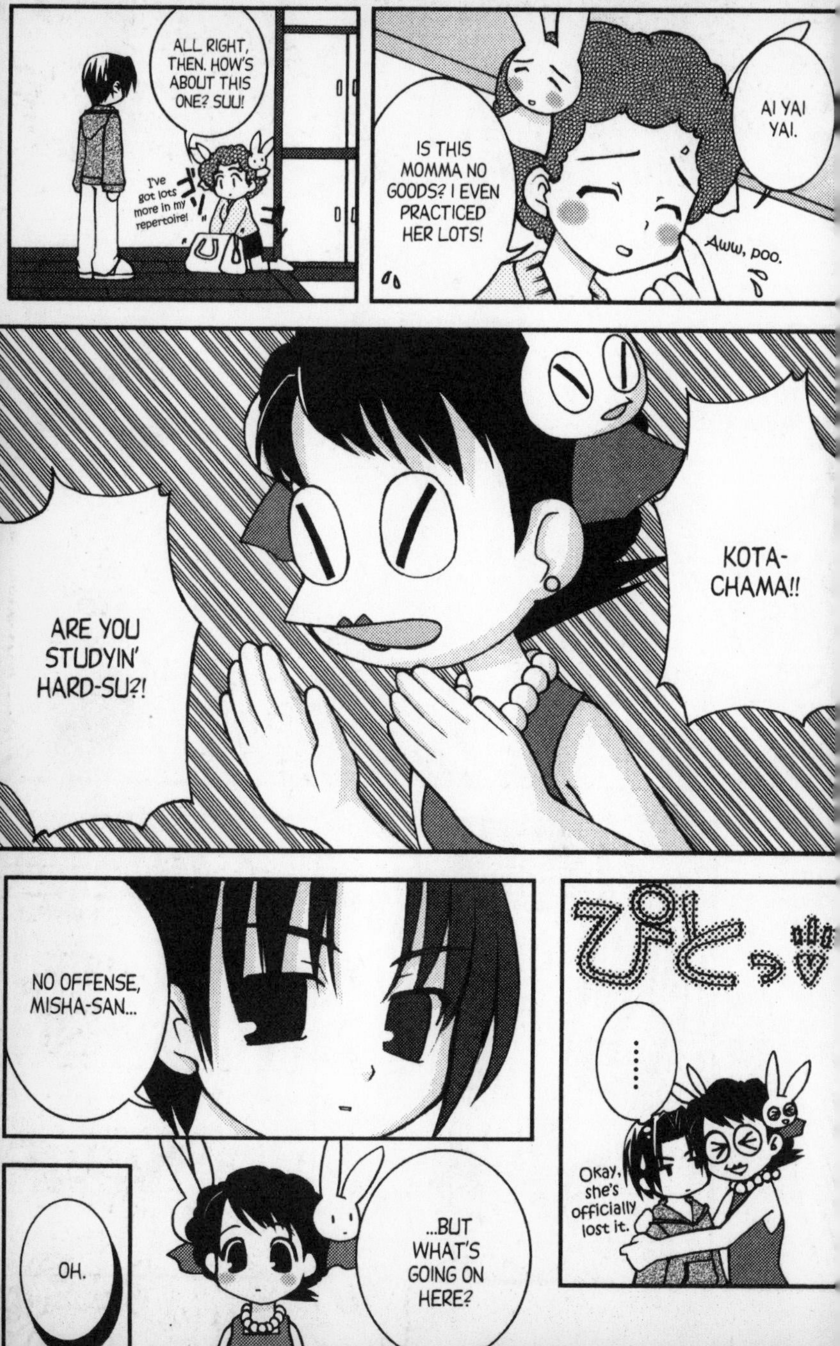
AI YAI YAI.
IS THIS MOMMA NO GOODS? I EVEN PRACTICED HER LOTS!
Aww, poo.
ALL RIGHT, THEN. HOW'S ABOUT THIS ONE? SUU!
I've got lots more in my repertoire!
KOTA-CHAMA!!
ARE YOU STUDYIN' HARD-SU?!
ぴとっ
......
Okay, she's officially lost it.
NO OFFENSE, MISHA-SAN...
...BUT WHAT'S GOING ON HERE?
OH.

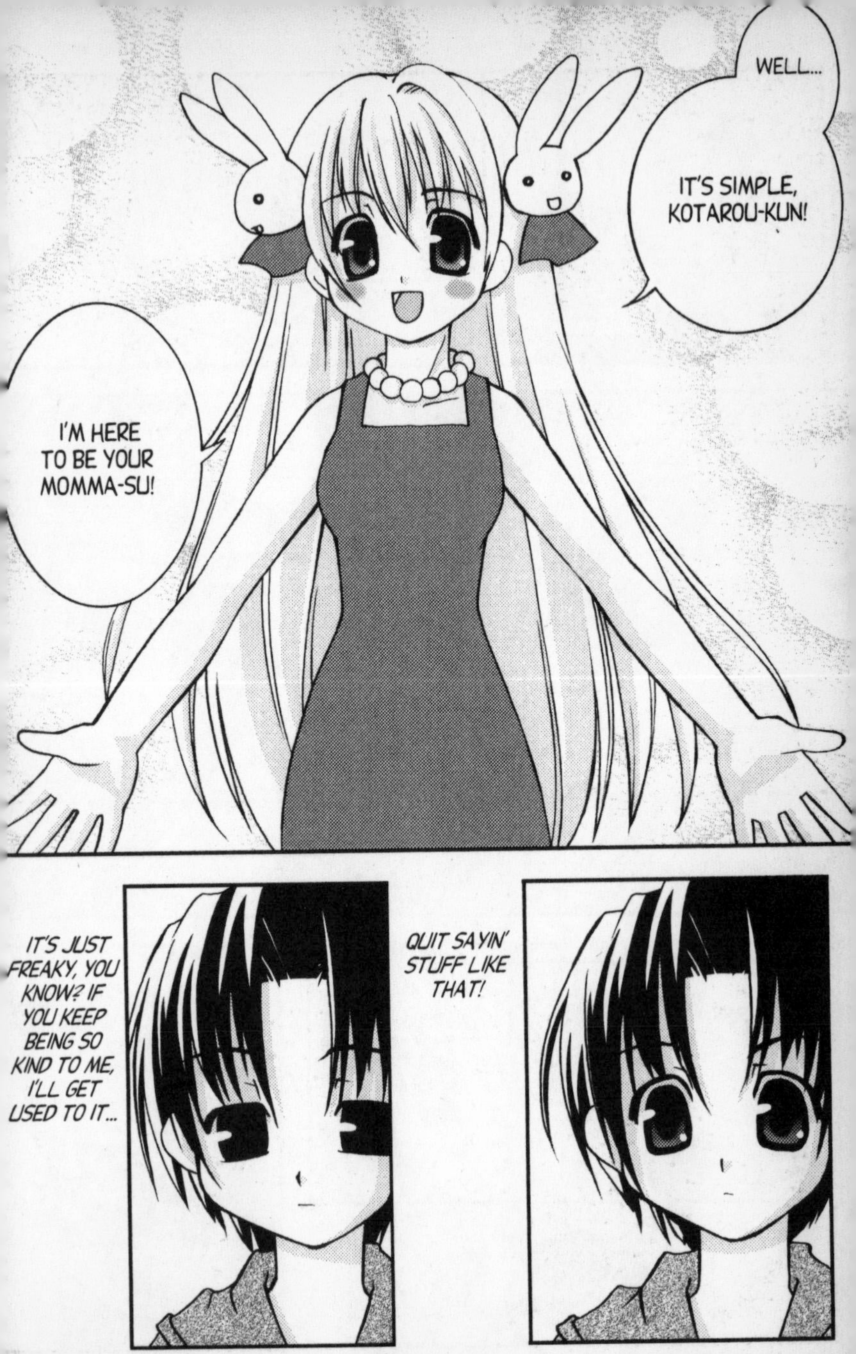
WELL...
IT'S SIMPLE, KOTAROU-KUN!
I'M HERE TO BE YOUR MOMMA-SU!
QUIT SAYIN' STUFF LIKE THAT!
IT'S JUST FREAKY, YOU KNOW? IF YOU KEEP BEING SO KIND TO ME, I'LL GET USED TO IT...

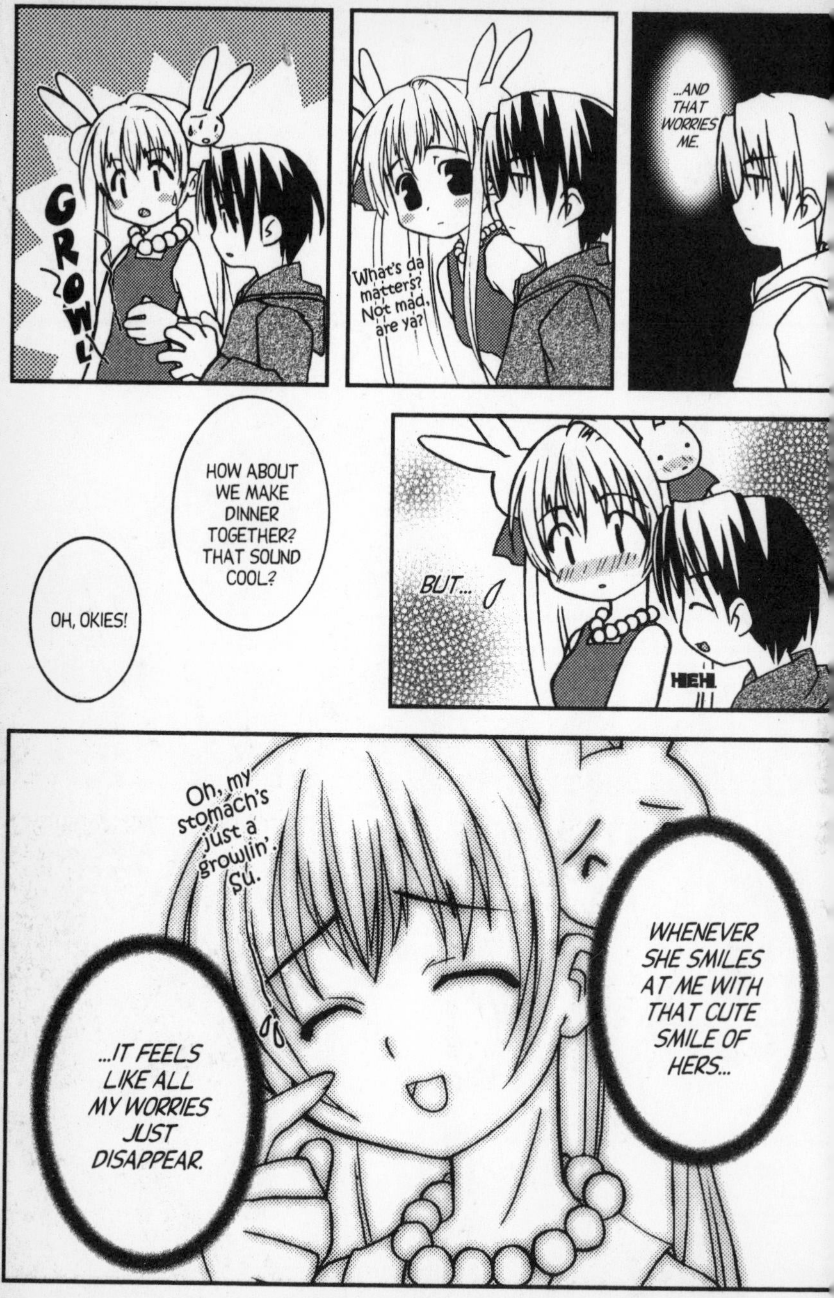
...AND THAT WORRIES ME.
What's da matters? Not mad, are ya?
GROWL
BUT...
HEH.
HOW ABOUT WE MAKE DINNER TOGETHER? THAT SOUND COOL?
OH, OKIES!
WHENEVER SHE SMILES AT ME WITH THAT CUTE SMILE OF HERS...
Oh, my stomach's just a growlin'. Su.
...IT FEELS LIKE ALL MY WORRIES JUST DISAPPEAR.

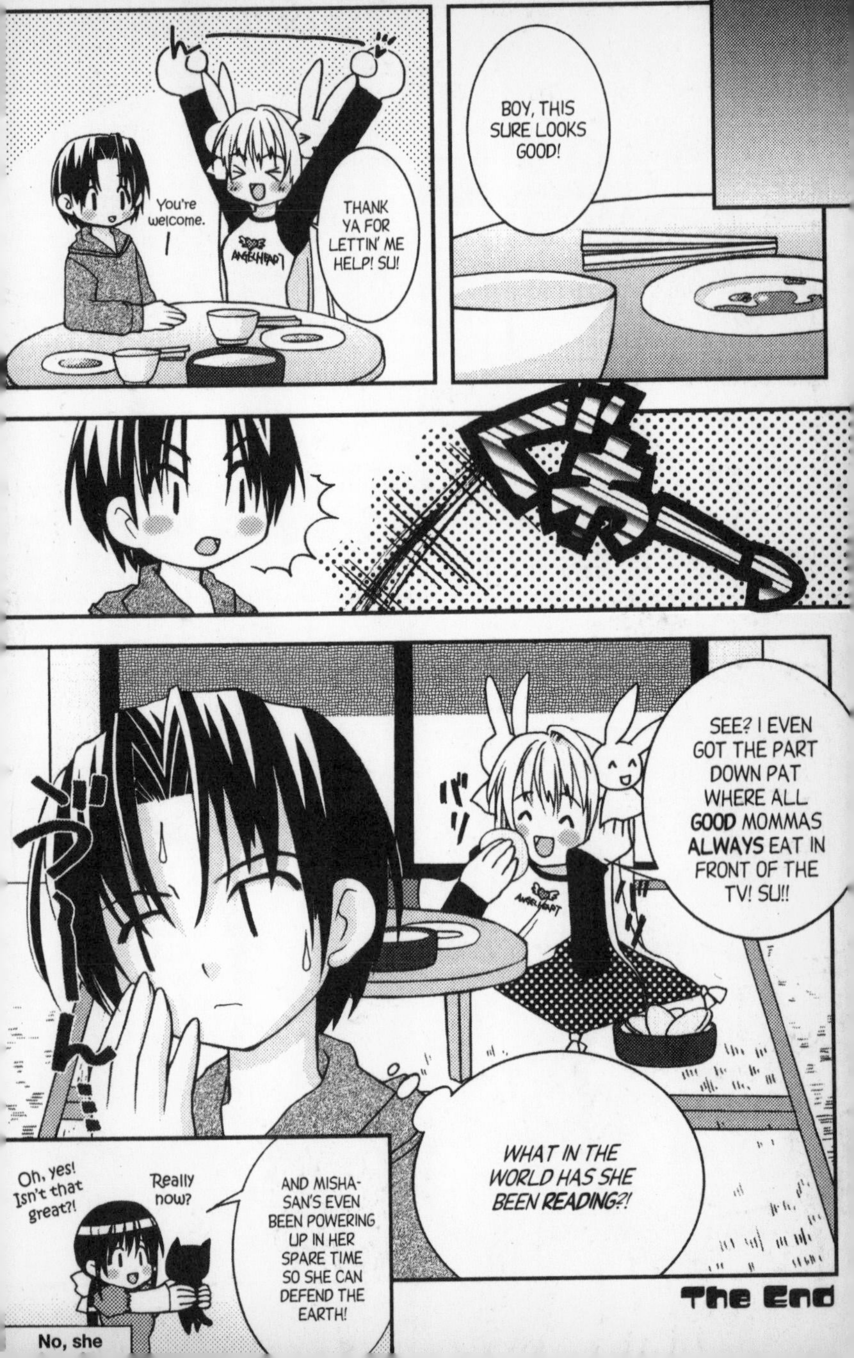
BOY, THIS SURE LOOKS GOOD!
THANK YA FOR LETTIN' ME HELP! SU!
You're welcome.
SEE? I EVEN GOT THE PART DOWN PAT WHERE ALL GOOD MOMMAS ALWAYS EAT IN FRONT OF THE TV! SU!!
WHAT IN THE WORLD HAS SHE BEEN READING?!
AND MISHA-SAN'S EVEN BEEN POWERING UP IN HER SPARE TIME SO SHE CAN DEFEND THE EARTH!
Really now?
Oh, yes! Isn't that great?!
No, she
The End

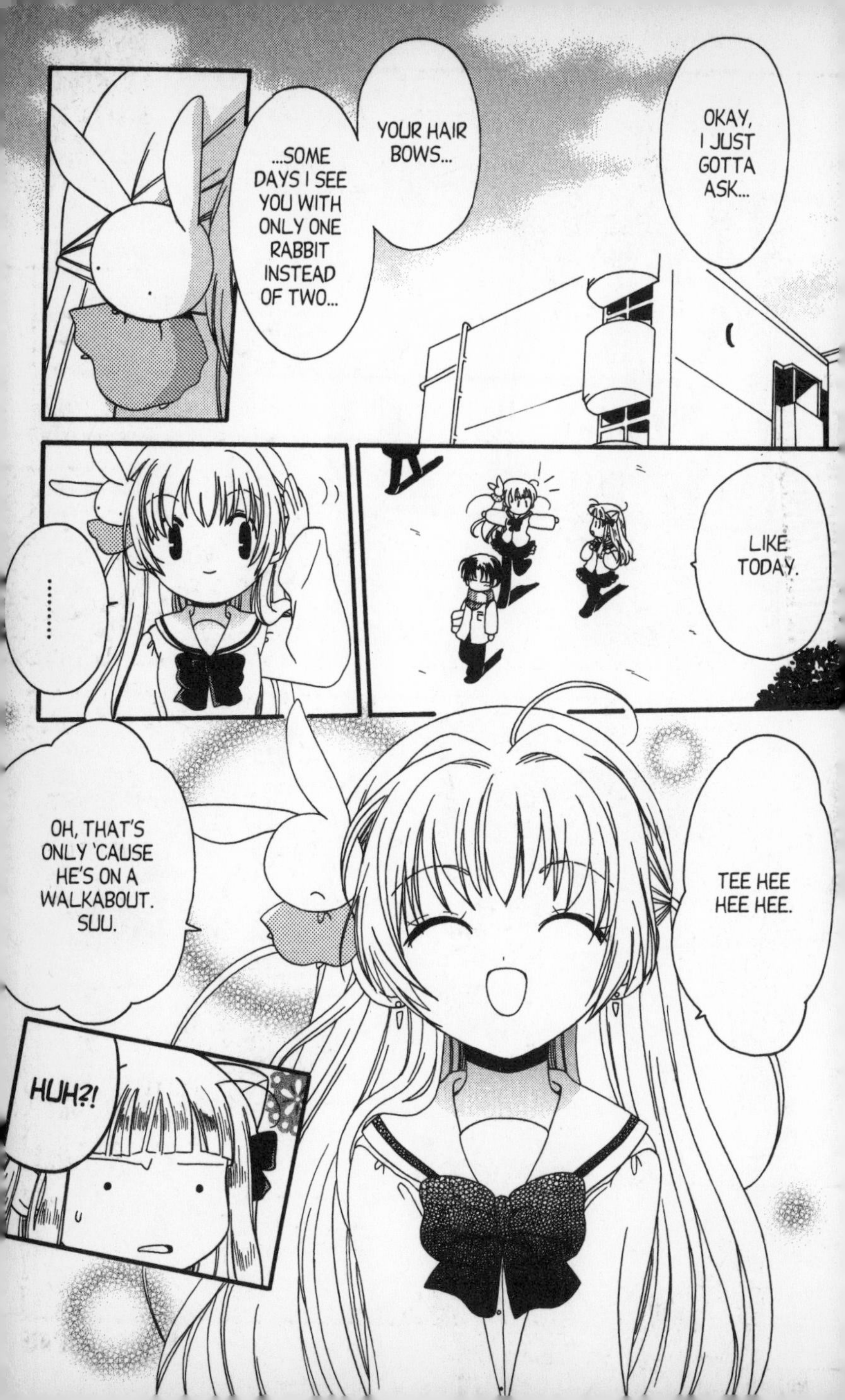
OKAY, I JUST GOTTA ASK...
YOUR HAIR BOWS...
...SOME DAYS I SEE YOU WITH ONLY ONE RABBIT INSTEAD OF TWO...
LIKE TODAY.
....
TEE HEE HEE HEE.
OH, THAT'S ONLY 'CAUSE HE'S ON A WALKABOUT. SUU.
HUH?!

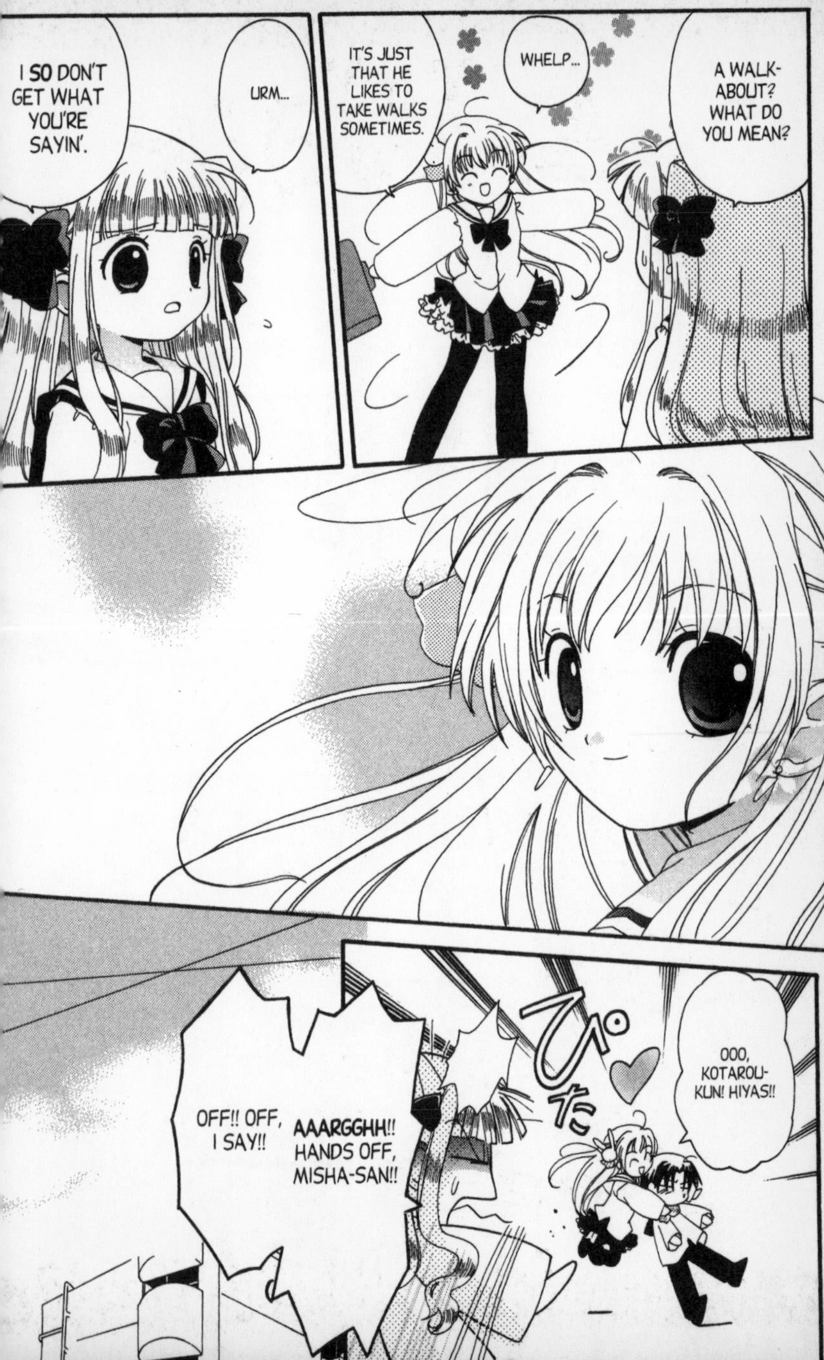
A WALK-ABOUT? WHAT DO YOU MEAN?
WHELP...
IT'S JUST THAT HE LIKES TO TAKE WALKS SOMETIMES.
URM...
I **SO** DON'T GET WHAT YOU'RE SAYIN'.
OOO, KOTAROU-KUN! HIYAS!!
ぴた
AAARGGHH!! HANDS OFF, MISHA-SAN!!
OFF!! OFF, I SAY!!

A Walk

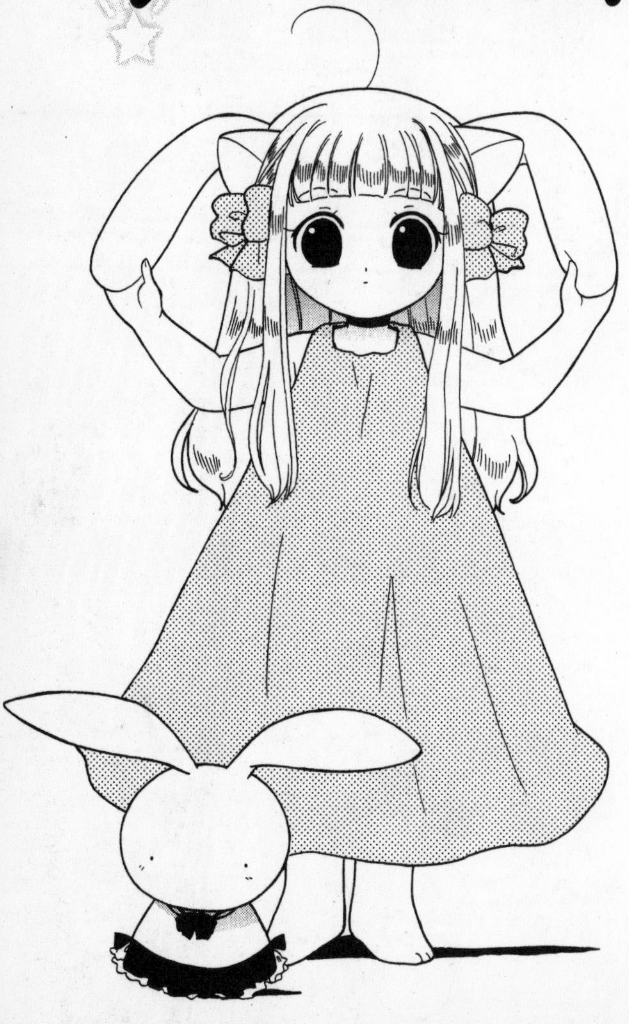

Mari Matsuzawa

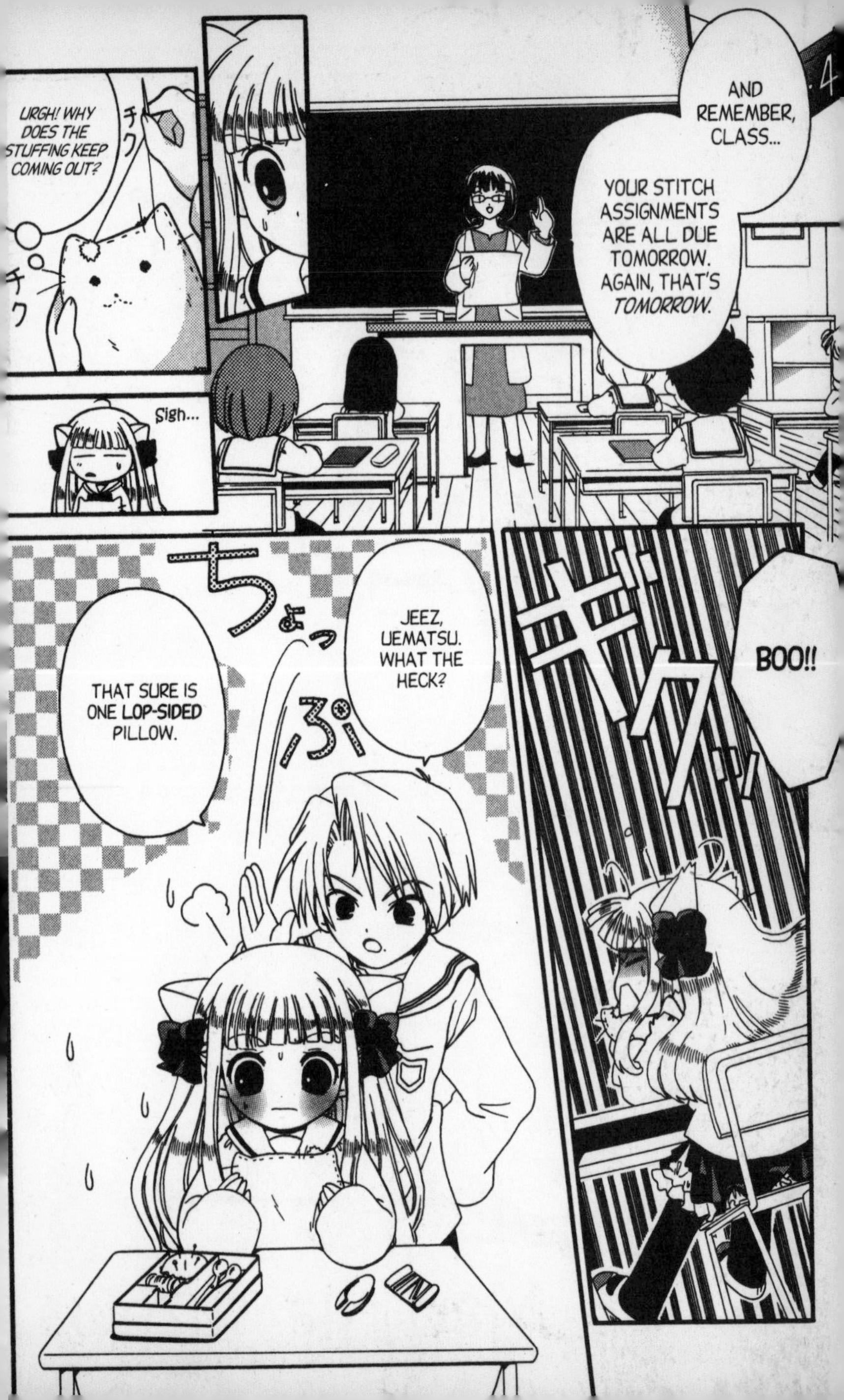
4
AND REMEMBER, CLASS...
YOUR STITCH ASSIGNMENTS ARE ALL DUE TOMORROW. AGAIN, THAT'S *TOMORROW.*
URGH! WHY DOES THE STUFFING KEEP COMING OUT?
チク
チク
Sigh...
BOO!!
ギクッ
JEEZ, UEMATSU. WHAT THE HECK?
ちょっ
ぷ
THAT SURE IS ONE **LOP-SIDED** PILLOW.

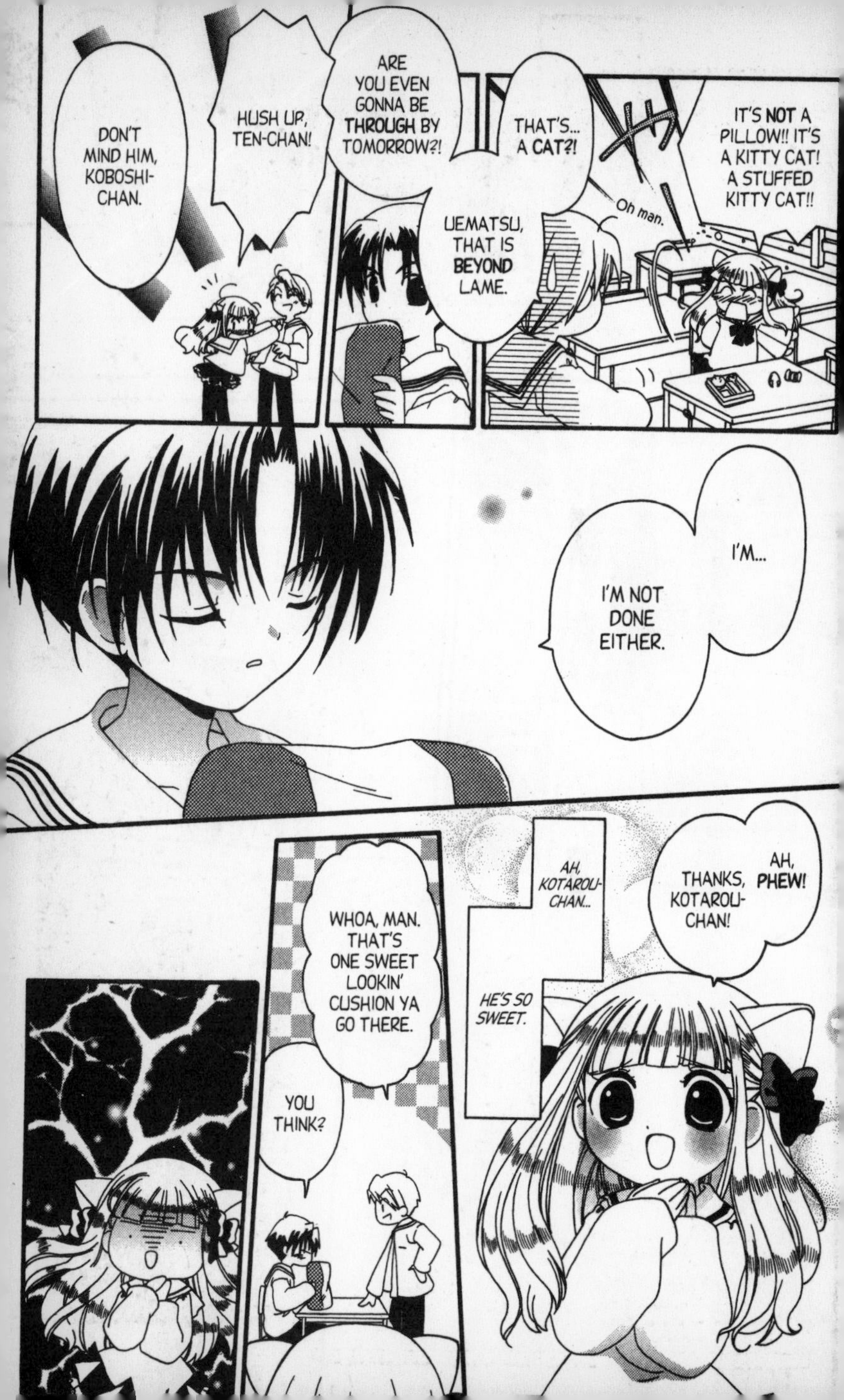
IT'S NOT A PILLOW!! IT'S A KITTY CAT! A STUFFED KITTY CAT!!
Oh man.
THAT'S... A CAT?!
UEMATSU, THAT IS BEYOND LAME.
ARE YOU EVEN GONNA BE THROUGH BY TOMORROW?!
HUSH UP, TEN-CHAN!
DON'T MIND HIM, KOBOSHI-CHAN.
I'M...
I'M NOT DONE EITHER.
AH, PHEW!
THANKS, KOTAROU-CHAN!
AH, KOTAROU-CHAN...
HE'S SO SWEET.
WHOA, MAN. THAT'S ONE SWEET LOOKIN' CUSHION YA GO THERE.
YOU THINK?

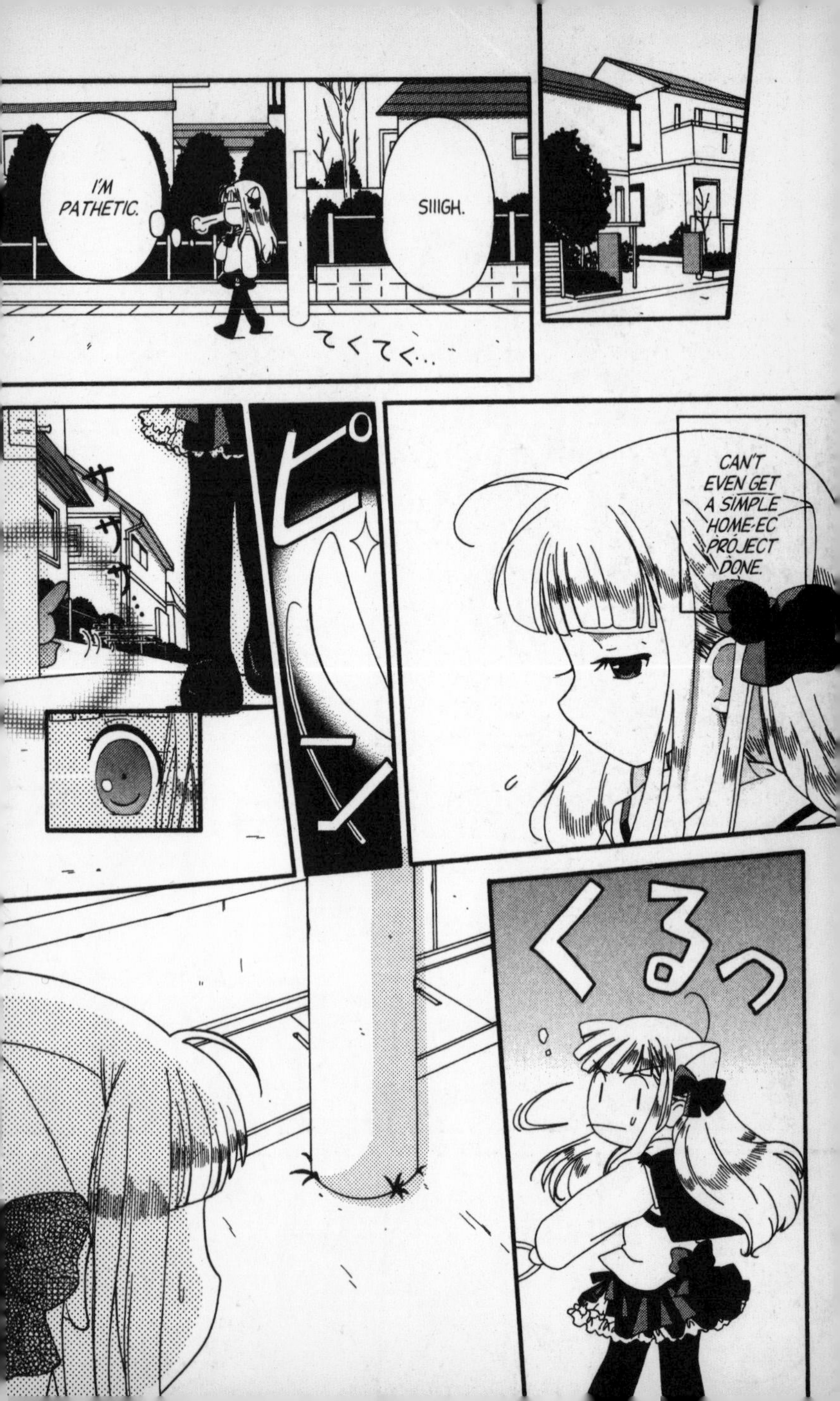
SIIIGH.
I'M PATHETIC.
てくてく…
CAN'T EVEN GET A SIMPLE HOME-EC PROJECT DONE.
ピーン
サササ
くるっ

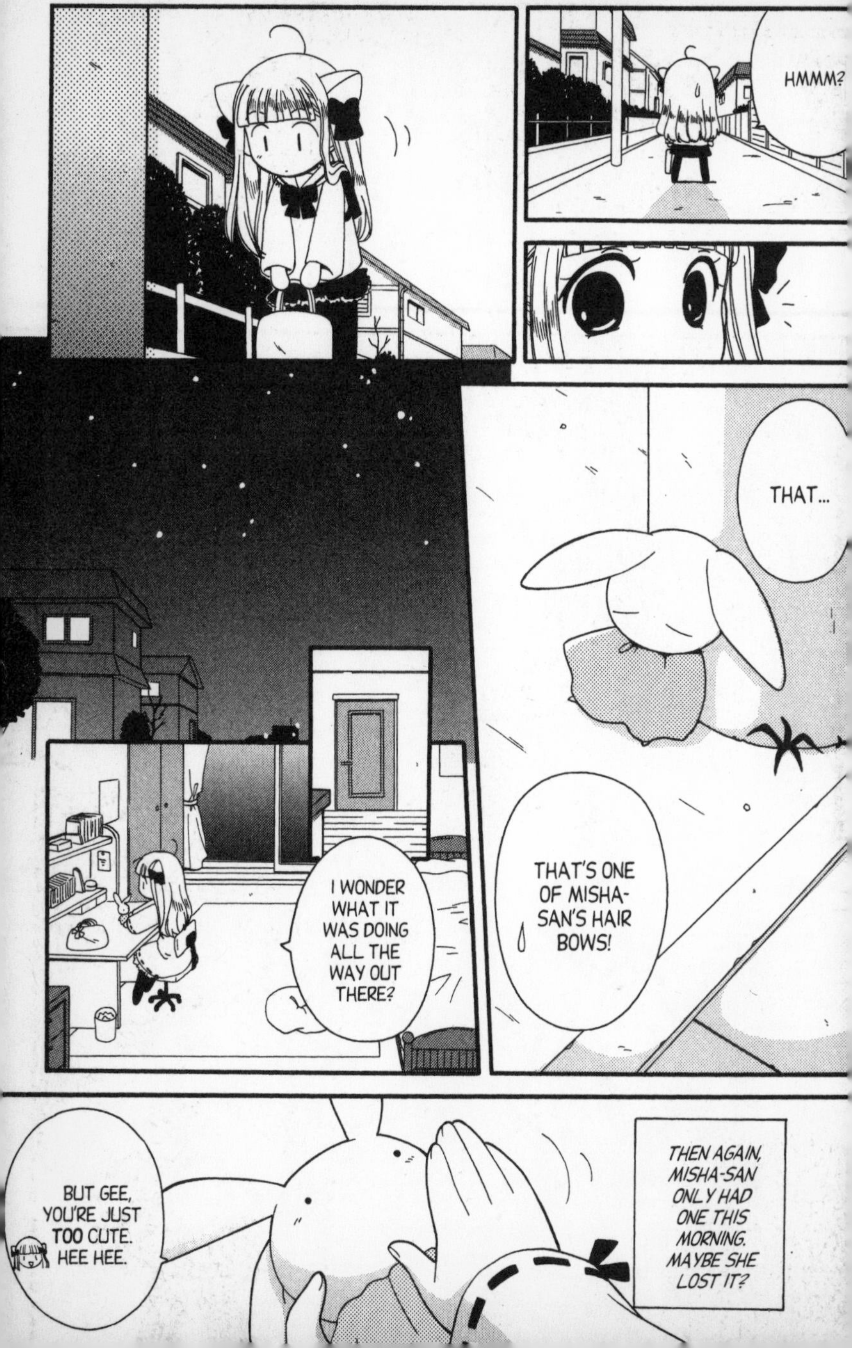
HMMM?
THAT...
THAT'S ONE OF MISHA-SAN'S HAIR BOWS!
I WONDER WHAT IT WAS DOING ALL THE WAY OUT THERE?
THEN AGAIN, MISHA-SAN ONLY HAD ONE THIS MORNING. MAYBE SHE LOST IT?
BUT GEE, YOU'RE JUST TOO CUTE. HEE HEE.

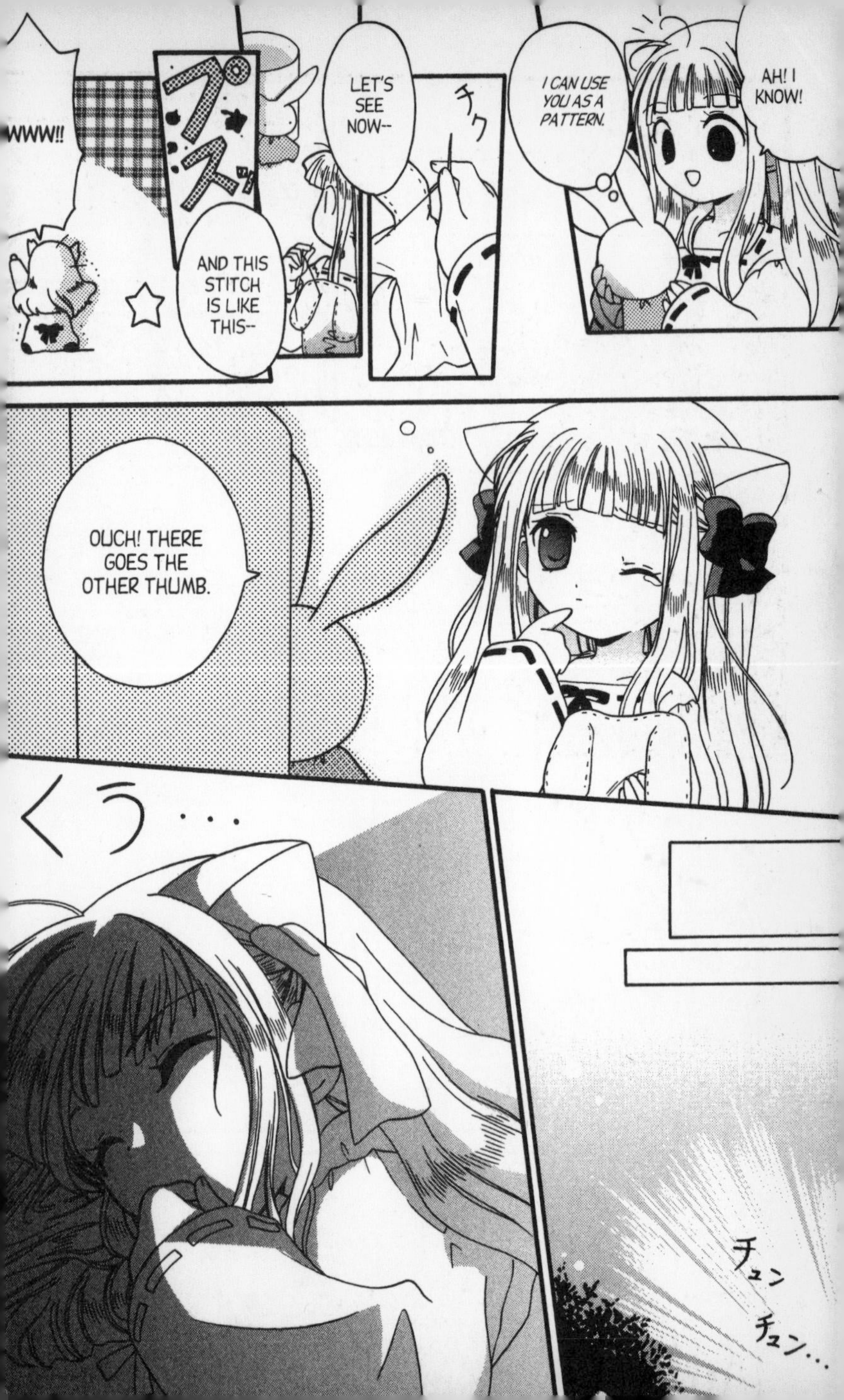
AH! I KNOW!
I CAN USE YOU AS A PATTERN.
チク
LET'S SEE NOW--
プスッ
AND THIS STITCH IS LIKE THIS--
WWW!!
OUCH! THERE GOES THE OTHER THUMB.
チュン
チュン…
くう…

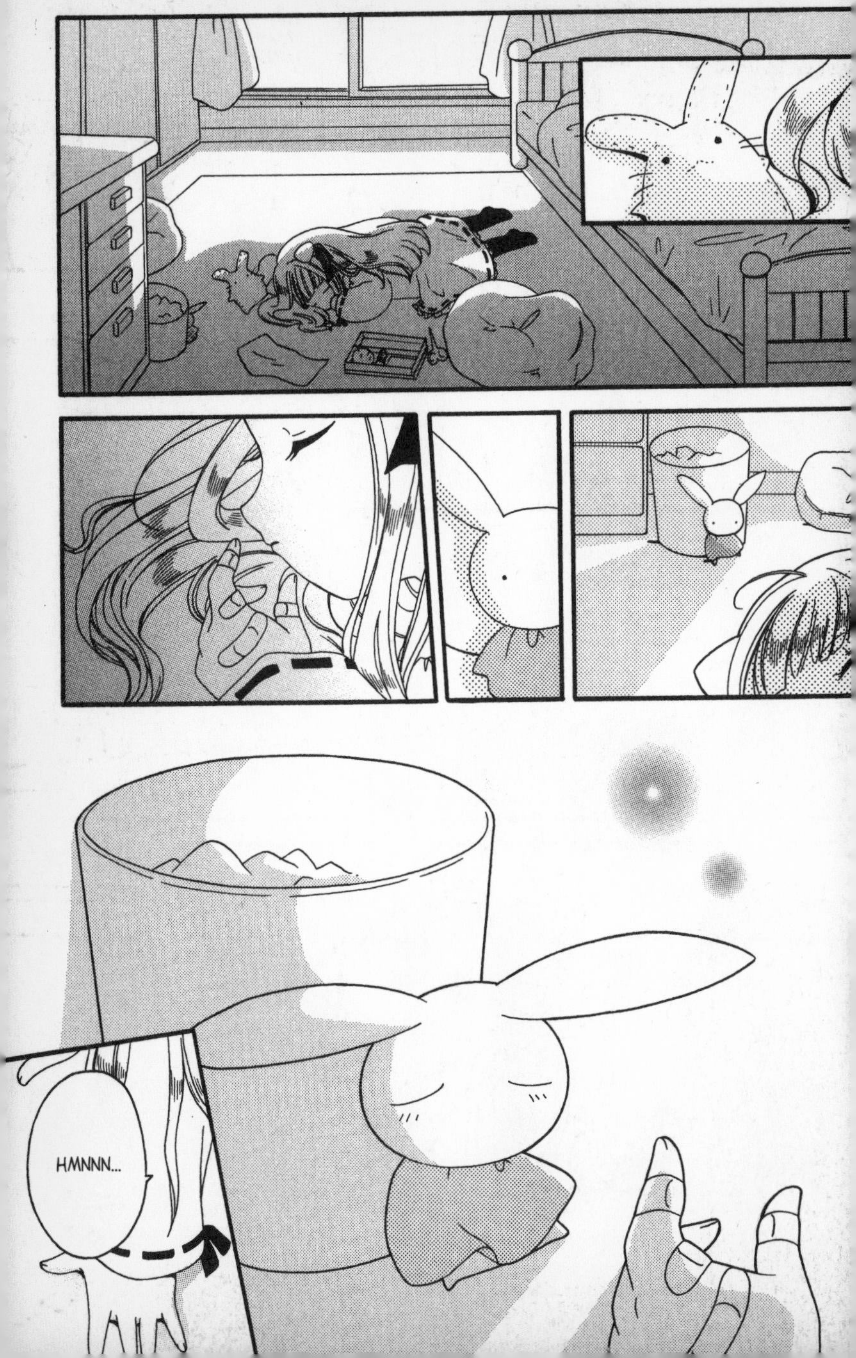
HMNNN...

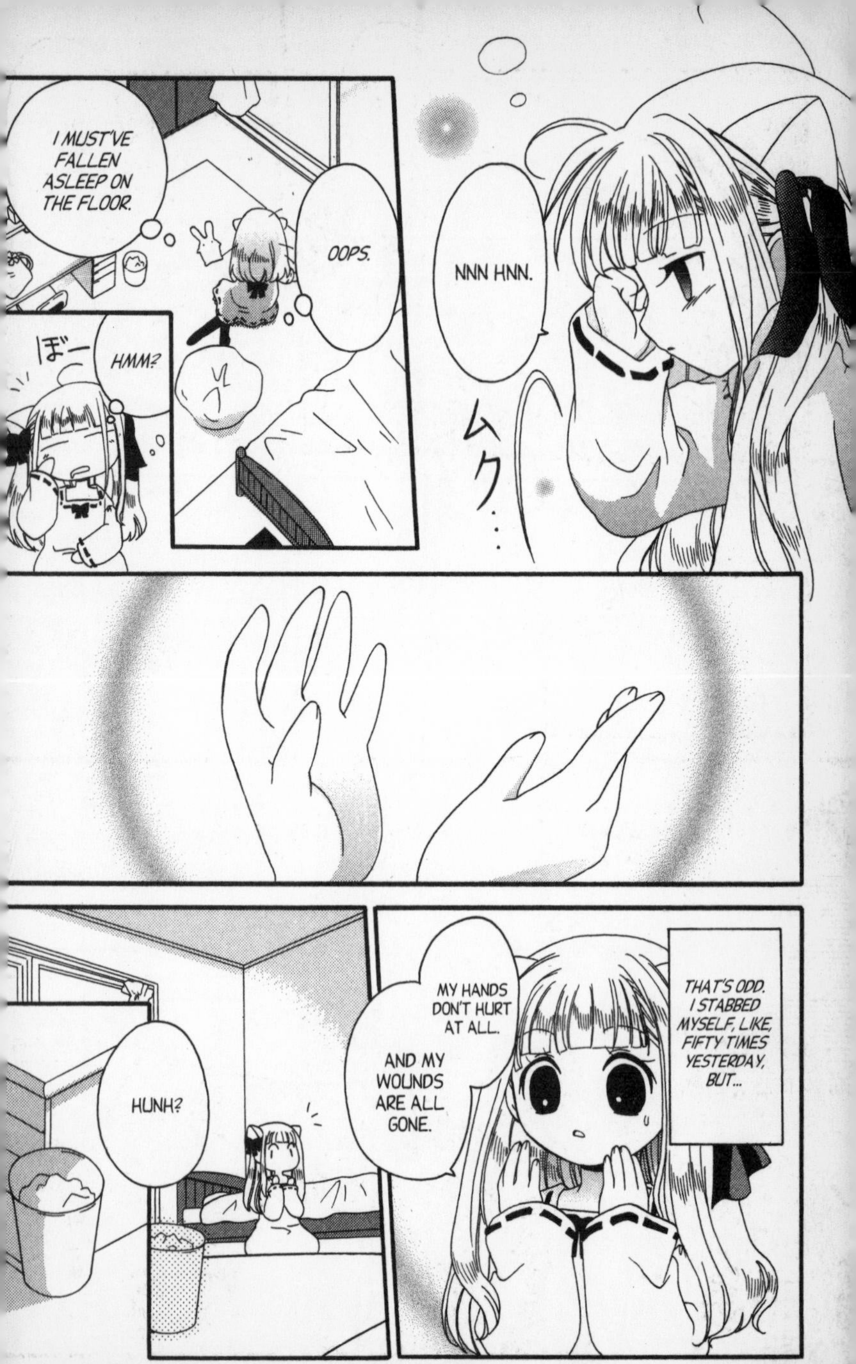
NNN HNN.
ムク...
OOPS.
I MUST'VE FALLEN ASLEEP ON THE FLOOR.
ぼー
HMM?
THAT'S ODD. I STABBED MYSELF, LIKE, FIFTY TIMES YESTERDAY, BUT...
MY HANDS DON'T HURT AT ALL.
AND MY WOUNDS ARE ALL GONE.
HUNH?

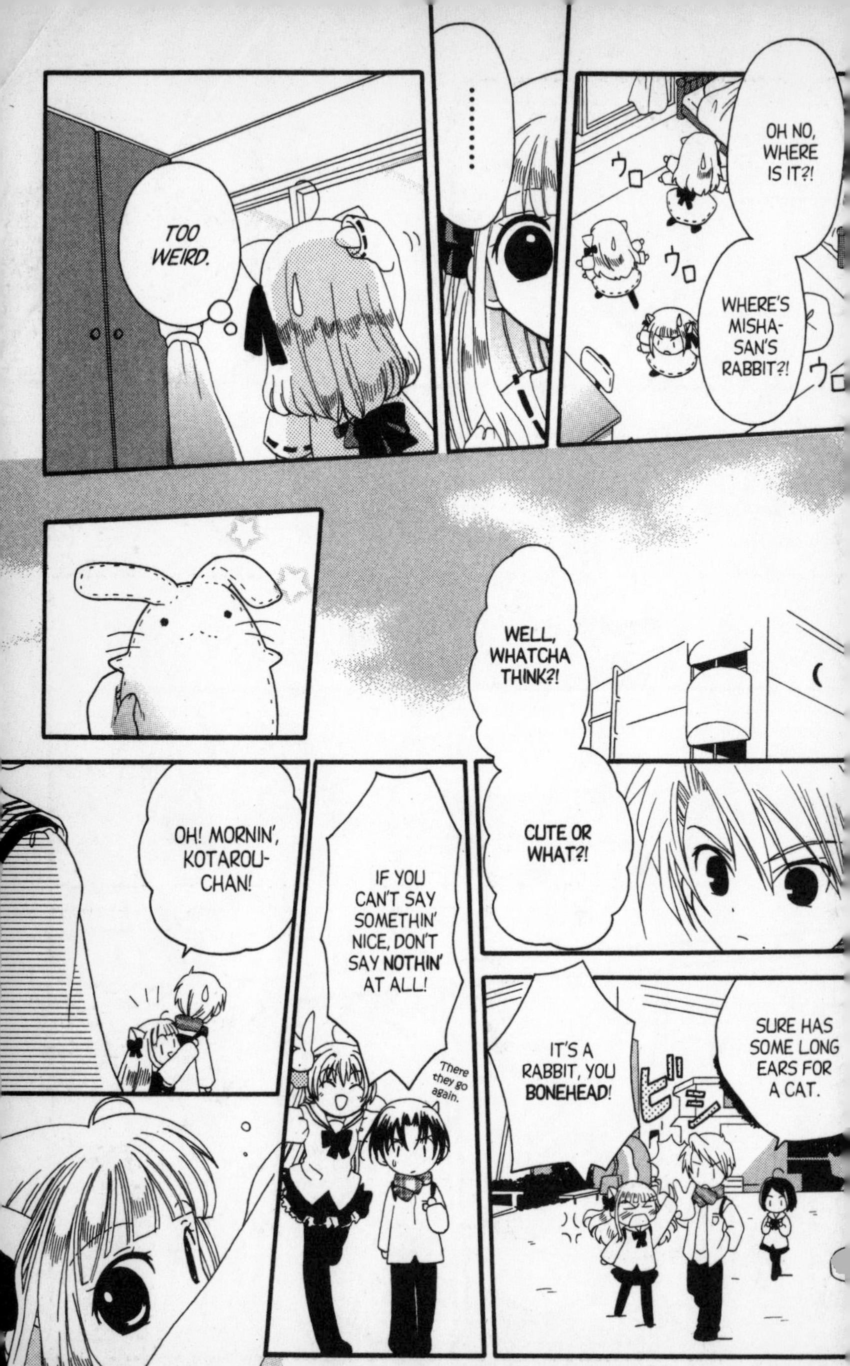

OH NO, WHERE IS IT?!
ウロ
ウロ
WHERE'S MISHA-SAN'S RABBIT?!
ウロ
....
TOO WEIRD.
WELL, WHATCHA THINK?!
CUTE OR WHAT?!
SURE HAS SOME LONG EARS FOR A CAT.
IT'S A RABBIT, YOU BONEHEAD!
ビシ
IF YOU CAN'T SAY SOMETHIN' NICE, DON'T SAY NOTHIN' AT ALL!
There they go again.
OH! MORNIN', KOTAROU-CHAN!

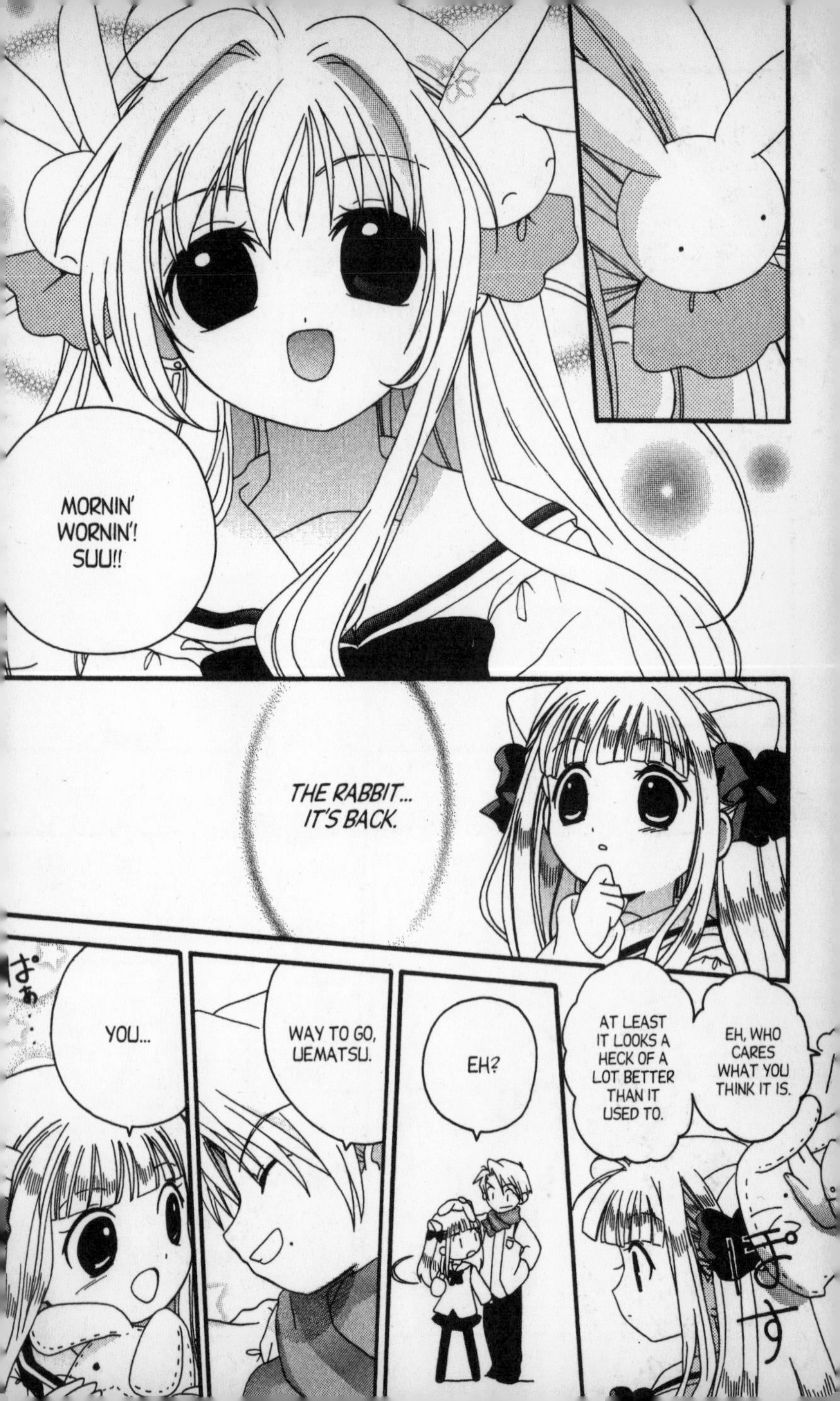
MORNIN' WORNIN'! SUU!!
THE RABBIT... IT'S BACK.
EH, WHO CARES WHAT YOU THINK IT IS.
AT LEAST IT LOOKS A HECK OF A LOT BETTER THAN IT USED TO.
ぽす
EH?
WAY TO GO, UEMATSU.
YOU...

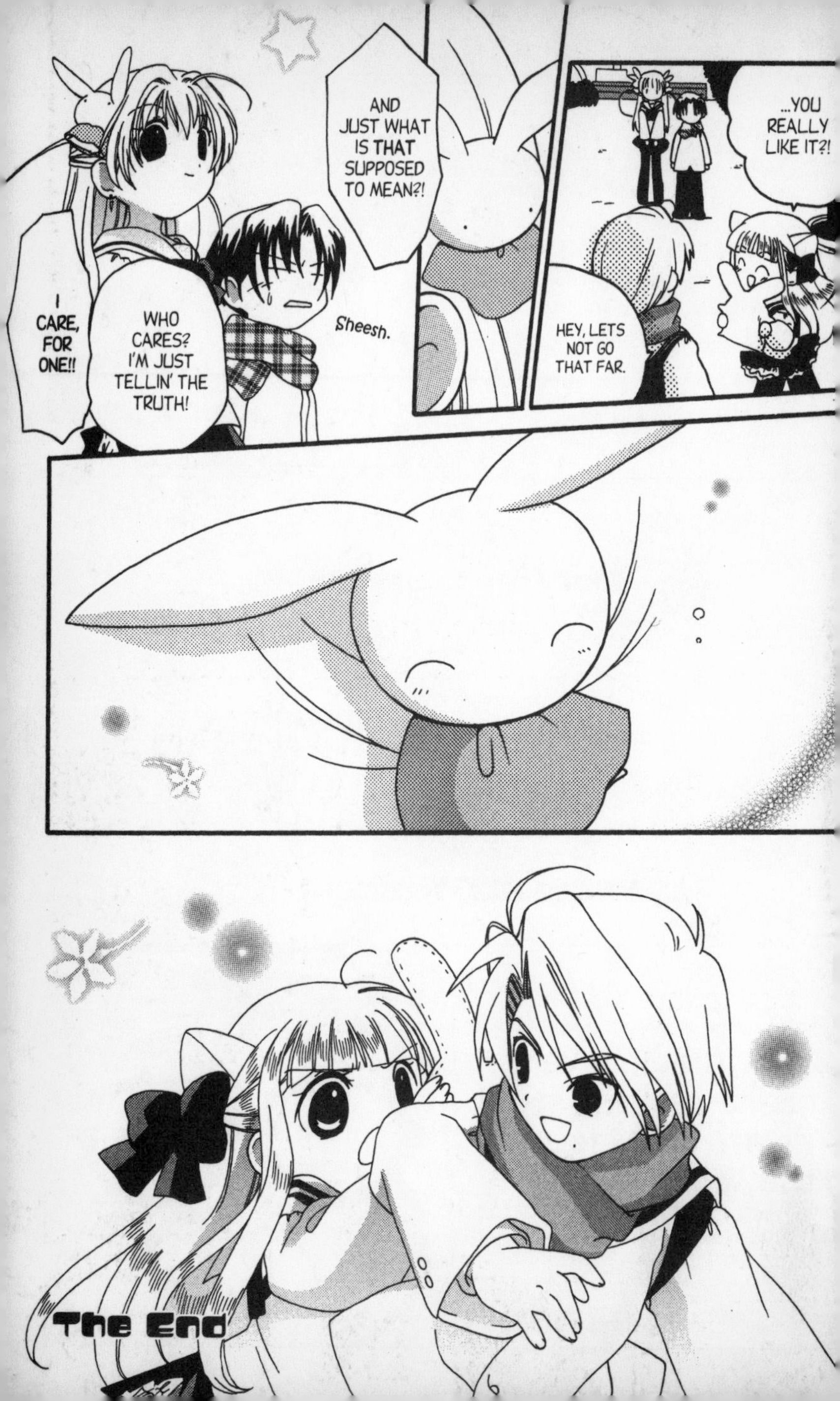
...YOU REALLY LIKE IT?!
HEY, LETS NOT GO THAT FAR.
AND JUST WHAT IS THAT SUPPOSED TO MEAN?!
Sheesh.
WHO CARES? I'M JUST TELLIN' THE TRUTH!
I CARE, FOR ONE!!
The End

Congrats on the *Pita-Ten* anime!

Thank you very much for letting me participate in this endeavor.

I had so much fun drawing this.

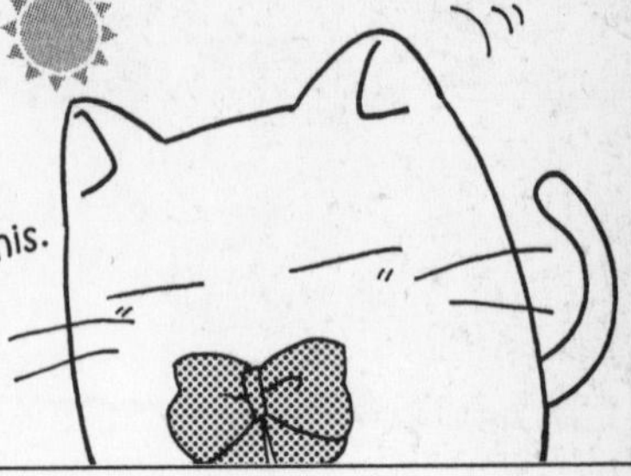

— Mari Matsuzawa —

p.133

Mari Matsuzawa

Writer's Talk

p.147

Masakazu Iwasaki

I've drawn a very heart-warming story. Please enjoy it with the family.

-Masakazu Iwasaki

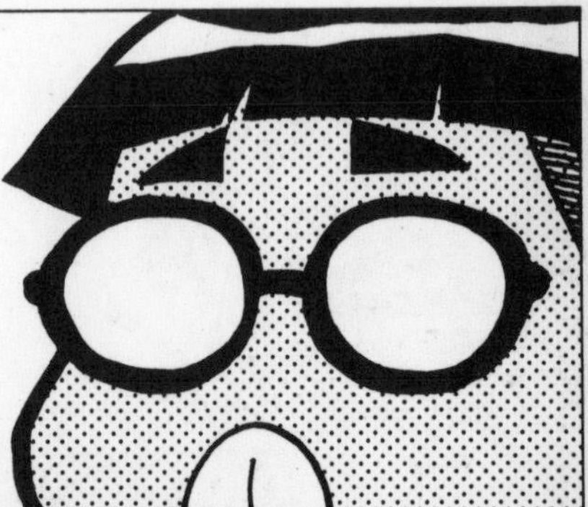

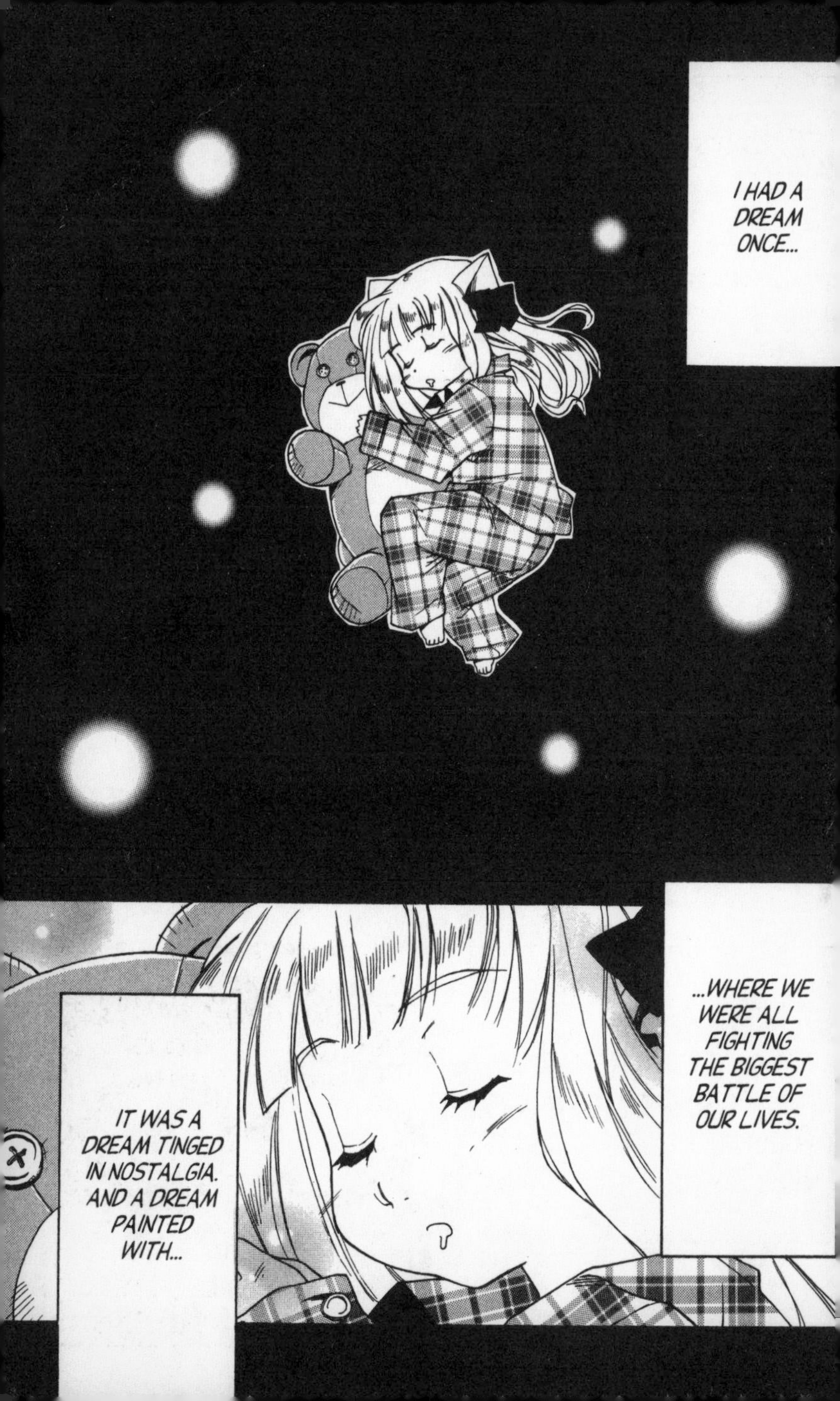
I HAD A DREAM ONCE...
...WHERE WE WERE ALL FIGHTING THE BIGGEST BATTLE OF OUR LIVES.
IT WAS A DREAM TINGED IN NOSTALGIA. AND A DREAM PAINTED WITH...

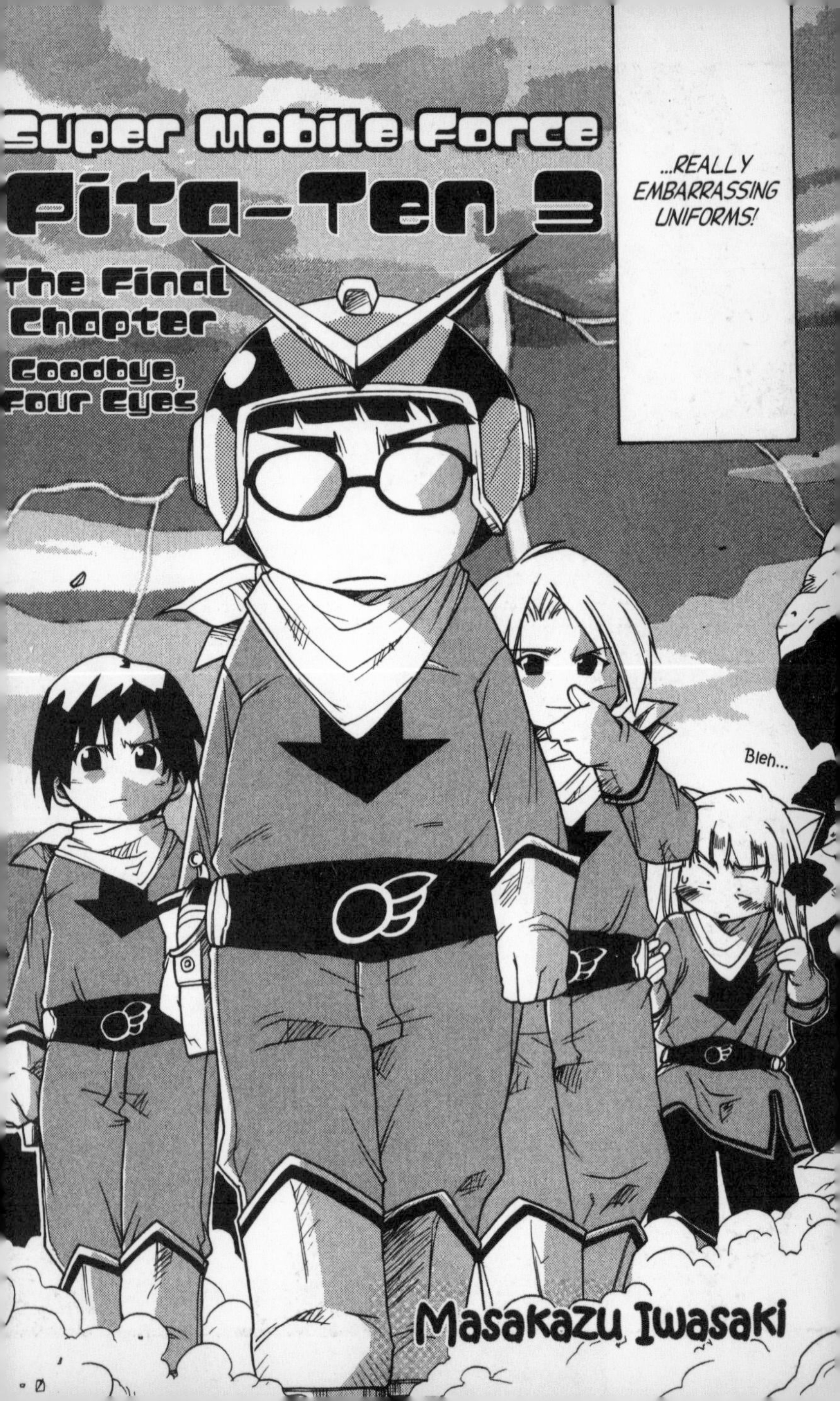
...REALLY EMBARRASSING UNIFORMS!
Super Mobile Force
Pita-Ten 3
The Final Chapter
Goodbye, Four Eyes
Bleh...
Masakazu Iwasaki

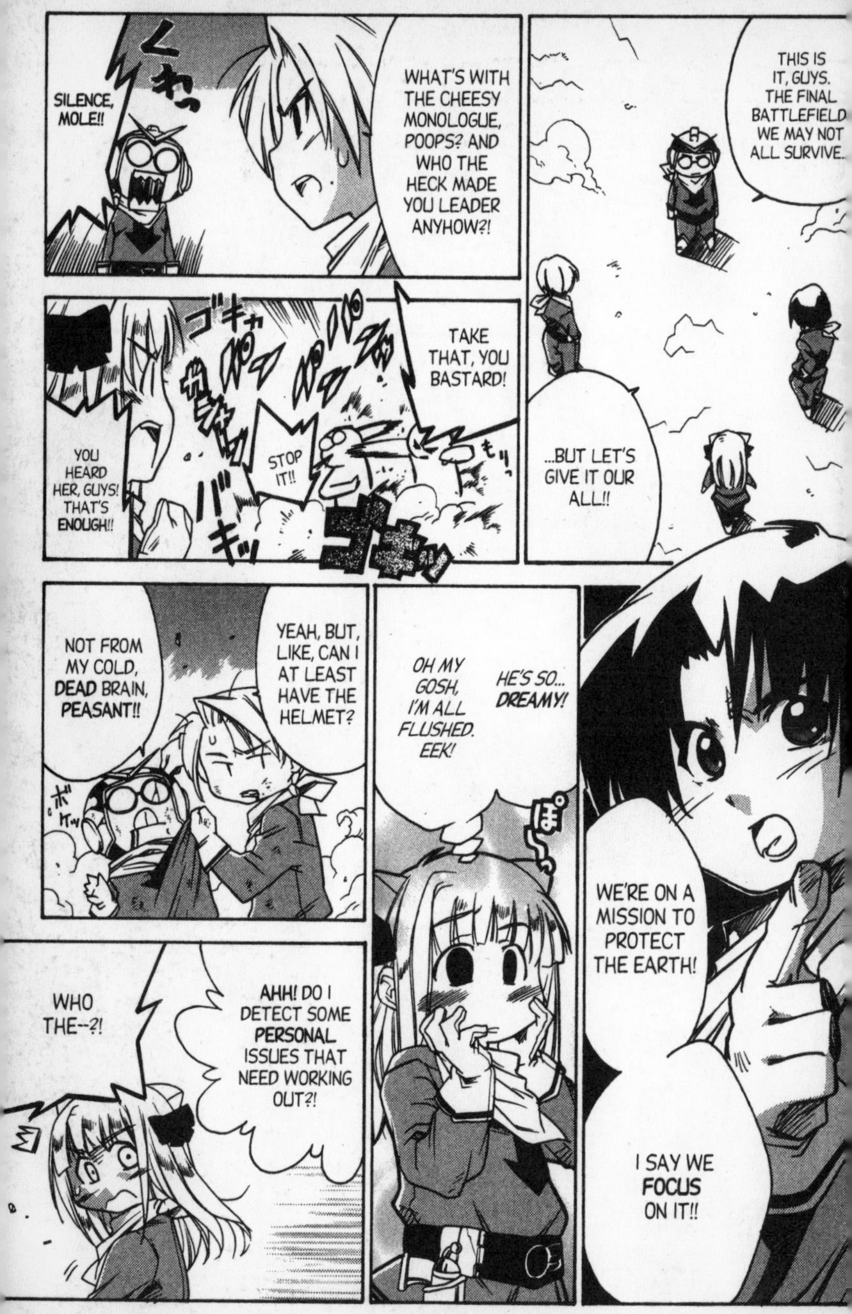
THIS IS IT, GUYS. THE FINAL BATTLEFIELD. WE MAY NOT ALL SURVIVE...
...BUT LET'S GIVE IT OUR ALL!!
WHAT'S WITH THE CHEESY MONOLOGUE, POOPS? AND WHO THE HECK MADE YOU LEADER ANYHOW?!
SILENCE, MOLE!!
TAKE THAT, YOU BASTARD!
STOP IT!!
YOU HEARD HER, GUYS! THAT'S ENOUGH!!
WE'RE ON A MISSION TO PROTECT THE EARTH!
I SAY WE FOCUS ON IT!!
HE'S SO... DREAMY!
OH MY GOSH, I'M ALL FLUSHED. EEK!
YEAH, BUT, LIKE, CAN I AT LEAST HAVE THE HELMET?
NOT FROM MY COLD, DEAD BRAIN, PEASANT!!
AHH! DO I DETECT SOME PERSONAL ISSUES THAT NEED WORKING OUT?!
WHO THE--?!

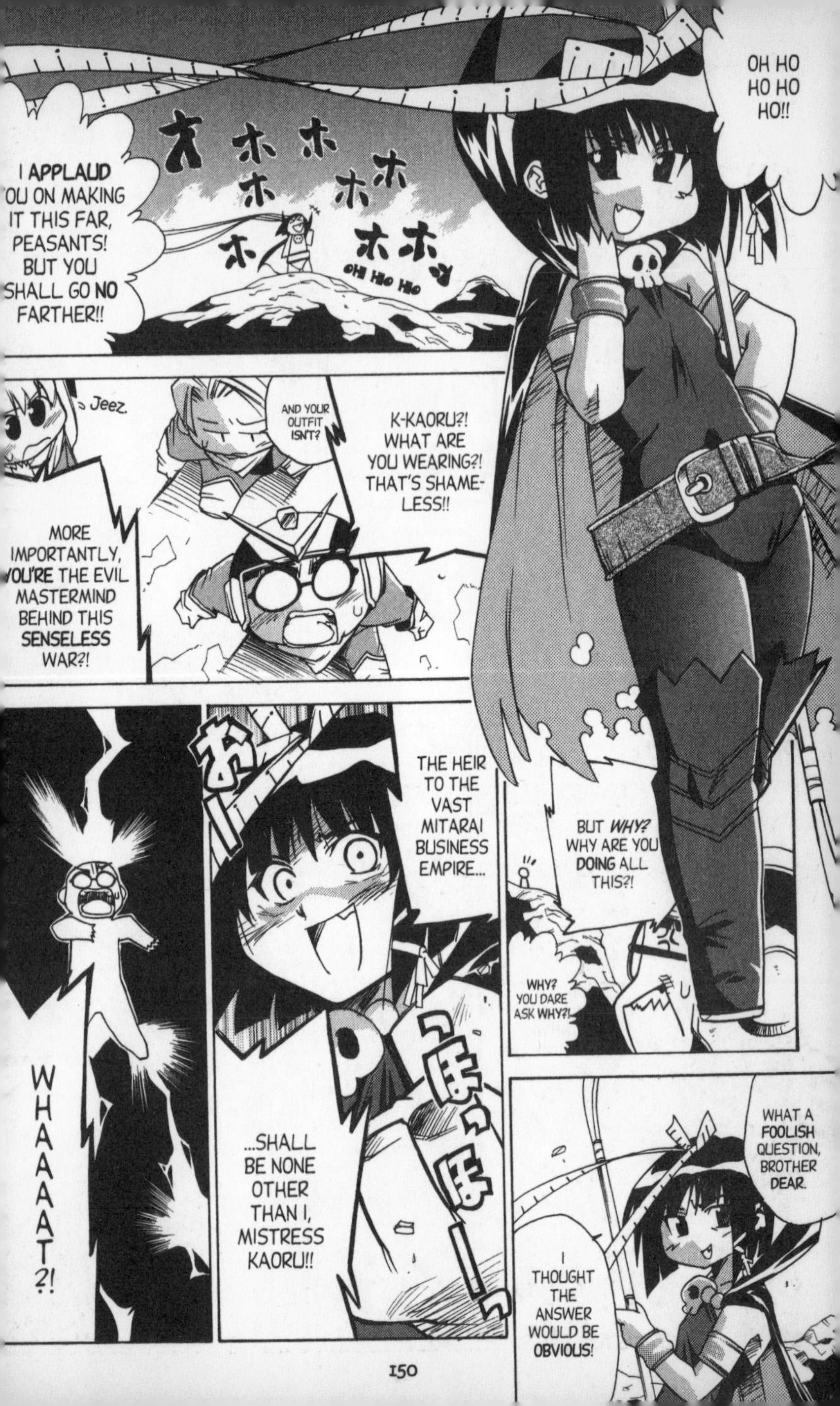
OH HO HO HO HO!!
OH HO HO
I APPLAUD OU ON MAKING IT THIS FAR, PEASANTS! BUT YOU SHALL GO NO FARTHER!!
K-KAORU?! WHAT ARE YOU WEARING?! THAT'S SHAME-LESS!!
AND YOUR OUTFIT ISN'T?
Jeez.
MORE IMPORTANTLY, OU'RE THE EVIL MASTERMIND BEHIND THIS SENSELESS WAR?!
BUT WHY? WHY ARE YOU DOING ALL THIS?!
WHY? YOU DARE ASK WHY?!
WHAT A FOOLISH QUESTION, BROTHER DEAR.
I THOUGHT THE ANSWER WOULD BE OBVIOUS!
THE HEIR TO THE VAST MITARAI BUSINESS EMPIRE...
...SHALL BE NONE OTHER THAN I, MISTRESS KAORU!!
WHAAAAT?!

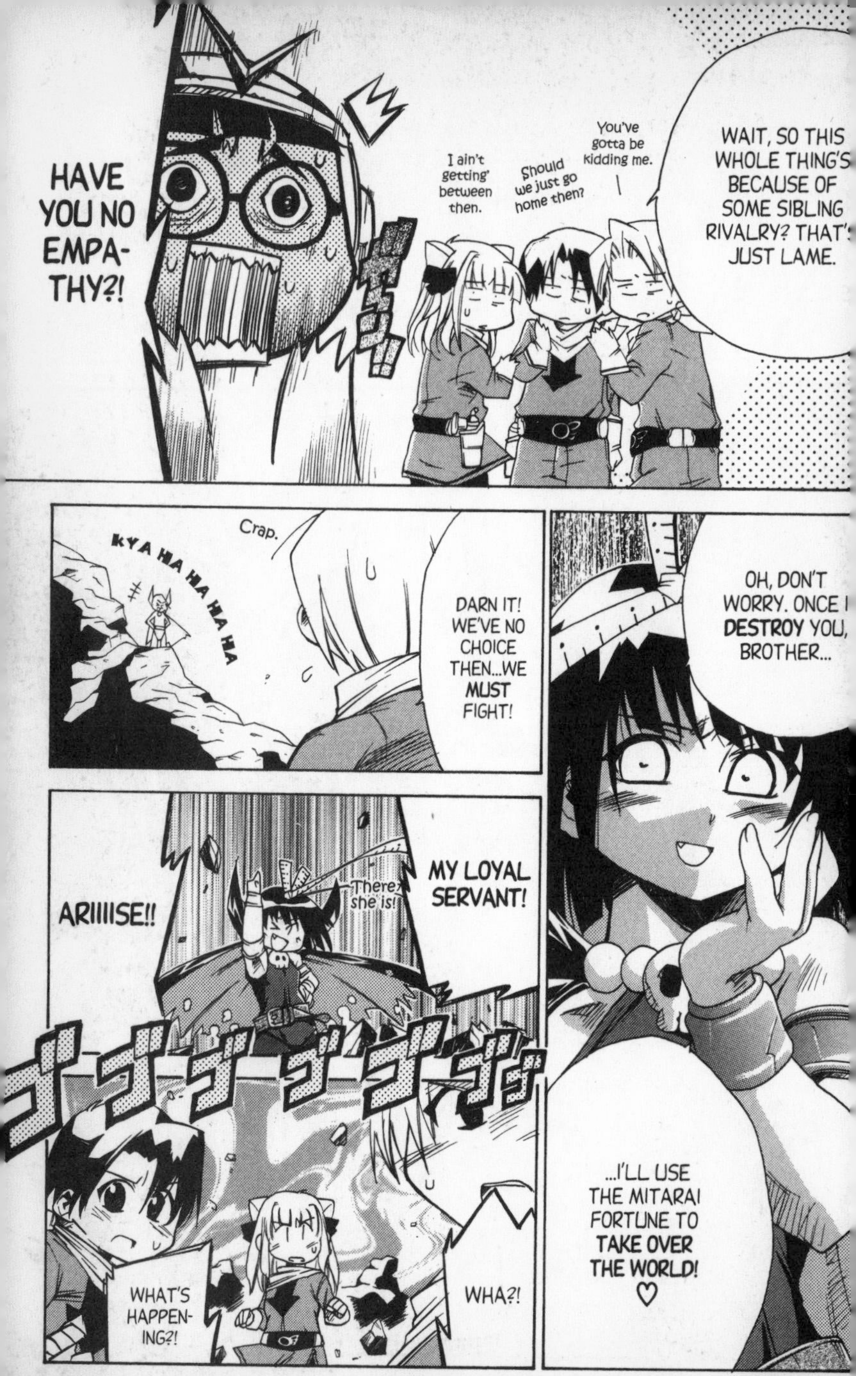

WAIT, SO THIS WHOLE THING'S BECAUSE OF SOME SIBLING RIVALRY? THAT'S JUST LAME.
You've gotta be kidding me.
Should we just go home then?
I ain't getting' between then.
HAVE YOU NO EMPA-THY?!
OH, DON'T WORRY. ONCE I DESTROY YOU, BROTHER...
...I'LL USE THE MITARAI FORTUNE TO TAKE OVER THE WORLD! ♡
DARN IT! WE'VE NO CHOICE THEN...WE MUST FIGHT!
Crap.
KYA HA HA HA HA HA
MY LOYAL SERVANT!
There she is!
ARIIIISE!!
WHA?!
WHAT'S HAPPEN-ING?!

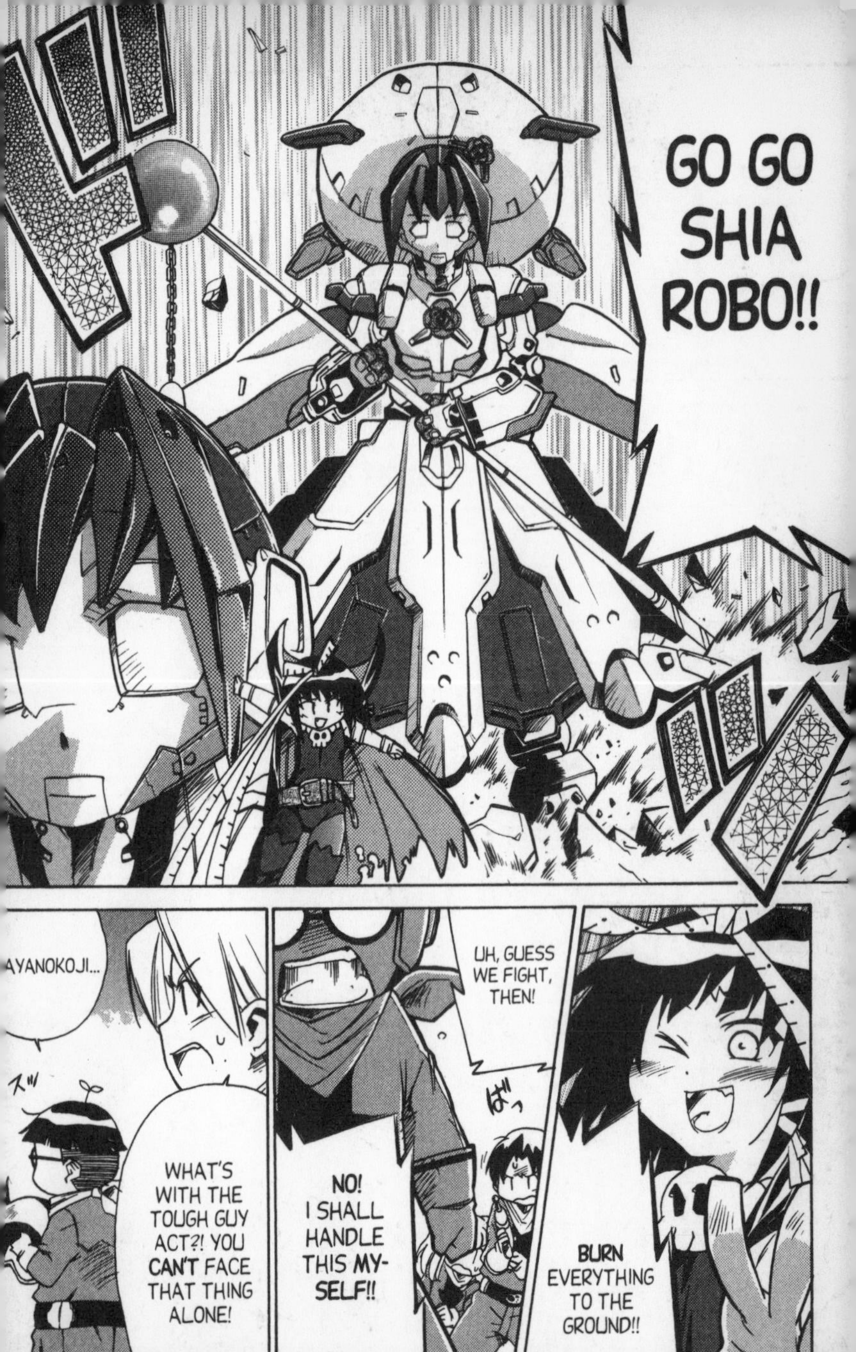
GO GO SHIA ROBO!!
BURN EVERYTHING TO THE GROUND!!
UH, GUESS WE FIGHT, THEN!
ばっ
NO! I SHALL HANDLE THIS MY-SELF!!
AYANOKOJI...
ズッ
WHAT'S WITH THE TOUGH GUY ACT?! YOU CAN'T FACE THAT THING ALONE!

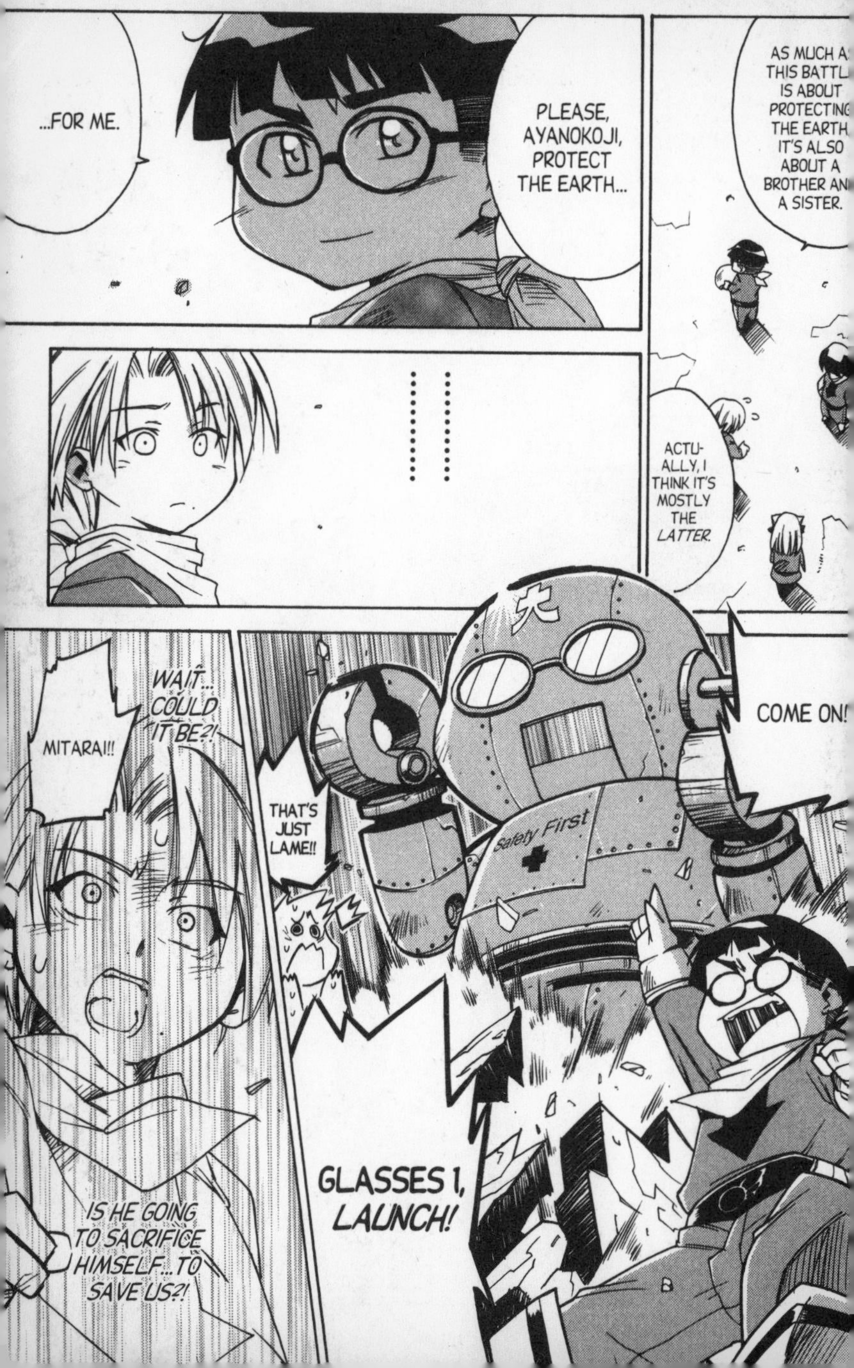
AS MUCH A THIS BATTL IS ABOUT PROTECTIN THE EARTH IT'S ALSO ABOUT A BROTHER AN A SISTER.
ACTU-ALLY, I THINK IT'S MOSTLY THE *LATTER.*
PLEASE, AYANOKOJI, PROTECT THE EARTH...
...FOR ME.
......
......
COME ON!
大
Safety First
THAT'S JUST LAME!!
GLASSES 1, *LAUNCH!*
MITARAI!!
WAIT... COULD IT BE?!
IS HE GOING TO SACRIFICE HIMSELF...TO SAVE US?!

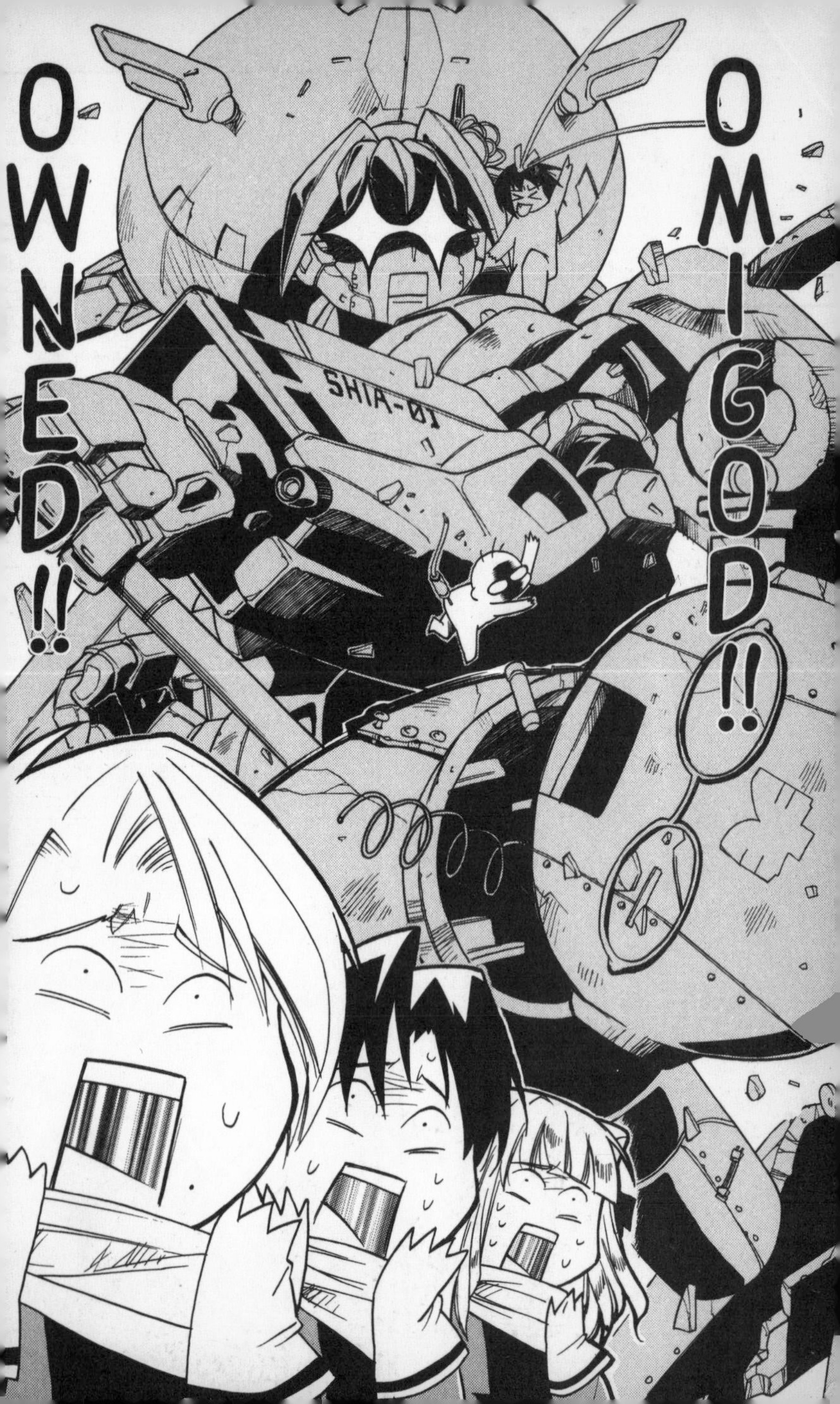
OMIGOD!!
SHIA-01
OWNED!!

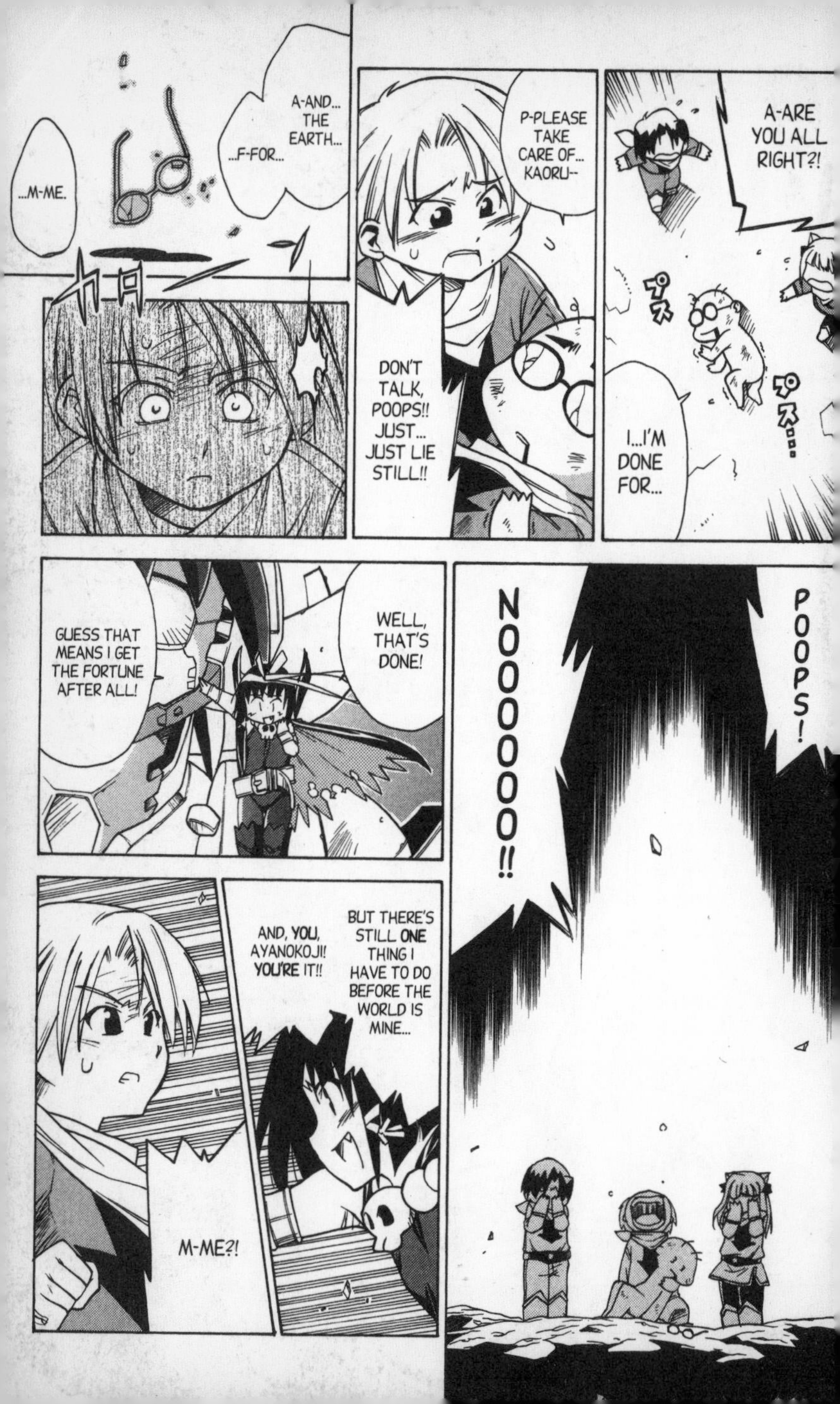

A-ARE YOU ALL RIGHT?!
I...I'M DONE FOR...
P-PLEASE TAKE CARE OF... KAORU--
DON'T TALK, POOPS!! JUST... JUST LIE STILL!!
A-AND... THE EARTH...
...F-FOR...
...M-ME.
POOPS!
NOOOOOOO!!
WELL, THAT'S DONE!
GUESS THAT MEANS I GET THE FORTUNE AFTER ALL!
BUT THERE'S STILL **ONE** THING I HAVE TO DO BEFORE THE WORLD IS MINE...
AND, **YOU**, AYANOKOJI! **YOU'RE** IT!!
M-ME?!

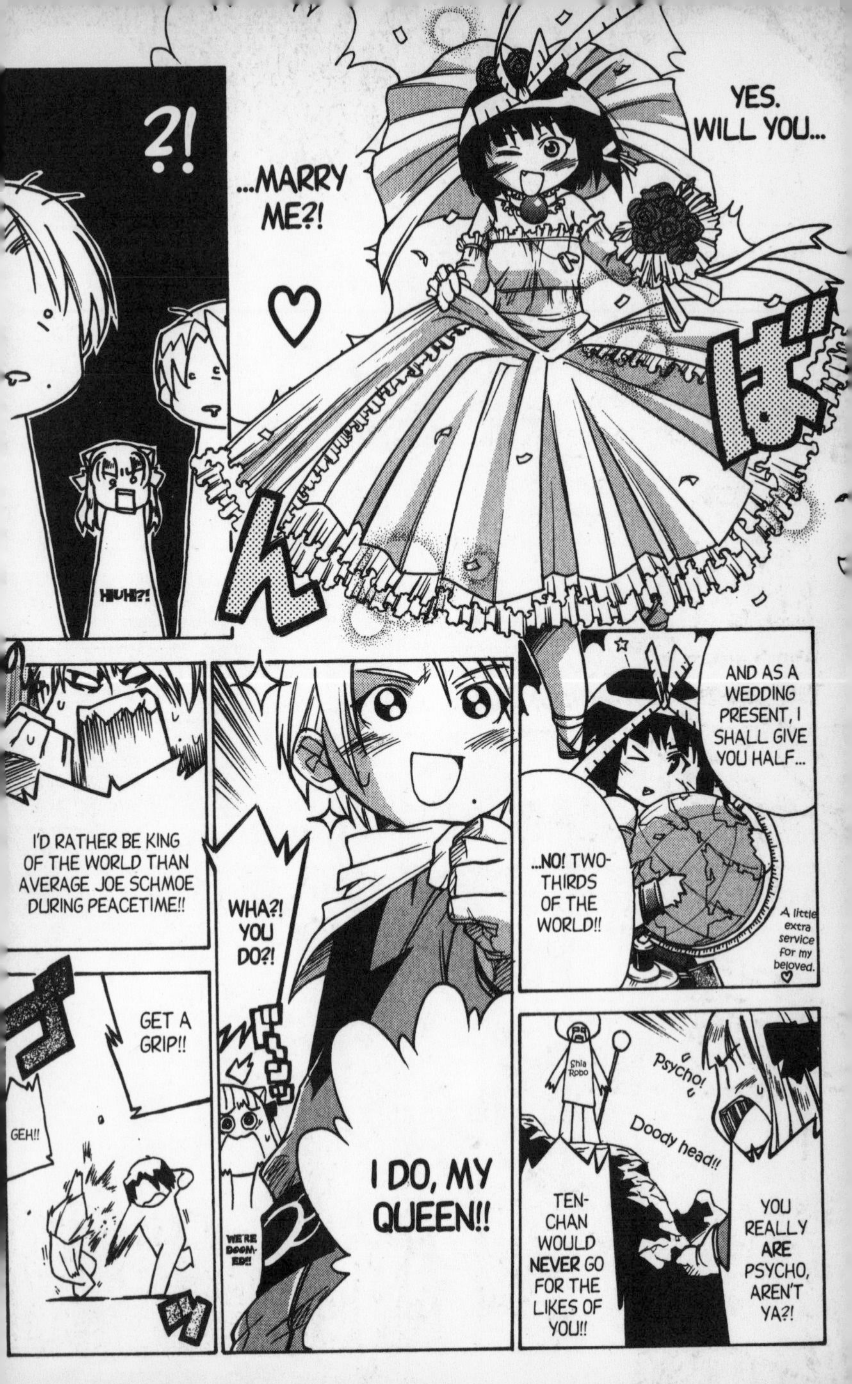

YES. WILL YOU...
...MARRY ME?!
?!
HUH?!
AND AS A WEDDING PRESENT, I SHALL GIVE YOU HALF...
...NO! TWO-THIRDS OF THE WORLD!!
A little extra service for my beloved.
Psycho!
Doody head!!
YOU REALLY ARE PSYCHO, AREN'T YA?!
Shia Robo
TEN-CHAN WOULD NEVER GO FOR THE LIKES OF YOU!!
WHA?! YOU DO?!
I DO, MY QUEEN!!
WE'RE DOOMED!!
I'D RATHER BE KING OF THE WORLD THAN AVERAGE JOE SCHMOE DURING PEACETIME!!
GET A GRIP!!
GEH!!

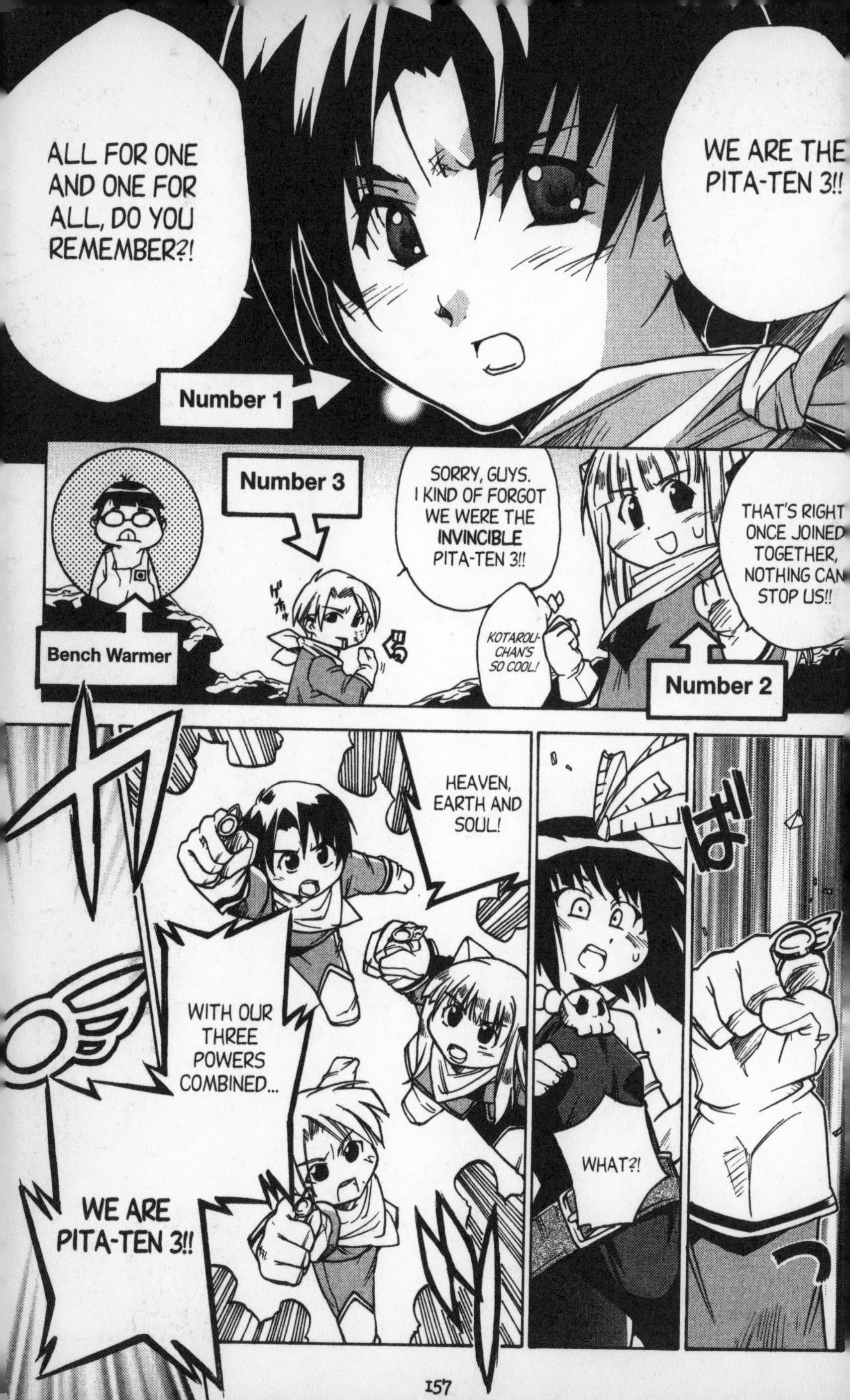
WE ARE THE PITA-TEN 3!!
ALL FOR ONE AND ONE FOR ALL, DO YOU REMEMBER?!
Number 1
THAT'S RIGHT ONCE JOINED TOGETHER, NOTHING CAN STOP US!!
Number 2
SORRY, GUYS. I KIND OF FORGOT WE WERE THE INVINCIBLE PITA-TEN 3!!
KOTAROU-CHAN'S SO COOL!
Number 3
Bench Warmer
WHAT?!
HEAVEN, EARTH AND SOUL!
WITH OUR THREE POWERS COMBINED...
WE ARE PITA-TEN 3!!

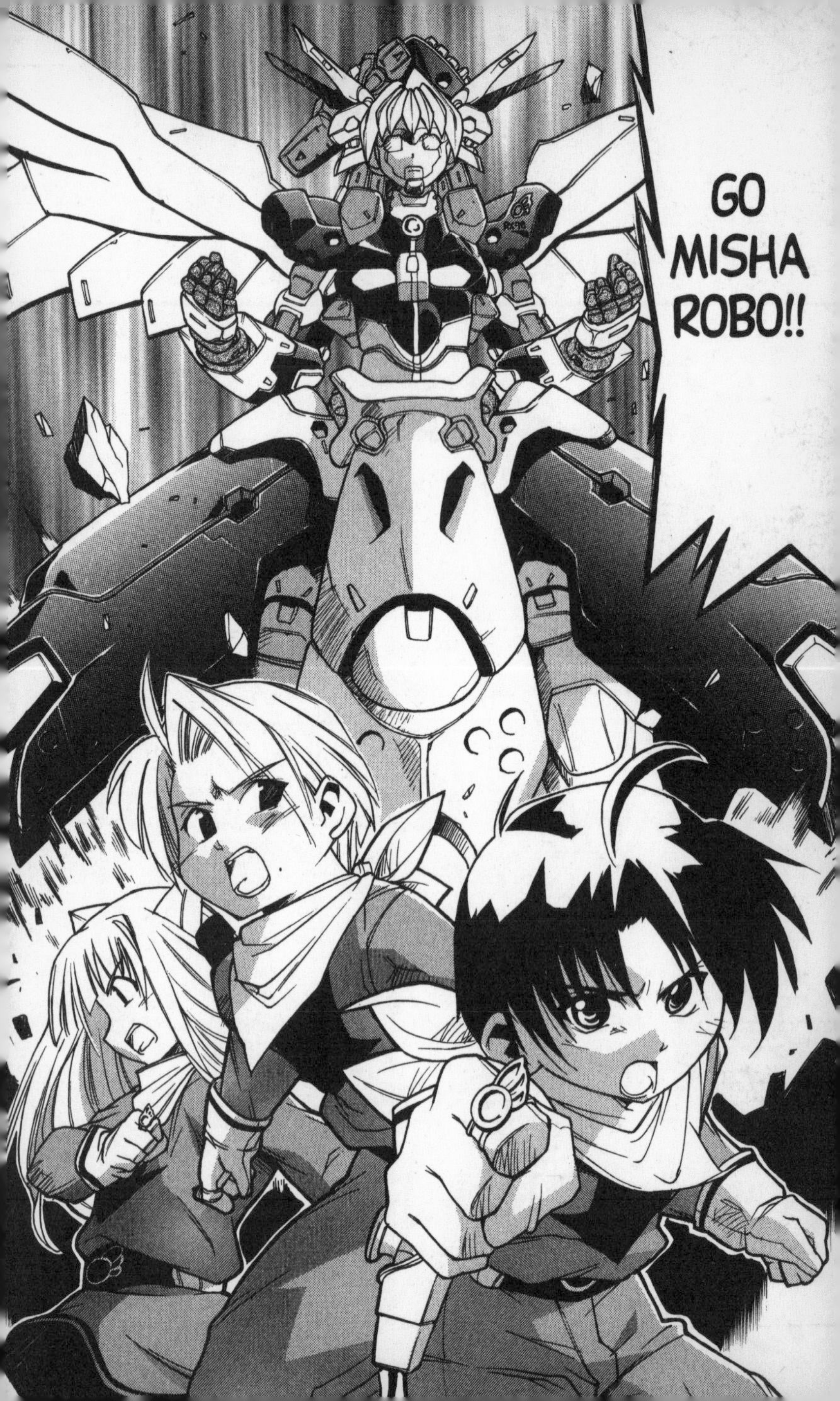
GO MISHA ROBO!!

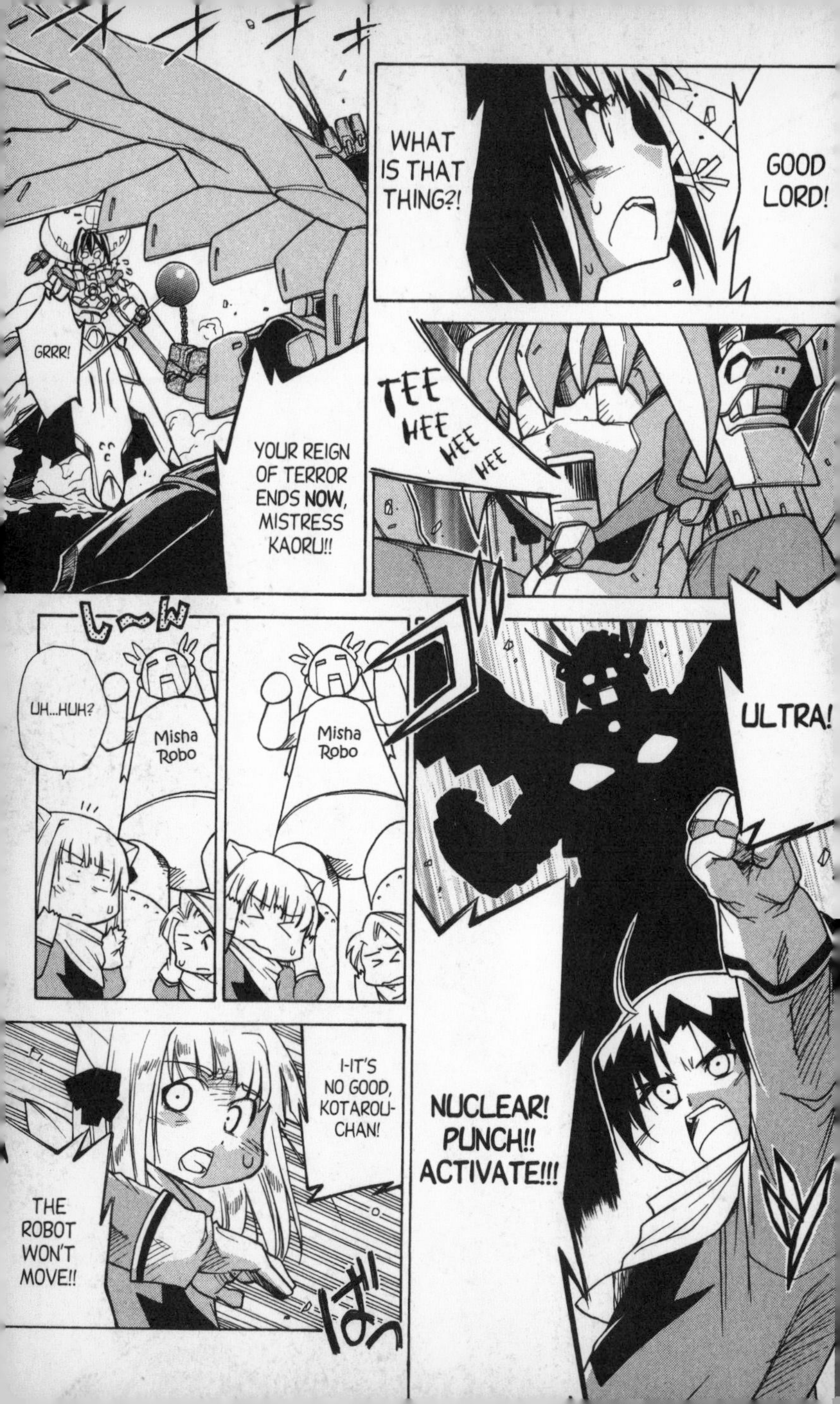
GOOD LORD!
WHAT IS THAT THING?!
TEE HEE HEE HEE
YOUR REIGN OF TERROR ENDS NOW, MISTRESS KAORU!!
GRRR!
ULTRA!
NUCLEAR! PUNCH!! ACTIVATE!!!
Misha Robo
し〜ん
UH...HUH?
Misha Robo
I-IT'S NO GOOD, KOTAROU-CHAN!
THE ROBOT WON'T MOVE!!

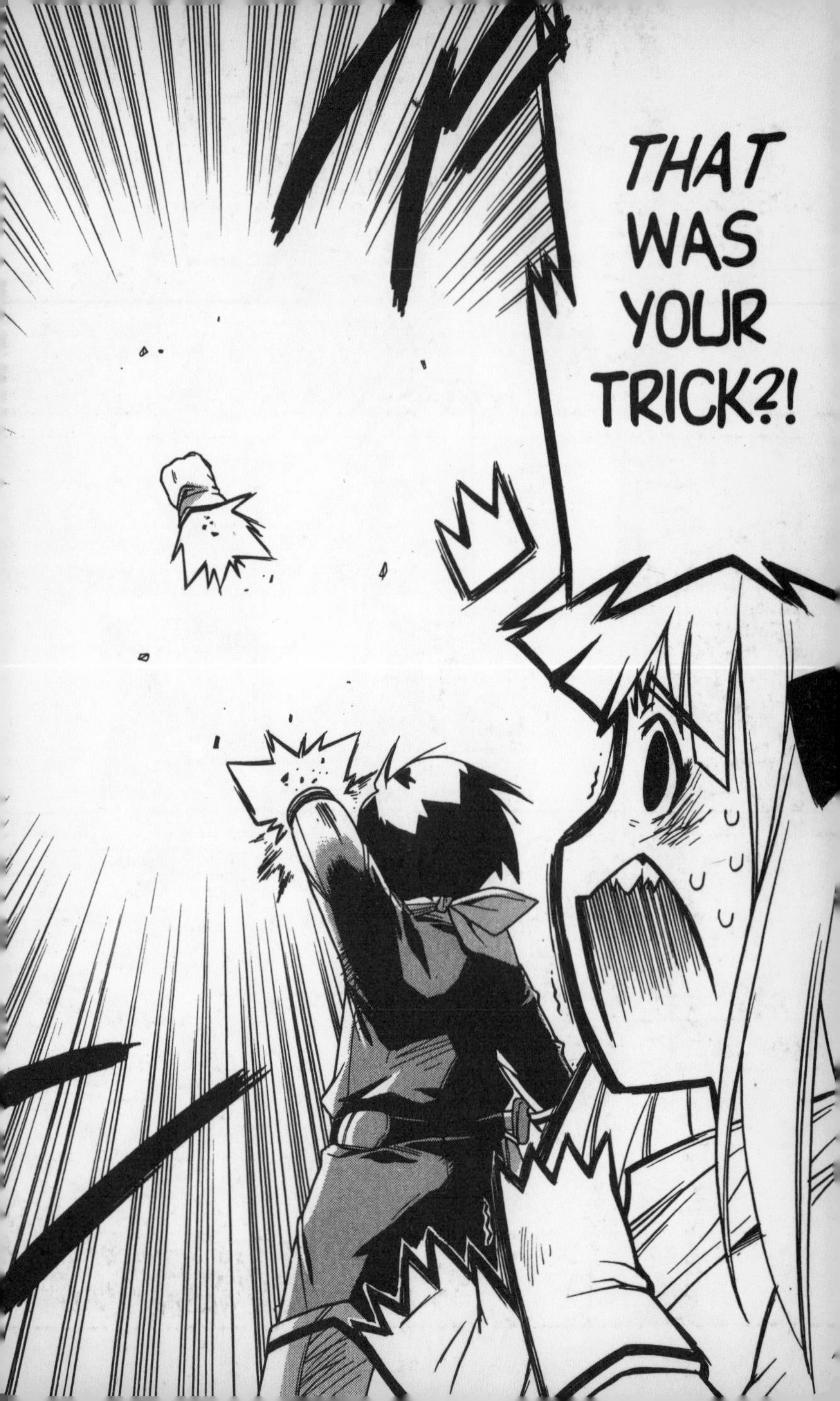
THAT WAS YOUR TRICK?!

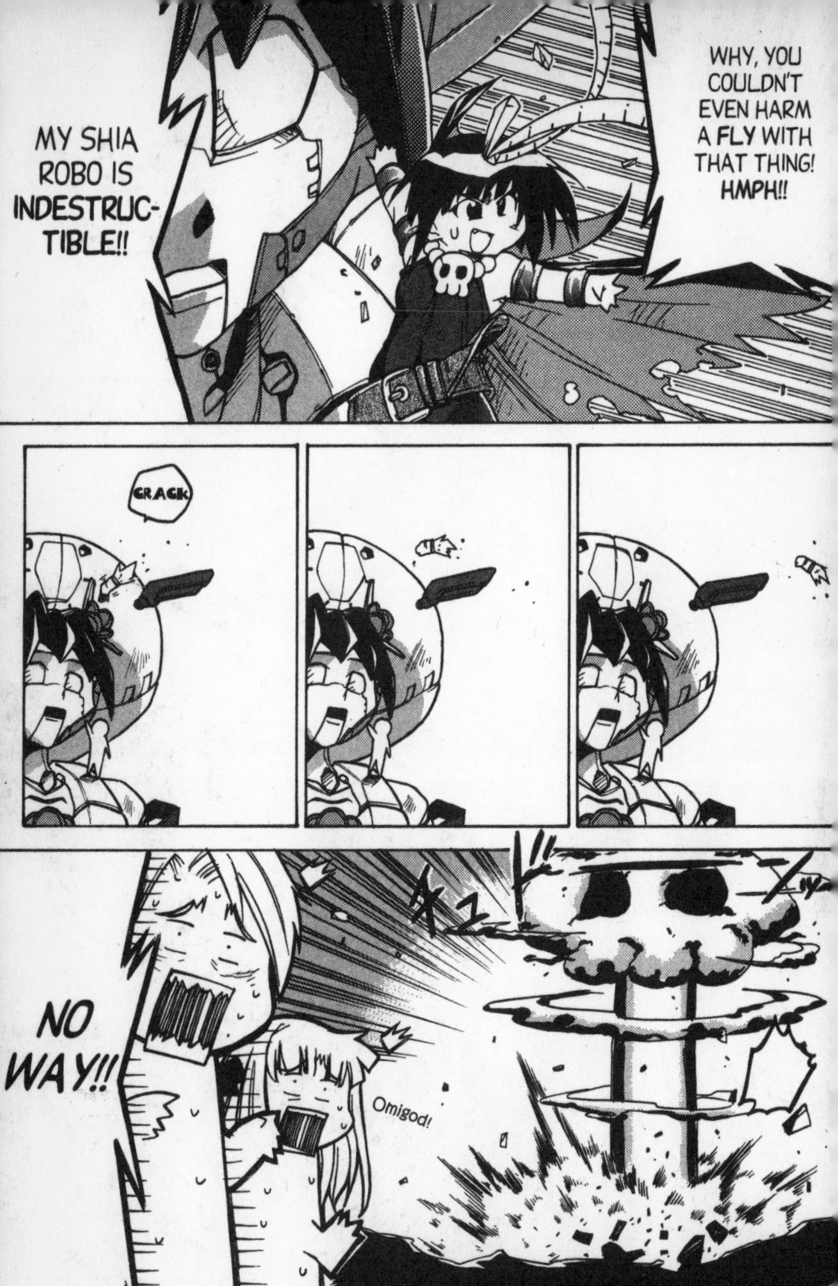
WHY, YOU COULDN'T EVEN HARM A FLY WITH THAT THING! HMPH!!
MY SHIA ROBO IS INDESTRUC-TIBLE!!
CRACK
Omigod!
NO WAY!!

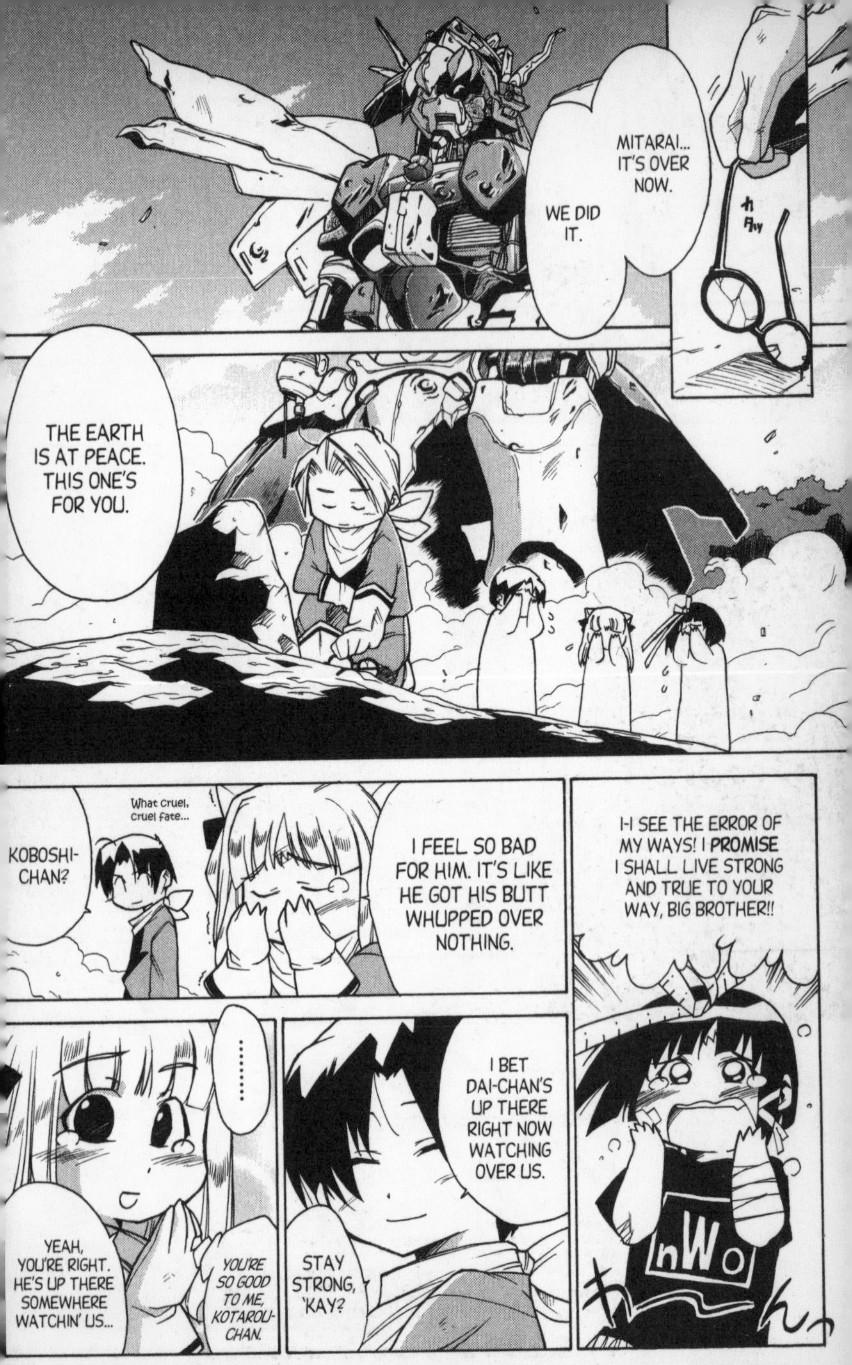
MITARAI... IT'S OVER NOW.
WE DID IT.
THE EARTH IS AT PEACE. THIS ONE'S FOR YOU.
I-I SEE THE ERROR OF MY WAYS! I **PROMISE** I SHALL LIVE STRONG AND TRUE TO YOUR WAY, BIG BROTHER!!
I FEEL SO BAD FOR HIM. IT'S LIKE HE GOT HIS BUTT WHUPPED OVER NOTHING.
What cruel, cruel fate...
KOBOSHI-CHAN?
I BET DAI-CHAN'S UP THERE RIGHT NOW WATCHING OVER US.
STAY STRONG, 'KAY?
......
YOU'RE SO GOOD TO ME, KOTAROU-CHAN.
YEAH, YOU'RE RIGHT. HE'S UP THERE SOMEWHERE WATCHIN' US...

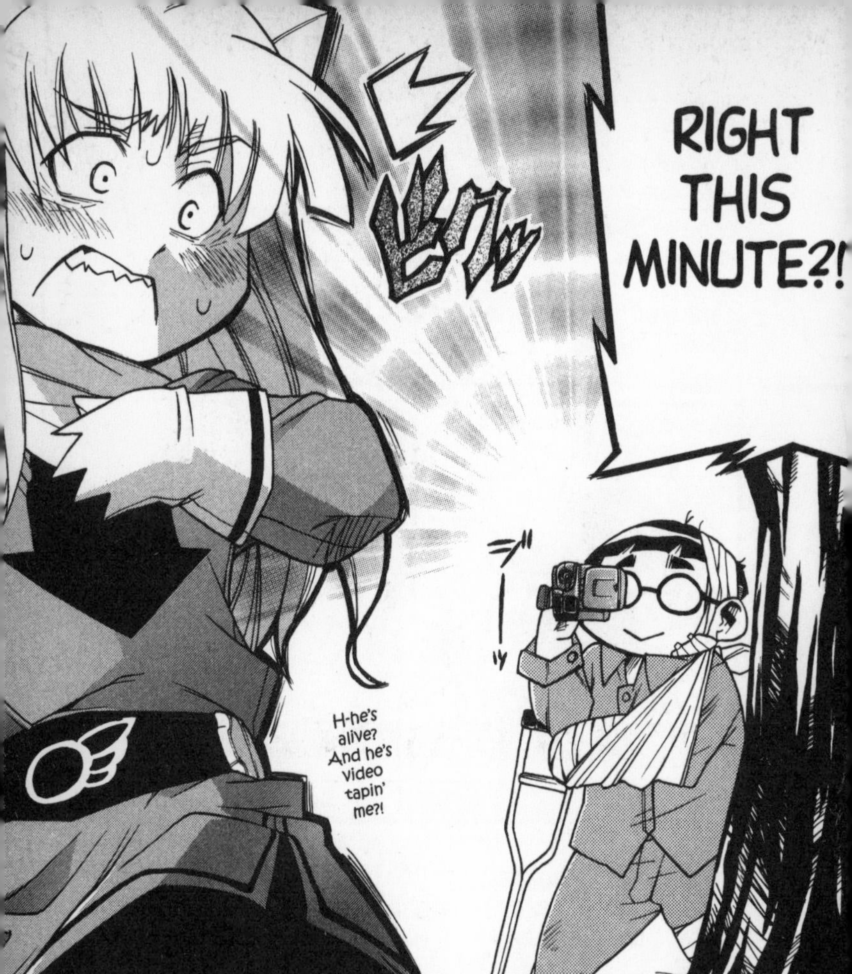
RIGHT THIS MINUTE?!
H-he's alive? And he's video tapin' me?!

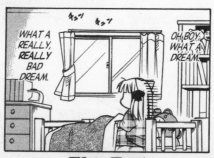

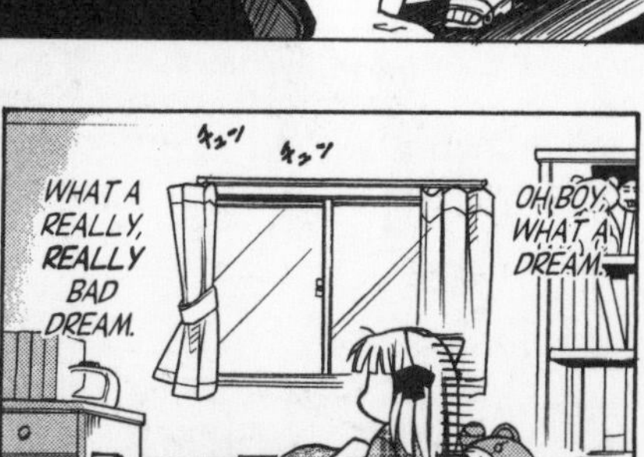
OH BOY, WHAT A DREAM.
WHAT A REALLY, REALLY BAD DREAM.

The End

Koge-Donbo

Drawing this story brought back memories of this old manga I read where this magician sawed someone in half. It kinda went something like this:

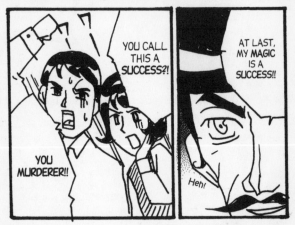

AT LAST, MY MAGIC IS A SUCCESS!!
Heh!
YOU CALL THIS A SUCCESS?!
YOU MURDERER!!

Now that I think about it, those old stories were really over the top and corny, but they were still fun. Very fun.

I'm so happy that my publisher started a *Pita-Ten* anthology for me. I can't wait to see what the next two batches of authors have cooked up! ♡

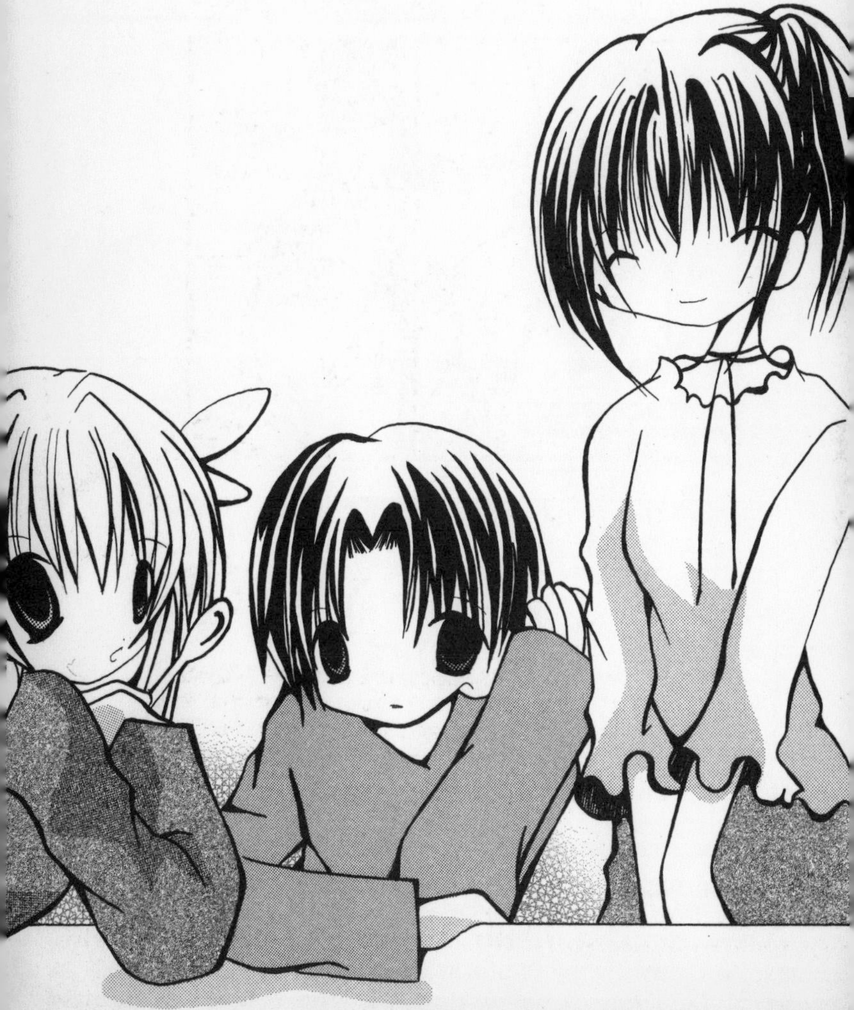

In volume 2 of...

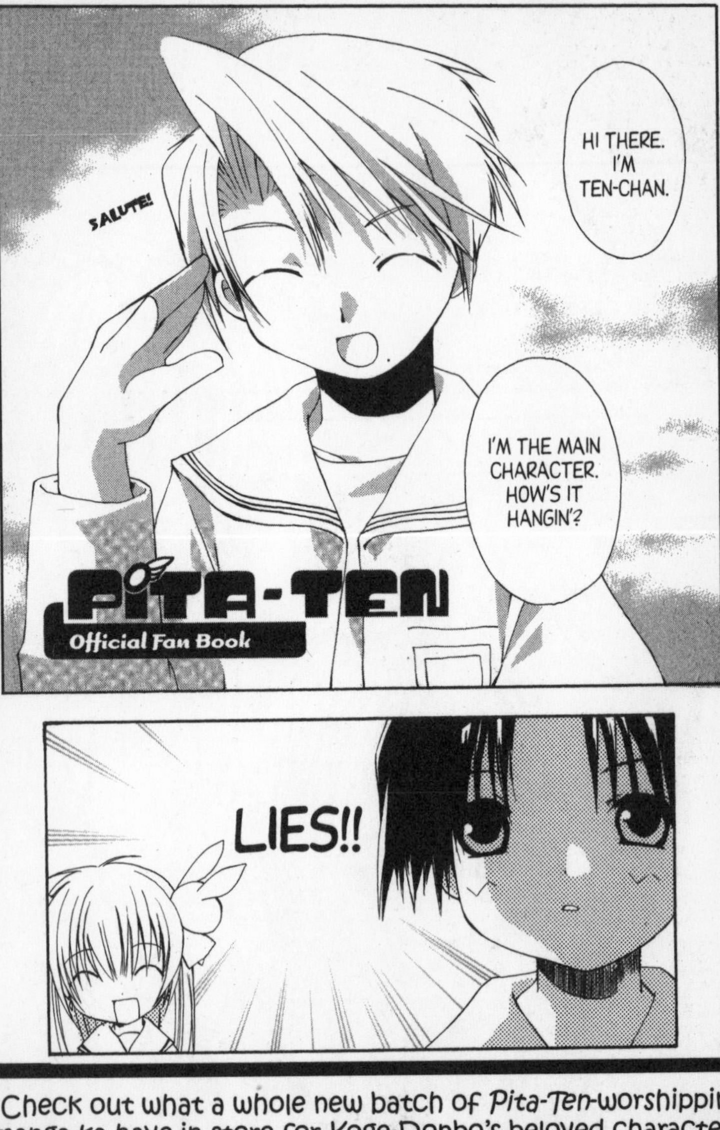
HI THERE. I'M TEN-CHAN.
SALUTE!
I'M THE MAIN CHARACTER. HOW'S IT HANGIN'?
PITA-TEN
Official Fan Book
LIES!!

Check out what a whole new batch of *Pita-Ten*-worshipping manga-ka have in store for Koge-Donbo's beloved characters! If they're not careful, they might even reveal the top-secret meaning of this manga's quirky title! Available March 2006!

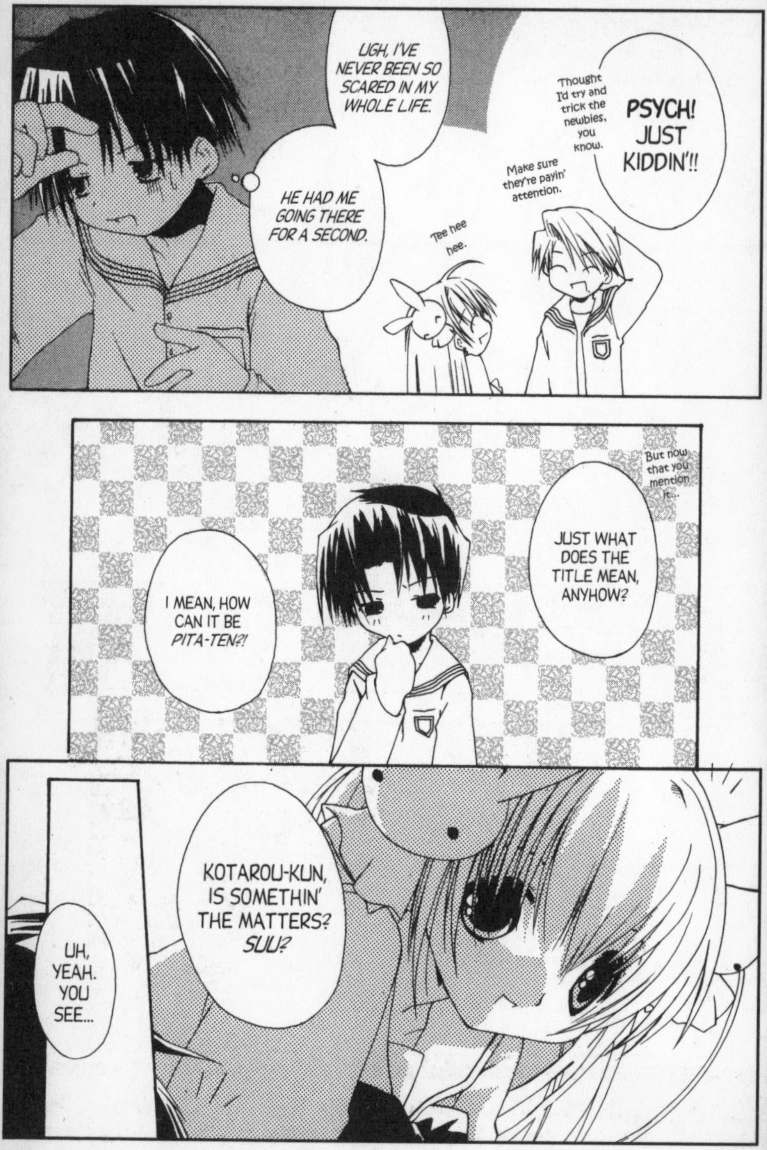
PSYCH! JUST KIDDIN'!!
Thought I'd try and trick the newbies, you know.
Make sure they're payin' attention.
Tee hee hee.
UGH, I'VE NEVER BEEN SO SCARED IN MY WHOLE LIFE.
HE HAD ME GOING THERE FOR A SECOND.
But now that you mention it...
JUST WHAT DOES THE TITLE MEAN, ANYHOW?
I MEAN, HOW CAN IT BE *PITA-TEN*?!
KOTAROU-KUN, IS SOMETHIN' THE MATTERS? *SUU?*
UH, YEAH. YOU SEE...

TOKYOPOP SHOP

WWW.TOKYOPOP.COM/SHOP

DRAMACON and other hot titles are available at the store that never closes!

HOT NEWS!
Check out the TOKYOPOP SHOP!
The world's best collection of manga in English is now available online in one place!

SAMURAI CHAMPLOO

KINGDOM HEARTS

DRAMACON

WWW.TOKYOPOP.COM/SHOP

```
00000 00000
```

- **LOOK FOR SPECIAL OFFERS**
- **PRE-ORDER UPCOMING RELEASES**
- **COMPLETE YOUR COLLECTIONS**

A MIDNIGHT™ OPERA

Immortality, Redemption, and Bittersweet Love...

For nearly a millennium, undead creatures have blended into a Europe driven by religious dogma...

Ein DeLaLune is an underground Goth metal sensation on the Paris music scene, tragic and beautiful. He has the edge on other Goth music powerhouses—he's undead, a fact he's kept hidden for centuries. But his newfound fame might just bring out the very phantoms of his past from whom he has been hiding for centuries, including his powerful brother, Leroux. And if the two don't reconcile, the entire undead nation could rise up from the depths of modern society to lay waste to mankind.

MARK OF THE SUCCUBUS

ASHLY RAITI & IRENE FLORES

Maeve, a succubus-in-training, is sent to the human world to learn how to hone her skills of seduction. But things get complicated when she sets her sights on Aiden, a smart but unmotivated student at her new high school. Meanwhile, the Demon World has sent a spy to make sure Maeve doesn't step out of line. And between Aiden's witchy girlfriend, his nutty best friend, and Demon World conspiracies, Maeve is going to be lucky to make it out of our world alive!

Here is a Gothic romantic fantasy set in one of the most menacing worlds known to humans: high school.

T TEEN AGE 13+

FOR MORE INFORMATION VISIT: WWW.TOKYOPOP.COM

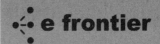

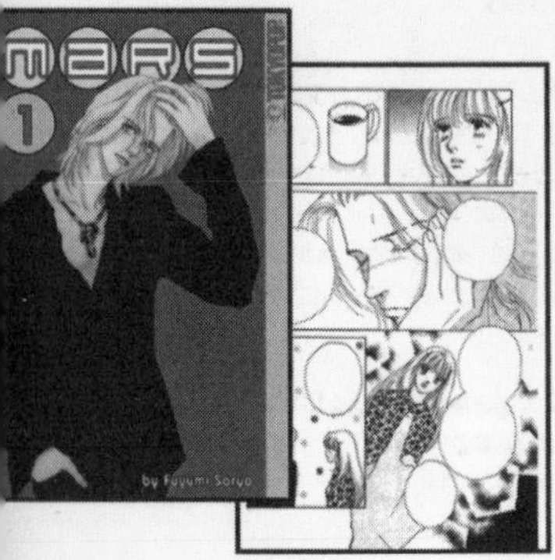
MARS
1
by Fuyumi Soryo

BY FUYUMI SORYO

MARS

I used to do the English adaptation for *MARS* and loved working on it. The art is just amazing—Fuyumi Soryo draws these stunning characters and beautiful backgrounds to boot. I remember this one spread in particular where Rei takes Kira on a ride on his motorcycle past this factory, and it's all lit up like Christmas and the most gorgeous thing you've ever seen—and it's a factory! And the story is a super-juicy soap opera that kept me on the edge of my seat just dying to get the next volume every time I'd finish one.

~Elizabeth Hurchalla, Sr. Editor

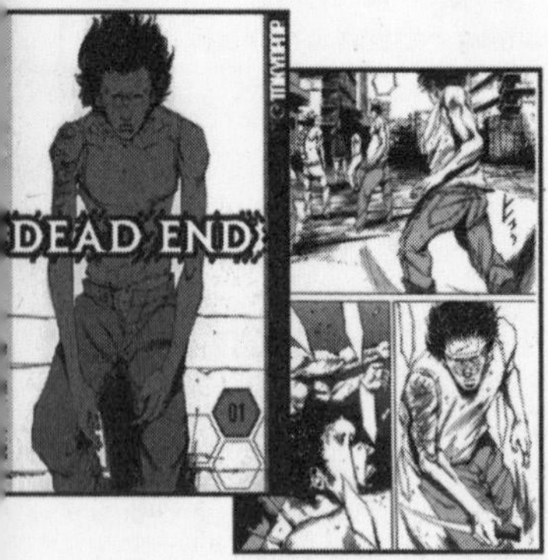
DEAD END
01

BY SHOHEI MANABE

DEAD END

Everyone I've met who has read *Dead End* admits to becoming immediately immersed and obsessed with Shohei Manabe's unforgettable manga. If David Lynch, Clive Barker and David Cronenberg had a love child that was forced to create a manga in the bowels of a torture chamber, then *Dead End* would be the fruit of its labor. The unpredictable story follows a grungy young man as he pieces together shattered fragments of his past. Think you know where it's going? Well, think again!

~Troy Lewter, Editor

© Rivkah and TOKYOPOP Inc.

STEADY BEAT
BY RIVKAH

"Love Jessica"... That's what Leah finds on the back of a love letter to her sister. But who is Jessica? When more letters arrive, along with flowers and other gifts, Leah goes undercover to find out her sister's secret. But what she doesn't expect is to discover a love of her own—and in a very surprising place!

Winner of the Manga Academy's Create Your Own Manga competition!

T TEEN AGE 13+

© MIN-WOO HYUNG

JUSTICE N MERCY
BY MIN-WOO HYUNG

Min-Woo Hyung is one of today's most talented young Korean artists, and this stunning art book shows us why. With special printing techniques and high-quality paper, TOKYOPOP presents never-before-seen artwork based on his popular *Priest* series, as well as images from past and upcoming projects *Doomslave*, *Hitman* and *Sal*.

A spectacular art book from the creator of *Priest*!

T TEEN AGE 13+

© 2003 Liu GOTO © SOTSU AGENCY • SUNRISE • MBS

MOBILE SUIT GUNDAM SEED NOVEL
ORIGINAL STORY BY HAJIME YATATE AND YOSHIYUKI TOMINO
WRITTEN BY LIU GOTO

A shy young student named Kira Yamato is thrown in the midst of battle when genetically enhanced Coordinators steal five new Earth Force secret weapons. Wanting only to protect his Natural friends, Kira embraces his Coordinator abilities and pilots the mobile suit Strike. The hopes and fears of a new generation clash with the greatest weapons developed by mankind: Gundam!

The novelization of the super-popular television series!

T TEEN AGE 13+

STOP!

This is the back of the book.
You wouldn't want to spoil a great ending!

This book is printed "manga-style," in the authentic Japanese right-to-left format. Since none of the artwork has been flipped or altered, readers get to experience the story just as the creator intended. You've been asking for it, so TOKYOPOP® delivered: authentic, hot-off-the-press, and far more fun!

DIRECTIONS

If this is your first time reading manga-style, here's a quick guide to help you understand how it works.

It's easy... just start in the top right panel and follow the numbers. Have fun, and look for more 100% authentic manga from TOKYOPOP®!